Linn's
U.S. Plate Number Coil Handbook

By
Ken Lawrence

Published by *Linn's Stamp News,* the largest and most informative stamp newspaper in the world. *Linn's* is owned by Amos Press, 911 Vandemark Road, Sidney, Ohio 45365. Amos Press also publishes *Scott Stamp Monthly* and the Scott line of catalogs.

033050

Introduction
and
Acknowledgments

The principal purpose of this book is to help collectors of modern United States coil stamps — specifically those issued in 1981 and afterward — to derive pleasure from their collections. That means mainly (but not exclusively) the coils issued with plate numbers printed, at regular intervals, on the stamps themselves. The choice of that focus reflects the fact that plate number coils have become the most popular specialized area of modern U.S. philately.

Despite that motive and focus, I have tried to write a book that will be useful to anyone who likes modern stamps and postal history. I have approached each stamp in its various contexts, examining each new item as philately, as postage, as postal history. That approach has dictated a chronological structure, which sets this book apart from other plate number coil references. Most plate number coil, or PNC, guides are organized according to features intrinsic to the stamps themselves, usually their common design features or consecutive denominations. These are useful as far as they go, but tend to skim over why the stamps exist in the first place, what they are intended to do, and how they are actually used.

Also, to use an organizing strategy based on qualities intrinsic to PNCs means eliminating those coil stamps that don't include plate numbers in the design, many of which have been issued since the beginning of 1981. Knowledge of those non-PNC coil stamps adds useful insights to the PNC issues, whether or not one chooses to collect them. For each year since PNCs began, I have included any non-PNC stamps issued that year in the overview portion of the chapter. That is followed by separate sub-chapters for each issue that does have PNCs. Alternating chapters discuss the philatelic significance of PNCs each year.

With rare exceptions, I have not used catalog numbers in this book, for several reasons. I don't like the tendency within the stamp hobby for catalog numbers to become a kind of in-group jargon, and in effect a language barrier to people who aren't steeped in it. As much as possible we ought to be using terms that can be readily understood by everybody, particularly those we would like to attract to our hobby and to the PNC specialty. To facilitate that further, I have included a glossary of terms with specific philatelic definitions, or with specialized meanings in the PNC context.

The most widely used catalog numbering system in the United States, the one owned by Scott Publishing Company and used in the *Scott Standard Postage Stamp Catalogue* and the *Scott Specialized Catalogue of United States Stamps,* has greater problems with PNCs than with other stamps. Scott has changed the numbers assigned to recent coil stamps on several occasions since 1981, and may make further changes. Any time the numbers are reassigned, texts based on the previously assigned listings become obsolete or confusing.

Also, when Scott breaks up a set for its own numbering convenience, as it has with the Transportation coil series, collectors who overemphasize catalog numbers tend to impose these arbitrary breaks on their collecting habits even when the breaks have no philatelic or postal meaning. An example is grouping the Transportation coils into "first series," "second series," and so forth, while the stamps obviously constitute a single continuing series.

Some PNCs are not listed at all by Scott. Some are mentioned but not numbered. And some — those called "precancels" by the Postal Service and by traditional precancel collectors — are listed only in used condition, although PNC specialists collect them both unused and used.

An alternative catalog numbering system devised by Stephen G. Esrati does designate every PNC, but it has problems of its own. Like Scott's, Esrati's system is evolving and subject to change. And like all such systems, it threatens to become an impenetrable PNC-ese, excluding the uninitiated from the clique's revealed truth. Also, the Esrati system wrenches PNCs out of their place, not only in U.S. philately generally, but even from the important context of coil stamps issued during the past decade. For Esrati, if they don't have plate numbers, they don't exist.

The only disadvantage to avoiding catalog numbers is that one must use a descriptive phrase instead of a group of numbers and letters. The advantages are clarity to veteran and beginner alike, and warm hospitality to all. This approach also has the virtue of freeing the author to define stamp issues differently from their catalog designations, and I have done so. For purposes of this book, a stamp is a distinct issue if it differs from similar stamps in overprint or service inscription text, image size, or tagging style, but not if the only constant detectable difference is the interval of a repeating feature.

To be specific, the plain tagged version of the 5.2¢ Sleigh coil is a different stamp from the untagged 5.2¢ Sleigh precancel. A subtler example is the two versions of the 12¢ Stanley Steamer precancel; on single stamps the Cottrell and B press versions can be difficult to tell apart, but the image is slightly wider on the Cottrell edition. On the other hand, Flag stamps printed on both the intaglio B and C (or D) presses are not distinct issues unless some other feature sets them apart, such as a precancel or tagging difference. Nor are the 25¢ Honeybee stamps different, despite being printed in two very different ways.

Although I have included a glossary at the end of this book, a couple of terms should be clarified in the beginning. Most important, since it is part of the specialty's name, is the word "plate." Plate has two overlapping meanings in this book, which should be clear from the context. First is a generic use, to refer to any printing base used on any press that contains coil stamp images, whether it is an actual printing plate in the specific, technical sense, or a printing sleeve or gravure cylinder.

Second is the narrow meaning of plate to differentiate a printing base that is manufactured on a flat surface and later curved to fit a press cylinder from printing bases that are manufactured directly on cylindrical surfaces to fit a mandrel. The latter are called sleeves when their inside dimensions are tapered and cylinders when they are not. (These are not the only kinds of printing bases, but others — such as chases with moveable type, mimeograph or silkscreen stencils, hecto-graph gelatins or spirit masters, and lithograph stones — have not been used to print United States postage stamps.)

Thus, a reference to plate number coils throughout this book can be taken to mean the numbers printed from plates, sleeves, or cylinders, depending on which press and printing method was used, but a dis-tinction between a flexographic plate and an intaglio sleeve used in combination printing on the Bureau of Engraving and Printing's inta-glio B press should be read as the narrow, exclusive meaning of plate.

Another term requires explanation mainly for collectors who are more familiar with the stamp-issuing policies of other countries than with those of the United States. I refer to the specific meaning of a stamp being "withdrawn from sale." Elsewhere in the world, that means taken off sale at all post offices with all unsold stock destroyed. Here it means no such thing.

When a U.S. stamp is withdrawn, it is removed from philatelic sale. Surplus stock still on hand at the Philatelic Sales Division in Wash-ington and Kansas City, and at retail philatelic counters in post offices throughout the country, are returned to central inventories, from which they are then distributed for regular sales by stamp window clerks until the supplies are exhausted.

For commemorative stamps, that ordinarily uses up the remainders as postage fairly quickly. But for odd values of definitive stamps, they may remain in storage vaults for years, available for future distribu-tion when a rate change requires a particular denomination that earlier fell into disuse. Thus, perfectly legal and legitimate sales of obsolete U.S. postage stamps at post offices can and do occur long after published withdrawal dates. The large-scale reintroduction of previously withdrawn stamps has taken place on several occasions.

Some stamps are ordered destroyed after withdrawal, usually decimal-denominated coil stamps bearing restrictive service endorsements whose rates are unlikely ever to return. But even those stamps turn up in Accountable Paper Depositories and Stamp Distribution Offices around the country. Some stamps stay on or are reintroduced to philatelic sale after withdrawal, as individual components of mint year sets, thematic sets, and other products. Besides those considerations, the United States has appointed private firms in certain foreign countries to act as agents, selling U.S. stamps, postal stationery and philatelic products at foreign-exchange equivalents of face value. These agents routinely ignore directives to withdraw items from philatelic sale. They often have stamps in inventory that U.S. post offices haven't sold for many years.

To minimize the inevitable confusion on this issue, this book gives the withdrawal dates as the dates stamps have been withdrawn from philatelic sale. Though it certainly has implications for the philatelic market, collectors should understand that almost any modern U.S. stamp could, in theory at least, show up and be legitimately sold at face value at any post office.

Without the assistance of many people, this book could not exist. No writer, certainly not this one, possesses the comprehensive knowledge, sustained verbal skill, or physical stamina to do the job alone. Charles Yeager was this book's nursemaid, and in a fair world he would receive a significant percentage of its royalties. Fortunately for me, the world isn't that fair yet. Charlie telephoned me almost every day for over a year to keep me on track, thus rivaling my wife, Elizabeth Sharpe, as a positive influence.

Various staffers at *Linn's Stamp News* in Ohio also kept me on track. Usually editor-publisher Michael Laurence would dangle the carrots while Donna O'Keefe, this book's editor, prodded with a sharp stick. Wayne Youngblood passed along helpful tidbits from time to time.

At the United States Postal Service, almost everybody involved in any way with coil stamps, philatelic marketing, and philatelic sales helped out, from Assistant Postmaster General Gordon C. Morison on down, including Donald M. McDowell, W.L. "Pete" Davidson, Joe Brockert, Linda Foster, Dickey B. Rustin, Frank Thomas, Hugh McGonigle, Kim Parks, Mary Margaret "Peggy" Grant, Peter Papadopoulos, Wayne Anmuth, Bill Halstead, John Spiehs, Robert G. Brown and Cindy Tackett.

Belmont Faries, who chairs the Citizens' Stamp Advisory Committee, wears many other hats. He has provided assistance in many areas of his knowledge and experience.

Help at the Bureau of Engraving and Printing was provided by the director, Peter Daly, and many others, including Ira Polikoff, Leah Akbar, Edward Felver, Carl D'Allessandro, Leonard Buckley, Ralph Payne, Jerry Hudson, and others in the postage stamp processing areas.

George V.H. Godin of the Bureau Issues Association, who edits the *Durland Standard Plate Number Catalog* and is BIA's reigning plate number expert, wasn't stumped by any of my questions, no matter how obscure. Kim D. Johnson's research for the BIA also helped. George W. Brett's quarrels with some of my preliminary findings have sharpened my wits considerably.

A number of plate number coil dealers and former dealers gave information and helped me track down scarce materials for illustration. They include Dennis D. Chamberlain, A.S. Cibulskas, Kim Cuniberti, Jon Denney, Ed Denson, Robert Dumaine, Stephen G. Esrati, Al Haake, Allen Hagen, Dale Hendricks, Max D. Hickox, Jerry Koepp, Joe R. Lane, William S. Langs, Vern Kraus, Stewart R. Kusinitz, Tom Maeder, Frank Marrelli, Robert Rabinowitz, Alan Rosenberg, D. John Shultz, and Lee Warzala, plus Rick Lancaster, who sells modern covers of all kinds.

The information on authorized false franking usage of coil stamps was supplied by everyone's expert source on United States postal rates and usages, Henry W. Beecher.

Specialists in particular areas of PNC collecting have done more than anybody else to keep me informed and abreast of the latest discoveries. John Greenwood's knowledge of imperforate PNCs is second to none, as is his collection. Glenn A. Estus and Thomas E. Gift pioneered the study of PNCs on first-day covers. Their information has been expanded by serious collectors, such as Wayne Anmuth, Larry W. Graf, and John A. Ziegler, and cachetmakers Gerry Adlman, Gary Dubnik, John Halliday, Ken D. Kribbs, Larry Newman, Ray Novak, Bill Toutant, and Mike Zoeller. Gerald Blankenship has done the same for PNCs on USPS Souvenir Pages. Larry G. Haynes has kept up with precancel gap positions since the beginning, and Robert Washburn has assumed responsibility for tracking the earliest known commercial use of each PNC.

Many fellow collectors have provided continuous encouragement, far too many to list. I have corresponded with more than 1,000 PNC collectors during the past five years, and all of them have contributed to my appreciation of PNCs. Those who deserve special recognition are Fred A. Anderson Jr., Paul Arnold, Louis Bartilotta, Tom Beschorner, Stanley W. Brown, James R. Callis Jr., Jiri Chytil, Michael A. Courtney, Allison W. Cusick, Ronald J. DeHaas, Don Eastman, Darrell Ertzberger, Walter P. Esparza, James D. Galceran, Richard Grant, William J. Griffiths, Myron G. Hill Jr., Robert A. Holcomb, John Hotchner, Conrad Keydel, Robert E. Kitson, George Kuhn, Douglas Landon, Tim Lindemuth, Eugene Y. Liu, Alan Malakoff, Bill

McMurray, Richard J. Nazar, Frank Norulak, Robert A. Olsen, William K. Phipps, James A. Rial Sr., Steven J. Rod, Philip F. Rose, Robert S. Rowe, Eric Russow, Dennis Ryan, Steve Schweighofer, Frank Shively Jr., David L. Smith, Gene Trinks, Dino Vardavas, Thom E. Wheeler, and Calvin V. Whitsel.

The editors who first encouraged me to write on plate number coils, Michael Green and Kyle Jansson of *Stamp Collector*, and Bill Welch of *The American Philatelist*, started a project bigger than any of us would have imagined. I'm sure I've forgotten many others who deserve mention, and I regret every such omission.

With all the wisdom gleaned from such an enthusiastic collective, there shouldn't be too many mistakes in this book, but I'll accept full responsibility for those that are found, and will welcome correspondence pointing them out.

CONTENTS

Chapter 1

Getting Started with PNCs

In the beginning, many of us fell into collecting plate number coils without an established system to guide us and with no comprehensive sources of supply. It was probably just as well that there were no albums, because we generally had to take what we could find, often nothing but line pairs with plate numbers on the left stamp. I don't know how many PNCs I soaked off envelopes to fill spaces in my used singles collection without paying any attention to the cancelation dates — even though I was also interested in acquiring as many numbers on cover as off.

Today's PNC beginners face an entirely different situation. Those who collect mint strips can decide from the start which standard format to collect, and how comprehensively. Some collectors prefer just one plate strip of each stamp without regard to its specific plate number. Scott publishes album pages for those collectors with spaces for mounting plate strips of three stamps. Stamps 'N' Stuff publishes similar album pages but with spaces for strips of five. For Transportation series coil stamps only, White Ace offers album pages with spaces for one pair and one strip of three of each stamp, alongside a descriptive writeup of the subject of each stamp.

For collectors who decide to indulge themselves fully in the pursuit of a mint strip of every stamp and every plate number, Scott has published a comprehensive album with illustrated spaces for strips of three. Lighthouse publishes a set of hingeless album pages, with protective mounts already in place, for every number in mint strips of five, including most precancel gap positions.

Wastebasket collectors and mixture sorters, who may pursue used singles of every plate number, can use the Scott comprehensive plate number coil singles album. All these commercial albums are periodically updated with supplements. Collectors who choose a more varied approach to PNCs often use stock sheets or customized album pages to house their collections.

Whatever format a collector prefers, it is wise to collect the highest quality material one can afford, as in any area of philately. Plate number coils are bought, sold and traded according to condition, yet we still don't have perfect agreement on grading standards. Some cynics have said that the rating depends on whether you're buying or selling.

Nevertheless, we've come a long way. When Dennis Chamberlain issued the very first mint PNC list in August 1983, he made no mention at all of centering. Before the year was out, Chamberlain defined fine-to-very fine centering this way: "Plate numbers will be whole and joint lines will touch perforations." The other early PNC dealers, Vern Kraus, Tom Myers and D. John Shultz, all tended to follow Chamberlain's lead.

Everybody agreed that cut plate numbers were not acceptable. More recently, some collectors have specialized in miscut coil varieties. This includes stamps with plate numbers entirely at the top, or split top and bottom, but such items are still usually excluded from basic PNC collections.

In June 1985, Al Haake mailed out his first price list. In a dramatic departure from his predecessors, he offered each mint PNC strip in three different grades, each priced accordingly. His definition of fine almost equaled Dennis Chamberlain's fine to very fine: "line touches perfs, numbers clear." For Haake, very fine meant "50 to 75 percent of line on perfs, numbers clear." His extra fine promised "85 to 100 percent of line on perfs, numbers clear. Those without lines, exceptional centering."

Haake later revised his criteria for extra fine, so that Cottrell press coils must have 100 percent of the joint line on the perforations to qualify. These definitions are the closest we have to a consensus, al-

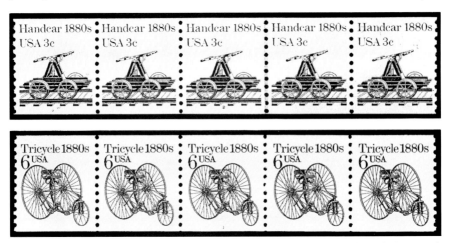

Both of these mint strips would be rated extra fine to superb under existing grading systems. The 3¢ Handcar strip has the entire joint line on the perforations; the 6¢ Tricycle is attractively centered in both dimensions.

though Stephen G. Esrati has criticized them for being concerned sole-ly with horizontal centering. His definitions are similar to Haake's, but Esrati adds a superb state: "line exactly centered inside perfs, height centered," and for those without lines, "design is perfectly cen-tered."

Many PNC dealers now have a basic fine-to-very-fine price, and then a specified percentage surcharge for extra fine or superb. Buy advertisements often work in reverse, offering a price for extra fine, with a specified discount for lower grades. Generally, these standards work pretty well. Sometimes, however, the placement of the joint line is not necessarily a gauge of overall centering. Another problem is that the centering often varies from stamp to stamp on a strip. That's why I personally always judge a mint strip by the overall centering, and don't care too much where the joint line falls.

The last Cottrell press stamps were issued in 1985. Stamps issued since that time, as well as earlier Flag issues and B press Transporta-tion coils, have no joint lines. As the numbers of coils issued without lines grows, traditional grading criteria are gradually asserting them-selves, with less attention to the lines even on the older stamps.

Grading used PNCs is a subtler and more complex activity, because additional variables, such as the quality of separation and cancelation, are as important as centering. Used precancels are normally cut and affixed by machine, and only rarely do the blades chop right down the center of the perforations.

For me, if a reasonably centered stamp is cut so the perforations are full on one side and well-indicated but short on the other, that's very fine. One straightedge reduces it to fine, but even two straightedges, which I'd call "average," are collectible in my opinion.

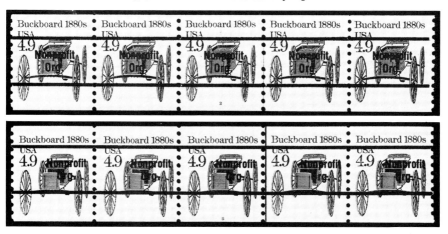

These 4.9¢ precancel strips illustrate a problem of grading. By usual PNC stand-ards, the plate number 2 strip would be graded as extra fine. The joint line is centered on the perforations. The plate number 5 strip, however, would be consid-ered barely fine since the line only grazes the perforations, but the stamp's design is actually centered on the plate number 5 strip.

The disappearance of the joint line on B and C press coils has brought PNC collectors back to mainstream grading criteria. Most would regard this plate 1 strip of the 5.3¢ Elevator stamp as extra fine to superb, although some who regard the plate number as a design feature would prefer higher placement of the image.

Manually separated stamps are a different matter. Determining how uneven the perforations can be, or whether one or two short perfs are acceptable, is a highly subjective judgment. So are cancels. Ideally, they should be clear, crisp, and well away from the plate number.

But choosing between two stamps when one has worse centering, better perforations, and disappointing placement of the cancel is highly subjective. And what about slogan cancels? Some collectors like them and others don't. Choosing between one with a slogan cancel and one with wavy lines would probably be made according to that preference, rather than to some objective ideal.

If you're soaking stamps, the decision is a purely private matter. If you're buying or trading, you're entitled to satisfaction. Refuse to accept any PNCs, mint or used, that don't measure up to your personal requirements.

Beyond collecting mint and used single stamps, pairs, and strips of various lengths, PNC collecting is as varied and challenging as any other philatelic specialty. Some collectors seek every plate number known to exist on first-day covers, or first-day ceremony programs, or USPS Souvenir Pages. Others collect PNCs as postal history, searching for interesting examples on non-philatelic covers, including the

These are typical used precancels. The plate number 1 stamp on the left was not properly aligned with the blade of the franking machine. A fairly typical problem, the perforations are cut off on one side. Alignment is better on the center stamp and best on the right stamp, although not perfect. Most used grading systems would rate the left stamp fine, and the other two stamps very fine or better.

By all objective standards of grading, this 4¢ Stagecoach would be rated very fine or better in almost anyone's collection.

earliest known dates for each number.

For those with large budgets, collecting imperforate PNCs can provide the ultimate philatelic fun. More modest spenders can still find many affordable varieties, including shifted perforations, miscut strips with numbers at the top instead of the bottom, constant plate varieties, and other assorted flyspecks.

Precancel gap position collecting has a growing band of committed adherents, especially since the appearance of the Lighthouse album that provides space for most of the reported positions. A few dedicated diehards insist on having each collectible gap in a strip long enough to include both paired Cottrell press plate numbers and beyond. Even collectors of the stick-on labels from coil rolls have their own study group and body of literature.

Few collectors dive right in collecting everything. But it's quite common for a collector who begins by building a collection of mint PNC strips of three, once having completed that goal, to branch out into another area, such as used singles, first day covers, and so forth. In that way, PNCs can be quite addictive.

Many collections have been built almost entirely through post office purchases and trades with other collectors. For trading to be a success-

The choice as to which of these 22¢ Flag plate number 10 coil stamps is better depends on whether the grader prefers the right stamp's better perforations or the left stamp's clear plate number.

5

Some collectors like slogan cancels; others shun them. That would probably be the biggest factor in determining which of these 20¢ Flag plate number 14 stamps to keep in a collection of used stamps.

ful strategy, it is best to seek out collectors who are at a similar level of achievement; otherwise it can be quite frustrating. Beginners only rarely have material that advanced collectors need. On the other hand, correspondence with more advanced collectors is encouraged, and the PNC community is among the friendliest in the entire hobby. Every PNC enthusiast should join the Plate Number Coil Collectors Club, the Bureau Issues Association, and the American Philatelic Society.

Chapter 2

The New United States Stamp Specialty of the 1980s

Plate number coils, or PNCs, are by far the most enthusiastically collected stamps issued by the United States in the past 50 years. Even though the stamps involved in this passion have all been issued since 1981, and include some of the most common of all U.S. issues, a few of them are already being bought and sold, in a highly competitive market, for thousands of dollars each.

No other intentionally issued recent U.S. stamps have realized such success in the marketplace. Prices of key PNCs rival those of classic 19th-century rarities and premium modern errors. No other area of U.S. collecting, including errors and classics, has experienced such phenomenal growth in recent years.

The factor that commands so much attention from collectors is a tiny number three-fourths of a millimeter high in the bottom margin of the stamp, which appears at regular intervals throughout the coil. For line-engraved (intaglio) stamps, the number is usually a single digit, but occasionally it's a two-digit number. In some cases so many of a particular engraved stamp are printed that 10 or more plates or sleeves are used to keep it in circulation. Usually plates are sent to

Tiny numbers printed on some modern coil stamps have sparked unprecedented collector interest in the new PNC specialty.

This stamp was in such demand that a large number of plates was required to keep it in production, so plate numbers reached double digits.

press in approximately consecutive order as earlier plates are damaged or wear out. For those issues, stamps with double-digit plate numbers eventually go on sale. Single-digit numbers also occur in combinations on some multicolored coil stamps printed by the gravure process, where each ink requires a separate printing cylinder.

What makes these coils distinctive, and unprecedented among U.S. stamps prior to 1981, is that plate numbers are included below the central design of certain stamps, not as marginal markings. On earlier U.S. coil stamps, plate numbers were printed in the selvage, which was trimmed off during processing. Collectors could not obtain plate numbers on properly manufactured coil stamps as they could with sheet stamps and certain booklet panes.

Foreign Forerunners

There are forerunners to modern PNC collecting. Certain 19th-century British stamps had plate numbers included in their designs. Like modern U.S. PNCs, certain of the old British plate number stamps are much scarcer and more valuable than others of the same issue, but unlike our PNCs, these British ancestors have plate numbers on every stamp. Ours occur only at predetermined intervals. The great majority of stamps in a roll have no number at all.

Early British stamps have another feature that some collectors have likened to our PNCs: the corner letters, which alphabetically code the position of each stamp on the sheet. But again, every stamp on the sheet had these letters, not just certain ones.

For Specialists Only: U.S. Forerunners

A more direct forebear of today's PNC collecting was the practice of some early United States coil specialists. They sought older coils that were miscut enough to show the plate number. If the stamp were properly trimmed, the number would not be seen. Such stamps were not easy to find. The majority of coils, even miscut, would reveal nothing more than part of the stamps from the adjacent row on the printed web of stamps. Only stamps from the very edge of the printed web could have a number. Finding a coil from that location, sufficiently miscut to show the entire plate number, was rare. But many were found with partial numbers, positioned at the top or bottom of horizontally wound "side coils," or at the left or right of vertically wound "end coils."

These forerunner plate number coils came mostly from two types of continuous webfed single-color rotary presses, the Stickneys and the Cottrells. Both involved two engraved curved plates mounted in tandem around the printing cylinder. Together the two plates formed a cylindrical printing surface. But because the plates never adjoined each other perfectly, ink would gather in the space between them and then print as a line between the stamps.

Coil line pairs, showing these joint lines in the middle, have been avidly collected by generations of U.S. stamp collectors. Those who collected plate numbers taken from miscut rolls found the plate numbers right beside the joint lines — not surprisingly, since the numbers were engraved at the edges of each plate. On Stickney press plates, the

The gravure process requires a separate plate cylinder for each color, so each of these digits represents a different plate.

Some 19th-century British stamps have plate numbers incorporated into the design. Shown is plate number 5.

numbers were entered at diagonally opposite corners of each plate, so only one plate number would adjoin the line. Side coils printed from Stickney plates were laid out with 170 subjects in 10 rows of 17 stamps each, so joint lines occurred at 17-stamp intervals throughout a roll. Plate numbers were placed above the first and below the last stamp on each plate. End coils came from similar 150-subject plates, with joint lines at 15-stamp intervals, and analogous plate number placement at the left and right. Complete or nearly complete plate numbers can sometimes be reconstructed by combining partial numbers from each position, top and bottom on side coils, left and right on end coils.

Collecting these freaks in their heyday was a difficult task, limited mainly to a handful of members of the Bureau Issues Association, an organization for collectors who specialize in U.S. stamps. In the March 1947 issue of the BIA's monthly journal, *The Bureau Specialist*, Norman W. Kempf wrote, "Because of this difficulty in obtaining them, interest in collecting these items is limited to a relatively few specialists. Surprisingly enough, fairly complete collections of the

The world's first postage stamp, Britain's Penny Black, issued in 1840, and other early British issues have letters in the corners identifying the stamp's position on the sheet. The B and C on this Penny Black specify its original placement as the third stamp in the second row.

numbers used on the Presidential issue have been formed by at least a dozen collectors, due to an excellent spirit of cooperation in exchanging numbers by collectors in different cities. The numbers are generally collected in strips of five, with the number in the middle. In this way, the top and bottom numbers can be completed and appear symmetrically in the middle of a 'block' of 10 stamps."

All Presidential series coil stamps were printed on the Stickney rotary presses. The Cottrell presses made their debut at the Bureau of

Engraving and Printing in October 1955, the year after the Liberty series stamps replaced the Presidentials as the standard U.S. definitives. These presses were three times as productive as the Stickneys, according to George W. Brett writing in the December 1956 issue of *The Bureau Specialist*.

The switch required a gradual transition in coil production, because the first coil stamps printed on the new presses had to be perforated, slit, and packaged on equipment designed to be compatible with the Stickneys. This meant that the full productive capacity of the Cottrells could not be realized immediately. For more than a year, coils were printed from 384-subject Cottrell press plates, laid out in 16 rows of 24 stamps. But the changeover to new examining and coil-processing equipment permitted the use of 432-subject coil plates, adding two rows, starting in early 1958. Either way, the joint line occurred at 24-stamp intervals.

On 384-subject plates, placement of plate numbers was similar to that used on the small Stickney plates. But the 432-subject plates were more crowded, so numbers were located under the first and last stamps in the bottom row only. Whole numbers cannot be reconstructed from this plate array. When miscut, two partial numbers appear, one on each side of the joint line, but only in the bottom position, or on the left side of end coils. In mint condition, these are usually collected in strips of six, with the joint line in the center.

For several Liberty series coil stamps, it is

This strip of the 2¢ John Adams end coil stamp from the Presidential series is sufficiently miscut to show a portion of plate number 22210.

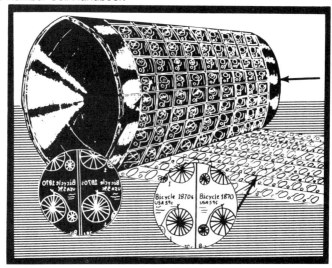

The Stickney and Cottrell presses required two curved plates to run. Ink would gather in the spaces separating the two plates where they adjoin, and print as a joint line.

therefore possible to collect miscuts with single plate numbers in strips of five from both Stickney and Cottrell presses, and with pairs of plate numbers in strips of six, also from the Cottrells. The dozen or so specialists who pioneered this field learned about production varieties on their stamps that were unknown to most U.S. collectors, and are still not well-developed in the *Scott Specialized Catalogue of United States Stamps*. Liberty series specialists differentiate between the wet printing of the Stickney press coils and the later dry printing of the Cottrells. These differences are noted in the *Scott Specialized* beginning with the 1989 edition.

Scott does not differentiate between the two different dry printing varieties. Besides the different positions of plate numbers, Cottrell press coils printed from 384-subject plates have measurably larger perforation holes than those printed from 432-subject plates.

Coil stamps in several subsequent definitive series were also printed on the Cottrell presses: the Prominent Americans, Americana, and Transportation series, as well as the 1963 George Washington and Andrew Jackson stamps.

Production varieties that fascinated the relatively few who collected

Coil line pairs have one stamp from each of the two plates astride the printed line where the plates meet.

Whole plate numbers are rare on older coil stamps, but it is sometimes possible to find matched positions of partial plate numbers that reconstruct the number when placed side by side, as is done here with plate 22101 side coils of the 10¢ John Tyler stamp of the 1938 Presidential series.

them at the dawn of the Cottrell era in the 1950s have been among the most widely noted features of modern PNC collecting, born during the Cottrells' twilight. When the last of the Cottrell presses was retired in late 1985, several coil stamp designs that had begun on its curved, paired plates were later reissued from single cylindrical sleeves, printed on the newer intaglio B press. They are called sleeves, as opposed to cylinders, because internally they are tapered to fit the press mandrel. Gravure printing cylinders are smaller and not tapered.

While these varieties are fairly easy to differentiate — Cottrell press coils have joint lines, B press coils do not — other coil stamps that have been printed on more than one press are next to impossible to differentiate.

For stamps printed on both the intaglio B and C (or D) presses, the B press 52-stamp interval between plate numbers conclusively differentiates it from the 48-stamp interval of the C or D press product, provided long enough strips are available for reference. But there are no handy guideposts to differentiate engraved coils printed on both the C and D presses, or gravure coils printed on the A and Andreotti presses. C and D press printing sleeves are interchangeable, as are A and Andreotti press gravure cylinders.

Today's plate number coils are usually collected in mint strips of three or five, with the plate, sleeve or cylinder number on the center

This miscut line pair of the 8¢ Eisenhower stamp shows portions of Cottrell press plates 32753 and 32754.

When Cottrell press end coils are miscut enough to show a portion of the plate numbers, they appear only on the left. This 3¢ Parkman coil pair shows parts of plate numbers 35763 and 35762.

stamp, or as used singles. (The Postal Service calls all three "plate numbers," as I shall do frequently in this book.) Some specialists also collect PNCs on cover, or in mint strips long enough to show various kinds of production varieties, including errors and freaks.

Coil Counting Numbers

One final forerunner is worth mentioning: coil counting numbers, a direct consequence of the shift in coil production from the Stickney to the Cottrell presses. Although counting numbers have been relatively unknown among United States coil collectors, they were certainly known to several of the people who helped devise the new plate number coil system, and may have influenced their thinking as they developed the single-digit small-number scheme.

During the interim period when the Cottrell presses were operating with 384-subject plates while the Bureau awaited new coiling equipment, coil processing remained largely a manual, labor-intensive operation. Counting numbers were added to increase efficiency and accuracy of coil-processing workers.

In an article in the January 1970 issue of *The United States Special-*

Plate number collectors of mint Cottrell press coils usually keep the examples with two partial numbers in strips of six. The strip of 9¢ Capitol coils in the Americana series shown here was printed from plates 36985 and 36984.

The customary formats for collecting modern plate number coils are in mint strips of three or five, with the plate number on the center stamp, or as used singles. Other configurations are less popular.

ist, E. Elsworth Post explained the format of these interim plates, the first to utilize the "dry" Cottrell printing method:

"The plate contained 16 rows of 24 subjects each; however, inasmuch as the coil processing equipment could not handle a web 16 subjects deep, the plate was arranged in two halves of eight rows each. For all practical purposes the top and bottom halves were identical, each with 192 subjects and with sufficient space between the halves to provide for the slitting of the printed web. During the process of slitting the printed and perforated web — better than two miles long — several cuts were made the other way, dividing the huge web into several smaller ones.

"These smaller rolls, now only 8 stamps deep, could be handled

In the early days of plate number collecting, imprint and number strips were popular, like this 1¢ Franklin example from 1898. Later collectors preferred plate number blocks.

These mis-slit 4¢ Lincoln stamps make up a continuous strip from one Cottrell press plate number to the next, printed from 384-subject plates. The strip is cut far enough into the top selvage, which should have been removed and discarded during processing, to show one complete plate number and nearly all of the next plus all five counting numbers in between. The stamps were in the collection of the late E. Elsworth Post.

on the coil processing equipment and were ready to be cut into lengths of 500, 1000 or 3000. Because there were now 24 stamps (divisible by 4) between the 'plate joint lines,' instead of the previous 17, counting numbers were added to the plate as an aid for faster and more accurate counting.

"As previously explained, the plate was made up of two halves of 192 subjects each. Each half has a plate number over stamp #1 (on the printed sheet) and each half has a plate number under stamp 192. There are four rows of counting numbers engraved on the plate. On the printed sheet these numbers are inverted at the top of each half of the plate but read normally at the bottom of each half. The numbers are 4, 8, 12, 16 and 20 with the plate number substituting for 24."

To make up coils of 500, a processor would count from a joint line 20 lines (20 x 24 stamps = 480) plus 20 (480 +20 = 500) and cut the web beside counting number 20. This would leave four stamps before the next line, so the next cut for a 500-stamp coil would be at counting number 16 (4 + [20 x 24] + 16 = 500), and so forth.

Coils printed on the Cottrell presses from 384-subject plates first appeared in 1956, processed in the manner described here. That system was in use until 1959, when the need for counting numbers endcd. The new Huck coil-processing equipment, capable of loading the 18-row printed webs all at once, combined slitting, perforating, and counting into a single mechanized operation. The new coils were printed from 432-subject plates, the format used for all coils printed on the Cottrell press from that time until they were retired and scrapped in 1985.

Except for the 25¢ Paul Revere coils, all denominations of Liberty-series coil stamps had been printed from 384-subject plates — the 1¢ George Washington, 1¼¢ Santa Fe, 2¢ Thomas Jefferson, 2½¢ Bunker Hill, 3¢ Statue of Liberty, 4¢ Abraham Lincoln, and 4½¢ Hermitage. The 1¢, 2¢, 3¢ and 4¢ values had earlier been "wet" printed from 170-subject plates on the Stickney presses. All Liberty coils, including the 25¢ Revere, were later printed from 432-subject Cottrell press plates.

The 384-subject plates were only used for a short time during the transition, but their single- and double-digit small counting numbers, only 0.07 inches high and never used before or since, may have planted some seeds in the memories of those who, 25 years later, put similar tiny numbers on the stamps themselves to give us plate number coils.

Plate Number Blocks

If only a handful of U.S. collectors have specialized in the pursuit of plate numbers on old British stamps or on pre-1981 U.S. coils, and

Plate block collecting soared in popularity in the 1950s when the Liberty series definitive stamps appeared.

even fewer have even known about coil counting numbers, the opposite is true of U.S. plate number blocks and plate number imprint strips. These have been collected almost as long as the hobby of philately has existed in this country.

A booklet published by the Bureau Issues Association quoted an 1896 price list: "Plate number collecting, so far as the United States stamps are concerned, is not a new thing. For many years some of our largest collectors have been adding plate number strips to their collec-

Finding all four positions of a number makes it possible to reconstruct the plate layout in miniature on an album page.

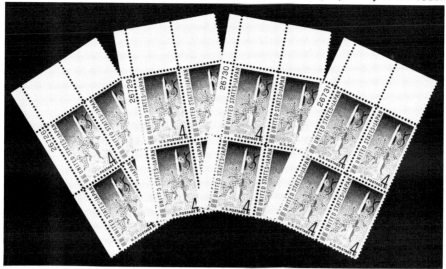

Collecting one example of every plate number on one stamp was another challenge for plate block enthusiasts.

tions, but during the past two years it has become a very popular branch of philately. Since the Bureau of Engraving & Printing, of Washington, D.C., has taken the contract for printing the adhesive postage stamps, the collecting of their plate numbers and imprints has become a regular fad with the collectors of U.S. stamps."*

Actually the dealer, J.M. Bartels & Company of Washington, got a bit carried away with his promotion. For the first half century of Bureau printings, plate number block collecting was mainly the province of specialists. According to Herman Herst Jr. in his book *Nassau Street*, plate number blocks were collected by a few but ignored by most collectors during the years of the Great Depression. The principal function of the Bureau Issues Association in the 1930s and 1940s was to circulate information on current plate numbers.

Eventually, though, plate number block collecting did become an exciting pastime embracing casual collectors and novices as well as experts. The craze soared in the 1950s and 1960s. Introducing the 1954 Liberty series definitive issue, the *Durland Standard Plate Number Catalog* states, "The advent of this series brought a sharp increase in the collecting of plate number blocks."

One factor that made this a popular field was its relatively low cost. In the days when the first-class letter rate was 3¢, a typical plate number block had a face value of 12¢. Collectors could match their collecting styles with their financial capabilities and levels of interest.

*Stanley B. Segal, *Errors, Freaks and Oddities on U.S. Stamps — Question Marks in Philately*, page 67.

Collecting plate singles has kept plate number fun within reach of those on a shoestring budget.

Usually casual collectors would be satisfied with just one plate block of each new stamp.

More advanced collectors would try to collect a matched set, representing a plate number from each position on the plate. On an album page, this would reconstruct the sheet in miniature. Others would try to get one example of each different plate number. The most committed plate block specialists tried to acquire every known plate number in every available position.

Less popular, but less expensive, is the pursuit of plate number singles. Even though this approach gets no encouragement from standard stamp catalogs, it retains an avid following.

Today's plate number coils offer a similar range of collecting styles. Some collectors are satisfied with only one plate number strip of each stamp, while others collect them comprehensively, attempting to acquire an example of every different plate number.

Eventually the popularity of plate block collecting waned. Today, although thousands of collectors still routinely collect plate number blocks of every new issue, this area of collecting has never regained its former status. Many large accumulations of plate number blocks that once were worth a significant premium have sold in recent years for less than face value on the discount postage market.

This decline was caused by the convergence of several factors, but principal among them was the advance in stamp printing technology. During the heyday of plate number block collecting, the great majority of stamps issued by the United States were printed in one color from engraved plates.

Toward the end of the 1960s, the Bureau of Engraving and Printing introduced new presses that allowed several colors to be printed simultaneously. The three-color intaglio sheetfed Giori presses were able to print up to three colors from a single line-engraved plate, while the six-color Miller offset sheetfed press and the seven-color Andreotti webfed gravure press required several plates or cylinders at a time, one for each ink used.

By the time that plate number block collecting hit its stride in the 1950s, tens of thousands of plates had been used at the Bureau, so each plate number consisted of five digits, substantially filling up the selvage space adjacent to the corner stamp. When multiple plates or cylinders were required, the plate numbers were strung out along the selvage, each number beside a different stamp. The more numbers that appeared, the larger was the block required to collect them, sometimes up to 20 stamps. Meanwhile, the first-class letter rate had crept up from 3¢ to 4¢, to 5¢, and to 6¢.

So from the early fifties, when the standard plate number block had 12¢ face value, to the end of the sixties, when a normal block would cost from 24¢ for a block of four to $1.20 for a strip of 20 6¢ stamps at the post office, the size of a plate block often grew to unwieldy, or at least unattractive, proportions. And that was just the beginning of the problem. Rates have continued to rise ever since, steadily pushing up the average price per stamp.

Meanwhile, another production innovation required large plate number blocks even on single-color stamps. Instead of a plate layout yielding four 100-stamp panes per revolution of the plate cylinder, some A press gravure cylinders, 23 stamps in circumference, yield a continuous roll of stamps without selvage in one dimension, either at

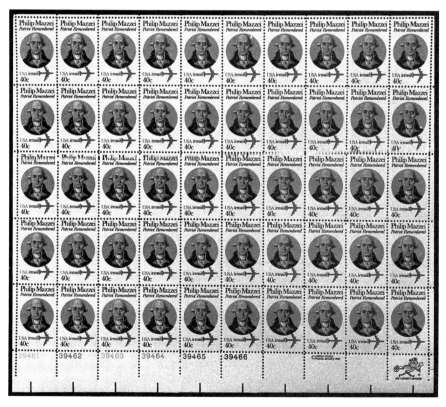

According to the Scott catalog, a plate number block of the 40¢ Mazzei comprises 12 stamps, with a face value of $4.80. Large expensive blocks like this were among the factors that turned many collectors away from plate number blocks.

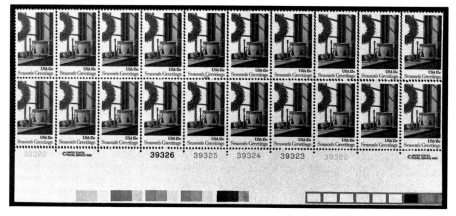

On some stamps printed on the A combination press, the plate numbers "float" to different positions, adding further confusion to plate block collecting.

the top and bottom, or at the left and right. When this web is cut into panes 10 stamps deep, the numbers appear to "float," from one pane to the next, to different positions along the selvage.

Some collectors believed that the Bureau of Engraving and Printing and the Postal Service were deliberately creating stamps in ways that required the purchase of large blocks. Others, who accepted the explanation that the larger blocks were simply the consequence of production innovations, nevertheless didn't like them, for a variety of reasons. Six- to 20-stamp strips do not have the same eye appeal as uniform corner blocks of four.

Gradually, many of the most avid plate number block collectors lost interest. By the end of the 1970s, a time when enthusiasm for U.S. stamp collecting and speculating in the market were reaching frenzied proportions, plate number block collecting collapsed. As we shall see,

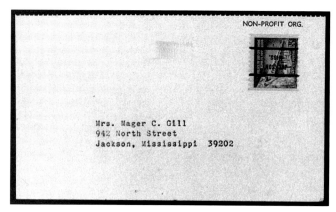

For more than 60 years, Bureau precancels consisted of a city and state inscription between parallel horizontal lines, overprinted on definitive stamps used mainly on bulk mail.

In 1969, 6¢ Christmas stamps were overprinted locally with precancels of four cities from plates supplied by the government, as an experiment.

it was out of the ashes of this once towering domain that the new plate number coil specialty arose.

Bureau Precancels

One other collecting specialty has played a significant role in shaping plate number coil collecting — precancels, especially precanceled stamps whose overprints are applied at the Bureau of Engraving and Printing.

Beginning in 1916, a Bureau precancel consisted of an overprint featuring a city and state inscription between a pair of parallel horizontal lines. The stamps were ordered as needed by the respective cities, to be sold exclusively to holders of bulk mail or other precancel

The 1970 6¢ Christmas Toys and Nativity stamps were precanceled with overprinted stylized killer bars but no city and state inscriptions.

23

The self-adhesive 1974 Christmas 10¢ Weather Vane stamp was inscribed "PRECANCELED" in the legend above the denomination, without any overprint.

user permits, who were instructed to use the stamps only for their designated postal purpose.

When those rules were obeyed, the only precancels that reached collectors legitimately were those that had done postal duty. Although some collectors managed to circumvent the rules to obtain mint precancels, the customary practice was to soak off the gum, so that such stamps could not be distinguished from legitimately acquired ones. Thus, precancels were collected as "used" stamps, even in cases where they had not franked mail.

There were exceptions to the basic policy. Experimental precancels of the 1969 6¢ Christmas stamps were overprinted in four cities from plates supplied by the government. The next year's Christmas stamps, a se-tenant block of Christmas toys and a Lorenzo Lotto Nativity Painting single, were precanceled with stylized killer lines but no

In the late 1960s and early 1970s these three airmail stamps were precanceled Washington, D.C., for the exclusive use of members of Congress. The 10¢ denomination was a local product, while the 11¢ and 13¢ values were overprinted at the Bureau of Engraving and Printing.

city/state inscriptions. The self-adhesive 10¢ Weather Vane Christmas stamps of 1974 were inscribed "PRECANCELLED."

In the late 1960s and early 1970s, three airmail stamps were precanceled Washington, D.C., for Congressional use. None of these required permits.

In September 1978 the Postal Service drastically revised its precancel format. Henceforth there would be no city/state precancels created at the Bureau of Engraving and Printing. The new Bureau precancels would have just a pair of plain lines, or lines and a service inscription

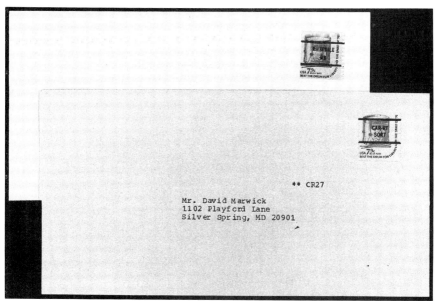

Before September 1978, Bureau precancels had city/state overprints. After that, the overprints consisted of plain lines or lines and service inscriptions.

Some stamps were overprinted in both of the new precancel styles, with plain lines and with service inscriptions between the lines.

such as "PRESORTED FIRST-CLASS." The same stamps would be valid on bulk third-class or quantity first-class mail anywhere in the country. All would be sold in mint condition to collectors through the Philatelic Sales Division. Henceforth there would be no need for subterfuge to acquire them, or to own them as mint stamps.

Once precancels achieved philatelic acceptance, specialists began to focus on elements besides the basic stamp and overprint combinations. One feature that attracted interest was the gaps in the precancel lines that occur at regular intervals. These were collected as coil pairs. At the same time, collectors who had no particular interest in precancels as such began collecting them as untagged varieties of modern stamps that otherwise exist only with phosphor tagging.

Because of the established traditions of Bureau precancel specialists, the relationship between them and PNC collectors has not been an easy one. On the one hand, PNC collectors have learned a great

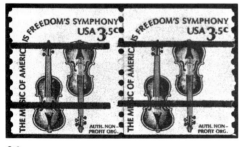

The 1978 change in precancel formats broadened the ways of collecting them. Gap pairs became items of interest to precancel specialists, while other collectors regarded precancels' lack of phosphor tagging as their defining feature.

deal from the traditional precancel specialists. But today, as the PNC throng greatly outnumbers all of its forebears, listings in the Scott catalog follow the old Bureau precancel modes of collecting. Plate number strips of precanceled coils are priced in the used column, even though virtually nobody buys, sells or collects them that way.

PNC collecting has borrowed from many of these earlier provinces of philately, but it has outstripped them all. It has pioneered a whole new approach to U.S. stamp collecting.

Chapter 3

New Plate Number System

The founding document of plate number coil collecting is a news release from the U.S. Postal Service dated December 10, 1980. Philatelic Release number 82 was titled "USPS ANNOUNCES NEW PLATE NUMBER SYSTEM."

It begins, "The U.S. Postal Service announced today that a new plate numbering system for U.S. postage stamps will be into effect January 1.

"Except in cases where more than four designs appear on a pane of stamps, the new system will establish a plate block as consisting of four stamps regardless of a number of inks used or the press used to print the stamps.

"The new system also will permit offset plate numbers to remain on the selvage of panes instead of being trimmed off during production as in the past, and will make possible the printing of plate numbers on booklet panes and the printing, at intervals, of plate numbers on coil stamps."

The purpose of the new policy was clearly to revive the flagging popularity of plate number block collecting. The stated goal was "to make plate number collecting a less expensive pursuit based on logic and consistency." Yet the approach deliberately embraced booklets and coils as well: "The Postal Service said that, to be based upon logic, a new plate numbering system should be applicable to all stamps in all formats. Therefore, it never considered sheet stamp-only 'solutions' such as stacking five-digit plate numbers in the selvage or curving them around the corners of panes."

The new system was designed, for the first time, to yield information about the production sequence of the particular stamp. That could be extrapolated from the old system only with great difficulty. "In the past, plate numbers (when they appeared) reflected an accounting-system sequence only. It was not possible, by looking at a pane of new stamps, to determine how that pane fitted into the manufacturing sequence for the issue."

The first eight pages of the announcement dealt almost exclusively with the plate number system on sheet stamps, concluding, "The consecutive numbering feature of the new system is expected to be popular with collectors . . . Consecutive numbers also will contribute to the attractive display of plate blocks."

Compared to sheet stamps, the new policy regarding plate numbers on coil stamps and booklet panes received little space in the announcement, less than one page in all. This actually represented more drastic change. For booklet panes, the change was to add the plate number to the upper binding stub, while for coils it was to place a plate number on the stamps themselves, at predetermined intervals. Had logic and consistency really guided the decision, we would probably have sheet and booklet stamps with plate numbers on a corner stamp, rather than in the margin.

These new plate number policies failed to rekindle interest in plate number blocks of the sort that prevailed in the 1950s and 1960s. Booklet collecting, although definitely growing in popularity, has so far not focused special attention on plate numbers. In fact, the announcement that every booklet would have a visible plate number on the binding stub made the numbers themselves incidental, except to that handful of collectors who seek all the different numbers for each booklet.

As time went on, booklet specialists reported various combinations of booklet cover varieties and plate numbers, numbers available on both top and bottom panes, and dozens of subtler differences. Those who collect them are as keen as any, but their specialty has not captured the imagination of ordinary U.S. collectors.

The opposite is true of coils. Although the original announcement devoted the least amount of space to the new coil numbering system, that has turned out to be the aspect that has caused all the excitement, embracing literally thousands of old and new collectors, and injecting an element of shared adventure that had virtually disappeared

The nondenominated D stamp, issued in 1985 to cover the 22¢ letter rate, was printed on the gravure section of the A press, using a 460-subject format, 20 stamps across the cylinder and 23 around the circumference, with plate numbers and other marginal markings floating from position to position because the 100-stamp panes are not even multiples of the cylinder impressions.

from philatelic life.

Some of Philatelic Release number 82's predictions were overly optimistic. The promise to "establish a plate block as consisting of four stamps regardless of the number of inks used or the press used to print the stamps" was thwarted for five more years by the A press "floaters."

The guarantee "that all plate blocks for a given issue, regular or commemorative, will have consecutive plate numbers" promised more than could be delivered. The Bureau of Engraving and Printing assigned plate numbers consecutively, but there's considerable distance between engraving plate numbers in order and putting plate blocks or strips into an album.

Some plates were never certified. Others, though certified, were never sent to press. Some went to press out of sequence. Still others would be taken out of production, repaired, and later returned to the press for a late run of an early number. And some plates that were printed had all their impressions destroyed.

On combination printings, offset plates frequently wear out faster than intaglio plates or sleeves, sometimes resulting in complex dou-

The 1982 State Birds and Flowers stamps were printed from five cylinders on the Bureau of Engraving and Printing's Andreotti gravure press. Thus the plate number consists of five digits, one for each process color — yellow, magenta, cyan and black — for the halftone picture image, and another black cylinder for the line inscription impression.

ble-digit sequences for the offset numbers, while the intaglio numbers stay low and orderly.

At this writing, one booklet has been issued, the 22¢ Flag with Fireworks design, that does not have the promised plate number in every booklet, this because it was adapted from a printing scheme intended for sheet stamp production.

In the case of Official stamps, the disparity between the legal limitations on the stamps' usage and the requirements of philatelic marketing caused the Postal Service to drop the numbers entirely, from both sheets and coils.

The brief reference to coils in the 1980 document said that "single-digit numbers will be printed at 24-stamp intervals on single-color coils and 52-stamp intervals on multicolor coils," anticipating production on the single-color Cottrells and the three-color B press, respectively. But by the end of the first year, we had double-digit single-color coils from the Cottrell presses. Later came 48-stamp intervals on C press three-color Flag coils, 38-stamp intervals on Andreotti press and A press single-color gravure coils, double-digit numbers on B, C and D press three-color Flag coils, and groups of four, five, and six single-digit combinations on multicolor gravure coils from the Andreotti press. The new system proved to be much more complex and varied than its inventors anticipated, but at the same time more interesting and challenging to stamp collectors. To be fair to USPS, rate changes precluded immediate implementation of the USPS number-

The 1984 Smokey the Bear commemorative was the first stamp to combine offset and intaglio printing on the D press. Because offset plates wear out faster than intaglio sleeves, offset plate numbers reached double digits, while only plate 3 has been reported for the intaglio.

ing system, while technological improvements added unforeseen nuances. The first collector reaction to the new numbering system was cautiously optimistic. Writing in the February 1981 *United States Specialist*, Kim D. Johnson wrote, "As is the case when any long-standing system is discarded in favor of something new, and as yet untried, there is something to be gained and something to be lost. One of the main criticisms of the new system will certainly be that it is a purely artificial means of satisfying the more vocal plate block collectors. What we are losing are the very real and meaningful five-digit numbers which have been in use at the Bureau since the first days of their stamp production. On the other hand, the inclusion of litho numbers into the system is a tremendous plus, as is the placement of plate numbers on coils and booklet panes."

As word of the new numbering system spread through the philatelic community, there were expressions of approval and disapproval from various quarters. The policy did succeed in provoking a discussion on how to collect the new products. The way to collect plate numbers on sheet stamps became corner blocks of four once again, except for the A press "floaters," which seem to have acquired one grou committed to strips of 20 and another to blocks of six. The booklet enthusiasts continued to collect plate numbers in complete panes or in unexploded booklets.

A debate immediately ensued among coil collectors, however. Those who were wedded to the traditional line pair opted for pairs, even on B press stamps that lacked joint lines. Since the Cottrell coil plates had plate numbers entered on the stamp designs in the last row at the right edge of the plate, the numbers appear in the final product on the stamp just left of the joint line, and thus on the left stamp in a line pair. By analogy, traditionalist collectors saved B press PNCs in

Strong demand for booklets in 1987 led the BEP to produce the 22¢ Flag and Fireworks by making do with sheet-format cylinders, therefore showing four gravure cylinder numbers on just one booklet in 10. The four-digit plate numbers occur only in upper left and lower left positions, as shown on these two panes.

pairs, with the plate number on the left.

Others argued that the new system made the plate number, not the joint line, the collectible "feature." This meant the numbered stamp should be kept at the center of a strip of three. Only a handful of collectors at that time opted for longer strips. Their voices were drowned out in the weekly philatelic press by the pair-versus-strip-of-three debate.

Among those who collected the larger formats, usually strips of five or six, were veterans of the search for miscut coils produced the old way, with single numbers saved in strips of five and double numbers in strips of six. Still others wanted their strips to show a combination of features, such as the Cottrell press plate pairings, which require strips of 25 or longer, or the varieties of precancel overprint type styles and gap locations, which require strips of varying lengths.

The transformation of coil printing methods eventually created a new consensus. At first there was some tension between those who were essentially collecting plate numbers and those who were essentially collecting coil stamps. This tension expressed itself in strong disagreements over the preferred format. Plate number collectors preferred a format that highlighted the number as the significant feature, and thus placed it at the center of a strip of three or more stamps. Coil collectors viewed the line as the significant feature, centered in a pair

All the Official stamps issued in 1983, both coils and sheets, had plate numbers. The 1¢ plate block shown here is an example. The nondenominated D contingency Official sheets and coils shown here, released for the 1985 rate increases, also had plate numbers, because they were actually prepared when the 1983 issues were printed. All subsequent Officials, beginning with the illustrated 22¢ coil and 14¢ sheet stamps, have none.

Surrey 1890s USA 18c	Surrey 1890s USA 18c	Surrey 1890s USA 18c	Surrey 1890s USA 18c	Surrey 1890s USA 18c	Surrey 1890s USA 18c

During the short span of 5½ months from the time the 18¢ Surrey was issued until the letter rate rose to 20¢, stamps from 16 of the plates were widely used.

or longer strip. But the very first PNC issue had no line, and a few years later, lines disappeared completely from coils, leaving only the number for either faction to feature.

Today some PNC enthusiasts collect longer formats, particularly mint strips of five. It is possible that among those who collect PNCs comprehensively, seeking an example of every different coil plate number, strip-of-five collectors may outnumber strip-of-three collectors. Specialist PNC dealers are not in agreement as to which is the more popular format, but there is no doubt that the failure of nearly every collector and dealer to anticipate the popularity of the larger format has had a dramatic effect on the coil market.

Before demand arose for strips of five, most accumulators broke down coils and saved the plate numbers in pairs or strips of three. They could not go back later and paste on additional stamps to create strips of five. Some of the first three years' coils, issued from 1981 to 1983, before PNC collecting hit its stride, are now relatively easy to find in pairs or strips of three, but very difficult in strips of five. This leads to large disparities in the retail values of those early numbers in the different formats. Others, which were still on sale in complete rolls after the popularity of the longer strips had become established, now cost only a small premium in strips of five.

All plate numbers of all stamps issued since 1983 are as readily available in strips of five as in the shorter formats. Some dealers end up breaking down a strip of five to fill an order for a single, a pair or a

Plate 4 of the 20¢ Flag coil was the first stamp printed on the intaglio C press at the Bureau of Engraving and Printing.

Plate numbers, spaced at 38-stamp intervals, are often difficult to find on the D contingency coil stamps. On this misperforated pair, the number 1 looks more like an inking flaw than an actual digit.

strip of three.

Even though strips of five are now established as the largest standard format, there are instances in which collectors may sacrifice a substantial portion of a roll's value by breaking it down into plate strips of that length. Some scarce precancel styles and gap locations cannot be shown on strips of five, because the gap or other feature occurs more than two stamps away from the plate number. Specialists normally collect these varieties in long strips of varying lengths, stretching from two stamps past the plate number at one end to two stamps beyond the other desired feature at the other. It is wise to

The highest number on a modern coil stamp is plate 22 of the 22¢ Flag stamp, printed on both the C and D presses.

check a gap scarcity chart before breaking down a roll of early PNC precancels.

One thing is certain: Despite all these collectible features and formats that have delighted PNC collectors during the early years of the specialty, we have not exhausted the possibilities. There are still discoveries to be made, even on the stamps that have been with us since the 1981 beginning.

Each of the six digits on the 21.1¢ coil stamp denotes a separate Andreotti press gravure cylinder.

35

Chapter 4

The Coil Stamps of 1981

When the new policy on plate numbers went into effect in 1981, the first-class letter rate was 15¢. The first stamps to use the new plate numbering system were the 15¢ Everett McKinley Dirksen and 15¢ Whitney Moore Young commemorative sheet stamps. The Dirksen issue was a single-color intaglio stamp, and the Young was a multicolor gravure stamp printed from six cylinders. Eight different plates of the Dirksen stamp went to press, but only one set of the Young gravure cylinders. No booklets or coils for the 15¢ rate used the new system, because there were no new booklet issues until after the next rate increase.

The year 1981 was a volatile one for the U.S. postal system. The cost of a prime-rate stamp went up twice, to 18¢ on March 22, and to 20¢ on November 1, and most other domestic rates changed with them. Each change required a flurry of new stamps to meet the new rates. At the same time, the years 1980 and 1981 had been chosen to phase out the Americana series of definitive stamps, first introduced in 1975, replacing them with the Great Americans series of sheet stamps and the Transportation coil series. A number of definitives from the earlier 1954 Liberty series and the 1965 Prominent Americans series were still in service, but scheduled to be replaced by stamps in the two new definitive series.

The rate changes disrupted the orderly introduction of the new system. In both cases, the non-denominated stamps, released to cover requirements until stamps of the proper denominations could be prepared, followed the old system. Both the B stamps, issued on March 15, and the C stamps, issued on September 30, have five-digit numbers on the sheet stamps, and no numbers on properly manufactured booklets and coils.

The reasons for this are easy to understand. The B stamps had been printed and stored as a contingency a few years earlier, shortly after

Only one set of six gravure cylinders printed the entire press run of 15¢ Whitney Moore Young commemoratives.

the non-denominated A stamps had been released to cover the May 29, 1978 rate increase from 13¢ to 15¢. Then, at the end of 1980, anticipating that rates would go up right after the first of the year, using up the B stamps, the Bureau of Engraving and Printing began preparing plates for the C contingency. That was before the new numbering policy was announced.

Other 1981 rate-change stamps using the old numbering system were the three issued to cover the new 12¢ postcard rate. One sheet stamp and two coil stamps were issued with a Torch design in the Americana series. The sheet stamp and one of the coils are common tagged stamps. The other coil is an untagged precancel overprinted

The nondenominated B (18¢) and C (20¢) contingency stamps issued in 1981 were being prepared in 1980, before the new numbering system was adopted, so the coil versions of those stamps do not contain plate numbers.

with two lines. The precancel was withdrawn from philatelic sale on November 30, 1984, and the tagged version on August 31, 1985. Another version of this stamp, with overprinted lines and a service inscription, was issued in 1983.

It seems difficult to understand why the Postal Service should have issued new stamps in the Americana series at the same time it had decided to phase that set out of circulation, but the planners had not lost their senses. Contingency plates for several values of Americana series and Flag definitive stamps had been made during the periods of uncertainty prior to the December 31, 1975 change, when the letter rate went from 10¢ to 13¢, and prior to the 1978 hike to 15¢. These included 11¢ and 12¢ Flag stamps, and 11¢ and 12¢ Liberty Bell stamps, employing the Americana series design that was eventually used for 13¢ booklet and coil stamps.

The 12¢ Torch stamps in the Americana series were printed from plates that had been prepared originally in 1976, but not used until 1981. Therefore plate numbers do not appear on the stamps, although mis-slitting sometimes reveals parts of the numbers that should have been trimmed off. This pair shows a fragment of one of its Cottrell press plate numbers, enough to identify it as number 37845.

BEP records state that no stamps were ever printed from the 11¢ and 12¢ Liberty Bell plates. There are no records as to whether the 11¢ and 12¢ Flag stamps were ever printed, but they were never issued. The first 12¢ Torch plates had been prepared during this same period. They had never been used, but with the rise of the postcard rate to 12¢, they were pressed into service, an alternative that was both more efficient and more economical than creating a new design.

One other 1981 coil stamp issued according to the old system, without plate numbers on any properly cut stamps, is difficult to explain. In this case, the mystery is not why the stamp does not fit the new policy, since its two plates were prepared in 1980, before the policy existed, but why the re-engraved 5¢ George Washington coil stamp in

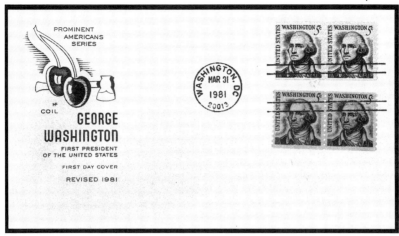

The re-engraved 5¢ George Washington coil stamp was placed on sale without prior notice. Despite the existence of "first-day covers" post-marked March 31, 1981, a survey conducted by Linn's Stamp News *in 1982 uncovered earlier usages in February and March. The March 31 cancel on this "FDC" was actually backdated by more than a year.*

the Prominent Americans series exists at all.

When the original version of the 5¢ Washington stamps was issued in 1966, 5¢ was the basic letter rate, replacing an earlier 5¢ Washington design that had been in use since 1962. Ever since the first U.S. stamps were issued in 1847, people had been accustomed to seeing George Washington's portrait on a widely used denomination. But the Prominent Americans version of Washington was not popular at all. It was criticized because the engraved detail in Washington's face made him appear dirty or unshaven, definitely unkempt. In response to widespread antipathy, the Post Office Department issued a "clean face" or "clean shaven" re-engraved version of the 5¢ Washington sheet stamp on November 17, 1967. This improvement was not applied to the coil version, however, until almost 14 years later.

By the time the re-engraved 5¢ George Washington coil stamp was issued, unannounced, some time in February of 1981, it served no essential postal purpose. Its principal use was as a changemaker in

The two different versions of the overprinted PRESORTED FIRST-CLASS precancel on the 13¢ Liberty Bell coil stamp are shown here. The narrow-spaced version on the right, with only ½-millimeter spacing between the lines of type, is scarce. It was discovered only after the stamps were obsolete and had been withdrawn from sale. No mint examples have been found.

postage vending machines. The original version, printed from 144 plates over the course of a long life, should have been sufficient for a while longer. If the Postal Service wanted a new 5¢ coil stamp, a design in the new Transportation series would have been more sensible, but that did not occur until 1983. The re-engraved 5¢ Washington coil stamp was withdrawn from philatelic sale on May 31, 1984.

Two other new coil stamps were issued in 1981, both unintentionally, and nobody even noticed until they were gone. They were new overprinted versions of two Americana series stamps, the 9¢ Capitol Dome and the 13¢ Liberty Bell coils. Previously both had been issued with plain precancel line overprints, with the inscription PRESORT-ED FIRST-CLASS between the lines. These precancels prepaid the first-class presort rate for mail sorted to three ZIP-code digits, 9¢ for postcards and 13¢ for letters of one ounce or less. Those rates had been in effect since May 29, 1978.

The new version was very similar to the earlier service-inscribed overprint, but on the original the two lines of type are spaced two millimeters apart, whercas the new version has narrowly spaced type, only ½ millimeter between the lines. The rates for which the stamps were issued ended on March 21, 1981, but collectors did not discover the variety until the following summer. By then the stamps were obsolete and had been withdrawn from sale. Eventually a few rolls of the narrow-spaced 9¢ precancel were found, but no mint examples are known of the narrow-spaced 13¢ precancel.

Although the Postal Service's December 10, 1980 news release had promised the new plate numbering system for 1981, including single-number digits printed at intervals on coil stamps, the first six 1981

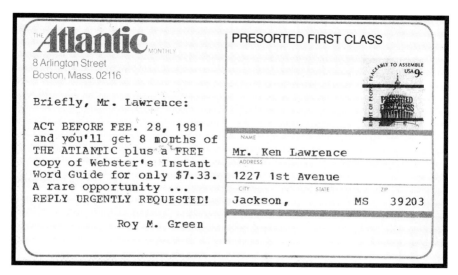

This cover bearing the scarce narrow-spaced overprint on the 9¢ Capitol Dome coil stamp of the Americana series proves that it was in use in early 1981.

coil issues did not have them. These were the non-denominated B coil; the re-engraved 5¢ George Washington coil; both versions of the 12¢ Torch coil, ordinary and precanceled; and the narrow-spaced 9¢ Capitol Dome and 13¢ Liberty Bell precancels. Later in the year, a seventh coil stamp, the non-denominated C contingency issue, also adhered to the old system. But on April 24, 1981, the plate number coil era arrived, and over the course of the year, eight coil stamp issues carried the new plate numbers. There were five regular tagged stamps, two untagged precancels, and one tagged, service-inscribed "philatelic edition" with no real postal purpose except as samples for distribution to Universal Postal Union member countries.

The 18¢ Flag "... from sea to shining sea" Coil Stamp

The 18¢ Flag coil stamp, issued on April 24, 1981, at Portland, Maine, was one of a four-stamp set (sheet, se-tenant booklet, and coil versions). Three of the stamps each illustrated a different line from the song "America the Beautiful." The fourth stamp in the set was a 6¢ change maker. The coil stamp was printed in red, blue and purple ink with block tagging on the B press, on paper pregummed with mint-flavored adhesive.

This 18¢ coil stamp was the workhorse for the 18¢ letter-rate period, from the day it was issued until the rate went up to 20¢ on November 1. It replaced the 15¢ Flag coil stamp in the Americana series. More than nine billion 18¢ Flag coil stamps were printed for use

The 18¢ Flag coil stamp was issued as one stamp in a four-stamp set. The three 18¢ Flag stamps — sheet, booklet and coil — each featured and illustrated a line from "America the Beautiful." The fourth, a 6¢ Stars stamp, came in se-tenant booklet panes to round the price of a booklet to $1.20 for vending machine sales.

during the relatively brief period. The stamps sold in rolls of 100, 500 and 3,000. Some of those that were still on sale after the November 1 increase were used in strips of three as the most convenient way to prepay the 54¢ rate for a first-class letter weighing up to three ounces.

All the 18¢ Flag coils were printed from a total of seven printing sleeves. An eighth was prepared, but never sent to press, so a total of seven plate numbers can be collected. Numbers 1 through 5 exist on

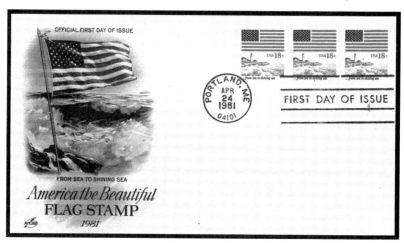

Plate 1 of the 18¢ Flag coil was widely available on the first day of issue.

first-day covers, although only the first three had gone to press before that date. Grace periods for submitting serviced first-day covers were extended to 45 days after the day of issue, because of the glut of new stamps to meet all the new rates. Even so, plate 5 did not go to press until June 9, the final day of the 45-day grace period, so it is likely that Colorano, the only company known to have this plate number on its cachet, was granted additional time.

Despite the huge numbers of 18¢ Flag coils printed, some plate numbers are very scarce. Plate 6 is the scarcest PNC of all, mint, used or on cover. For the other numbers, scarcity is to some extent a matter of the format a collector prefers. Plate 1, for example, is relatively common in used condition but much more difficult to find in mint strips. Since most people who saved mint strips at the time the stamp was current kept strips of three, strips of five are disproportionately difficult to find, and far more expensive. The same situation holds true for plate 3, for the same reasons, except that in each of the three standard formats plate 3 is scarcer and more expensive than plate 1, even though considerably more stamps were printed from plate 3, according to USPS plate activity reports.

Plates 2, 4 and 5 are all relatively common, because all three remained in the inventories of large post offices around the country long

Plate 5 of the 18¢ Flag coil did not go to press until 45 days after the date of issue for that stamp; yet, first-day covers with that plate number exist on Colorano envelopes.

after the denomination was needed, and could be purchased at face by anybody who knew where to look.

At one time number 7 was thought to be scarce, and for a while it was the most expensive number, but after large quantities were found in post offices in Chicago and in the East in the fall of 1986, prices dropped back and stabilized at modest levels. Actually, during the formative period of the PNC specialty, the most difficult 18¢ Flag number seemed to rotate. First it was number 7, then number 6, then number 3, then number 1. For a time number 3 and number 6 seemed about equally tough. But here and there a roll or two of 1 and 3 would

This 18¢ Flag plate 7 cover was canceled November 9, 1981, with the purple ink characteristic of that period of time. It is the earliest usage reported for this number; yet it should have been assessed postage due because the first-class letter rate had increased to 20¢ on November 1.

turn up, while there have been very few new finds of number 6. So 6 is now the key item in any PNC collection.

Sleeves 6 and 7 did not go to press until September 9, 1981. By the time they were placed on sale in post offices, the rate was changing. The 20¢ letter rate went into effect on November 1, and as of this writing no cover has ever been reported showing an example of number 7 used during the 18¢ rate era. The November 7 earliest-known-use cover bears a purple machine cancel typical of the time.

Plates 2 through 5 exist imperforate. The imperf strip of plate 3 is thought to be unique. Next in scarcity is plate 2. Imperf strips are widely available from plate 4. Plate 5 imperforates, while not com-

This 18¢ Flag coil plate 3 imperforate strip is believed to be unique.

mon, are less expensive than normal mint strips of plates 1, 3 and 6.

Plate 3 seems to be the most difficult 18¢ Flag FDC to obtain, followed by plates 4, 5, 2 and 1, in that order. None of them are common.

The 18¢ Flag coil stamps were withdrawn from philatelic sale on July 31, 1982. Taking them off sale at postiques and dropping them from the Philatelic Sales Division's mail-order catalog meant relatively little, however. Besides the large quantities that remained in the USPS Accountable Paper Depositories and Stamp Distribution Offices in many parts of the country, others were placed back on sale through philatelic outlets when the 1981 Definitive Mint Set was put on the market in July of 1982. Pairs of all 18¢ Flag plate numbers, including the scarce ones, were found in those mint sets.

Other finds continue to be reported, but none of them sufficient to halt the steady climb in value of most 18¢ Flag PNCs since the fall of 1986. The scarce numbers, mint and used, are certainly the blue chips of recently issued United States postage stamps.

The 18¢ Surrey Stamp

The first stamp in the popular Transportation coil series made its debut on May 18, 1981. The 18¢ Surrey stamp depicts the 1890s vehicle that, Postal Service advance publicity pointed out, evokes memories of the "Surrey With the Fringe on Top" from the Rodgers and Hammerstein musical *Oklahoma*. A discontinued post office at Notch, Missouri, closed since 1932, was commissioned for a day to host the first-day ceremony, borrowing the ZIP code of Reed Springs for the occasion. The stamps were printed in brown, with overall tagging, on Cottrell presses, as a second denominated coil stamp to meet the 18¢ letter rate. They were issued in coils of 100, 500 and 3,000 stamps.

By contrast with the pioneer plate number coil issue, the 18¢ Flag, the 18¢ Surrey had many attributes that were more conducive to sparking collector interest in the plate numbers. The 18¢ Flag coil, a product of the B press, would contain, at most, two copies of the same plate number stamps on a coil of 100. But a coil of 100 Surrey stamps would contain four or five numbered stamps, with two plate numbers alternating at 24-stamp intervals. A joint line appeared at the right of each plate number stamp. From one $18 roll, a collector would get two plate strips to keep and two or three duplicates to trade.

The first 10 numbers have all been found on first-day covers, although only plates, 1, 2, 3 and 4 had been sent to press before the issue date. Plates 9 and 10 went to press for the first time on June 18, 1981, more than a month after the release date, but July 3 was the deadline for submitting serviced covers for cancelation under the terms of the extended grace period. The scarcest plate numbers on FDCs are 3 and 4, but 7, 9 and 10 can be very difficult to find. Numbers 5 and 6 are

Although plates 9 and 10 went to press on June 18, 1981, more than a month after the issue date, first-day covers with those numbers exist on several cachets, because the deadline for obtaining cancelations was extended by the Postal Service to July 3.

Plate 3 and its companion on the Cottrell press, plate 4, are the scarcest 18¢ Surrey numbers on first-day covers.

next in line, more frequently available but expensive. Plate 8 was once easy to find, but not any more. Plates 1 and 2 are still widely available; 2 is more common than 1, because there is approximately one cover with a plate 2 pair or strip for every cover serviced with plate 1, but there are also plate 2 FDCs made from the pairing with plate 8.

In all, 24 plates were prepared for the 18¢ Surrey, but only the first 18 were sent to press. Numbers 19 through 24 were canceled with no recorded impressions. The first 16 numbers were placed on sale and widely used on mail during 1981, but not 17 and 18. Fewer of those were printed than any of the other numbers. Although all of them had been printed between September 16 and 26, 1981, for a long time

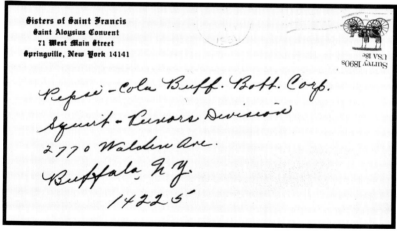

All 18¢ Surrey plate numbers from 1 through 16 were distributed and used as postage during the period when the 18¢ letter rate was in effect.

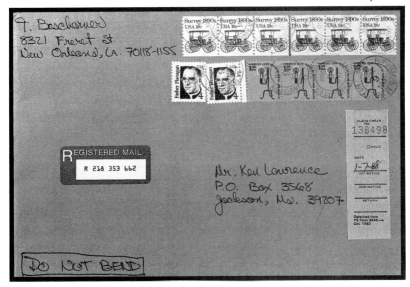

Plates 17 and 18 were only on sale through philatelic channels, and only long after the letter rate had risen to 20¢, so their use on mail was restricted mainly to stamp collectors and dealers. This cover with a plate 18 strip was sent from one collector to another.

nobody could find them. They first appeared in USPS 1981 Definitive Mint Sets in the summer of 1982.

The philatelic history of these two numbers has been like a roller coaster ride, rising high with creeping suspense, then suddenly, with little warning, crashing downhill with breathtaking speed, leaving some collectors with a rare thrill and others near heart failure, many of the latter vowing never to ride again. For everyone concerned, it was an object lesson in how to search for elusive PNCs.

After the mint sets confirmed the collectibility of plates 17 and 18, the search was on. Collectors found small supplies in Washington and Chicago in the summer of 1983 and the fall of 1984, respectively. One enterprising dealer located the two numbers in the Philatelic Sales Division stock at the end of 1984 or the beginning of 1985, when most collectors were unaware that the numbers could be found there. He advertised them for sale, offering mint strips of five for $40 to $70 depending on centering. At the time, that was a record price for any PNC; in those days even the scarce 18¢ Flag numbers didn't cost that much. For a few months, prices hovered in that range. Even a used single of plate 17 or 18 went for $50.

But then, just as nearly every plate number coil collector grudgingly agreed that maybe these stamps were sufficiently scarce to justify such high prices, word spread that collectors could purchase them at face value from the Philatelic Sales Division in Washington. Ninety cents was a much better price for five stamps than $70, and those who had resisted the hype congratulated themselves. Their patience had been rewarded. Others, not so lucky, were thunderstruck to see the value of their most expensive PNCs plummet virtually overnight. More than one collector abandoned the field, disheartened. Most, however, stayed the course and over the next few years saw far more increases than declines in PNC values.

None of the other 18¢ Surrey plate numbers experienced such sharp swings in price, but the relative prices did shift around quite a bit. After the dust settled, plate number 1 emerged as the most expensive, with plates 3, 4 and 7 also very desirable. Next in availability are numbers 11 through 17 in mint condition. The market in used singles breaks this group down further, because in mixtures of U.S. stamps, plate numbers 11 and 12 are more common than 13 and 14, which in turn are more common than 15 and 16, representing mainly the amount of time each was available in post offices before the rate increase to 20¢. Used examples of numbers 17 and 18 are available only when created deliberately by collectors, so their prices are very close to mint prices. Below these groups arc plate numbers 2, 5, 6, 8, 9 and 10, all of which are fairly common, mint or used.

Many of the discrepancies in availability are a result of the Cottrell press plate pairings. Plate 8 was used with plate 7 on some press runs, with 2 on others. Plate 2 was paired with 1 as well as with 8. According to a 1985 report by Francis J. Janeczek, then acting manager of the USPS Stamp Management Branch, to Stephen G. Esrati, plate 2 was also paired with 3. No one has ever found a roll exhibiting this combination. If it exists at all, it is very rare, and would be a prize to find. Collectors have found number 3 only on coils with number 4. USPS plate activity reports show that 129 more impressions were printed from plate 3 than from plate 4. If the entire excess exists in coils of the 2-3 pairing, that would be 1,114 coils of 100 at most, or the equivalent smaller quantity of larger coils. Otherwise, the combinations are consecutive pairs: 5 with 6, 9 with 10, 11 with 12, 13 with 14, 15 with 16, and 17 with 18.

Besides basic collections of PNCs in mint strips, as used singles, or on covers, collectors have identifed many collectible varieties. Constant plate varieties can occur on any kind of stamp, but a certain variety called a "gripper crack" is a frequent feature of Cottrell press

This 18¢ Surrey error-freak combination plate strip goes from fully imperforate to perforated, with the perfs through the middle of the design.

coils. According to the Scott catalog, a gripper crack "is caused by the cracking of the plate over the slots cut in the under side of the plate, which receive the 'grippers' that fasten the plate to the press." These occur only on curved Cottrell plates. They are found in the row of stamps adjoining the plate seam. They appear on the printed stamp as light jagged colored lines, usually parallel to the plate joint line. On PNC strips, the stamps adjoining the joint line are the plate number stamp and the one to its right, so all gripper cracks will appear on one or the other of these. Gripper cracks have been reported on plates 1, 9 and 10.

Imperfs are known with plate numbers 2, 8, 9 and 10. All are rare.

One often overlooked source of 18¢ Surrey PNCs is non-FDC souvenir covers. Although these covers were deliberately created as collectors' items, the stamps were often incidental to the pictorial cancels and cachets, since few people were paying close attention to the plate numbers in 1981. These are often the most neglected items at stamp

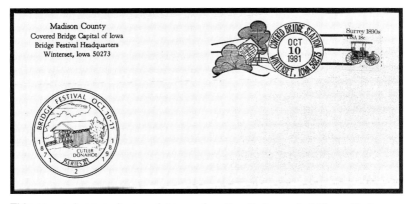

This souvenir cover has a plate number 5 coil stamp, but it's unlikely anybody paid much attention to the PNC at the time it was made.

bourses, flea markets, and the tiny tourist museums and gifts shops that dot our country.

The 18¢ Surrey coil stamps were withdrawn from philatelic sale on February 28, 1986, but that had little meaning, because there were millions — not thousands, but literally millions — of these stamps in post offices and Postal Service Accountable Paper Depositories and Stamp Distribution Offices all over the country until late in 1988, when all were ordered destroyed. More than 3.1 billion were printed, the largest quantity of any Transportation series stamp. At least some rolls of every plate number were unearthed by collectors and dealers who searched them out during 1987. Until those supplies are exhausted, it is unlikely that any of the 18¢ Surrey plates will approach the lofty heights reached by the three top 18¢ Flag numbers.

The 17¢ Electric Auto Stamps

The second design in the Transportation coil series, the 17¢ Electric Auto, depicts in blue ink an actual 1917 Detroit Electric coupe owned and driven by Edgar E. Rohrs of Manassas, Virginia. The stamp design was used on stamps issued for two quite different postal purposes. The first was a regular version with overall tagging, in coils of 100, 500 and 3,000 stamps, released at a first-day ceremony in Greenfield Village, Michigan, on June 25. The second was an untagged precanceled version with a black overprinted inscription, "PRESORTED FIRST-CLASS," issued without fanfare in coils of 500 and 3,000 the following November. All stamps in both forms were printed from the same seven Cottrell press plates. The tagged version replaced the tagged 13¢ Flag Over Independence Hall and the tagged 13¢ Liberty

Only plates 1 and 2 of the regular 17¢ Electric Auto stamp exist on first-day covers. Higher numbers and precancels did not appear until several months after the date of issue.

Bell coils. The precanceled version replaced the various overprinted 13¢ Liberty Bell coils.

The tagged stamp was issued to meet the 17¢ rate for each additional ounce of first-class mail after the first, up to 12 ounces, a rate that remained in force while the first ounce rate was 18¢, then 20¢, then 22¢, making it the most durable U.S. postage rate of the 1980s.

The 17¢ additional-ounce rate lasted through three basic letter rates — 18¢, 20¢ and 22¢ — so PNCs reflecting that intended usage can be found over a period of almost seven years. The plate 4 line pair on this cover paid the second and third ounces in December 1985.

During the first five months the stamp was in circulation, only plates 1 and 2 had been to press, so those are the only ones found on first-day covers.

Plates 3 and 4 were sent to press in late October for the precancel run, to meet the 17¢ first-class presort letter rate that went into effect on November 1, 1981. Official notice of their availability was published in the November 19 *Postal Bulletin*, and they were offered for sale to collectors in the December 1, 1981-January 31, 1982 *Philatelic Catalog*. There was no official first-day ceremony or cancelation for the precancels, and no early date-canceled covers are known to exist.

During the next year, collectors found rolls of the tagged stamps printed from plates 3 and 4, and precanceled rolls of the plate 5 and 6 pairing. It wasn't until 1984 that tagged versions printed from plates 5 and 6 turned up, and plate 7 of the precancel paired with plate 5. In 1985 the 5 and 7 pairing appeared in rolls of tagged stamps, and in 1986, the year after the last Cottrell press was retired, collectors finally found precanceled rolls of plates 1 and 2, so that all seven plates were known both tagged and precanceled. It might appear that a collection of 14 strips would complete the book on the 17¢ Electric Auto stamps, but that's not the case at all. In fact, there are so many variations in precancel overprints alone, to say nothing of subtler collectible features, that some collectors have built large specialized collections of this one stamp design in all its manifestations.

Three different overprint type styles exist, originally described and named by PNC specialist dealer Dennis Chamberlain, whose terminology is now universally accepted. The difference is in the fonts, the printer's term for type styles, but most easily identified by measuring the width of the word PRESORTED with an accurate millimeter ruler. The font of Type A precancels is condensed, so that the letters are 2.2 millimeters high, but PRESORTED measures 11 millimeters across. On Type B the letters are medium strength so that they are

The easiest way to verify the precancel overprint type on the 17¢ Electric Auto is to measure across the word PRE-SORTED with an accurate millimeter ruler.

shorter, 2 millimeters high, but PRESORTED measures 12.5 millimeters across. Type C is bolder than either of those, measuring 2.1 millimeters high but 13.5 millimeters across PRESORTED.

When Dennis Chamberlain reported the discovery of 17¢ Electric Auto precancels with both types B and A together on the same roll of stamps in July 1984, it created a sensation among plate number coil collectors. It was also this discovery that led a number of PNC enthusiasts to focus attention on the gap in the precancel overprint, and on the fact that it can occur in many different positions. Some began to collect every precancel style and gap position, no matter how long a

Both plate 6 strips of the 17¢ Electric Auto precancel are Type BA, with the Type B overprint on the stamps to the left of the precancel gap and the Type A to the right, but the position of the gap is different on each. For many collectors, the discovery of the se-tenant overprints was their first encounter with precancel gap positions as collectible varieties in their own right.

strip might be required to show those features. Others switched from strips of three to strips of five, realizing that the larger format could better showcase the Type BA combination overprint, se-tenant with Type B to the left of the gap and Type A to the right.

For those who collect strips of three or five, the Type BA precancel associated with plates 5 and 6 are the only se-tenant overprints, and they are the most expensive of the 17¢ Electric Auto precancels. Type BA can be collected with numbers 3 and 4 also, but only on longer strips, because the gap is located four stamps to the right of the joint line (called "gap four right" or "4R" by specialists). Type AB (A on the left, B on the right) can also be collected on longer strips with plate numbers 5, 6 and 7 at position 4R. Other BA and AB locations exist also; a comprehensive listing is given in the Appendix. None of the se-tenant overprint precancels can be considered common.

On strips of five or shorter, Type A exists with plate numbers 3, 4, 5, 6 and 7. These are all widely available, but number 7 is a bit scarcer and more expensive than the others. Type B is found in coils printed from plates 3, 4, 5 and 6, which are all scarcer than any of the Type A numbers. But 3 and 4 are more difficult to find than 5 and 6, and are exceeded in price only by the se-tenants. Type C is found on every plate except 6. Numbers 3 and 4 are common ones, while 1, 2, 5 and 7 cost more. Collectors who require particular gap positions may have to pay considerably more than the basic plate number and precancel type price, because some are rare. The availability of used singles of 17¢ Electric Auto Type A, B and C precancels mirrors the mint strip ratios of those varieties.

The situation with the tagged stamps is simpler. Numbers 1 through 5 are common, number 7 less so, and the price of number 6 has been climbing significantly, as mint strips. As used singles, numbers 1 through 4 are cheap, because lots of them are found in inexpensive mixtures, but 5, 6 and 7 are not so readily available and cost more.

Imperforates exist of tagged number 1, 2, 3 and 4 strips and of number 3 and 4 Type A precancels.

The 17¢ second-ounce rate outlasted the supply of 17¢ Electric Auto coil stamps, and they could not be reprinted from these plates

Plate 7, which is widely available in mint strips from PNC dealers, is relatively uncommon in mixtures of used stamps.

because the Cottrell presses were taken out of service and scrapped in November 1985. As a result, the Electric Auto coils were replaced in 1986 by the 17¢ Dog Sled issue. As the remaining stocks of the 17¢ Auto dwindled, they were withdrawn from philatelic sale, coils of 100 on April 30, 1987, and coils of 500 on October 31.

The 17¢ presort rate ended on February 16, 1985. Mailers were authorized to continue using the precanceled 17¢ Electric Auto stamps, plus an additional payment at the time of mailing, to cover the 18¢ rate that went into effect on the following day, a usage called "false franking." This false franking authorization was originally granted until August 18, 1985, and later extended until January 1, 1986, when the Electric Auto stamps' validity to prepay quantity mail expired. The precanceled stamps were withdrawn from philatelic sale on June 30, 1987.

The 20¢ Fire Pumper Stamp

The third Transportation coil stamp, the 20¢ Fire Pumper, was issued in Alexandria, Virginia, on December 10, 1981, to cover the 20¢ first-class letter rate that had gone into effect on November 1. It depicts an 1860s Amoskeag fire pumper that had been purchased by the City of Alexandria for use by the Alexandria Volunteer Company, later know as Columbia Engine Company Number 4, a volunteer fire-

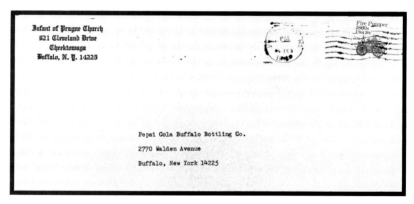

Plate 2 of the 20¢ Fire Pumper was widely used, but it has become a scarce number in mint condition. This example, postmarked February 16, 1982, at Buffalo, New York, illustrates the messiness often associated with purple machine cancels that caused many collectors to complain.

fighting association in Alexandria. All 20¢ Fire Pumper stamps were printed on the Cottrell presses in red ink, issued in coils of 100, 500 and 3,000.

The 20¢ rate held for more than three years, so the Fire Pumper stamp, which replaced the 18¢ Surrey coil stamps, did a lot of postal duty. Somewhat paradoxically, all the 20¢ Fire Pumper stamps were printed from 16 plates, while 18 plates were required for the 18¢ Surrey stamps, whose rate lasted less than a year.

Plate numbers 1 through 8, and also 10, have been collected on first-day covers. The first six stamps had been printed before the stamp was issued, but 7 and 8 did not go to press until January 22, 1982. Evidently the extended grace period for submitting serviced FDCs accounts for these covers, known only on Bazaar-cacheted en-

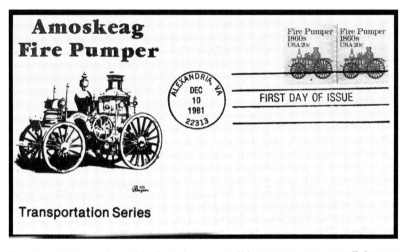

The plate 8 line pair on this first-day cover did not go to press until January 22, 1982, six weeks after the issue date. Plates 7 and 8 have been found only on Bazaar FDCs, and are believed to be scarce.

velopes. They are scarce and have sold for four-figure prices. Plate 10 did not go to press until February 6, 1982. Only one FDC is known with that number, discovered in 1989. Either its maker, the late George Alexander, was granted an extension of time beyond the grace period, or else it was canceled as a replacement for a damaged cover.

All the other PNC FDCs of this issue are more common. Numbers 3 and 4 are easier to find on FDCs than numbers 5 and 6. First-day covers prepared with number 1 and 2 stamps are difficult to find, and expensive, even though they seem to be the most frequently used numbers on collector-serviced covers. When they do appear on the market, plate 2 FDCs usually sell for a higher price than covers with plate 1. There should be approximately equal numbers of covers with these two plates, but collectors who are aware that plate 2 is scarcer than plate 1 in mint or ordinary used condition (because of later plate pairings in production) may be mistakenly thinking that the same ratios hold true for FDCs. However, there is at least one instance in which a collector paid a stiff price for an FDC with plate 2 in a strip of four in order to soak the stamps off for his used PNC collection.

Printing impression totals vary widely from plate to plate. Numbers 12 and 14 were paired on press and occur on the same rolls. These two plates have the lowest number of recorded impressions of any Transportation coil issues released so far — 58,177 each, which multiplies

Rolls printed from plates 12 and 14 became plentiful on the collector market in 1988, after 20¢ paid the second-ounce letter-rate, but covers with these numbers used during the 20¢ first-ounce letter-rate period are scarce, like this Long Beach, California, example dated August 31, 1983.

out to a maximum of 1,065,186 PNCs, if the plate activity reports issued by the Postal Service are accurate.

During the 20¢ first-class rate period, plates 12 and 14 received spotty geographic distribution, which made them difficult to collect. Prices climbed steadily, and by March of 1986, plate strips of three were selling for over $100 apiece and strips of five were virtually unknown to the market. But just as collectors were despairing of ever acquiring affordable copies, eight 3,000-stamp coils turned up at the main post office in Baltimore.

Retail prices quickly dropped to approximately $40 for a strip of five, but then started to rise again. After the 20¢ Fire Pumper stamps were withdrawn from philatelic sale on October 31, 1987, prices soared to $300 or more for a mint strip of three or five. But the withdrawal proved to be one of the shortest on record. After the April 3, 1988 rate increase, when 20¢ became the second-ounce first-class rate, the 20¢ Fire Pumpers were placed back on sale in vending machines and at philatelic counters, replacing the 17¢ Electric Auto and 17¢ Dog Sled coil stamps.

Almost immediately there were several large discoveries of plates 12 and 14. The first and largest find was a hoard of 48 rolls at the Indianapolis postique. For the second time in two years, prices plummeted to a fraction of their peak level, and once-scarce numbers seemed to be available in sufficient quantity to remain reasonably priced for the foreseeable future. Meanwhile, though, throughout all these dizzying ups and downs, plates 12 and 14 remained the scarcest and most expensive Fire Pumper plates in used condition and on cover during the 20¢ rate era.

The return to sale of the 20¢ Fire Pumper coils after their philatelic withdrawal, and the reappearance of plates 12 and 14 in quantity, sparked a heated controversy. Some dealers and collectors, evidently unaware that the Postal Service may ship previously withdrawn definitive stamps when the need arises, felt betrayed by USPS as they saw the value decrease on some of their most expensive PNC stamps. But this is inherent in the postal purpose of definitive stamps, which is not limited to fixed printing totals or sale dates as is done with commemoratives. It is quite possible that the same experience will recur with other plate numbers in the future. In the May 16, 1988 *Linn's,* editor-publisher Michael Laurence called upon the Postal Service to disclose which obsolete stamps were being held for possible re-release. Assistant Postmaster General Gordon Morison replied with a letter promising that the information would be made public, and it was, but not until January 1989.

With prices high on mint examples of plate 2, a forger evidently thought used examples would bring high prices too. The stamp shown was advertised for $50 at a time when genuine examples cost about $5 each. The counterfeit plate number is enlarged with a genuine number shown at upper right.

Today the scarcest and most expensive number for collectors of mint strips is plate 2, which is still a relatively common number in used condition. That plate, paired with plate 1 on the press, was canceled after 241,235 impressions. That is a lot of stamps — potentially 4,342,230 PNCs, so nobody should be surprised if more of them turn up some day. Evidently because plate 2 is a scarce number in mint condition, forgeries of this number in used condition appeared on the market in late 1987, selling for $50 each, which was 10 times the price of the genuine stamp. (The story of the forgeries is told in Chapter 5.)

Plate 4 was one of the most common numbers, mint and used, during all periods of the 20¢ Fire Pumper's usage.

After plate 2 was canceled, plate 1 was rechromed and paired with plate 5. More stamps were then printed from this pairing, to make a total of 622,953 impressions of plate 1. That ought to be enough to make it common, but prices for mint strips of five have been creeping steadily upward for four years, and probably won't come down unless significant quantities reappear in post offices.

Plate 5 must have been made from a good piece of steel, because it became the Bureau's utility plate for Fire Pumper press runs. After Plate 1 was canceled, it was paired with plate 6, and, still later, with plate 13. Although BEP plate activity reports released by the Postal Service credit plate 5 with just 167,732 impressions, the reports are clearly erroneous. The Plate Number Coil Study Group estimates the true figure should be 935,909, making it the champion. Plate 13's other printing cylinder mate, plate 11, was actually its partner for most of the stamps printed from plate 13. All the other 20¢ Fire Pumper plates were paired consecutively on press: 3 with 4, 7 with 8, 9 with 10, and 15 with 16. Production varied widely on these, from a low of 264,702 impressions of plates 15 and 16 to a high of 634,419 of plates 3 and 4.

The reported number of 560,318 impressions for plates 7 and 8 cannot be accepted as valid, because those were the plates that were mounted on the press on March 5, 1982, when a fire broke out in the Bureau of Engraving and Printing annex building at 2:45 a.m. The fire was severe enough that two of the Cottrell presses had to be scrapped as a result, while two others were only slightly damaged and were back in production within 72 hours. Plates 7 and 8 of the 20¢ Fire Pumper were ruined. Perhaps some or all of the stamps printed during that press run were lost, which might help explain why these numbers have always seemed scarcer than the plate activity figures indicate.

Plates 1, 2, 3, 4, 5, 9, 10, 15 and 16 have all been collected imperforate. Priced at $1,000 or more in strips of five, none are common. Plate 2 imperforates are known only as pairs. Gripper cracks exist on plates 2, 3, 11 and 15. Image doubling caused by set-off has been reported on plate 15 and 16 rolls. (Information on the cause of doubled set-off images is found in Chapters 6 and 12.)

The last Fire Pumper plate was canceled November 21, 1984, after more than 3 billion of the stamps had been printed.

The 9.3¢ Mail Wagon Stamps

The first fractional denomination to appear in the Transportation coil series was the 9.3¢ Mail Wagon stamp, on December 15, 1981. Printed in red ink, the stamp depicts a mail wagon of the 1890s, in use during the period when Rural Free Delivery was being inaugurated. The 9.3¢ coil stamps were issued in precanceled form in coils of 500 and 3,000, to prepay the third-class, five-digit ZIP code sort bulk mail rate that had been introduced on November 1. That rate tier had existed since March 22, 1981, but no stamp had been issued to prepay the earlier 8.8¢ rate. The Postal Service had authorized mailers to use precanceled 8.4¢ Piano coil stamps to prepay that rate, with the balance due at the time of mailing, until the 9.3¢ Mail Wagon stamps were available. Even after that, the 8.4¢ Piano stamp continued to serve as false franking for the costlier basic presort rates until the following year.

The 9.3¢ rate proved to be the most durable of the modern bulk mail rates, lasting until February 16, 1985. Technically, it was the cost per piece, not the rate, that remained unchanged, because the incentive discount increased as the basic rate increased. Originally, when the basic bulk rate for mail presorted to three digits was 10.9¢, the discount for presorting to five digits was 1.6¢, which equaled 9.3¢. When the basic presort rate increased to 11¢, the five-digit discount

The precanceled 9.3¢ Mail Wagon stamps carried third-class bulk rate mail for 3½ years. This cover, with a plate 3 stamp, is a typical example.

increased by the same amount to 1.7¢, keeping the per-piece cost at the same 9.3¢ level. The stamps themselves were valid even longer, because the Postal Service authorized false-franking usage from February 17 until June 16, 1985, at the new 10.1¢ rate, with the balance of the postage to be paid by the sender at the time of mailing.

The Postal Service also issued a tagged philatelic edition of the stamp, without overprinted precancel lines, for collectors and for distribution as samples to postal administrations that are members of the Universal Postal Union. This version of the stamp went on sale in Shreveport, Louisiana, the first-day city. Nearly all first-day covers bear the tagged stamps. FDCs with PNCs have either plate number 1 or plate number 2 or both, except for a small number of collector-

Tagged editions of the 9.3¢ Mail Wagon coils, without precancel overprints, were issued for collectors and sold exclusively as philatelic items. Not surprisingly, the used examples that exist are almost all from collector mail. The cover shown here, with plate strips of numbers 3 and 4, was sent from one collector to another.

Despite the strange configuration of stamps and the odd placement of plate numbers, the two covers shown here are the only reported examples of the 9.3¢ Mail Wagon plates 3 and 4 on a first-day cover.

serviced covers bearing numbers 3 and 4. Oddly, numbers 3 and 4 are the only plate numbers known on USPS Souvenir Pages, which also bear the first-day-of-issue cancel.

A very small number of FDCs was prepared using precancels, and Ken D. Kribbs, the cachetmaker who serviced them, believes he used a plate 4 line pair on one cover, but this has never been confirmed. If it does exist, it is a true modern rarity. BEP plate activity reports issued by the Postal Service indicate that plate 4 did not go to press for a precancel run until January 20, 1982, so none should have been available during the time period for submitting FDCs.

Two easily discernible ink shades are found on 9.3¢ Mail Wagon stamps: brownish rose and carmine rose.

In their philatelic (tagged, not precanceled) press runs, the Cottrell press plate pairings were: 1 with 2, 3 with 4, and 5 with 6. The first numbers issued, plates 1 and 2, are the most commonly found numbers. Plate numbers 3 and 4 are a bit less common, while numbers 5 and 6, the last ones to appear before both versions of the stamp were withdrawn from philatelic sale, are now scarce and expensive, both as mint strips or as used singles.

Precancel press runs used the same plate pairings as the tagged versions, plus these others: 2 with 4, and 4 with 8. Plate 8 is known only as a precancel. A BEP plate activity report issued by the Postal Service also shows a run that paired 1 with 4, but the impression totals for each plate are fully accounted for by the pairings listed above, so this is apparently an erroneous report.

Precancel availability is almost the reverse of tagged. At present, plates 5 and 6 are the most common, followed by plate 4, then plate 2. Plate 3 is next in scarcity, followed by plate 1. Plate 8, which did not go to press until November of 1984, had the lowest press run, and is now getting scarce and expensive.

Although some large stocks of 9.3¢ Mail Wagon precancels continued to turn up in the years after the stamp was withdrawn, most of the remainders were destroyed in 1985, because the chance of this decimal rate being reintroduced is nil. Unlike the experience with the scarce 20¢ Fire Pumper numbers, there isn't much the Postal Service can do to disrupt the market for mint strips of these stamps. Posterity stocks retained for possible inclusion in future mint sets were destroyed in 1988, after USPS officials decided the mint sets would not be issued.

Since the stamps were going off sale on June 30, 1985, just at the time that PNC collecting was on the verge of its great burst of popularity, supplies have never been as plentiful as they are for more recent issues. Even plate numbers that are easy to obtain now may become scarce as interest in PNCs continues to grow.

Collectible varieties include imperforates of the plate 1, 2, 3 and 4 precancels, and gripper cracks on or adjacent to the plate 1, 2 and 3 numbered stamps.

The 20¢ Flag Over Supreme Court Coil Stamp

The second Flag coil to appear with plate numbers printed on the stamp below the design was the 20¢ Flag Over the Supreme Court stamp, issued in Washington, D.C., on December 17, 1981. The companion sheet and booklet stamps used the identical design, unlike their 18¢ Flag predecessors. The stamps were printed in black, blue and red ink from a single seamless intaglio sleeve, and issued in coils of 100, 500 and 3,000 stamps.

The first three 20¢ Flag coil sleeves sent to press were printed on the intaglio B press, just as the 18¢ Flag coils had been. All three exist on first-day covers, with plate 1 the most common, plate 2 getting

There are probably fewer than 30 20¢ Flag first-day covers with plate 3.

scarce and expensive, and plate 3 very difficult to find. Both 2 and 3 went to press after the date of issue. There are probably fewer than 30 plate 3 FDCs in existence.

Sleeve number 4 added a new wrinkle to PNC collecting, because it was the first stamp printed on the intaglio C press. The Goebel C press introduced a new 960-subject plate layout, 20 stamps across and 48 in circumference, as opposed to the 18x52 configuration on B press sleeves, processed into 100-stamp coils on new Goebel coiling equipment. The 48-stamp interval guaranteed at least two, and sometimes three, sleeve numbers would appear on each 100-stamp coil. The C press very quickly became the Bureau's most productive printing press for prime-rate stamps issued in coils of 100. Unfortunately we cannot rely on BEP plate activity reports to learn about the debut of this all-important machine, because they say that plate 4 did not go to press until October 1, 1982. But the stamps are known on covers with dates earlier than that, the earliest reported so far being July 16, 1982.

By the time plate 4 was canceled, on January 24, 1985, the Bureau had recorded a total of 6,254,632 impressions — using an arcane system of record-keeping in which the subject size is not the number of stamps printed by one revolution of the sleeve, but rather an imaginary "sheet" of 480 subjects, legacy of the Cottrell press system where one impression printed two plates. Using those figures, more than 62½ million PNCs were printed from plate 4; yet today mint strips of this number are the scarcest and most expensive of all the 20¢ Flag numbers. Ironically, imperforate mint strips cost just a little more than properly perforated examples. Despite the huge numbers of stamps printed from this plate, there must have been a lot of waste, as Bureau workers tried out the new press. Also, with 20 stamps across the web, a high percentage of imperforates got past workers as they learned to use the new, automated Goebel coil-processing equipment for the first time.

Plate number 6, second in scarcity to number 4 in mint condition, was the next C press sleeve to go into production. The shortage of these seems to be a consequence of a lower printing total, 1,984,593 impressions, rather than from any lingering startup problems. Plate 7 was assigned to the C press, but never certified and used. Plate 8, the third Flag sleeve actually put on the C press, was the most durable of all the 20¢ Flag sleeves, with 15,539,861 reported impressions. The plate activity report got the dates wrong again, however, showing plate 8 as having gone to press for the first time on July 29, 1983, but covers exist showing continuous availability of this number beginning in early January of 1983. Number 8 is the most common PNC in used condition, but is no longer plentiful in mint strips.

Plates 9, 10 and 12 were also run on the C press, while numbers 5, 11, 13 and 14 were assigned to B press sleeves. Plate 11 had the fewest printed impressions, and at one time was the scarcest, but a large supply of 3,000-stamp coils turned up on the market in the fall of 1986, which has kept prices stable ever since. On the other hand, it is the scarcest and costliest number in used condition, which bears out the plate activity report, although used examples of all the 20¢ Flag

Bureau of Engraving and Printing plate activity reports issued by the Postal Service state that plate 8 did not go to press until July 29, 1983, but covers show that this number was in continuous use beginning in January.

PNCs are common enough that a complete set can be purchased for just a few dollars.

Two truly exotic varieties of the 20¢ Flag have been collected. One is an imperforate strip of three 20¢ Flag coils spliced to an imperforate strip of three 17¢ Electric Auto coils. The splice was probably made to facilitate threading one roll of 20¢ Flag stamps through the Huck coiling equipment as a roll of 17¢ Autos was being completed. It would have been removed and destroyed. The other item, the only

This combination error probably occurred because a roll of 20¢ Flag coils was spliced to the tail end of a 17¢ Electric Auto stamp roll to thread the Flag roll through the Huck coiling equipment.

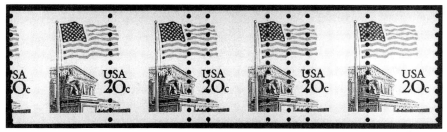

This freak triple perforation was probably created at the start of a processing run on the Goebel coiler's stroke perforator.

triple perforation variety on a modern U.S. coil stamp, probably occurred on the Goebel coiler's stroke perforator before the roll had been fully registered at the start of a run.

Imperforates of every 20¢ Flag plate number have been collected. Numbers 1, 11 and 14 are considered rare, with only two examples of each reported to date. Number 8, 9 and 10 imperfs are relatively common for major U.S. errors. The rest fall somewhere in between.

A plate flaw called the "Q" variety exists on some plate 14 stamps, on both regular and later precanceled versions. The zero of the denomination has a tail at the lower left, making it appear to be a mirror image of the letter Q.

Another item that has sparked a lot of collector interest is the "brick-red" variety, in which that color replaced the normally black portions of the image. This happened when red ink dripped into the press's black ink fountain and blended with it. The mistake occurred only on plate 8 rolls. Mint examples are known because James Payne, a collector in Washington state, discovered the "brick-red" stamps while he was sorting through about 150,000 business covers he had

A plate flaw that appears to add a tail to the zero of the denomination on some plate 14 20¢ Flag coils is called the "Q" variety.

acquired in Seattle. Using the return addresses and postmarks on the covers, he backtracked the stamps to the people who had bought and used them, and to the post offices where the rolls had originated.

Writing in the September 1986 issue of *The United States Specialist*, Tim Lindemuth reported on a similar variety, "the slate-blue coil, first cousin to the brick-red variety." It is known from three different printing sleeves, numbers 3, 5 and 8. That means these slate-blue stamps were printed on two different presses, since 8 was a C press sleeve, while 3 and 5 ran on the B press. Like its brick-red counterpart, the slate-blue variety was caused by ink contamination and blending. Neither the slate-blue nor the brick-red is an actual error of color, but both are handsome freaks.

Even without a plate number example, C press Flag coils can be differentiated from B press versions by measuring the tagging blocks. On the B press, the blocks are 21.1 millimeters high by 18.2 millimeters wide with 3.9-millimeter gutters. C press tagging surfaces are 20.6 millimeters high by 15.6 millimeters wide with 6.5-millimeter gutters. These are measurements reported by Robert L. Kugel. The Bureau of Engraving and Printing actually operates on the English system of measurement — feet, inches and decimal fractions of inches. Even though the phosphor applications vary somewhat from these measurements, C press tagging is visibly narrower than B press tagging, when the two are viewed together under shortwave ultraviolet illumination. It's easy to check an unknown stamp against a known. The details of this technique were first published in an October 1984 *United States Specialist* article by Kugel.

Another collectible 20¢ Flag coil variety described by Tim Lindemuth is image doubling on plate 2 coils caused by set-off, probably from a tagging roller or chill roller.

In 1982, the Postal Service introduced a packaging innovation for 100-stamp coils of Flag stamps. Previously all the coils had been wrapped in cellophane, sealed with plain or imprinted paper labels, and packed into chipboard trays, fifty 100-stamp rolls per tray (or equivalent numbers of the larger rolls). The new containers were

Until the Postal Service introduced perforated plastic trays that yielded 50 bubble-packs of 100-stamp 20¢ Flag coils in 1982, coil stamps had all been wrapped in cellophane sealed with paper labels and packed in chipboard trays for shipment.

transparent plastic trays that also replaced both the cellophane and the labels. Each contained 10 rows of five coils each, rouletted in both directions to allow easy separation of any number of coils, but leaving each separate coil sealed inside its own bubble. The bottom of each single coil container was embossed

100 — USA 20¢
$20.00
© USPS 1981

Later, in response to complaints from postmasters, the plastic trays were redesigned to make them safer and easier to use. The original

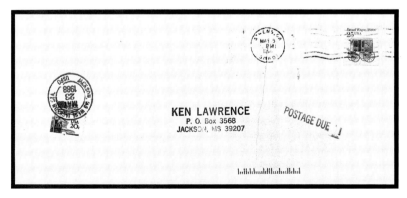

By the time rates were increased on April 3, 1988, postage due stamps had been phased out, but any ordinary stamps could be used instead. Here a plate 14 20¢ Flag coil pays postage due on an overweight letter.

version had sharp corners, and the individual containers were often difficult to separate. The new ones came with rounded corners and deeper rouletting. Pull tabs were added to make it easier to remove the transparent seal that covered each molded cell. These have since become the standard containers for letter-rate coils, and more recently for other 100-stamp coils as well. When the adhesive seal is broken, the adhesive becomes clouded, providing a security feature showing a bubble package has been opened.

The 20¢ Flag stamps were withdrawn from philatelic sale on October 31, 1985. Then, like their 20¢ Fire Pumper counterparts in the Transportation series, they were placed back on general sale after the Easter 1988 rate increases to cover the second-ounce letter rate, replacing the 17¢ Electric Auto and Dog Sled coil stamps. Prices on a few plate numbers declined after their reappearance, but these were relatively minor, and caused little disruption in the marketplace.

In 1984, the Postal Service issued an untagged precanceled version of the 20¢ Flag Over Supreme Court coil stamp. That version is described on Page 125.

Chapter 5

The Key — 18¢ Flag Number 6

The scarcest and most expensive modern United States postage stamp, excluding errors, is plate 6 of the 18¢ Flag coil. Just six years after these stamps were issued, dealers were quoting prices of $2,400 for mint strips of five, $1,700 for mint strips of three, and $500 for sound used singles, making this item truly "the King of the Coils." Prices have held at approximately those levels ever since.

No single factor alone can explain the apparent scarcity and high prices of plate 6, but a number of factors taken together provide a plausible explanation.

Sleeve number 6 was certified and sent to press on September 9, 1981, just seven weeks before the 18¢ letter rate expired. Only 491,500 impressions were printed from it, the fewest of any 18¢ Flag coil printing sleeve. Adding additional time necessary to complete the rest of the manufacturing and packaging process, and then time to distrib-

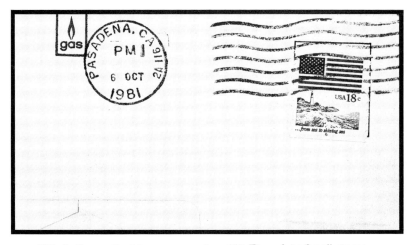

This is the earliest known use of an 18¢ Flag plate 6 coil stamp.

ute them, the stamps probably could not have gotten into circulation until the first week of October at the earliest. The earliest reported usage is a cover postmarked October 6, 1981, on a utility payment envelope mailed at Pasadena, California.

Any discussion of this stamp, the key item of any comprehensive PNC collection, mint or used, is incomplete unless it also embraces number 7, which went to press on the same date as number 6. In some instances, rolls of stamps printed from these two sleeves were included in the same shipments from Washington, and later both numbers turned up in 1981 Definitive Mint Sets. The earliest reported cover bearing number 7, not mailed until after the rate increase, has a purple cancel from Industry, California, dated November 9, 1981.

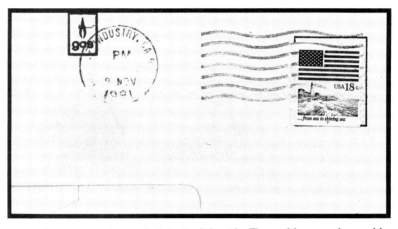

The earliest reported use of plate 7 of the 18¢ Flag, with a purple machine cancel of Industry, California, is dated November 9, 1981, nine days after the letter rate had risen to 20¢.

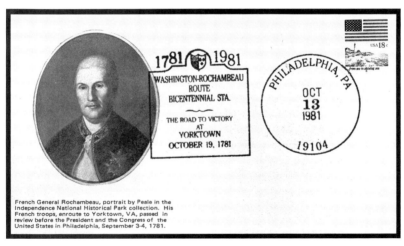

One of the very few covers franked with plate 6 of the 18¢ Flag coil is this National Park Service commemorative cover.

In addition to the Pasadena cover, two covers showing number 6 canceled during the 18¢ rate period have been reported. One is on a souvenir cover that never went through the mail, with a commemorative cancel of Philadelphia, dated October 13, 1981. The other is on a Southern California Gas Company return envelope mailed at Marina del Ray, with an October 15, 1981, purple machine cancel.

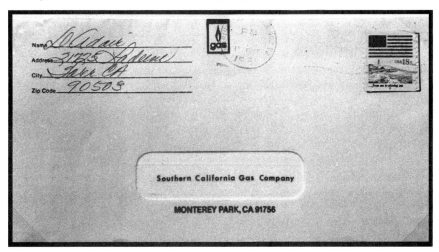

The faint cancel on this cover is Marina del Rey, California, October 15, 1981. Of the known covers with plate 6 Flag stamps, this is the only one so far reported with a purple machine cancel. A blowup of the stamp portion is shown below the cover.

A number 6 cover postmarked November 12, 1981, at Santa Ana, California, addressed to a publisher in Portland, Maine, has 2¢ postage added to meet the new 20¢ rate. There are probably other number 6 covers waiting to be found.

A pair of covers, one with number 6, the other with number 7, were both postmarked at Pasadena on December 8, 1981. Both have 2¢

Americana stamps to complete the required postage, and both of those 2¢ stamps are the original "greenish paper" versions, as the Scott catalog calls them, not the "cream paper" reprints issued in late 1981 specifically for the needs created by the rate change. Another number 7 cover, also from California, has a December 13, 1981 cancel.

As of January 1990, these seven covers are the only confirmed examples of numbers 6 and 7 used during 1981, but others are rumored, and more probably exist. The others that are known, on or off cover, bear dates in 1982 or later. The five commercial covers on Southern California Gas Company envelopes were found originally by James D. Galceran of the Bureau Issues Association, and all now reside in collections of other BIA members.

The cacheted souvenir cover with the Philadelphia commemorative postmark belongs to a well-known East Coast collector who asked not to be named. Here is his story of its discovery:

These two covers show nonphilatelic usage of the scarcest PNC stamps — the 18¢ Flag stamp from plates 6 and 7. Both went to the same address, postmarked with the same city and date, an amazing coincidence.

"We were showing some friends around the Independence Hall historic area in the summer of 1982. They wanted to stop at the gift shop (which we rarely visit on our own).

"While waiting for them, I noticed a tray on a counter which contained a number of those cacheted covers commemorating special events. One group of these was franked with the 18¢ Flag coil, so I quickly looked through them — about 30 or so — to see if there was a plate number single.

"Imagine my surprise when I found a cover with a copy of plate number 6. Needless to say, I bought it. Thus alerted that plate number 6 had been sold locally, I intensified my search of area dealer stocks. I was rewarded a few weeks later with a couple of strips of three of plate 6. I promptly traded one of these for a strip of number 7, which had similarly been found in a dealer's stock by one of my friends. All of this happened some time before Escue's find of number 7."

In 1982 and 1983, number 7 was very tough to obtain, and seemed scarcer than number 6. In 1984 Jeff Escue, an Illinois collector, found a quantity of them. Most mint strips sold by dealers before the fall of 1986 came from Escue's find.

Only one other cover bearing number 6 has been confirmed, but it's a beauty, with a plate strip of five, number on the center stamp, mailed from a dealer to a collector, Eugene Lopp. It has two postmarks, an August 19, 1982, Smithtown, New York, roller cancel, and an indistinct August 20 machine cancel.

The other early usages of these stamps are off-cover examples with readable dates in their cancels. The largest group of these was discovered by Paul Arnold, a Florida collector. He found 36 of plate 7 and eight of plate 6 in one mixture, along with dozens of more common plate numbers — and thousands with no numbers at all.

These provide clues to a usage quite different from Jimmy Galceran's covers. All of Paul Arnold's examples were strips of three, with plate number stamps randomly distributed on left, center or right positions. Every strip came on an identical distinctive type of laid

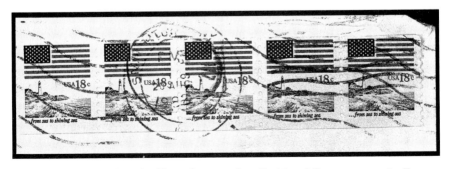

An enlargement of the 18¢ Flag plate number 6 strip of five on cover to Eugene Lopp. If this was a three-ounce piece with minimum insurance, the 20¢ + 17¢ + 17¢ + 45¢ fee was 1.4¢ overpaid and the cover contains an inexact endorsement.

This scarce strip of three probably carried a bulky three-ounce letter.

paper, and all were machine affixed with clipped perforations at the left. They bore postmarks dated February, March and April 1983, from every part of the United States.

Since this could have been the easiest way to machine-frank for the three-ounce 54¢ rate then in effect, I presume that these stamps originated on return envelopes for something pretty bulky, perhaps a marketing survey. They probably came from large rolls, coils of 500 or 3,000. I believe that the majority of collectors of used PNCs who added the scarce Flag numbers to their collections during 1984 and 1985 got their stamps through trades with Paul Arnold.

Douglas Landon, an Alabama collector, found two copies of number 6. One is a strip of three canceled Prince George's, Maryland, on February 19, 1982. This is probably an early example in which these stamps paid the 54¢ three-ounce rate. His second example of number 6 is a single, showing the tell-tale characteristics of a bulk-mail operation: a clean, slightly curved cut on both sides, clipping the perfs short

The slightly curved cuts at left and right, not perfectly aligned with the perforations, indicate that this plate 6 stamp was affixed by machine, part of a commercial bulk mailing.

at the right and long on the left. It seems likely that this would have been used in 1981 before the rate increasesd, but without a dated cancel there's no proof.

Al Haake, a stamp dealer who specializes in mint PNCs, supplied an even longer used multiple, probably from a parcel. The four-bar handstamp cancelation shows that plate 6 rolls were available in San Diego in the fall of 1982.

How many large multiples of plate 6 exist used during the time that the stamps were in circulation? The handstamp cancellation suggests it came from a parcel.

Besides these finds, collectors who search through common mixtures of used U.S. stamps have continued to find the key stamp, with reports coming in at a rate of about one per month — a bonanza for the finders, but not enough to supply the ever-growing demand, so prices have continued to rise.

Mint examples are another matter. Part-time PNC dealer Tom Maeder took an informal census based on the experience of knowledgeable dealers, and concluded there are 332 copies of number 6 in mint strips of five. He wrote, "If that is accurate, then it is 180 times scarcer than a set of Zeppelins."

In all probabillity, more were kept as strips of three than strips of five, because that was the typical format for the majority of early PNC collectors. By the time strips of five became popular, most of the finds of number 6 were history. It was therefore the good fortune of everybody who collects strips of five that the largest discovery of number 6 was unearthed by Jiri Chytil, a Colorado collector who specialized in strips of five and longer.

It was early December 1983, more than a year after the USPS had withdrawn the 18¢ Flag coil from philatelic sale. Chytil asked for them at the Denver post office Mile Hi philatelic counter, and was surprised that there was a supply in stock, rolls of 100 and 500. He bought one 100-stamp coil and checked it. Imagine his surprise to find plate 6!

It took another month before he had enough spare cash to buy them all, but every one turned out to be plate 6 — 83 plate strips total. Some of the numbered stamps were near the ends of the rolls, so a few of those wound up as strips of three, six of those with straight edges at one end.

Some of the mint singles and pairs on the PNC market today may have been deliberately saved that way by collectors who preferred those formats, but a lot of them resulted from being positioned at or near the end of a roll, or adjacent to damaged stamps, and also, of course, some were found in the 1981 Definitive Mint Sets in pairs, with the number as frequently on the right stamp as the left.

Plate 7 remained fairly scarce and was becoming increasingly more expensive, until the fall of 1986. The first to find them at that time, somewhere in New England, was Wayne Chevery, a Maine dealer. His colleagues estimate that he found three or more boxes, each containing 50 100-stamp coils, for a total of about 300 strips. Chevery's discovery was dwarfed in September 1986 by Father Ken Opat, a Minnesota PNC enthusiast, in Chicago. Father Opat's find eventually yielded approximately 2,700 mint strips.

These 1986 discoveries, added to whatever stocks remained from Jeff Escue's 1983 group, were sufficient to bring the price on number 7 down to a fraction of its mid-1986 level, which had been over $100 per strip. But despite a zealous group of stamp collectors pursuing every lead, nobody turned up any new stores of number 6 until 1988, when a mysterious man from the Seattle area, who insisted on absolute anonymity and cash payments, sold approximately 30 mint strips to PNC dealers.

With prices reaching high levels, it was almost inevitable that philately's criminal element would see a situation too good to pass up. In the fall and winter of 1987, a Canadian advertiser offered to sell used singles of number 6, first for $200 each, and later for just $100, at a time when the retail price was far higher. Collectors who ordered from the man's classified advertisement in *Linn's* received excellent forgeries, with bogus "plate numbers" added to ordinary genuine stamps. But the scheme came to an end when a forged plate 6 first-day cover was offered to Bill McMurray, a Connecticut collector.

Fortunately McMurray had a genuine copy of the 18¢ Flag number 6 coil in his collection. When he compared the two stamps, he became suspicious, and forwarded the FDC to me for examination. His suspicions were fully justified. The plate number on the cover was slightly misplaced, a fraction of a millimeter too high and to the left of its placement on a genuine stamp, and slightly off in the curvature of the

Although the stamp on this first-day cover is genuine, the number 6 is fake. It was offered to Bill McMurray, a Connecticut collector. This example now stands as the most convincing plate number coil forgery to date despite that a number 6 probably could not appear on a first-day cover.

numeral. Even without those differences, the cover would have to be regarded as probably fraudulent, because plate number 6 went to press for the first time on September 9, 1981, four and a half months after the stamp was issued, and is not known to have gone on sale until October.

Some FDCs are known of plates 4 and 5, which went to press three weeks and five weeks after the issue date, respectively, so the possibility of a back-dated FDC from an even later plate cannot be ruled out entirely, but it certainly seems unlikely.

On McMurray's cover, the color and texture of the counterfeit digit, and the width of the stroke, are remarkably accurate reproductions of the genuine article — even under high magnification. When the stamp is viewed through a 30-power microscope with a very shallow depth of field, using low-angle cross illumination, it is possible to demonstrate that the forged portion is not recess printed, because the numeral comes into focus in the same plane as the paper fibers rather than at the level of the raised ink image.

The real danger of a fake like this is that most potential purchasers do not have another copy of the rare stamp for comparison, and this forgery looks exceptionally good to the naked eye.

Since the forgery originated in Canada, Keith A. Wagner, executive director of the American Philatelic Society, advised *Linn's* to contact Michael Millar of Barrie, Ontario, chairman of the Royal Canadian Philatelic Society's stamp theft committee. In Canada, this type of forgery investigation is a provincial matter. Millar brought the problem to Corporal Michael Sharland, an intelligence officer with the Ontario Provincial Police. Bill McMurray forwarded the cover to Sharland for analysis.

Meanwhile, Millar arranged to have the prominent Toronto stamp firm, R. Maresch & Son, standing by to provide him with an expert opinion on the cover. As it turned out, that wasn't necessary. Sharland took the cover instead to Brian Dalrymple, the senior forensic analyst at the police Forensic Identification Services laboratory. Within five minutes, they had established conclusively that the plate number was counterfeit, even though neither Sharland nor Dalrymple has any philatelic knowledge.

Sharland told me, "He put the stamp under a video camera, with a laser on it, and then changed filters until everything on the stamp that was legitimate disappeared. The 6 stayed on the screen, proving it wasn't part of the original image."

Dalrymple explained how this expertizing system works. "I used the infrared luminescence characteristics of the printed image, viewed under an infrared-sensitive video camera. The argon laser produces only blue-green light, with no infrared. Some of the material in the ink luminesces in the infrared. Luminescence is a generic term encompassing both fluorescence and phosphorescence. What it means is that the compounds absorb the light and re-emit it at a different wavelength.

"Here we were looking at infrared luminescence. Since our eyes can't see infrared, we use the video camera to see it for us. We use filters over the lens to block the reflected light, and to transmit only the infrared luminescence. The pigment of the (fake number) 6 luminesced at different wavelengths than the rest of the stamp's image, proving the number was a different ink. I don't know about stamps, only physics and the luminescence characteristics of inks and pigments. Here you have two inks, both blue. Our eyes don't detect subtle differences between them. But one luminesces strongly, the other hardly at all. There is no way the two images could have come from the same ink."

Dalrymple said that although he used high technology equipment worth $100,000 to perform the test, a system adequate to detect stamp fakes like this could be assembled for about $4,000.

Sharland discussed the matter with the supplier, and considered the problem of the fake PNCs solved. He planned no further action unless new ones turn up. But Bill McMurray didn't get the fake PNC back. It was seized by Her Majesty Queen Elizabeth and forwarded to the Royal Canadian Mounted Police Central Bureau of Counterfeiting in Ottawa for eventual destruction. Sharland explained that in Canada it is a crime to counterfeit currency or other "tokens of value," which includes stamps, Canadian or foreign. "Anything counterfeit becomes the property of the Crown automatically," he said. "It would be illegal for me to give it to anybody else."

The same week that McMurray's cover appeared on the front page of *Linn's*, Dino Vardavas, an Ohio collector who had purchased a batch of used single PNCs from the same source, received a panicky call from the supplier, telling him to destroy all copies of a shipment of number 6, which, as it happened, he had not yet received.

The 18¢ and 20¢ Flag number 6 forgeries shown here appear to have been made from the same device. A genuine number of each stamp is shown in the upper right corners; the forged number is shown blown up at left center.

"At this point I rushed to my mailbox and sure enough a package was waiting," wrote Vardavas. "He was requesting $100 in cash for the [fake number] 6s. If I hadn't read your articles, and if he didn't call, I would probably have put a hundred dollar bill in an envelope and mailed it — for that kind of bargain no collector would hesitate." The package included forgeries of other PNCs too, including plates 2 and 5 of the 20¢ Fire Pumper, and plate 6 of the 20¢ Flag. Vardavas forwarded the fakes to *Linn's*. Shortly afterward he received a full refund from the supplier, who claims to have found all the forgeries in large mixtures.

If anything, the fact that an ordinary stamp issued in 1981 with a face value of 18¢ has reached such lofty heights, even to the extent of becoming an object of a forger's attention, would seem to have earned plate number coil collecting a place in philately's first rank.

Until 1988, the possibility existed that 18¢ Flag coil stamps stored in Postal Service vaults might have been reissued at a future time. But after some dealers and collectors protested the re-release of previously withdrawn 20¢ Fire Pumpers, Postal Service officials decided to destroy the remaining stocks of 18¢ Flag coils, and that was done. Some pairs of the key number 6 stamp are probably in 1981 Definitive Mint Sets that are still on sale at many post office philatelic counters.

It is ironic that despite the tremendous popularity of the Transportation series, which has fueled the PNC boom more than any other single factor, the key item for PNC collectors is a Flag stamp.

Chapter 6

The Coil Stamps of 1982

Compared to the turbulence of 1981, with its two major rate-increase packages, 1982 was a relatively relaxed year for the Postal Service. But for United States philately, it was the worst year on record. Catalog prices reached record levels in their 1982 editions, reflecting the peak of a four-year binge of wild speculation in stamps. But just as these catalogs were rolling off the presses, the stamp market collapsed. By year's end, collectors and dealers alike had seen more than a quarter of the value of their stamps evaporate into thin air. The crash of 1982 was the rude beginning of a three-year decline in U.S. stamp prices, accompanied by the departure of thousands of shocked and disillusioned collectors from the hobby's ranks.

The new plate number system on coil stamps was not an immediate hit with stamp collectors, who may have been somewhat distracted by larger concerns, but it did receive its first significant nudge in the 1982 edition of the *Minkus New American Stamp Catalog*, which listed and priced the 18¢ Surrey and 17¢ Electric Auto coils as line/number strips of three rather than as line pairs. For the 18¢ Flag coil, Minkus specified no preferred format, but noted, "Plate number incorporated into roll." By contrast, the *Scott Specialized Catalogue of United States Stamps* for 1982 continued its traditional methods by listing and pricing the first two Transportation coils as line pairs, noting the presence of the plate numbers on them, and making no mention at all of a format for collecting plate numbers on stamps that lacked a joint line. Scott stubbornly stuck with that policy until its 1987 edition.

Although the major postal rates that require stamps did stabilize after 1981, some discounts for bulk mailings by nonprofit organizations fluctuated up and down during 1982. The basic nonprofit bulk third-class minimum rate per piece rose from 3.8¢ to 5.9¢ on January 10, then dropped to 4.9¢ on July 28. Nonprofit mail sorted to five-digit ZIP codes went from 2.9¢ up to 5¢, then down to 4¢ on the same dates, while the carrier-route sort went from 1.9¢ to 4¢ to 3¢. And although new stamps had not been issued to cover many of the new rates, because the Postal Service had been mainly preoccupied with the stamps needed for first-class mail, the lull provided an opportunity to catch up on some of the bulk-rate stamps.

The initial Postal Service intent was to use new designs for new rates, in which case the new stamps would all have conformed to the new plate numbering scheme introduced in 1981. But once again fate intervened to thwart such well-laid plans. After several of the bulk rates had proven to be less stable than anticipated, the Postal Service resorted to older stamp designs, but with new overprints, to meet some of the needs.

The third-class carrier-route sort rate had risen to 7.9¢ on November 1, 1981. A coil stamp in the Americana series depicting a drum

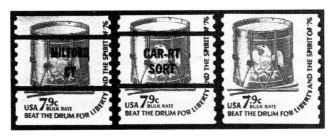

The 7.9¢ Drum coil stamp in the Americana series included the BULK RATE endorsement as an element of the stamp's design. The original 1976 version, printed in deep carmine on rich yellow paper with glossy corn-dextrin "wet" gum, was precanceled with city and state overprints. The 1982 version, printed in lighter carmine ink on lighter yellow paper with matte-textured Davac PVA "dry" gum, included the service inscription CAR-RT SORT in the overprint, further restricting the usage. Both versions were also issued without precancel overprints for philatelic sales.

had been issued back in 1976 for a different 7.9¢ third-class rate. At that time the USPS was using a two-tier bulk rate structure, where the first 250,000 pieces from a mailer (in a calendar year) went for a minimum of 7.7¢ each, and any additional pieces went for 7.9¢. Those rates, in effect from December 31, 1975, through July 17, 1976, could be prepaid with precanceled stamps, and the 7.9¢ Drum coils had been overprinted with a total of 108 different Bureau precancels for use in 107 different cities. (The Jersey City, New Jersey, overprint came two ways, with and without periods in the state abbreviations.)

New Cottrell press plates were prepared from the old dies, and sent to press in June and July. When this printing was shipped to philatelic units and went on sale August 13, some collectors and cachetmakers prepared covers marking the occasion, even though there was no official first day of issue. The new stamp differed from the original in several respects. Both the yellow paper and the carmine ink were

Several cachetmakers prepared "first day covers" post-marked on August 13, 1982, the date the reissued 7.9¢ Americana returned to philatelic sale. This House of Farnam cachet shows the correct design but wrong denomination.

lighter in hue. The original issue stamps had shiny gum; the reissue had dull gum. The new overprinted CAR-RT SORT service inscription further restricted the BULK RATE endorsement in the stamp's design legend.

Precancel specialists were surprised to see that the typeface of the overprint was unfamiliar. The reason, they later learned, was that the rubber mats, ordered in the past from the Government Printing Office, had been manufactured by the Baumgarten Company of Washington, D.C., supplier of rubber stamps and canceling devices used by the Postal Service. The research that led to this disclosure, by precancel specialists James R. Callis Jr. and Horace Q. Trout, eventually also explained the three different precancel styles on the 17¢ Electric Auto stamps.

After the third-class carrier-route sort rate dropped to 7.4¢ on May 22, 1983, the 7.9¢ precancels remained valid as false franking to cover the new rate, with the difference refunded to the mailer. Initially the false franking was permitted until October 1, 1983, but no 7.4¢ stamps had been issued by then, so the usage was extended "until further notice." After a stamp in the 7.4¢ denomination finally appeared, the 7.9¢ Americanas were no longer needed. They were withdrawn from philatelic sale on July 31, 1984.

Another older stamp that got dusted off and returned to duty was the 3¢ Francis Parkman coil from the Prominent Americans series. This design had already appeared on several different kinds of stamps since its initial release as a tagged sheet stamp for makeup postage in 1967. The sheet version was also issued in untagged precanceled form for use in 11 cities.

The regular tagged version of the 3¢ Parkman coil made its debut on November 4, 1975, in anticipation of the letter rate increase from

The 3¢ Parkman coil began as a plain tagged stamp for use when the letter rate jumped from 10¢ to 13¢ on December 31, 1975. Precancels appeared according to changing USPS specifications. Before September 1978, they included city and state overprints, and plain lines after that.

10¢ to 13¢, and for many years through many rate changes it also served as a changemaker in stamp vending machines, to round odd values to the nearest nickel (17¢ plus 3¢, for example). Its second makeup tour of duty came when the letter rate went from 15¢ to 18¢ in 1981. Besides the changemakers, seven city-state overprints had been issued on untagged 3¢ Parkman coils precanceled for bulk-mail use by 1978.

The Postal Service changed its policy for precancel overprints in September 1978, replacing the city/state designations with a plain pair of solid horizontal lines. The 3¢ Parkman coils, called upon to prepay the very first nonprofit carrier-route presort rate, in use from April 23 until July 26, 1980, had been overprinted in the new precancel style.

The 1982 return of the 3¢ rate was actually not as simple as it seems. At the time of the original 1980 experiment, the basic nonprofit rate for mail presorted to three Zip-code digits was 3.1¢, with an additional 0.1¢ discount for presorting to carrier routes. The basic nonprofit rate introduced on July 28, 1982, was 4.9¢, with a 1.9¢ carrier-route discount. Both calculations equaled 3¢, but were arrived at from significantly different base rates, with a much larger discount incentive to mailers in 1982.

The 1982 editions substituted dull gum for the shiny gum of the earlier ones, and the precancel overprint included the Nonprofit Org. CAR-RT SORT service inscription.

Also, the Bureau of Engraving and Printing had changed its paper and adhesive specifications, and the Postal Service had further modified its precancel policy, so the 1982 versions of the 3¢ Parkman coil, printed from previously used Cottrell press plates, came out with dull gum on both tagged and precanceled versions, and the precancels carried the service inscription "Nonprofit Org. CAR-RT SORT" between the lines of the overprint.

This time the 3¢ rate lasted from July 28, 1982 until January 8, 1983. The new precancels went to press for the first time on November 5, and they were available for distribution after November 22. There was no official date of issue, and no dated early use covers have been reported. When the rate rose to 3.3¢, false franking with the 3¢ Parkman stamps, and the balance due paid at the time of mailing, was authorized by the Postal Service until July 6, 1983, and later extended "until further notice."

After the rate rose again to 3.4¢, the service-inscribed Parkmans were authorized for false franking at that rate until June 16, 1985, by which time a 3.4¢ coil stamp was ready. Both tagged and precanceled versions were withdrawn from philatelic sale even earlier, on May 31, 1984. Although authorization to use the precanceled stamps expired in June 1985, the tagged stamps remained in general circulation in post office vending machines, and saw widespread use as late as 1988, when the letter rate increased from 22¢ to 25¢.

Many versions of the 3¢ Parkman coil exist imperforate, but the most common and least expensive is the service-inscribed edition issued in 1982.

The Postal Service announced that it would issue a precanceled version of the 5¢ George Washington coil stamp in the Prominent

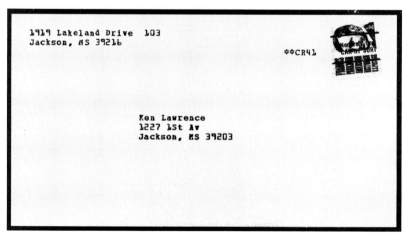

This proper use of the service-inscribed 3¢ Parkman is actually an example of false franking. It arrived on October 25, 1984, after the carrier route-sort rate had risen to a minimum of 3.3¢ per piece, a denomination for which no stamp was ever issued.

Americans series on August 13, but did not state whether it would be the "dirty face" original or "shaved" re-engraved version. As things turned out, the stamp was not issued, because the nonprofit bulk rate fell to 4¢ on July 28.

The rest of the year's new coil stamps conformed to the new numbering system, providing eight additional stamps for plate number coil collections, five tagged and three precanceled.

The 5.9¢ Bicycle Stamps

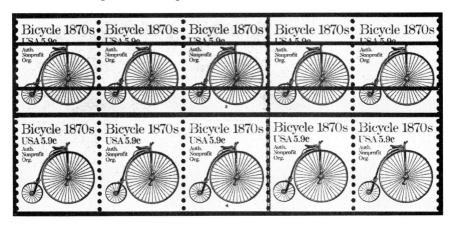

The blue 5.9¢ Bicycle stamp depicted a high-rider bicycle of the 1870s. It was issued with the legend "Auth. Nonprofit Org." as part of the stamp's design inscription, indicating its purpose, when precanceled, to prepay the basic nonprofit presort bulk rate introduced on January 10, 1982. It replaced the 3.5¢ Weaver Violins stamp in the Americana series, issued in 1980.

The Bicycle stamps were issued in Wheeling, West Virginia, on February 17, 1982, along with a 5.9¢ embossed envelope, but no first-day ceremony was held. Only plates 3 and 4 were available in the beginning, so those are the only numbers actually placed on sale in Wheeling on the issue date. Untagged precancels, for use on bulk mail, issued in rolls of 500 and 3,000 were made available immediately afterward. Precancels exist on first-day covers submitted for cancelation within the grace period, but only one or two of each number are known to have PNCs of the precancels.

Plates 1 and 2 were certified, but were never sent to press. They were canceled before the stamp was issued. Plates 5 and 6 were sent to press in June, and were printed only with precancel lines. Plates 7 and 8 were also assigned, but were never needed.

Far more stamps were printed from plates 3 and 4 than from 5 and 6 — 582,553 impressions of the pairing of 3 and 4, but only 75,740 from the 5 and 6 pairing. Over a period of time, dealer prices of mint strips have reflected this discrepancy, but early in 1986 a large supply

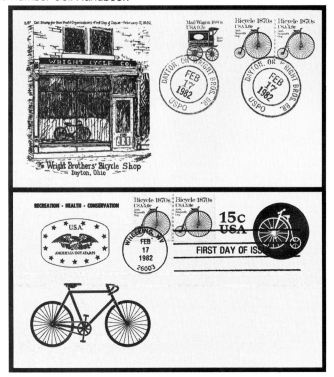

Collectors exercised their creativity in preparing first-day covers of the 5.9¢ Bicycle stamp. The upper cover, with a plate 3 pair, was prepared by Allison W. Cusick. It combines a Weddle cachet showing the Wright brothers' bicycle shop in Dayton, Ohio, with unofficial cancels of the Wright brothers' branch post office in Dayton. The cover below, issued by the American Topical Association's Americana Unit, combines a plate 4 pair of the Bicycle stamp with the similar 15¢ embossed envelope issued in 1980.

of plate 5 and 6 coils turned up in rolls of 3,000, which depressed the value of those numbers for more than a year. In used condition, plate 5 and 6 precancels are scarce, but plates 3 and 4 often turn up in mixtures. The tagged stamps, issued only in coils of 500, are normally available only on collector mail. The cost of used examples is usually close to mint prices.

The 5.9¢ rate lasted only until July 27, 1982, when it dropped to 4.9¢. Mailers were authorized to use the 5.9¢ Bicycle precancels as false franking for the new rate until December 31, 1982, with a refund of the overpayment to the mailer. No stamps were issued for that 4.9¢ rate, and on January 10, 1982, the nonprofit basic presort rate increased to 5.2¢. The Postal Service authorized the 5.9¢ stamp to be used as false franking for that rate too, with a refund, until July 6, 1983. On August 4 that authorization was extended "until further

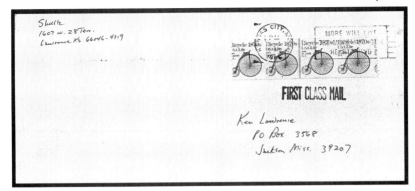

*The tagged collector edition of the 5.9¢ coil would under normal circum-
stances only be found on collector mail. The plate 4 strip on this cover has
a three-millimeter perforation shift.*

notice," although a 5.2¢ precancel was issued on March 21, 1983. The
5.9¢ precancels were dropped from the list of stamps available to be
shipped from the Bureau in October, and both versions of the stamp
were withdrawn from philatelic sale on January 31, 1984. The Bicycle
was thus the first Transportation coil to go off sale.

Ironically, the 5.9¢ Bicycle stamp was available for more than a
year to pay rates other than its face value, while it prepaid its intended
rate for only five and one-third months. It is quite likely that any
existing non-philatelic covers with plates 5 or 6 would be examples of
false franking, since those plates were sent to press shortly before the
5.9¢ rate came to an end. As rare as such covers are, it would be folly
to pay much money for one. Since precancels are not regularly tied to
covers with dated postmarks, anyone can create such a cover simply
by sticking the desired stamp on a likely looking envelope.

This cover, a subscription offer from the socialist weekly newspaper In
These Times, *technically qualified for the nonprofit rate as a Capp Street
Foundation fund appeal. The envelope shows the characteristic "bite" of
the affixing machine to the right of the stamp.*

Precanceled versions of plates 3 and 4 exist imperforate. Examples are both scarce and expensive. The 5.9¢ Bicycle narrowly edged out the 5.2¢ Sleigh as the favorite Transportation series coil stamp when members of the Plate Number Coil Collectors Club were polled in 1989.

The 10.9¢ Hansom Cab Stamps

On March 26, 1982, the violet 10.9¢ Hansom Cab coil stamp was issued at a ceremony in Chattanooga, Tennessee, held at the Chattanooga Stamp Club's 50th anniversary show, CHATTAPEX 82. It depicted a lightweight two-wheeled 19th-century carriage designed by Joseph Aloysius Hansom. The "Bulk Rate" legend in the stamp's design indicated the intended use for the basic third-class presort rate that had gone into effect on November 1, 1981. The new stamp replaced the 8.4¢ Steinway Grand Piano stamp in the Americana series, issued in 1978. Precanceled 10.9¢ Hansom Cab stamps overprinted with plain lines were produced for bulk mailers in coils of 500 and 3,000. Philatelic editions in coils of 500, without the precancel overprint, were phosphor tagged.

Four Cottrell press plates were prepared. Plates 1 and 2 were used to print both tagged and precanceled versions, and those are the only numbers known on first-day covers. The precancel FDCs are scarce.

Only precancels were printed from the plate 3 and 4 pairing. According to USPS plate activity reports, more than twice as many impressions were printed from plates 3 and 4 as from 1 and 2 — 285,706 to 108,000, respectively — yet mint strips of plate numbers 3 and 4 have been scarce as long as PNC collecting has been popular, selling for hundreds of dollars each, while numbers 1 and 2 have always been readily available. Even as used singles, numbers 3 and 4, while not really scarce, are far less common in mixtures than numbers 1 and 2. The tagged versions would normally only have been used by collec-

This first-day cover is believed to be the only one with a 10.9¢ Hansom Cab plate 2 precancel. The handpainted cachet is by Ken D. Kribbs of Jekyll Island, Georgia.

tors, so prices tend to follow the retail level of mint strips.

The 10.9¢ third-class basic presort rate went into effect on November 1, 1981, and was raised to 11¢ on May 22, 1983. After that, the 10.9¢ Hansom Cab precancels were valid as false franking for the 11¢ rate, first until October 1, and then extended "until further notice." New 11¢ precancels finally became available on February 3, 1984, and both tagged and precanceled 10.9¢ coils were withdrawn from philatelic sale on March 31, 1984.

Imperforates exist of plate 1 and 2 precancels. They are scarce and expensive. But one of the most interesting varieties on any Transportation coil stamp is much more common, a low entry of the stamp to the left of the numbered plate 2 stamp on one row of the web. It can easily be overlooked, since it is misaligned by only about ½ millimeter, which explains how it escaped notice for the first five years of the stamp's existence. Once you know what to look for, it's easy to spot.

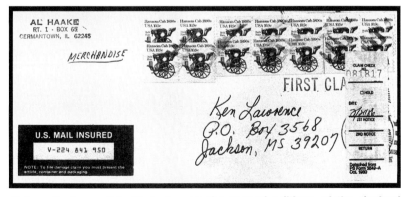

Only collector mail is likely to use the tagged editions of the decimal-denominated coils. This plate 1 cover from a dealer to a collector got by with overlapping stamps, contrary to postal regulations.

This is a typical commercial cover franked with a 10.9¢ Hansom Cab pre-cancel. The stamp is a number 2 PNC.

Although the 10.9¢ stamps were valid by themselves to frank bulk mail at the new 11¢ third-class rate, with the extra amount paid at the time of mailing, a mailer in Redwood City, California, created a "postmaster's provisional" handstamp to indicate that the proper postage had been paid. This unauthorized postmark was ordered withdrawn after a short period of use, but 500 or more of the covers were sold to stamp collectors.

On the average, it would be found on one plate 2 strip in every 18.

Some plate 1 and plate 2 coils show doubling caused by setoff, probably from a chill roller or tagging cylinder. An assortment of gripper cracks is known on some plate 2 stamps, and one on the adjacent stamp to the right of the line, therefore actually a crack near the left edge of plate 1.

The 20¢ Consumer Education Stamp

A true anomaly among Cottrell press plate number coils is the blue 20¢ Consumer Education stamp, a design that originated for political reasons, and was unveiled during the waning days of Jimmy Carter's losing bid for re-election as president. Its issue date was delayed until the second year of Ronald Reagan's first term. As originally envisioned, there would have been two versions, one in English, the other in Spanish, but the bilingual concept was scrapped before the stamp

This plate 2 20¢ Consumer Education stamp is canceled with a purple machine cancel typical of its time.

made its debut. This was on April 27, 1982, at a ceremony in the Old Executive Office Building in Washington, in conjunction with the observance of National Consumer week. The English version retained the planned design features, a tag labeled "Consumer Education" beneath the slogan, "Wise shoppers stretch dollars."

Only four plates were prepared, and all four were sent to press before the issue date, plate 1 paired with number 2, and number 3 with number 4. All four plate numbers exist on first-day covers.

This strip of the 20¢ Consumer Education plate 4 is both miscut and imperforate.

Since these were issued in coils of 100, 500 and 3,000 to cover the regular first-class letter rate, they were widely used on mail, and all four numbers are commonly found in mixtures. Line/number pairs are common, but not enough were saved as plate strips. Strips of three are widely available to anyone willing to pay the price, but strips of five have become quite scarce and costly. More stamps were printed from plates 1 and 2 than from 3 and 4, 533,673 impressions to 381,110, yet numbers 1 and 2 are somewhat scarcer and more expensive than 3 and 4. All four exist imperforate.

The Consumer Ecucation stamp was not popular with users. It was voted the worst stamp in 1982 in the annual *Linn's* Stamp Popularity Poll. Few mourned when it was withdrawn from philatelic sale on November 30, 1983.

The 2¢ Locomotive Stamp

The black 2¢ coil stamp depicting an 1870s vintage steam locomotive was issued at a ceremony held in Chicago's Union Station on May 20, 1982. The stamp was issued in rolls of 500 and 3,000 to serve as utility makeup postage and changemakers, replacing the tagged 2¢ Jefferson coil stamp of the Liberty series issued in 1968. (The untagged version had been issued in 1954.)

Looking back, it seems likely that the stamp may actually have been intended for much earlier release, as add-on postage when the letter rate increased from 18¢ to 20¢ in 1981. But by the time it was actually issued, more than six months after the rate increase, there wasn't really much need for it.

The first plate numbers to appear were 3 and 4, which are the only numbers known on first-day covers. Later coils paired plate 2 with plate 6 and plate 8 with plate 10. According to USPS, 4,327 impressions of plate 1 were printed. But apparently the plate was defective, and all printed work was shredded and never left the Bureau of En-

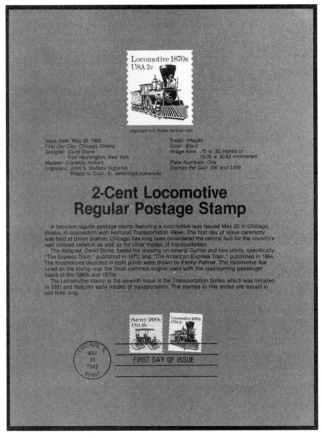

USPS Souvenir Pages with first-day cancelations are available only on a subscription basis, with plate numbers by pot luck. Because the 2¢ Locomotive Souvenir Pages carried only one of that stamp, plate numbers appeared on an average of only one page in 24, making this plate 4 example scarcer than most.

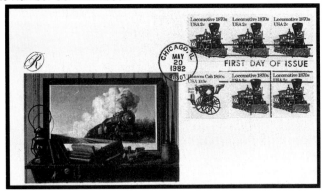

This plate 3 first-day cover is notable to first-day cover spe-cialists as the first cachet by Remarque.

graving and Printing.

An even smaller press run was reported for plate 5 — 1,440 impres-sions — paired on press with plate 3, and the fate of those printed impressions has never been conclusively announced, although USPS says the printed work was "probably" shredded. If they exist, plate 5 examples of the 2¢ Locomotives would be the rarest of all PNCs. Plates 7 and 9 were both canceled without ever having been certified.

Although the 2¢ Locomotive stamps were issued too late to see much duty as makeup postage for the 20¢ rate, they were widely used

The 2¢ Locomotive stamp became important as makeup postage after the letter rate rose from 20¢ to 22¢ as this plate 10 example was used.

in conjunction with 20¢ stamps on letters after the rate rose to 22¢ on February 17, 1985.

A re-engraved version, printed on the B press, was issued in 1987. The B press version has no joint line, and its sleeve number repeats at 52-stamp intervals. The re-engraved design has no "c" for cents in the

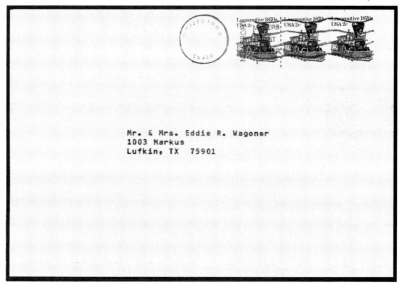

To prepay the 6¢ nonprofit bulk rate, this cover has three 2¢ Locomotive stamps, one showing plate number 8. To the Postal Service, this is considered a precancel usage, because the stamps had already been canceled before being delivered to the post office.

denomination, and the numeral 2 is much larger than in the original design. The report on that stamp begins on Page 208.

One of the first constant plate varieties reported on any Transportation coil was the "Smoking t" gripper crack on plate 3. Reports of "double transfers" turned out to be false alarms. Actually they are set-offs. Imperforates exist from plates 3, 4, 8 and 10.

A subtle constant plate variety is unequal spacing between subjects on the same row. Normally the designs are approximately 2.5 millimeters apart, but on some coils printed from plates 3 and 4, the stamps in positions 12 and 13 to the right of the plate 4 stamp measure just 2 millimeters between subjects, while the position 16 and 17 subjects are 3 millimeters apart.

This constant plate variety, a gripper crack rising from the "t" of Locomotive, is one of the first to have been reported on any Transportation coil stamp. It is usually called the "Smoking t" variety.

The 4¢ Stagecoach Stamps

STAMPSHOW, the annual meeting of the American Philatelic Society, held in 1982 in Milwaukee, was the site for the first-day ceremony to launch the brown 4¢ Stagecoach coil stamp. The stamp was issued August 19, the show's opening day. Stamps printed from Cottrell press plates 1 paired with 2 and 3 paired with 4 were available from the beginning, and all four numbers are easily obtainable on first-day covers.

In some ways the 4¢ Stagecoach seems to have emerged as a lucky accident. At the time it was in the planning stages, 4¢ per piece was the correct bulk rate for third-class nonprofit mailings presorted to the local carrier route, but that rate dropped to 3¢ on July 28. The nonprofit 5-digit sort rate conveniently dropped from 5¢ to 4¢ at the same time, so the stamp was still needed, but with a different precancel overprint. Five-digit presort nonprofit discounts had existed since March 22, 1981, but this was the first time a stamp had been issued for this tier of the rate structure.

Both tagged and precanceled stamps were printed before the issue date, but the precancels, overprinted "Nonprofit Org.," were not placed on sale until after November 22. No legitimate first-day covers of the 4¢ precancels can exist, and no dated early usages have been reported. Plate pairings of the precancels are 3 with 4 and 5 with 6.

Covers showing the 4¢ Stagecoach precancels in their intended usage are probably scarce, and might be nearly impossible to document, unless the cover was date-canceled for some reason such as returned-to-sender. The stamps did not go on sale until late in November 1982, and the rate ended on January 8, 1983. After that the stamps were authorized for false-franking use to cover the 4.3¢ rate, with additional postage paid at the time of mailing, until July 6, 1983, later extended "until further notice." No stamp was ever issued in the 4.3¢ denomination, and the rate rose to 4.9¢ two years later, on February 17, 1985. The 4¢ Stagecoach precancels were then authorized to false-

Often false frankings don't obey the rules. The authorization for using the 4¢ precancels expired on August 18, 1985, because precanceled 4.9¢ stamps had been issued to cover the then-current five-digit presort nonprofit bulk rate. When the rate rose in 1986, first to 6.3¢ on January 1, then to 7.2¢ on March 9, and then dropped to 7.1¢ on April 20, the 4.9¢ precancel was the authorized stamp to use for those rates. Nevertheless, the cover shown here was mailed in July of 1986, almost a year after the 4¢ precancel was no longer valid for the purpose.

frank that rate until June 16, 1985, extended to August 18, 1985. By then a 4.9¢ stamp had been issued, and the 4¢ Stagecoach precancels were withdrawn from philatelic sale on August 31, 1985. They had been available to prepay an actual 4¢ rate for only seven weeks, but legitimately covered subsequent higher rates for two and a half years.

The tagged 4¢ Stagecoach stamps covered no rate, although some mailers used them on nonprofit bulk mailings canceled with a mailer's postmark, an acceptable form of precanceling to the Postal Service. One large mailer, Disabled American Veterans, used huge quantities

This nonprofit bulk-mailed cover is franked with a pair of tagged 4¢ Stagecoach coil stamps, but the Postal Service considers the mailer's permit postmark a precancelation. The contents of the envelope indicate that it was probably mailed at the short-lived 7.4¢ nonprofit rate between January 1 and March 9, 1986. No stamp was issued for that rate. (The 7.4¢ Baby Buggy coil covered a commercial bulk rate between 1983 and 1985.)

of unprecanceled 4¢ Stagecoach stamps in strips of five on return envelopes sent out with their fund appeals (later, strips of five plus a 2¢ Locomotive single for the 22¢ rate). DAV's usage, larger than all others combined, gradually consumed the quantities that had been printed from the first four plates. After that, plates 5 and 6, previously available only on precanceled stamps, were sent to press for a run of regular tagged coils. Some of those were shipped to northern Virginia, where they were used on nonprofit mailer's postmark fund appeal letters, but as before, a large quantity was shipped to Cincinnati for use by DAV. That was where they turned up in January 1986, and most of the strips available to collectors originated there.

The tagged plate 5 and 6 rolls must have been among the last stamps printed on the Cottrell presses, which were retired in November 1985. But DAV's needs continued, and eventually the Bureau filled the continuing orders with 4¢ Stagecoach stamps printed from a re-engraved sleeve printed on the B press — not a bad history for a stamp that met no rate. The image size was reduced for the re-engraved B press version of the 4¢ Stagecoach stamp. This has no joint line, and the single sleeve number repeats at 52-stamp intervals. The report on the re-engraved stamp begins on Page 174.

The first stamps to exhibit image doubling, leading to false reports of "double transfers," were 4¢ Stagecoach coils found in March 1983. Although these turned out not to be double transfers (which are a type of constant plate variety), but offset or set-off images (a production problem), they did alert collectors to the existence of subtle but interesting features that could be found by carefully scrutinizing stamps.

Rare imperforates exist on plate 5 and 6 precancels.

Chapter 7

The Hansom Cab Mystery

The 1982 coil stamps left us with an intriguing mystery. Why do plates 3 and 4 of the 10.9¢ Hansom Cab stamp, known only as precancels, seem to be so scarce?

Only 108,000 impressions were reported printed from plates 1 and 2 of the 10.9¢ Hansom Cab stamp, while more than twice as many, 285,706, were reported from plates 3 and 4. The plate 1 and 2 pairing included all the tagged stamps for collectors as well as precancels for bulk mailers, whereas only precancels were printed from plates 3 and 4. Yet the latter are many times scarcer than the former, and are among a handful of the most expensive Transportation series PNCs.

Reasoning backward from this evidence, most PNC specialists have concluded that the bulk of the rolls printed from plates 3 and 4 were probably printed late and unevenly distributed. The trouble with that is that USPS plate activity reports show that all four plates had been sent to press before the issue date of the stamp. Bureau of Engraving and Printing data released in the plate activity reports show that plates 1 and 2 were used on seven dates in 1982 and 1983, beginning on February 25, 1982, and that plates 3 and 4 were sent to press twice in 1982, on March 15 and July 23. There were no later reports of plates 3 and 4 on press.

On this evidence, we could more easily speculate that plates 3 and 4 appeared early, not late, and that they were mostly used on mail before collectors became interested in them. That is supported by a report from Stanley W. Brown, a collector who has saved every PNC cover he's found since 1982, who had the foresight to record the dates on covers without dated postmarks. Brown found one 10.9¢ Hansom Cab plate 4 cover, mailed at Livingston, New Jersey, on October 5, 1982, and plate 3 and 4 covers, both mailed at Washington, D.C., on January 21, 1983. The last cover he found with a bulk-mailed Hansom Cab PNC was a plate 2 example received on June 2, 1984.

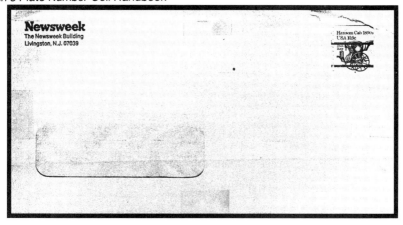

Stanley Brown retrived this 10.9¢ Hansom Cab plate 4 cover from a post office wastebasket on October 5, 1982.

The philatelic evidence seems to clash with the plate activity reports. Also, for each of the plate pairings, collectors have found five different precancel gap positions. If each of those represents at least one separate press run, and probably more than one, it is clear that the plate activity reports are far from complete.

Here's the clincher: By multiplying out all the impressions listed in

This plate 4 strip has the precancel gap four stamps to the right of the joint line, one of the scarcer gap positions for this issue.

the plate activity reports for all four plates, we arrive at a total of 340,161,984 stamps printed (if none at all were spoiled). But that's just a fraction of the number shipped by the Bureau of Engraving and Printing. These are the totals reported in the annual reports of the USPS Stamps Division for each fiscal year:

	Tagged	Precanceled
FY 1982	13,925,000	276,284,000
FY 1983	4,525,000	249,455,000
FY 1984	300,000	85,408,000
TOTAL	18,750,000	611,147,000

Plainly, any estimate of a maximum number of 10.9¢ Hansom Cab PNCs projected from Bureau reports will be much, much lower than the actual number. But let's suppose that BEP correctly reported the totals for plates 3 and 4, while drastically understating the totals for plates 1 and 2. This might plausibly have happened if only the 1982 press runs were included in the totals. In that case, there would have been more than 420,000 precancel impressions of plates 1 and 2, along with 21,700 tagged impressions.

If those figures are approximately right, the result would have been a lot of precanceled PNCs from all four plates in circulation, but those printed from plates 3 and 4 would be less plentiful than plates 1 and 2, and would have been used up early. That pretty well matches the philatelic evidence. Plates 3 and 4 are less common in mixtures and on covers than plates 1 and 2, but not in proportion to the apparent scarcity of plates 3 and 4 as mint strips of three or five. Four years after the denomination was obsolete, mint rolls of 10.9¢ Hansom Cab precancels turned up in post offices and bulk mailers' inventories in widely scattered parts of the United States, further proof that they were once widely available.

The solution to the mystery is this: Plates 3 and 4 of the 10.9¢ Hansom Cab coil stamp are not truly scarce. Large quantities were printed, distributed, sold and used on mail. The apparent scarcity in the PNC market stems from the fact that PNC collecting had not yet caught on during the time these particular numbers were in general use.

Chapter 8

The Coil Stamps of 1983

In the third year of plate number coils, all but one of the new stamps obeyed the PNC policy. The exception, lacking plate numbers on properly manufactured stamps, was a new version of an old stamp, the 12¢ Torch precancel. This stamp from the Americana series had

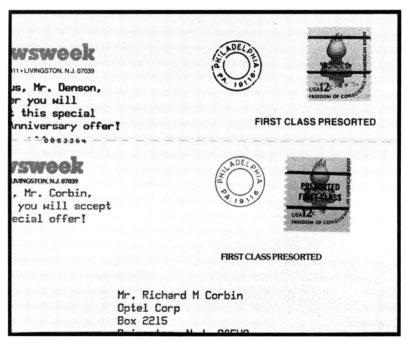

The 12¢ Torch stamp precanceled with plain lines, issued in 1981, was still in use in 1983, as the upper postcard shows. But when those supplies were exhausted, a new version overprinted PRESORTED FIRST-CLASS was issued, shown on the lower card.

made its belated debut in 1981 as a tagged sheet and coil stamp, and as a precanceled coil. But the 1981 version of the precancel had just the plain parallel lines overprint. The new version added the inscription PRESORTED FIRST-CLASS between the lines of the overprint.

The 12¢ presort plates went to press on February 8, 1983, and the stamp went on sale later that month, to cover the same postcard presort rate as its plain-lines predecessor. That rate continued in effect until April 2, 1988, but the service-inscribed 12¢ Torch precancel was withdrawn from philatelic sale on August 31, 1985, five months after it had been replaced by a Transportation series stamp, the 12¢ Stanley Steamer precancel.

All the other 1983 coil issues carried plate numbers.

The 20¢ Official Stamp

Beginning on February 1, 1983, two agencies of the United States government were authorized and required to use Official stamps, postal stationery or meter stamps as postage in place of the traditional envelopes and labels imprinted with penalty indicia. The agencies were the Soil Conservation Service of the U.S. Department of Agriculture and the U.S. Air Force.

This was a Postal Service experiment whose announced purpose was to provide "total official mail accountability and the collection of proper postage revenue from official mail users." The surprise announcement was made September 14, 1982, at the National Postal Forum in Washington, D.C.

Although the authorized usage did not begin until February 1, the new Officials were given a formal philatelic issue date of January 12. Sheet stamps were issued in 1¢, 4¢, 13¢, 17¢, $1 and $5 denominations, along with 20¢ embossed envelopes.

The 20¢ stamp, issued only in coils of 100, was the workhorse of the entire array, since it prepaid the first-class letter rate then in effect. But even that usage was not common, because only the two agencies used the Officials, and because their larger offices usually used meters instead of stamps.

The basis of the design is the Great Seal of the United States, slightly cropped, with the vignette printed dark blue and the inscription in red and black. One odd aspect of the design is that "USA" appears twice for no apparent reason.

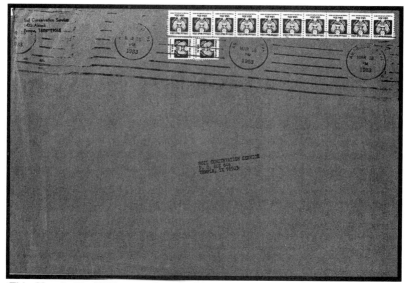

This March 18, 1983 cover has $2.08 postage, overpaying by 1¢ the first-class rate for up to 12 ounces. The third stamp from the left has a plate number, making this cover the earliest reported non-philatelic usage of an Official plate number coil.

All 20¢ Official coils were printed from sleeve 1 on the intaglio B press, block tagged, with numbers at 52-stamp intervals. Since no one outside the government could legally use these stamps on mail, the Philatelic Sales Division waived its minimum purchase requirement for collectors. Those who desired plate numbers could obtain them by buying single stamps or strips of any desired length, in any quantity, without having to buy extraneous "scrap." Even so, not enough people stocked up, and retail prices shot up quickly after the 20¢ coils were withdrawn from philatelic sale on August 31, 1985, after the letter rate had risen to 22¢.

In April 1988, after the second-ounce letter rate rose from 17¢ to 20¢, line-engraved 20¢ Official coils briefly reappeared, but they were quickly withdrawn from use and replaced by a new stamp of similar design printed by offset lithography — without plate numbers. During that opening, sizeable quantities of PNC strips again made their way into the hands of collectors and dealers.

Only one partial roll of imperforate 20¢ Officials, yielding just one plate strip, has ever been reported. All remaining unsold stocks of the original 20¢ Officials were recalled to Washington in May of 1988 for destruction.

The 5.2¢ Sleigh Stamps

On March 21, 1983, the Postal Service issued two new items, a red 5.2¢ coil stamp featuring an antique sleigh typical of those used during the 1890s, and an embossed envelope in the same denomination, to

cover the third-class basic presort rate that had gone into effect on January 9. Both items were released in Memphis, Tennessee, but no formal first-day ceremony was held.

The 5.9¢ Bicycle coil stamp was the last one issued for this rate. No stamp had been issued when the rate fell to 4.9¢ on July 28, 1982.

A poll among members of the Plate Number Coil Collectors Club (PNC3) in 1989 judged the 5.2¢ Sleigh to be the Transportation coil with the most appealing color, and it ran second to the 5.9¢ Bicycle as the overall favorite by just one vote.

The stamps have the service inscription "Auth Nonprofit Org" included in the design. Collector editions of the stamps are tagged, and the untagged precancels for bulk mailers are overprinted with parallel horizontal black lines. The tagged stamps were issued in coils of 500, the precancels in coils of 500 and 3,000. Plate numbers 1 and 2, both tagged and precanceled, occur on first-day covers. The precancels are

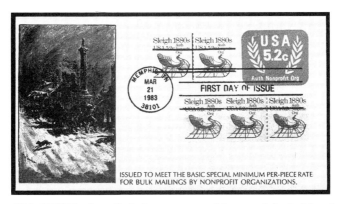

This KMC Venture first-day cover combines a plate 1 strip of three of the tagged 5.2¢ Sleigh coil with a 5.2¢ plate 2 line pair on a 5.2¢ embossed envelope. This scarce cover is one of the very few with a hand-colored cachet.

quite scarce on FDCs and have sold for hundreds of dollars.

An FDC variety came about because the Postal Service asked two of the largest first-day cover firms to cancel their own covers in order to help the Philatelic Sales Division with its "workload problem." Both Washington Press, owner of Artcraft cachets, and Unicover, owner of Fleetwood cachets, did so during 1982 and 1983. Collectors discovered this arrangement when several of the Fleetwood in-house cancels were non-standard-size reproductions of those applied by the Postal Service.

No coil stamps were given non-standard-size first-day cancels, but the simulated machine cancels applied by Fleetwood through a flexographic process can be differentiated from normal Pitney-Bowes machine cancels. The Fleetwood imitations have the boldness of

This Fleetwood first-day cover with plate 1 and 2 line pairs of the 5.2¢ Sleigh coil bears a first-day-of-issue postmark designed to look like a Pitney-Bowes steel die machine cancel, but it was actually applied by a flexographic plate.

handstamp postmarks. PNC covers bearing these cancellation varieties occur in two formats, first with two pairs of 5.2¢ Sleigh stamps, and second with a strip of three on a 5.2¢ embossed envelope. The only other coil stamp covers canceled in-house are FDCs of the 3¢ Handcar stamp.

Eight Cottrell press plates were manufactured for the 5.2¢ Sleigh stamps, and numbers 1 through 6 were sent to press. Plates 7 and 8 were certified, but were canceled with no impressions printed. All six of the plates used are widely available on precancels, but the tagged collector editions are only known from plates 1, 2, 3 and 5. The plates were paired on press as follows: 1 with 2, 3 with 5, and 4 with 6.

Precancels in large quantities were printed from all six plates. Ironically, plates 3 and 5 are the most common precancels but are in short supply in unprecanceled form.

The 5.2¢ Sleigh stamps were issued to cover the third-class basic presort rate for qualified nonprofit bulk mailers. This rate went into

The May 28, 1985 dated contents inside this cover prove that the plate 3 5.2¢ Sleigh precancel is an example of false franking, used after the basic sort rate had risen to 6¢.

effect on January 9, 1983, and lasted until February 16, 1985, when it rose to an even 6¢ per piece. After the 1985 increase, the 5.2¢ stamps were authorized for false-franking use, with the balance paid at the time of mailing, until June 16, 1985. By then a 6¢ coil stamp had been issued to cover the new rate, and the 5.2¢ Sleigh stamps were withdrawn from philatelic sale on June 30, 1985.

It is mildly surprising that no imperforates have ever turned up on this stamp, which was widely used over a two-year period. One interesting constant plate variety, a gripper crack on plate 2 stamps, was dubbed the "sleigh whip" by collectors.

Precancel gap position collecting had just begun to achieve popularity as these stamps were being withdrawn. Because the plates were returned to press so many times to satisfy heavy demand from nonprofit mailers, numerous gap positions exist. Some of them that were very common and widely used on mail have become difficult to find in mint strips, evidently because they were mostly gone before collectors focused attention on gap positions. Perhaps there will be more discoveries yet to come regarding this handsome stamp.

This plate 2 single shows the gripper crack known as the "sleigh whip," a constant plate variety.

107

These two plate number singles found in common mixtures of used U.S. stamps both show the precancel gap. The plate 3 stamp at the left has the gap at the joint line, hence it's called a "Line Gap." The plate 5 stamp at the right has it one perforation row to the left of the line, hence it's called "Gap One Left." Both are common in used condition, but difficult to obtain on mint strips.

The 3¢ Handcar Stamp

Just four days after issuing the 5.2¢ Sleigh stamp in Memphis without a ceremony, the Postal Service issued the 3¢ Handcar stamp with full honors, at the ROPEX 83 stamp show in Rochester, New York, on March 25, 1983. The 3¢ Handcar coil was printed in green ink from four Cottrell press plates, paired 1 with 2 and 3 with 4. All four numbers are found on first-day covers. Two additional plates were prepared, numbers 5 and 6, but these were canceled without ever having been sent to press.

The 3¢ Handcar, as well as the other coil stamps issued during the rest of 1983, met no postal rate. It was issued as a changemaker in coils of 500 and 3,000. The handcar shown on the stamp is a manually operated conveyance for railroad crews and supplies, manufactured in

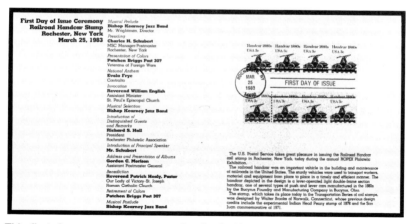

This first-day ceremony program for the 3¢ Handcar coil includes a plate 1 stamp at the lower left.

The wobbly waves of the cancel are the tell-tale sign of a mailer's postmark used to precancel this plate 2 single of the 3¢ Handcar stamp.

the 1880s by the Bucyrus Foundry and Manufacturing Company of Bucyrus, Ohio. It was driven by one or two men pushing the teeter-totter bar up and down.

Although no Bureau precancels were printed using this 3¢ coil design, some mailers used it in pairs to prepay the 6¢ third-class non-profit bulk rate. In those cases, the stamps must be precanceled, either with a city-state handstamp device obtained by the local postmaster or else, and more typically, by a mailer's postmark. The majority of used 3¢ Handcar PNCs found in common mixtures seem to have originated this way.

After the cost of postage for a first-class letter rose to 25¢ in 1988, the remaining stocks of 3¢ Handcar coils (and all other available 3¢ stamps) were pressed into service as makeup postage that, combined with leftover 22¢ stamps, met the new rate. But as 25¢ and 20¢ coil

After the first-class letter rate increased to 25¢, the 3¢ Handcar could make up the extra postage when using up the obsolete 22¢ stamps. Here a plate 2 single does the job.

stamps replaced 22¢ and 17¢ values in the vending machines, these changemakers were phased out, except in private vending machines that charge more than face value for stamps. The 3¢ Handcar coils were withdrawn from philatelic sale on August 31, 1988.

The Handcar design was intended to replace the tagged 3¢ Parkman coil issued in 1975, but the Postal Service actually continued to ship large quantities of the Parkman coil throughout the life of the Handcar. During two of those years, fiscal 1984 and fiscal 1988, quantities of the Parkman shipped exceeded the Handcar quantities. Both were eventually superseded at the same time, when the 3¢ Conestoga Wagon stamp was issued in 1988.

The initial use of the 3¢ Handcar, as well as its 3¢ Parkman predecessor, was to allow coin machines to vend 17¢ Electric Auto stamps for 20¢ to people who needed postage for overweight letters. Since there was no logical use for such a stamp, purchasers would often leave them dangling from the vending machine after taking and using the 17¢ coil.

The 1¢ Omnibus Stamp

On August 19, 1983, the 1¢ Omnibus coil stamp, depicting a horse-drawn urban mass-transit vehicle used during the 1880s, made its debut at the national convention of the American First Day Cover Society in Arlington, Virginia. Printed on the Cottrell press in purple ink, it was released only as a tagged stamp in coils of 500 and 3,000.

Nine Cottrell plates were manufactured with this design, but only the first six were actually used, plate 1 paired with plate 2, 3 with 4, and 5 with 6. Only plates 1 and 2 exist on first-day covers.

This stamp proved to be a more versatile changemaker than its 3¢ Transportation series counterpart, and many more 1¢ Omnibus coils were shipped. It replaced the 1¢ Inkwell and Quill coil in the Americana series, and the 1¢ Jefferson coil in the Prominent Americans series, both of which were still in use in 1983. For the duration of the 20¢ letter-rate period, vending machines dispensed three 1¢ Omnibuses along with one 17¢ Electric Auto stamp, or two Omnibuses along with a 13¢ coil for use on a postcard. After the 1985 increase to 22¢, the machines gave three 1¢ Omnibus stamps as change along with one 22¢ Flag coil or one 17¢ Electric Auto coil, and one Omnibus along with a 14¢ Iceboat coil, the new postcard stamp.

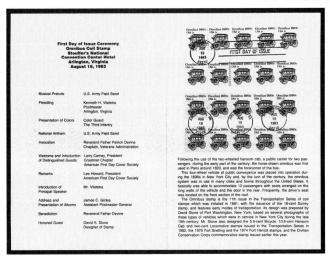

First-day ceremony programs of the 1¢ Omnibus stamp are the only ones featuring coils that are scarcer without a PNC than with one. The program shown here, however, has plate number 1, on the second row, second stamp, and plate number 2 on the top row, left-end stamp.

Although a lot of 1¢ Omnibus stamps were left dangling at post office vending machines, many of them were used as makeup postage with 20¢ stamps after the letter rate became 22¢ in 1985, and again with 22¢ stamps when the rate rose to 25¢ in 1988. Additionally, postal clerks used them to revalue 13¢ postal cards to 14¢ in 1985 and 14¢ cards to 15¢ in 1988.

Plates 5 and 6 exist imperforate. Gripper cracks exist on or adjacent to numbers 3 and 6. Some of the most spectacular image doubling

A plate 4 line pair of the 1¢ Omnibus served as makeup postage on this cover after the letter rate increased from 20¢ to 22¢.

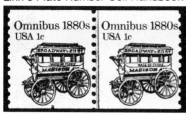

Offset, also called set-off, image doubling, evidently caused by ink deposited on chill rollers or tagging rollers, then transferred to stamps already printed, is very strong on this plate 2 stamp.

known on any Transportation coil issue has been found on plates 1 and 2 of the 1¢ Omnibus, evidently caused by set-off from the chill roller or from the tagging roller.

Eventually supplies of this stamp were depleted in 1986, but by then the Cottrell presses had been scrapped. A new redesigned version of the 1¢ Omnibus was issued in 1986, printed on the B press. As the last of the Cottrell printings ran out, the original 1¢ Omnibus stamps were withdrawn from philatelic sale on June 30, 1988. The B press version has no joint line, and its single sleeve number repeats at 52-stamp intervals. It was re-engraved, with no "c" for cents. The denomination numeral is much larger than in the original design. The report on that stamp begins on Page 195.

The 5¢ Motorcycle Stamp

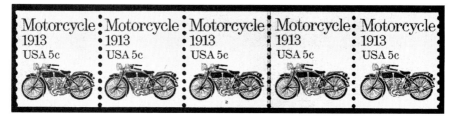

On October 10, 1983, the 5¢ Motorcycle stamp was issued at the annual convention of the Envelope Manufacturers Association of America in San Francisco. It quickly replaced the two versions, original ("unshaven") and re-engraved ("shaved"), of the 5¢ George Washington coil stamp in the Prominent Americans series that were still in general use.

The greenish-gray stamps depict a 1938 Pope "Model L" motorcycle housed at the Smithsonian Institution in Washington. Six Cottrell press plates were prepared, but only the first four were sent to press. Plate 1 was paired with 2, and 3 with 4. Plates 1 and 2 are commonly found on first-day covers. Plates 3 and 4 also exist on FDCs, but they are rare.

The 5¢ Motorcycle stamp was issued only in a tagged version, in coils of 500 and 3,000.

This unofficial 5¢ Motorcycle first-day cover was prepared by Ronald J. Traino, owner of Fulton Stamp Company. The machine cancel slug, "Stamp Collecting A Hobby for Everyone," had been placed into service just before these stamps were issued, to promote National Stamp Collecting Month. The 5¢ Motorcycle coil was the first new issue after this slogan went into use.

These new 5¢ coils matched no postal rate, but they were useful changemakers in vending machines that accepted quarters and vended 20¢ letter-rate stamps. There are no Bureau precancels of the 5¢ Motorcycle. Unlike the 2¢ Locomotive and 3¢ Handcar stamps, they did not lend themselves to nonprofit bulk mail usage when canceled with a mailer's postmark, although theoretically one 5¢ Motorcycle plus one 1¢ Omnibus could have been combined to meet the 6¢ rate. The local precancels that exist are interesting philatelic creations, and their usage is similar to the usage of tagged decimal denominated coils.

Imperforate examples of the 5¢ Motorcycle appeared shortly after

The plate 4 strip of the 5¢ Motorcycle coil stamp bears the tell-tale marks of a vending machine, with crescent-shaped cuts at each end and partially separating each stamp in the strip.

Collectors who desired precancels of every Transportation coil usually had to make their own for this issue. This plate 1 line pair was precanceled with the Redondo Beach, California, device.

the stamp was issued, one strip of fewer than 80 stamps with perforations at one end and a spliced portion near the other, yielding just one plate number strip each of plates 1 and 2, making this one of the scarcest modern coil errors.

A more widely available, popular variety was caused by imperfect ink blending, resulting in a darker gray and less greenish than the

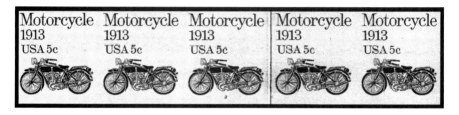

This imperforate strip of the 5¢ Motorcycle coil is owned by John Greenwood.

approved color. In response to a query from Frank Norulak, who initially discovered rolls of the dark gray variety, a Bureau of Engraving and Printing official responded that Norulak's stamps appeared "to have a higher percentage of black pigmentation in the green ink than Motorcycle stamps which were printed with the correct color." By the standards of traditional U.S. philately, this would probably be regarded as a distinct color shade.

By the time stocks of the 5¢ Motorcycle were running low, they could not be reprinted on the Cottrell presses, which were no longer in service. Postal service policy had changed too, so that instead of issuing a re-engraved version of the same design printed on the intaglio B press, an entirely new design was released, the 5¢ Milk Wagon, in 1987. The 5¢ Motorcycle stamps were withdrawn from philatelic sale on February 28, 1989.

Five years after the 5¢ Motorcycle was issued, Jack Williams, USPS program manager for philatelic design, gave the 5¢ Motorcycle as an example of a poor design, "a good example of the artwork being too small, thus making the type much too large." In later years of the Transportation coil series, areas for the inscriptions were blocked out first, in order to establish the "series look." The designer then fit the art into the remaining available space.

Chapter 9

Year One of PNC Collecting

The year 1983 was a milestone in coil collecting. For the first time, plate number coils achieved a special status in the world of U.S. philately.

In April, Dennis D. Chamberlain published a lively pamphlet titled, "The Great Philatelic Treasure Hunt." Chamberlain trumpeted his discovery: "RARE STAMPS!!! Millions of rare stamps! They are in homes and offices! They are in post offices and philatelic centers! There are more than 50 different varieties! Some varieties may be worth hundreds of dollars! Rare stamps are being used every day to mail letters! Rare used stamps are being destroyed every day and are becoming rarer! They have been issued since 1981, and they are still being printed!"

Chamberlain included a list of every PNC that had been reported at the time, and he urged collectors to keep them as strips of three or four. The pamphlet was handsomely illustrated with mint pairs and strips, used singles, and one first-day cover. The most charming passage was Chamberlain's description of how he had first stumbled upon PNCs, as he unwound a roll of 2¢ Locomotive stamps.

"Twenty of the identical little engines in a row reminded me of a strip of motion picture film. I looked at each stamp. A thought crossed my mind that had many times before while looking through other new lots of stamps or coins. 'It would be nice,' I thought, 'if one of these stamps was in some way different than the others.' This time, there it was! There was a small number '4' at the bottom of one of the stamps! I started looking for more numbers. Twenty-four more stamps down the strip I found another number! It was a '3'!"

Chamberlain offered his booklet for sale, for $10, in a *Linn's* display advertisement that ran for three weeks. He sold only 11 copies, and one customer demanded a refund. Undaunted, Chamberlain decided to become a stamp dealer, the first to specialize in plate number coils. His earliest price list, issued in August 1983, offered mint PNCs

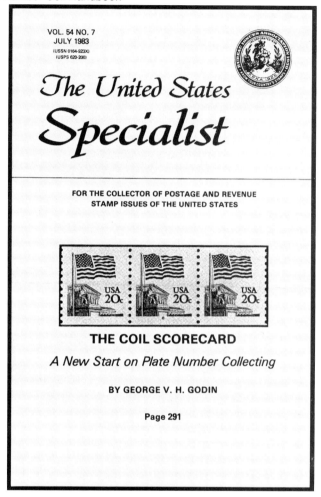

The July 1983 issue of The United States Specialist *gave a boost to plate number collecting. The cover featured a strip of three of the 20¢ Flag coil.*

in pairs, strips of three, and strips of four. The most expensive item was an 18¢ Flag plate 1 strip of three, for $3.50. A 10.9¢ Hansom Cab precancel plate 3 or 4 strip of four sold for $2, and a 20¢ Official plate strip of three was priced at $1.50.

If Chamberlain's career as an author was disappointing, his PNC business was an immediate hit. By the time his second price list appeared, the cost of an 18¢ Flag plate 1 strip of three had risen to $4.50, while the most expensive items, 20¢ Fire Pumper plate 12 and 14 strips of four, sold for $6 apiece. PNC collecting had a small but avid following.

Meanwhile, the specialty got a big boost among established, serious collectors of United States stamps. The July issue of *The United States*

Specialist, monthly journal of the Bureau Issues Association, carried an article by George V.H. Godin titled, "The Coil Scorecard, A New Start on Plate Number Collecting." Godin, the man who edits the *Durland Standard Plate Number Catalog* and keeps track of every known plate number on any U.S. stamp, waxed enthusiastic.

"At the suggestion of James D. Galceran, we are pointing out the fact that right now YOU have the opportunity to get in on the ground floor of a new specialty collection. We are presenting the full story on another page headed 'Coil Scorecard' where you may select either all or any part of the data to form your own collection showing the beginning of the current plate numbers on coil stamps as part of the design. You may collect these numbers in any manner that pleases you as an individual. For openers you may want either mint or used single stamps showing the number; you may decide that line pairs are THE thing; perhaps you are turned on by strips of three with the number on the middle stamp; you may like strips of five better or you might want to go for strips of six to balance your original collection of 432 coils by having three stamps on each side of the line. It is your collection, so YOU collect whatever you like."

Jimmy Galceran, who prodded Godin to view PNCs as something new, rather than simply as an extension of traditional plate number collecting, has since become well-known among PNC collectors as the man who can often track down and supply a new plate number long before it shows up in dealer inventories. All of us who collect PNCs today owe a debt of gratitude to these three pioneers — Dennis Chamberlain, George Godin, and Jimmy Galceran.

Linn's followed up on George Godin's initiative by publishing it's first PNC checklist in the August 22, 1983 issue, and Robert Rabinowitz hailed PNCs as a "major new area of U.S. philately" in his November 7 *Linn's* "Plate Numbers" column.

Chapter 10

The Coil Stamps of 1984

Although the policy of including plate numbers in the bottom margin of all coil stamp new issues had been announced in 1980 and the first examples had been released in 1981, 1984 was actually the first year that every new coil included plate number stamps. It had taken the previous three years for the Postal Service to catch up after the flurry of activity caused by two general rate increases in 1981 and a series of up-and-down bulk rates after that, complicated by the introduction of a new all-coil definitive set, the Transportation series. Finally, in 1984, a year of relative calm had arrived.

Only two new coil stamp designs were released in 1984, creating a grand total of five new coil stamps when the overprinted editions are counted separately. But this was a year of change nonetheless. None of the new coils were printed on the Cottrell presses; all were printed on the intaglio B press.

In 1983, 20¢ Bighorn Sheep booklet production had been moved from the Cottrells to the B press. Then, as the Cottrells were phased out, the 20¢ Flag booklets were moved from the B to the C press to make the B press available for more coil work.

Now it was time to start shifting coil production from the Cottrells to the B press, anticipating the Cottrells' 1985 retirement. This posed some technical problems, because none of the earlier B press stamps, whether booklets or coils, had been issued as precancels, so a method of applying the precancel overprint had to be devised. A makeshift routed-out seamless tagging cylinder was used to overprint the 11¢ Caboose and 20¢ Flag stamps with plain double-line precancels. Except where the roller's raised image sustained minor damage, there were no gaps in the precancel overprints on those stamps. The 7.4¢ Baby Buggy was the first to employ paired 468-subject flexographic plates to print precancel lines and a service inscription. This method was used on all subsequent overprinted B press coils. With the new B press system, precancel gaps occur at 26-stamp intervals rather than the 12-stamp gap spacing on Cottrell precancels.

The consequences of modernization ranged from the disappearance of joint lines on monochrome as well as multicolored coil stamps to the phasing out of precanceled sheet stamps. Worst of all from the collector's standpoint, it was now necessary to buy more than double the number of each new Transportation coil issue to assure that the strip would include a plate number. That blow to the hobbyist's pocketbook undoubtedly exacerbated a crisis that erupted mid-year.

In June, word leaked out that the Postal Service intended to invalidate as first-class postage all 10 previously issued service-inscribed, tagged coil staps that had been printed for collectors: the 3.1¢ Guitar, 3.5¢ Violins, 7.7¢ Saxhorns, 7.9¢ Drum, and 8.4¢ Grand Piano stamps in the Americana series; and the 5.2¢ Sleigh, 5.9¢ Bicycle, 9.3¢ Mail Wagon, 10.9¢ Hansom Cab, and 11¢ Caboose stamps in the Transportation series. It turned out that, although no directive had yet been circulated to postmasters, the stamps had been invalidated on April 7, the issue date for the 7.4¢ Baby Buggy coil. The Baby Buggy was only the second decimal-denominated stamp not to carry a restrictive inscription in the stamp's basic design (first was the 6.3¢ Liberty Bell coil issued almost 10 years earlier).

The reason for issuing the order was said to be that the stamps were confusing postal patrons and postal clerks handling mail bearing them. That was a weak excuse, since nobody seemed to have similar difficulty when other stamps with restrictive inscriptions, such as "Airmail," were used in unintended ways. A precedent existed for disallowing service-inscribed special delivery stamps as first-class postage, but at least they could be used for their intended postal pur-

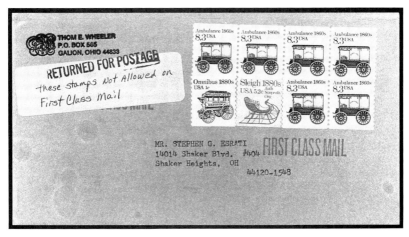

The refusal of some postal clerks to accept tagged, bulk-rate stamps with restrictive service inscriptions led to a U.S. Postal Service order annulling the postal validity of these stamps, a ruling later reversed after a strong protest from stamp collectors.

pose. There was no intended postal purpose for unprecanceled, tagged "Bulk Rate" or "Auth Nonprofit Org" stamps. They were purely philatelic creations, although in theory a bulk-mail permit holder could still have legally used the tagged 5.2¢ Sleigh, the 10.9¢ Hansom Cab (as false franking), and the 11¢ Caboose by having them locally precanceled or by canceling them with a mailer's postmark. The others had been invalidated earlier for use on bulk mail. But aside from that obscure usage, all 10 stamps were theoretically worthless as postage after April 7, 1984.

In effect, top brass at the Postal Service had decided to ratify the actions of their most ignorant clerks who had wrongly rejected mail franked with these special stamps issued for collectors. This was especially galling to collectors since the Philatelic Sales Division had always required a minimum purchase of 10 of any decimal-denominated stamp, and therefore 30 to guarantee getting a plate number or joint line on Cottrell press coils. To be certain of getting a plate number on the 11¢ Caboose required a purchase of at least 52 stamps.

In comparable cases of stamps that collectors could not use as postage, the Postal Service had sent mixed signals. Official stamps had no minimum purchase requirement to get plate numbers or marginal markings; anyone could order 1,000 plate singles without having to buy any scrap. But the rules for purchases of postage due stamps were the same as for any other sheet stamps: To guarantee getting a plate number or other marginal markings required a minimum purchase of 100 1¢ to 13¢ stamps; 20 30¢ or 50¢ stamps; and four $1 or $5 stamps. The big difference, however, was that nobody had bought these expecting to use them on mail legally. With the special-service coils, the Postal Service had changed the rules without prior notice and without even a grace period to allow collectors to use up their surplus.

The response was immediate and furious. Mail and phone calls protesting the policy change flooded the Postal Service and the philatelic press. On June 11, *Linn's* editor-publisher Michael Laurence sent a strongly worded letter to Postmaster General William F. Bolger decrying the ruling, and followed with a blistering editorial in the June 18 issue of *Linn's*. After a period of "we're studying the problem" equivocation, Stamps Division manager Don McDowell telephoned *Linn's* on June 26 to read a letter from Bolger to Laurence dated June 25. Bolger wrote, in part:

"I have reviewed our policy in light of the information brought to our attention by your editorial and the letters we have received from concerned stamp collectors. A clear statement permitting the use of these postage stamps on mail is obviously in order.

"I will see to it that our employees are notified of this decision through our internal communications. I appreciate your having taken the time to share your thoughts and those of your readers with me on this subject. I hope this resolution will be satisfactory to all."

When it arrived, the new directive read:

"The Domestic Mail Manual Section 142.3 will be amended to incorporate the following provision: Unprecanceled bulk-rate stamps and non-profit rate stamps may be used to pay regular postage and fees for special services providing the mailing piece is endorsed above the address and below the postage to indicate the appropriate class of the mailing piece."

Collectors could now legally use their stamps with the proper endorsement. If they wrote "First Class" below the stamps and above the address, such mail would not receive the slower third-class service and would not be opened for postal inspection.

Although the decision to demonetize these stamps was rescinded, the service inscription as an element of a coil stamp's engraved design did not return until 1986, and even after that, collector editions remained devoid of those slogans until 1988.

After the furor died down, the enduring consequence of the 1984 innovations was the onset of a five-year process, gradually weaning collectors from their Cottrell coil expectations of alternating plate numbers, dramatic plate varieties, and a proliferation of easily collectible precancel gap positions.

The 11¢ Caboose Stamps

On February 3, 1984, the 11¢ Caboose stamp was issued, without a ceremony, at the Chicago Philatelic Fair '84, the American Stamp Dealers Association Midwest Show, in Rosemont, Illinois. There was some confusion surrounding its issue because USPS news releases originally named Chicago as the first-day city instead of Rosemont, the suburb near Chicago's O'Hare Airport. To the Postal Service, Rosemont was actually a finance station of Des Plaines, Illinois.

As a tagged collector edition of a bulk-rate stamp, the 11¢ Caboose was the first to carry a round denomination without a decimal fraction of a penny, and the last to bear a restrictive service inscription. Henceforth the service inscriptions, whether overprinted or included in the stamp's basic design, would only be seen on the untagged coils actually intended for bulk or quantity mail.

The attractive red stamp features a small narrow-gauge railroad caboose, vintage 1890s, used by a logging company in the Sierra Nevada mountains of California. The tagged collector editions, which were exceptionally popular thematic stamps to collectors in many

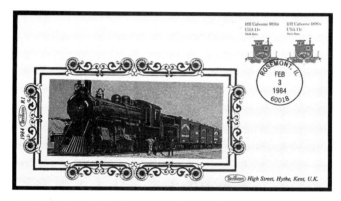

This Benham first-day cover has a plate 1 pair of 11¢ Caboose stamps postmarked with the plain bull's-eye cancel. It was a popular thematic item in Great Britain.

countries, came only in coils of 500, while the precancels were issued in coils of 500 and 3,000.

Only one printing sleeve was ever prepared and sent to press, so only number 1 can be collected in any form — tagged or precanceled, mint or used, on or off cover. As the first monochrome coil stamp printed on a three-color press, the 11¢ Caboose was a straightforward job relatively free of production problems. No imperforates were ever reported, but a couple of interesting plate varieties have stirred some interest.

I reported the first one in the April 23, 1984 issue of *Stamp Collector*, and Stephen G. Esrati promptly dubbed it the "Brake Shoe." Esrati then came up with another he called "Hoseline." Both names were attempts to invest these scratches and gouges on the printing sleeve with pictorial meaning as if they had been intentionally included in the design, a traditional practice among flyspeck variety lovers for generations.

Previously, PNC collectors had identified the location of coil plate varieties by using the Cottrell press joint line as the reference point, counting the number of stamps to the right or the left of the line, just as precancel gap positions were described. But, since the B press coils have no joint line, the new convention imagine it to be at the right of the plate number, and then counts from that imaginary line. The

Two 11¢ Caboose constant plate varieties are dubbed "Hoseline," shown at the left, and "Brake Shoe," shown on the right. "Hoseline" has been found only on precancels.

"Brake Shoe" location is 17 left. The "Hoseline" is 31 left, but has only been found on precanceled rolls.

The 11¢ Caboose stamp was issued to meet the basic third-class bulk rate that had been in effect since May 23, 1983, replacing the 10.9¢ Hansom Cab in use prior to the increase. That rate was raised again to 12.5¢ on February 17, 1985, and the 11¢ Caboose stamps were authorized as false-franking for the new rate, with additional postage paid at the time of mailing, until August 18, 1985. They were withdrawn from philatelic sale on August 31, 1985.

The 7.4¢ Baby Buggy Stamps

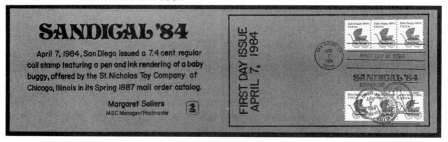

A first-day ceremony for the 7.4¢ Baby Buggy stamp was held at Sandical 84, a San Diego stamp show, but Postal Service headquarters did not prepare a ceremony program souvenir. This souvenir folder, distributed by the San Diego postmaster, has a plate 2 strip canceled "First-Day-of-Issue."

A small first-day ceremony for the 7.4¢ Baby Buggy coil stamp was held at SANDICAL 84, a San Diego, California, philatelic exposition, on April 7, 1984. The brown stamp pictures an 1880s baby carriage, also known (especially in England) as a perambulator, or "pram" for short. The plain tagged edition, available to collectors in coils of 500, was the first decimal Transportation coil issued without an engraved service inscription. Untagged coils were precanceled for third-class bulk mailers in coils of 500 and 3,000.

The endorsement "Blk. Rt. CAR-RT SORT" was provided on the bulk-mail version as part of the precancel overprint, just as had been done previously with the service indicators on the 4¢ Stagecoach and 17¢ Electric Auto precancels.

But those predecessors had been printed on the Cottrell presses, with overprints applied by precancel mats each 12 stamps across by nine stamps in the rotary dimension. As the first B press stamps with this style overprint, a new system was employed, using a 468-subject flexographic plate. B press precancel gaps occur at 26-stamp intervals.

According to BEP plate activity reports issued by the Postal Service, sleeve 1 was sent to press twice, once to print tagged stamps and a second time for a precancel run. The report shows a total of 55,100 impressions from sleeve 1, but that number has never been found by

The "blown tire" plate gouge is one of the most interesting constant varieties found on a B press Baby Buggy coil stamp.

collectors. It is possible that the sleeve may have been faulty, in which case all stamps printed from it were probably destroyed.

The only other sleeve was number 2, and all rolls known were printed from this sleeve. Therefore it's the only plate number that can be collected, whether mint or used, tagged or precanceled, or on cover. One spectacular plate flaw, found 15 stamps to the left of the imaginary joint line, is called the "Blown Tire" variety, a good description of its appearance.

In the annual *Linn's* Stamp Popularity Poll, the 7.4¢ Baby Buggy stamp was voted the least necessary issue of 1984.

The 7.4¢ Baby Buggy coil met the third-class carrier-route sort bulk rate that had gone into effect on May 22, 1983, succeeding the 7.9¢ rate that had been covered by the re-released version of the 7.9¢ Drum stamp overprinted for carrier-route sort use. That rate changed to 8.3¢ on February 17, 1985. The 7.4¢ stamps were valid for false-franking the new rate, with the balance paid at the time of mailing, until August 18, 1985. They were withdrawn from philatelic sale on August 31, 1985.

The Precanceled 20¢ Flag Over Supreme Court Coil Stamp

On July 9, 1984, the Postal Service issued an untagged precanceled version of the 20¢ Flag coil stamp, printed from the final B press sleeve used to print the earlier, tagged version of that stamp, number 14. Despite the advance announcement of its appearance, no first-day covers of this stamp are known, nor any dated early commercial covers. The only important plate variety is the previously noted "Q" on tagged versions of the stamp. The overprinted lines were applied by the same makeshift routed-out tagging cylinder manufactured for the 11¢ Caboose precancel press runs.

The Bureau of Engraving and Printing once required a minimum of 250,000 coil stamps for a precancel order and twice that for a sheet stamp. It was widely rumored that "a bulk mailer in Virginia" placed the initial order for the precanceled 20¢ Flag coils, but none of the people passing that story around could confirm it. It may, however, have been a euphemistic reference to the Republican Party. Several different Republican campaign and fund-raising organizations used the precanceled 20¢ Flag coils during the 1984 campaign season. The stamps were eventually also used by mailers in other parts of the

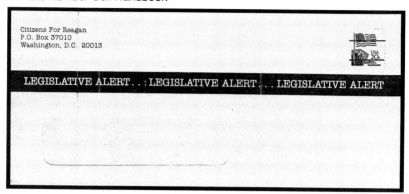

This Citizens for Reagan political cover shows a typical usage of the pre-canceled 20¢ Flag coil stamp.

country, including Oklahoma, Minnesota and Texas.

The quantity of precanceled Flag stamps shipped — 43,760,000 in all, in coils of 500 and 3,000 — significantly exceeded the minimum requirement. Of those, 14,000,000 were in 500-stamp rolls, which is approximately the amount of new coil stamps usually needed for philatelic sales, but even by itself is much larger than most special-order precancel press runs.

When the overprinted 20¢ Flag was issued, precancel expert Horace Q. Trout, who is responsible for the new-issue listings in *The Noble Catalog of Bureau Precancels*, wrote in the October 1984 issue of *The United States Specialist*, "This precancel is also the beginning of a new era in Bureau precancels. For the first time the Bureau has precanceled a 'non series' definitive, unless you want to consider the Defense and War stamps of 1940-43 in this category." Trout might better have called it the end of an era, the era of sheet stamp precancels.

The 20¢ Flag precancel replaced the overprinted 20¢ George C. Marshall stamp in the Prominent Americans series. Supplies of a few other sheet-stamp precancels were still on hand, but in the new context they were anachronistic.

The 20¢ Flag precancel replaced this stamp, the precanceled 20¢ George C. Marshall stamp in the Prominent Americans series. Today, all current Bureau precancels are coil stamps.

Collectors had not fully grasped the new system, however. In February 1982 Trout noted, "The USPS is currently in the process of introducing new definitive stamps. Actually they are being issued as two separate series — one for ordinaries, another for the coils. The ordinary stamps have been dubbed the 'Great Americans' series and the coils represent various modes of travel and have been named the 'Transportation' series. Since I have no way of predicting which of these denominations will be Bureau precanceled I have decided to assign new 'Noble' numbers to each of the stamps as they appear. We are going to number the Great Americans in the '1000' series, the Transportation coils in the '1100' series." None of the 1000 series numbers were needed, because all subsequent Bureau precancels were coils, including the one that surprised Trout, the 20¢ Flag.

The last new sheet-stamp precancel was the 30¢ Schoolhouse stamp in the Americana series, which went to press on February 20, 1981. Previously manufactured tagged stamps, already cut into single panes and stored, were recalled from the vault and overprinted on a Miehle flatbed letterpress, using a handset brass rule form locked up in a chase, typographic technology that dates back to the time of Gutenberg. This may have been fine for a stamp fulfilling such a small need that it wasn't shipped to postmasters until the following year and wasn't noticed by collectors until the summer of 1983, at which time it was placed on sale at the Philatelic Sales Division. But it was no way to run modern stamp production. When the need arose for first-class letter-rate precancels, the horse-and-buggy days quickly drew to a close, although the Postal Service continued to ship previously printed sheet-stamp precancels until 1986. The very last ones — overprinted, tagged 30¢ Schoolhouse (total quantity shipped was 2,400,000) and 50¢ Iron "Betty" Lamp stamps — were withdrawn from philatelic sale on April 30, 1987.

Presumably if a large-quantity mailer such as Reader's Digest requested a precanceled edition of a sheet stamp, the Postal Service would comply. Such an event seems unlikely now that automated bulk-mailing systems use coil stamps, embossed envelopes or imprinted envelopes, so we have probably seen the last of the special-order sheet-stamp precancels.

The 20¢ Flag precancel did not meet a special postal requirement. It was used on large first-class mailings by users who wished to speed mail to its destination, avoiding the time required for post office cancelation. The 20¢ letter rate expired on February 16, 1985, and the stamps were withdrawn from philatelic sale on October 31, 1985, along with their tagged counterparts.

Chapter 11

Collectors Move Toward Coils

If 1984 was a slow year for the appearance of new coil stamps, it was just the opposite for the development of collector interest in U.S. coils as a philatelic specialty.

Linn's reprinted the coil scorecards periodically updated by George Godin in *The United States Specialist*, the forerunner of the PNC checklist that eventually became a monthly feature. *Linn's* also conducted a poll to learn "collector preference for size of strips from modern coils which include the tiny plate number at the bottom at regular intervals." The result appeared in the March 19 issue. Strips of three handily beat pairs, with or without a joint line. Dennis Chamberlain again was instrumental in luring collectors to PNCs, this time with his discovery of the se-tenant Type BA overprints on the 17¢ Electric Auto precancels. This also established precancel gap collecting as a specialty.

Building on the popularity sparked by Chamberlain and Godin in 1983, Ron Bowman of Baldwinsville, New York, drew a huge response to his letter, published in *Linn's*, seeking members for the newly organized U.S. Coil Collector Society. The first issue of his *Coil Collector* newsletter appeared in January 1984 and came out once a month thereafter until the final issue dated September 1985. By the time Bowman quit, the U.S. Coil Collector Society had more than 200 members (subscribers, really), and he had corresponded with about 500 coil enthusiasts.

The monthly grind was more work than Bowman could manage, and nobody else immediately came forward to continue the newsletter, so it folded. But throughout 1984 and most of 1985, this was the clearinghouse for specialists. Bowman himself was interested in all U.S. coils, but the majority of buyers, sellers and traders who met one another through his pages were PNC people. Here we could see an 18¢ Flag number 7 strip of three offered for $12.50 in April 1984, a record price for a PNC at that time, and then soar to $17.50 in

May. These records fell in November as 20¢ Fire Pumper number 12 and 14 strips of six were offered for $20 each. Finally, extra-fine 18¢ Flag number 6 strips sold for $30 in December, the year's high. Bowman's newsletter had become the principal marketplace for serious PNC collectors.

On the downside, some dealers were selling plate 17 and 18 18¢ Surrey strips for prices ranging from $40 to $70 each, while they were on sale at the main philatelic sales counter in Washington, D.C., at face value. The word of their easy availability took a while to spread, but when Stephen G. Esrati reported it in the April 1, 1985 issue of *Linn's*, the cat was finally out of the bag. Some collectors felt cheated and quit collecting PNCs.

Esrati organized the Plate Number Coil Study Group in 1984, a small but durable working collective with a closed, by-invitation-only membership to compile and exchange information on every aspect of PNC collecting. Esrati systematically sought to recruit experts on each facet, no matter how arcane: imperforates, first-day covers, precancel gaps, plate activity, expertizing and so forth. The group debated findings through correspondence circulated in a round-robin printout from Esrati's computer.

The core of the study group was made up of collectors, including Esrati himself, who had previously specialized in collecting the West German Buildings definitive stamps of 1948, a lithographed set that seemed to have a nearly infinite number of collectible varieties in negative, blanket and plate flaws; perforation styles; watermark orientations; and the like. Though the collectors lacked specialized knowledge of United States stamps at first, they brought a special slant to PNC collecting that has persisted, particularly a zeal for flyspeck varieties that has contagiously spread to a larger-than-usual number of U.S. collectors.

PNC collecting had not yet reached the hobby's mainstream, but it was steadily advancing in that direction.

Chapter 12

The Coil Stamps of 1985

If 1984 was a slow year for coils, 1985 was the opposite, setting a record for the number of new coil stamp issues. In fact, it set a record for new definitives of all formats — sheets, booklets and coils. For the previous decade, commemorative issues had outnumbered definitives by more than four to one, but in 1985 the U.S. Postal Service released 32 new definitive designs and only 24 new commemoratives. When precancels are counted and Officials are added to the total, 24 new coils appeared in 1985.

The principal reason for so many new stamps was the set of across-the-board rate changes introduced on February 17. Although some third-class rates had fluctuated during the previous three years, this was the first major rate restructuring since November 1, 1981. In addition, a first-class incentive discount for quantity mailers using 9-digit ZIP-coded addresses got its own stamp for the first time — the 21.1¢ Letters coil inscribed "ZIP+4." And finally, one new stamp that met no postal rate, the 11¢ Stutz Bearcat coil, was issued at the request of the Stamp Vendors Association to meet the changemaking requirements of merchants whose profit comes from coin-machine sales of postage at prices above the stamps' face value.

All but one of the 1985 coils have plate numbers on the stamps. The exception is the denominated 22¢ Official stamp released on May 15, representing the first deliberate change in USPS coil stamp policy since PNCs were introduced in 1981. By this time PNC collecting had become so popular that a large percentage of stamp orders received by the Philatelic Sales Division were for PNCs. The policy of permitting collectors to obtain plate numbers on Official stamps without requiring them to purchase an additional quantity of unnumbered stamps filling the interval between the numbers meant that huge quantities of those stamps were wasted.

The nondenominated D contingency Official stamps had already been printed with plate numbers on them, but as those were replaced

130

with stamps bearing the new denominations, plate numbers were eliminated from Officials in both coil and sheet formats.

The flurry of new stamp issues put a lot of pressure on the Bureau of Engraving and Printing. There simply was not enough production capacity on its modern presses to meet so many different needs all at once. The answer was to take the old Cottrell presses out of retirement and place them back in service. The last time any new stamps had been printed on the Cottrells had been 1983. The 1984 Transportation series stamps — the 11¢ Caboose and 7.4¢ Baby Buggy coils — had been printed on the intaglio B press. But the return of the Cottrells was only for the short term; they were dismantled and scrapped before the year was out. As a result, when supplies of certain 1985 issues were depleted in 1986 and 1987, they were replaced by stamps of the same designs — the 14¢ Iceboat, 8.3¢ Ambulance, and 12¢ Stanley Steamer issues of the Transportation series — using sleeves made from the transfer rollers of the original engraved dies, printed on the B press.

This was also the period when two previously issued Cottrell-press stamps, the 1¢ Omnibus and 2¢ Locomotive, were in great demand as makeup postage, and two others, the 3¢ Parkman and 3¢ Handcar, as vending machine changemakers. Stocks of all four proved sufficient for the changeover period, so new B press designs were not needed for those denominations until 1986 and 1987.

One other 1985 event affects plate number collectors, although they are often unaware of it. The five-digit serial numbers assigned to each successive printing image carrier or printing base (plate, sleeve, or cylinder) were replaced by six-digit numbers as the Bureau adopted a new system of keeping records. The 1981 innovations had eliminated the full numbers from finished stamp products, replacing them with suffixes, usually single digits, so the change did not create a collectible difference. But those who follow plate activity reports took notice.

After 1985, another three years passed before there was a comparable wholesale upheaval in the rate structure. The experience of 1985 taught Bureau and Postal Service planners important lessons, which were taken to heart. A planned, orderly transition to the 1988 rates was the result, and is a matter of pride to both agencies.

The Nondenominated D Coil Stamp

Nondenominated D contingency stamps in sheets, coils, booklets and embossed envelopes had gone into production even before their predecessor C stamps were issued in 1981. The stylized Eagle design was similar to that of the earlier (15¢) yellow A, (18¢) violet B, and (20¢) brown C stamps, but printed in green ink. The inscription "Domestic Mail," added to the C stamps to indicate that nondenominated postage is not valid on international mail, was retained.

The Postal Service Board of Governors had announced the rate changes on December 13, 1984, providing ample time to distribute the D stamps to meet the 22¢ letter rate set to go into effect on February 17, 1985. The stamps and stamped envelopes were actually issued on February 1 in Los Angeles, but no first-day ceremony was held.

The first D stamp coil plates were prepared for the Cottrell press but were never actually used, probably because the Cottrells were working overtime in 1981 and 1982 to meet the needs generated by the 1981 rate increases. If those plates had been used, the sharp, line-engraved result would have been more attractive than the somewhat indistinct product eventually placed on sale, printed by the gravure process from two cylinders used interchangeably on the Andreotti and A presses. These were the first coil stamps printed by gravure, and thus the first to appear on coated (slick glossy) paper familiar to commemorative collectors for many years.

As the first gravure-printed PNCs, they were especially disappointing, because the blurring of the image often left a puzzling blob as the cylinder number. Several collectors reported finding number 3, and one reported number 6, but close examination under magnification always proved them to be misshaped 1s or 2s. The search for plates 1 through 6 was fueled by the plate activity reports showing that those plates had been manufactured in the Cottrell-press format. Sleeves numbered 1 and 2 were also manufactured for the B press. No stamps printed from them have ever been found, although a *Stamp Collector* article on D stamps reported that the coils were B press products.

Cylinders 1 and 2 were both printed on the Andreotti gravure press and on the gravure section of the A press. Approximately two-thirds of the entire order were run on the Andreotti. The rest, printed on the A press, had an extra step added to the production sequence. The delivery end of the A press wound the paper web gum side out, rather than the usual design side out, so BEP installed a rewind roll stand to reverse the facing.

After processing, A press rolls were wound clockwise, looking at the top of the coil. Normally coils are wound counterclockwise. Holding a D coil with the design upright, stamps from the A press will unwind to the left; those made on the Andreotti press will unwind to the right. When loaded into stamp-affixing machines used by bulk mailers, the

Because nondenominated D coil stamps printed on the gravure section of the A press were wound counterclockwise, opposite those printed on the Andreotti gravure press, bulk mailers' stamp-affixing machines fastened them upside down on envelopes, as shown with this plate 2 example.

A press coils are fastened to envelopes upside down.

Nondenominated (22¢) D coil stamps were issued in coils of 100, 500 and 3,000. Both cylinder numbers 1 and 2 were made available during the initial distribution. Both exist on first-day covers, and imperforate errors of both have been collected. The coil version of the D stamps was the most widely used form of first-class postage immediately after the basic letter rate was increased to 22¢, until stamps of that denomination could be manufactured and distributed. All the nondenominated D stamps and postal stationery were withdrawn from philatelic sale on December 31, 1985.

The Domestic Letter Rate D Official Stamp

Government agencies also needed contingency stamps to use between the time the rate increases went into effect and the time that stamps issued in the correct denominations became available. Two had been prepared in 1983, at the time the first group of modern Officials was being produced — a coil stamp to meet the first-class letter rate, and a sheet stamp to meet the postcard rate.

The coil stamp is inscribed "Domestic Letter Rate D," and the sheet stamp is inscribed "Postal Card Rate D." The latter is a misnomer, since stamps are not required on postal cards, which by definition have imprinted stamp indicia to prepay postage. "Post Card Rate D" would have been correct. Except for the inscriptions, the nondenominated Officials perfectly matched the 1983 set's design, printed in red, blue and black. The first day of issue was February 4, 1985, in Washington, D.C. No ceremony was held.

This was also the time when the Postal Service changed these stamps' designation from "Official" to "Penalty Stamps," an allusion to the inscription they all carry, "Penalty for private use $300." The inscription itself is not technically correct, because it is borrowed from the older imprinted government stationery, which read, "Penalty for private use to avoid payment of postage, $300." Since the stamps are actually purchased by their users, replacing the system of estimated postage for users of Penalty envelopes and labels, a private user would not be avoiding payment. The regulation that applies was not intended to apply to an unauthorized user of properly purchased stamps (obtained from the Philatelic Sales Division, for example), but to people who attempted to defraud the government by avoiding payment for postage. Despite the switch in Postal Service terminology, stamp collectors continue to call these stamps Officials, the proper philatelic term.

The coil stamps were printed on the intaglio B press, all from sleeve number 1, issued only in coils of 100. With an interval of 52 stamps between numbers, a roll usually has two PNCs, but some have only one. First-day covers exist with D Official PNCs. They are not common, but they are much easier to collect than PNCs on covers actually used to mail official business.

Although distribution of the nondenominated Official stamps be-

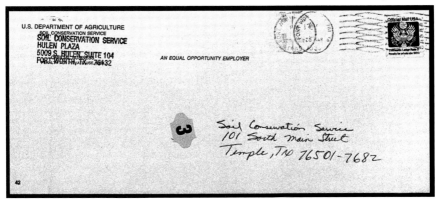

This March 28, 1985 cover is the earliest reported nonphilatelic usage of a nondenominated D Official PNC.

gan almost two weeks before the cost of a first-class letter rose from 20¢ to 22¢, it took additional time before they saw much postal duty. At first, most authorized users continued to frank letters with their existing supplies of 20¢ Officials, adding 2¢ makeup postage. No 2¢ Officials have been issued, so it was done by adding two 1¢ Officials to each letter. Naturally, some other combinations also were used, such as one each of the 17¢, 4¢ and 1¢ Officials, or a 13¢ Official with a 1¢ and a pair of 4¢ Officials, but the typical sender started with a 20¢ stamp and added the required amount. Even though more than 12½ million 1¢ Officials were shipped in 1985, in contrast to only 100,000 the year before, supplies were quickly depleted. Many government mailers used ordinary 1¢ and 2¢ stamps in combination with 20¢ Officials, so these covers with mixed frankings also postponed the switch to the D Officials in some offices. Another factor that slowed circulation was the paperwork involved in ordering them. The users can't just walk into a post office and buy them from a window clerk. To date, the earliest reported non-philatelic Official D cover is postmarked March 28, 1985, more than five weeks after the 22¢ rate went into effect.

Nondenominated D Official stamps were widely used for only a short time before being replaced by the denominated 22¢ Official stamps, the first new coil design to appear without plate numbers. Exceptions occur, however, and some covers mailed in 1989 have been found franked with D Officials and the necessary makeup postage.

No significant varieties have been reported for these stamps. They were withdrawn from philatelic sale along with the rest of the D stamps and postal stationery, on December 31, 1985.

The 14¢ Iceboat Stamp

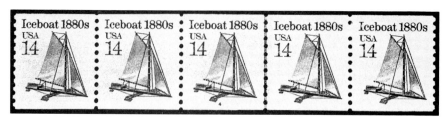

On March 23, 1985, the 14¢ Iceboat coil stamp was issued at a ceremony at ROPEX, the annual stamp show held in Rochester, New York. The design shows an 1880s iceboat printed in blue ink that does an exceptionally fine job of evoking an icy impression. Processed into coils of 500 and 3,000, the Iceboat stamps met the new domestic first-class postcard rate.

These stamps represented a combination of new and old elements. They were the first in the Transportation series to appear without a "c" to indicate "cents" in the inscription design. They also were the first since 1983 to be printed on the Cottrell press, bringing back the joint line where the two plates meet and the familiar alternating plate numbers at 24-stamp intervals.

Six plates were manufactured, and the first four were sent to press, pairing number 1 with number 2, and 3 with 4. All four exist on first-day covers; but 1 and 2 are common, while the covers with numbers 3 and 4 may be unique. So far only one of each has been reported. Plates 3 and 4 went to press after the official issue date, but may have been available during the grace period allowed for submitting FDCs to be canceled.

The 14¢ postcard rate proved to be more durable than the supply of Cottrell-printed stamps, and when inventories ran low in 1986 the Cottrells were just a memory. A sleeve was prepared for the intaglio B press using a transfer roller made from the original 14¢ Iceboat master die, but with a single plate number on the seamless 52-stamp circumference. The B press 14¢ Iceboat stamps are a fraction of a millimeter narrower than the Cottrell version, because the Cottrell press plates were engraved on pieces of flat steel. Bending them into the curved shape required to fit the press stretched each image. B press sleeves, on the other hand, are engraved on the cylindrical surface. A more obvious difference is that the B press version has block tagging, applied by a letterpress plate, while the Cottrell press version has overall block tagging applied by a roller. The report on the B press stamp begins on Page 188.

Imperforate plate 1 and 2 strips are known, and coils printed from plates 3 and 4 have been found with double images caused by ink set-off from a press roller. The original 14¢ Iceboat coil stamps were withdrawn from philatelic sale on February 28, 1989.

The 22¢ Flag Over Capitol Coil Stamp

For three years, the most widely used United States postage stamp was the 22¢ Flag Over Capitol coil. It was issued at a ceremony on Capitol Hill, in the Caucus Room of the Cannon House Office Building, on March 29, 1985, along with its sheet-stamp counterpart.

The third stamp of the set, a commemorative-size booklet stamp, was issued on the same day almost 800 miles away, in Waubeka, Wisconsin. Waubeka has no special connection to the U.S. Capitol. In the face of overwhelming contrary historical evidence, the Postal Service declared Waubeka the location of the first observance of Flag Day. All three stamps share a common design printed in red, blue and black.

Dividing the ceremonies made it difficult for first-day cover collectors to make FDCs of the entire three-stamp set in combination. Sleeve numbers 1 and 2 of the coil stamp exist on first-day covers. Most collector-serviced PNC covers and those prepared by smaller cachetmakers have number 1, a C-press product, issued in coils of 100 with numbers spaced at 48-stamp intervals. Most that were prepared by the large FDC companies have number 2, because those servicers usually buy the larger 500- and 3,000-stamp coils, which are printed

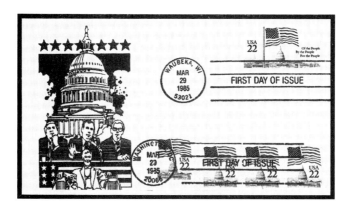

The coil and sheet versions of the 22¢ Flag Over Capitol set were issued in Washington, D.C., while the booklet version was issued in Wabeka, Wisconsin, all on the same day. Rick Chase's DRC first-day cover includes all three, with a plate 1 single of the sheet stamp and a plate 1 coil strip.

on the B press with plate numbers spaced 52 stamps apart. That's also why only plate 2 is found on USPS Souvenir Pages.

In reality, we can't be certain that any particular 22¢ Flag coil stamp was printed on the C press, because C press printing sleeves were also run on the D press, a press that went into service for the first time in 1984. The basic C and D presses are identical, but the D press has the ability to print six colors by the offset process in addition to its three-color intaglio capability. The first D press stamp, the 20¢ Smokey the Bear commemorative issued on August 13, 1984, combined both processes. But a Bureau of Engraving and Printing report to the Citizens' Stamp Advisory Committee in March 1984 noted that the D press "can be used to print coil and book issues during heavy demand periods such as a rate change."

The 22¢ Flag stamp was the first coil to be printed on the D press. During the three years when the letter rate was 22¢, no other coil stamp was issued in that denomination except for a test coil with an identical design, but with a small T printed in the bottom margin, printed on phosphored paper, treated as a separate issue both by the Postal Service and by stamp collectors. Earlier and subsequent first-class rates offered users a choice of coil stamps. Since the 22¢ rate did not, and since it lasted for three years, it is no surprise that a total of 21 different sleeves were sent to press and have been collected.

Sleeves numbered 2, 4, 6, 10, 13, 14, 15, 16 and 21 were used only on the B press. Those numbered 1, 3, 5, 7, 8, 11, 12, 17, 18, 19, 20 and 22 were used either on the C press or the D press; doubtless some were printed on both at various times. Sleeve 9 was manufactured, but was never sent to press and was canceled without any impressions having been printed.

These stamps were appearing just as several well-known dealers in United States stamps began to take an interest in plate number coils. At first some offered them for sale regardless of plate number while others stocked and sold as many different numbers as possible, but either way they needed to build up their inventories. Individual collectors most often preferred to purchase coils of 100 to acquire their PNCs, but for dealers the larger coils of 500 and 3,000 were more convenient. Only gradually did both collectors and dealers learn that they need to take strips from large and small coils alike, because the C and D press sleeve numbers occur only on coils of 100, while the B press Flag coils normally occur only on coils of 500 or 3,000. (Exceptions were sleeves 2 and 4 of the 22¢ Flag, which were packaged in all three roll sizes.) By the time sophistication began to spread, during the year 1986, the small rolls of early numbers had been used up. Those who had collected them during 1985 had found them to be common at the time. They have never been difficult to find in used condition, but dealers have not had an easy time stocking mint strips of numbers 1 and 3, so prices on those have risen disproportionately to the quantities printed and known to have been available. Another C/D press

138

product, number 7, had a smaller press run and has been subject to hoarding, speculation and manipulation of the supply, so that one too has risen in price even though most dealers have been able to obtain supplies easily.

Paradoxically, sleeve 6, a B press product, ought to be the scarcest number of all, but it isn't. A total of 56,036 impressions of sleeve 6 were printed, the smallest number of any PNC actually issued to date. (Some sleeves and plates have printed fewer stamps, but those have never been found, and it is generally assumed that all were destroyed.) By mid-summer 1985, the first five numbers were in collectors' hands, and specialists knew that sleeve 6 had been manufactured. For several months it was widely rumored to exist, but nobody could prove it with an actual example.

When *Linn's* inaugurated Stephen G. Esrati's monthly plate number coil column on November 18, 1985, the accompanying checklist included numbers 1 through 6 of the 22¢ Flag coil. Sleeves 7 and 8 were found and added to the list, but in the March 17, 1986 column, Esrati dropped 6, saying its existence could not be proven. The following month Esrati had seen it with his own eyes, and it went back on the *Linn's* checklist on April 21, 1986. When the data were finally released to *Linn's* Washington correspondent Charles Yeager, we learned in the June 23, 1986 issue that sleeve 6 had not been sent to press until November 18, 1985, and was canceled less than a month later, on December 13, after a short press run. Only coils of 3,000 stamps printed from sleeve 6 were found, and only in Texas, South Carolina and Florida.

Despite the short press run, the geographically limited distribution, and the late discovery, mint strips of number 6 are plentiful and are usually reasonably priced, because huge quantities were discovered in

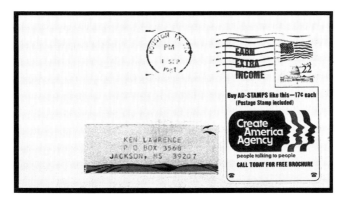

This plate 6 cover indicates what may have been the intended destination for most of the coils printed from that sleeve. The scuff that deleted the Capitol cupola and part of the USA inscription might have been typical problems had the Ad-Stamp labels actually been marketed.

139

the Houston area, where nearly the entire quantity was purchased and wholesaled to PNC dealers across the country. But number 6 is almost impossible to find used on a commercial cover during the time it was current.

Why Houston? One likely theory holds that an especially large shipment of 22¢ Flag coils of 3,000 was sent there to fill an order placed by American Discount Stamp (ADS), a company set up by three Houston advertising executives in 1982 to sell stamps affixed to labels at a discount: packages of 20 labels for $3.40, or 17¢ for each 22¢ stamp. Large corporations were expected to make up the rest, plus ADS's profit, by purchasing the 2-inch by 3-inch space on the labels to advertise their products and by including coupons in the packages. ADS expected to sell the advertising stamp packages in more than 2,400 7-Eleven stores nationwide.

Although the plan was conceived in 1982, ADS did not receive Postal Service approval until the end of 1985, precisely the time period (November 24 to December 1, 1985) when Texas post offices were authorized to order stamps directly from Washington instead of from Regional Stamp Distribution Offices, and when the sleeve 6 rolls were being shipped. But after that, ADS hit several snags. The proposed deal with Southland Corporation, owner of 7-Eleven stores, fell through. Next, Create America Agency of San Francisco signed a contract to distribute the Ad-Stamps, and promotional samples were prepared. Create America Agency then set up a pyramid marketing system to create a distribution and sales network for the product.

In May 1986, just as this long-delayed plan seemed to have cleared its final hurdle, the Justice Department notified ADS that its labels probably violated a federal law that forbids anyone to attach any advertisement to a U.S. "obligation or security," which includes postage stamps. A few months later, the Postal Inspection Service obtained an order prohibiting the Create America Agency from marketing its distributorships, and requiring it to return all money received from the public. Create America was charged with false representation for having claimed that USPS approved of its plan and that it had signed up well-known large companies as participants in the Ad-Stamp program. It seems ironic that an overly ambitious scheme to combine postage stamps with advertisements, which degenerated into a small-time direct-mail marketing swindle, helped prevent plate 6 of the 22¢ Flag coil from becoming rare. The large quantity shipped to Houston for the aborted Ad-Stamps became the principal source of that number for PNC collectors.

Two other B press sleeve numbers — 13 and 14 — have been mildly elusive. Both had relatively short press runs, but it is also possible that additional stocks remain in Postal Service vaults awaiting future distribution.

Imperforates have been confirmed for strips of all numbers except

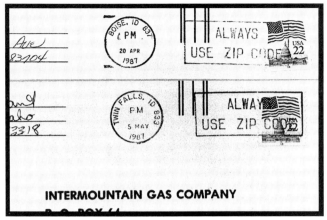

Plates 13 and 14 are difficult to find used on cover during the 22¢ letter-rate period.

13, 14, 16, and 21. One plate 19 imperforate strip contains a splice that has two numbered stamps with only one non-numbered stamp between them.

Two color varieties have received significant attention and acclaim. The first substitutes blue for black; the second substitutes black for blue. The slate blue variety is a freak caused by blue ink contaminating the black, with the result that the Capitol building, the inscription, and the plate number all appear to be printed to match the blue color of the flag's blue field. The other variety is an error. The blue field of the flag is rendered black because black ink was mistakenly loaded into the blue ink fountain. Contamination is not a possibility, because the blue ink fountain is located above the black ink fountain on the press.

The slate blue variety tells us something interesting about the plate number coil specialty. The original discovery was made by David Hackley of Sharpsburg, Maryland, on a cover mailed from Poughkeepsie, New York, in December 1985. It was reported in William H. Hatton's Basics & Beyond column in the May 19, 1986 issue of *Linn's*. A second discovery by Eugene Kiehlmeier of Erie, Pennsylvania, was reported on the front page of *Linn's* five months later by

This spliced imperforate strip, photographically cropped from a longer strip of nine, has two plate 19 stamps with just a single non-numbered stamp in between.

Stephen G. Esrati. Kiehlmeier's find included used singles on piece and mint plate 4 rolls of 100, an unusual package size for a B press coil.

Despite Hackley's much earlier discovery, and several later discoveries in other parts of the United States, the slate-blue variety of the 22¢ Flag coil is almost universally known as the "Erie blue" among PNC collectors. Evidently the specialty took greater notice of the article by Esrati than the one by Hatton, even though Hatton's had described a discovery of importance to all coil buffs. This seems to indicate that PNC collectors are more receptive to information pertinent to their interests when it is published by one of their fellow PNC enthusiasts, but that they may miss it if reported by someone else.

The other major variety is a true error. The field of the flag is rendered in black without a trace of blue ink where it belongs, confirmed by a spectrophotometric analysis at the Bureau of Engraving and Printing. It is the first multicolored engraved stamp error of color the Bureau has acknowledged — a C or D press coil from sleeve 8 issued in coils of 100.

The tour of duty for the 22¢ Flag stamps ended on April 3, 1988, when the cost of a first-class letter rose to 25¢. The stamps were withdrawn from philatelic sale on February 29, 1989, but a January 1989 report to the philatelic press showed that the postal service has stored 953,924,000 22¢ Flag coils in its vaults for re-release in the future if they are needed. If the second-ounce letter rate or the postcard rate becomes 22¢, these stamps will be placed back on sale at post offices throughout the country. If that happens, plate numbers that seem scarce now might re-appear and become more common, as happened in 1988 when the Postal Service reissued its contingency stocks of 20¢ Flag and 20¢ Fire Pumper coils that had been in storage since 1985.

The 12¢ Stanley Steamer Stamps

This House of Farnam first-day cover bearing a plate 1 line pair of the precanceled version may be unique. No other precanceled PNCs have been reported.

On April 2, 1985, the Postal Service issued the 12¢ Stanley Steamer coil stamp at a ceremony in Kingfield, Maine, the hometown of the twin brothers, Francis E. and Freelan O. Stanley, who designed and built the famous classic automobile depicted on the stamp. Printed in blue ink on the Cottrell press, the 12¢ Stanley Steamer stamps were made available in coils of 500 as tagged, unprecanceled stamps for collectors, placed on sale on the actual issue date.

A short while later, untagged precancels, overprinted PRESORTED FIRST-CLASS in black ink between parallel lines, were released nationwide in coils of 500 and 3,000. The February 28, 1985 *Postal Bulletin* announced, "This 12-cent Stanley Steamer stamp meets the First-Class presort rate for postal cards." It should have said "postcards." Postal cards have no need for adhesive stamps, since they already have imprinted stamp indicia.

Four Cottrell-press plates were manufactured, but only plates 1 and 2 were ever used. Both numbers on tagged stamps are commonly found on first-day covers, but only plate 1 of the precanceled version has been reported on FDC.

The 12¢ presort postcard rate had been in effect since November 1, 1981. It proved to be one of the more durable rates during a period of frequent fluctuations for other third-class bulk-mail rate tiers. For the first four years, two versions of the Americana series 12¢ Torch coil stamps had been available — one overprinted with plain black lines, the other with lines and the PRESORTED FIRST-CLASS legend in the overprint. By 1985, supplies of the 12¢ Torch precancels were running low. Rather than printing more, the Postal Service replaced them with a Transportation series stamp.

Even these eventually proved insufficient to meet mailers' needs. When additional supplies were needed in 1987, the Cottrell presses no longer existed, so a B press sleeve was prepared on one of the BEP's

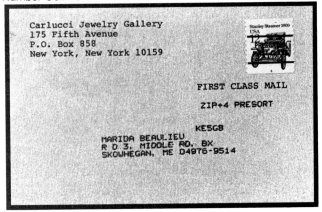

Carlucci Jewelry Gallery
175 Fifth Avenue
P.O. Box 858
New York, New York 10159

FIRST CLASS MAIL

ZIP+4 PRESORT

KE5GB

MARIDA BEAULIEU
R D 3. MIDDLE RD. BX
SKOWHEGAN, ME D4976-9514

Postcards showing the intended use of the 12¢ Stanley Steamer precancel are not easy to collect. This plate 2 example is probably an example of false franking, with a refund due to mailer, since the endorsement says "Zip+4 Presort." That rate would have been 11.5¢ per piece.

Destouche machines from a transfer roller made from the original master die, and shipped out without prior notice. The original Cottrell-press version has a printed joint line where the two plates meet, and the numbers alternate at 24-stamp intervals. The B press version has no joint line; its single sleeve number repeats at 52-stamp intervals. The report on the B press stamp begins on Page 213. The rate finally ended on April 2, 1988. The March 25, 1988 *Postal Bulletin* neglected to mention the 12¢ stamps in its announcement permitting use of other obsolete denominations as false franking until new stamps were issued. In practice, mailers used the 12¢ Stanley Steamer precancels to prepay the 13¢ rate until the 13¢ Patrol Wagon stamps became available on October 29, 1988. They were withdrawn from philatelic sale on February 28, 1989, but 16,839,000 of the tagged stamps were stored in Bureau of Engraving and Printing and Postal Service vaults for possible future use. It is unlikely they will ever meet an actual rate, with the possible exception of the non-standard-size surcharge, but they may eventually be useful as changemakers or makeup postage, either for USPS or private vending machine usage.

The 12.5¢ Pushcart Stamps

Two stamps were issued simultaneously without a ceremony in Oil Center, New Mexico, on April 18, 1985. The 12.5¢ Pushcart and 10.1¢ Oil Wagon coil stamps were needed in precanceled form to prepay the two most widely used third-class bulk rates that had gone into effect on February 17, 1985. The 12.5¢ rate met the cost per piece for bulk mail satisfying the minimum presort requirements, to three ZIP-code digits; the 10.1¢ rate met the five-digit presort cost per piece. The 12.5¢ rate replaced the 11¢ rate covered by the 11¢ Caboose coil stamp.

The 12.5¢ coil stamps, depicting an 1880's version of a two-wheeled street vendor's pushcart, were printed in olive ink on the B press with plate numbers appearing at 52-stamp intervals. Tagged collector editions of the stamp printed from sleeve 1 were issued in coils of 500. These are the only PNC's of this issue known on first-day covers. Untagged precancels overprinted "Bulk Rate" between parallel lines in black ink were issued in coils of 500 and 3,000. A second sleeve, number 2, was manufactured in 1987 and sent to press late that year to print precancels.

William K. Phipps of Hoffman Estates, Illinois, was the first collector to discover the 12.5¢ Pushcart imperforate, on part of a precanceled coil printed from sleeve 1. Phipps owns a bulk mailing firm. When an employee complained that the stamp-affixing machine had jammed, Phipps discovered that the roll had an imperforate section.

When the basic third-class bulk rate rose to 16.7¢ on April 3, 1988, the Postal Service authorized mailers to continue using the 12.5¢ precancels as false franking, with the balance to be paid at the time of mailing, until October 9, 1988, by which time stamps of the new denomination were available. Precanceled 12.5¢ Pushcart stamps were withdrawn from philatelic sale on April 30, 1989.

The initial announcement stated that the tagged 12.5¢ Pushcarts would also be withdrawn on that date. But on April 17, less than two weeks before the deadline, William Griffiths, a medical doctor, discovered plate number 2 on a tagged pair of 12.5¢ coils. They had been used on an envelope carrying payment from a patient. When Griffiths reached his patient by phone, he learned that the man had retrieved the stamps from a *Reader's Digest* sweepstakes mailing. The stamps had been supplied as an incentive to return the entry.

Less than a week after Griffiths' discovery, PNC dealer Robert Rabinowitz located the post office in the Hartford, Connecticut, district

This is how Reader's Digest *distributed pairs of tagged 12.5¢ Pushcart coil stamps in its sweepstakes mailing.*

where the stamps for *Reader's Digest* had been shipped. These turned out to be the first tagged decimal-denominated coil stamps ever issued in coils of 3,000. With the eleventh-hour discovery, the Postal Service reversed itself and kept these stamps on sale to avoid creating an artificial rarity. Collectors could then buy rolls or strips of sleeve 2 12.5¢ Pushcart stamps from the Philatelic Sales Division by mail or in person, at face value.

The 10.1¢ Oil Wagon Stamps

Along with the 12.5¢ Pushcart stamp, the 10.1¢ Oil Wagon stamp was issued without a ceremony at Oil Center, New Mexico, on April 18, 1985. Obviously the location was chosen for its name as a tie-in with this coil, since there was no logical connection whatever to the Pushcart. The 10.1¢ stamp took the place of the 9.3¢ Mail Wagon stamp that met the previous rate.

The design depicts an 1890s oil wagon, usually drawn by horses, from which vendors dispensed fuel for home heating, cooking and lantern lighting in towns and rural areas. The stamps were printed in blue ink on the B press. Single sleeve numbers repeat at 52-stamp intervals. A tagged, unprecanceled version was issued for collectors in coils of 500 printed from sleeve 1, the only PNC of this issue on first-day cover. Soon afterward, untagged precancels overprinted with the inscription "Bulk Rate" between parallel black lines was issued nationwide in coils of 500 and 3,000. Number 2, on precanceled rolls only, appeared in 1987. Imperforate copies exist of the precancels printed from sleeve 1.

The five-digit presort rate per piece for third-class bulk mail was 10.1¢ from February 17, 1985, to April 2, 1988, when the rate increased to 13.2¢. Mailers were permitted to continue using the 10.1¢ Oil Wagon precancels with the black Bulk Rate overprinted service inscription until October 9, 1988. By then stamps in the proper de-

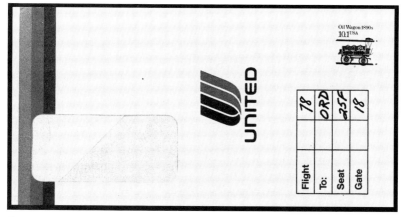

Many bulk mailers availed themselves of the five-digit sort discount, which saved an additional 2.4¢ per piece over the basic presort third-class bulk rate. This plate 2 cover is an example.

147

nomination for the new rate were in circulation. In the meantime, a new version of the 10.1¢ Oil Wagon stamp had been issued for third-class bulk-rate mail sorted to the individual carrier route. These were overprinted in red ink, "Bulk Rate Carrier Route Sort," without pre-cancel lines. The report on that stamp begins on Page 233. The 10.1¢ Oil Wagon coils with the black precancel overprint were withdrawn from philatelic sale on October 31, 1988, and the tagged, unprecan-celed stamps were withdrawn on December 31, 1988.

The 6¢ Tricycle Stamps

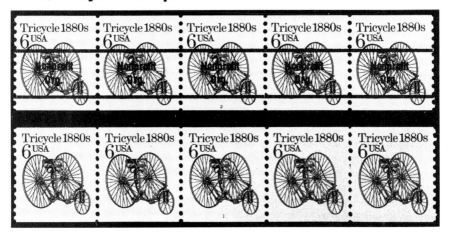

On May 6, 1985, the 6¢ Tricycle coil stamp was issued without a ceremony in Childs, Maryland. That location was chosen because tri-cycles are means of locomotion used by children. But that is today. It was not true for the 1880s Tricycle illustrated in brown ink on the stamp, which was an adult vehicle designed to overcome the instabili-ty of that era's high-rider bicycles, so the designated first-day site is really a mismatch.

The 6¢ Tricycle coil was printed on the intaglio B press. Single sleeve numbers repeat at 52-stamp intervals. The Tricycle stamp was issued in tagged, unprecanceled form printed from sleeve 1 for collec-tors, in coils of 500. Those were the only stamps actually placed on sale on the first day, according to Rachel Racine, the Childs postmas-ter. Untagged 6¢ Tricycle stamps overprinted in black ink with the inscription "Nonprofit Org." were released nationwide soon after that date, to prepay the basic third-class bulk rate per piece that had gone into effect on February 19, 1985, for mailings by nonprofit tax-exempt religious and charitable organizations and authorized political bodies. This replaced the rate covered by the 5.2¢ Sleigh coil stamps.

Nearly all PNC first-day covers of this issue have plate 1 strips of the tagged edition, but two years after the date of issue, a number of covers appeared on the market bearing plate number strips of both tagged and precanceled versions, on Artcraft envelopes canceled with a first-day-of-issue handstamp. The firm that offered these covers for sale, at prices ranging from $125 to $300, was R & D Enterprises of Rockville, Maryland. The late appearance of these covers seemed strange, but the factor that aroused the most suspicion was that these first-day covers, ostensibly manufactured at a time when only a small handful of collectors were seeking plate number coils on FDCs, were only known to exist with plate number strips.

Other cachetmakers had prepared FDCs of earlier Transportation coil precancels, notably Bill Olvey, owner of KMC Venture cachets, and Ken D. Kribbs, owner of Kribbs Kovers. But most of the KMC and Kribbs precancel FDCs were prepared with no special attention paid to the plate number. The PNC copies appeared in proportion to their frequency on the roll. But the R & D Enterprises covers did not exist with just plain 6¢ Tricycle precancels, only with plate strips. And they appeared only after the KMC and Kribbs covers, bearing numbered precancels, had soared in value.

I undertook an investigation for *Linn's Stamp News,* and the results were published in the September 12, 1988 issue of *Linn's.* As it turned out, Russ Draper, the proprietor of R & D Enterprises, was actually Wayne Anmuth, a senior marketing specialist in the Philatelic Marketing Division at U.S. Postal Service headquarters in Washington. Anmuth was a leader in the Ben Franklin Stamp Clubs sponsored by the Postal Service to promote stamp collecting among young people. He was a serious first-day cover collector, owner of a prize-winning

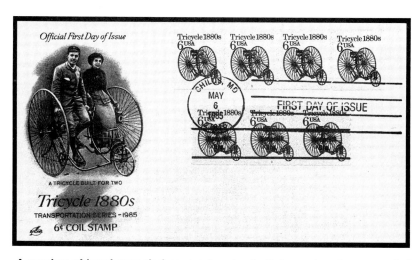

A number of hand-canceled covers bearing both tagged and precanceled plate 1 6¢ Tricycle strips were placed on the market by R & D Enterprises long after the issue date. They were manufactured by Wayne Anmuth, a high-level employee of the Postal Service, who gave conflicting accounts of their origin and scarcity. The expertizing committee of the American First Day Cover Society refused to certify this as a genuine first-day cover.

exhibit of PNC first-day and commercial covers, and an authority and lecturer on PNC FDCs, with a regular column on that subject in *First Days* magazine.

Anmuth refused to answer questions about the source of the 6¢ Tricycle precancel FDCs, but the *Linn's* investigation revealed that the first-day handstamper for these covers still existed more than two years later, and that Anmuth could have had easy access to it.

The Postal Inspection Service followed up with its own year-long investigation. During that time, Anmuth was transferred out of Philatelic Marketing and detailed to the William F. Bolger Management Training Academy, a USPS facility in Potomac, Maryland, as he had requested earlier. Anmuth denied any wrongdoing; he said he had submitted the 6¢ Tricycle FDCs to the Philatelic Sales Division facility at Merrifield, Virginia, to be canceled during the grace period allowed, the first 30 days after the stamps had been issued. This story differed from the one he had told his R & D Enterprises customers. Postal Service officials at Merrifield doubted that the covers had been canceled there. There were no records to confirm Anmuth's story, but laboratory analysis of one of his covers was inconclusive.

As a result of the Postal Inspection Service investigation, the Postal Service initiated disciplinary action against Anmuth. Just before press time, *Linn's* Editor-Publisher Michael Laurence received a letter from Stephen A. Leavey, General Manager, Headquarters Personnel Division of the Postal Service. Leavey wrote, "Mr. Anmuth is currently in a nonpay, nonduty status, pending the outcome of an administrative appeal which he initiated. Due to the pendency of this appeal, we believe that no further comment is appropriate at this time."

The cover was also submitted to the expertizing committee of the American First Day Cover Society. The committee ruled that it is not a genuine first-day cover of the 6¢ Tricycle precancel, but avoided the controversy surrounding its actual origin. During the course of its deliberations, the committee decided that a first-day cover of any stamp must meet three objective criteria: 1) The stamp must be on sale in the designated first-day city on the official first-day date; 2) the stamp must be available to collectors during the grace period allowed by USPS for covers to be submitted for servicing; and 3) an official first-day date must have been designated by the Postal Service. In the committee's judgment, the Anmuth cover failed to meet the first criterion, because the Childs, Maryland, postmaster confirmed that no precancels had been on sale there. The committee was satisfied that the stamps were on sale during the 30-day grace period, thus meeting its second criterion. A letter from Don McDowell, general manager of the USPS Stamps Division, said that detailed records of when the precancels had first been shipped had not been retained. McDowell added that "*nonprecanceled* stamps were intended to service first-day covers." Based on that, the committee concluded that "official dates were not designated for the precanceled coils under consideration.

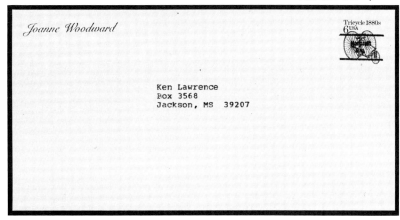

Covers bearing plate 2 6¢ Tricycle precancels appeared before stamp collectors had found mint rolls of that number.

Therefore, the true first-day dates of these issues would be the dates when they were first sold across a postal counter," and that the date for the 6¢ Tricycle precancel is "as yet unknown." A detailed description of the expertizing committee's ruling was published in the March 1, 1989 issue of *First Days*, in an article by the committee's chairman, Allison W. Cusick.

Sleeve 2 of the 6¢ Tricycle coil was manufactured and sent to press in 1985, but only to print precanceled stamps. Imperforate strips of this number are known.

The 6¢ nonprofit rate ended on December 31, 1985, but after that, the 6¢ Tricycle precancels were authorized as false franking, with the balance due at the time of mailing, for the 7.4¢ rate in effect from January 1, 1986, to March 8, 1986; for the 8.7¢ rate in effect from March 9, 1986, to April 19, 1986; and for the 8.5¢ rate that went into effect on April 20, 1986. The authorization to use the 6¢ Tricycle precancels at the 8.5¢ rate initially lasted until October 19, 1986, but was extended to March 31, 1987. By then new stamps had been issued in the proper denomination. The 6¢ Tricycle precancels were withdrawn from philatelic sale on December 31, 1988, and the tagged version on February 28, 1989.

The 3.4¢ School Bus Stamps

151

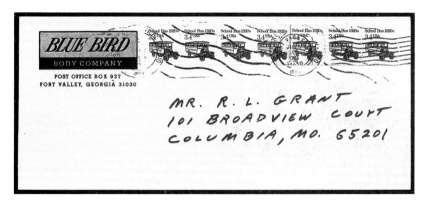

On June 8, 1985, the 3.4¢ School Bus coil stamp was issued at a ceremony at the NAPEX stamp show in Arlington, Virginia. It was printed in green ink on the Cottrell press. Two plate numbers alternate at 24-stamp intervals. Tagged, unprecanceled 3.4¢ School Bus stamps were issued for collectors in coils of 500. The untagged edition for bulk mailers in coils of 500 and 3,000 has the overprinted inscription "Nonprofit Org. CAR-RT SORT" between parallel lines in black ink.

Eight Cottrell press plates were manufactured, but only numbers 1 and 2 were actually used. Both numbers, in tagged editions, are known on first-day covers. One plate activity report stated that plates 4 and 6 had been printed. A Postal Service representative later stated that the report was erroneous, but not before collectors had undertaken a coast-to-coast search for the nonexistent stamps.

The stamps depict a 1920s school bus built by Blue Bird Body Company of Fort Valley, Georgia. One of the most interesting PNC covers reflects that aspect of the stamps, since its envelope bears the black and yellow corner advertising cachet of that bus manufacturer. The cover was mailed to Richard Grant by his father, now deceased, who was a history professor at Fort Valley State College in 1985. The cover is postmarked on the date of issue, Saturday, June 8. Some purists in the FDC community do not recognize this as an actual first-day cover, since the stamps were supposed to be sold only in Arling-

Both cancels on this plate 2 cover are dated June 8, 1985, the day the 3.4¢ School Bus stamp was issued. The bus shown on the stamp was manufactured by the Blue Bird Body Company of Fort Valley, Georgia.

ton on that date, and not until Monday, June 10, in other places.

The 3.4¢ School Bus stamp met the per-piece rate for third-class bulk mail from nonprofit organizations sorted to the local carrier route, which was in effect from February 17 until December 31, 1985. It replaced the overprinted 3¢ Francis Parkman stamps used when the rate had been 3¢ and 3.3¢. From January 1 to March 8, 1986, the 3.4¢ School Bus stamps were authorized as false franking to cover the 4.8¢ rate, with the balance paid at the time of mailing. From March 9 to April 19, false franking with this stamp met the 5.7¢ rate, and from April 20 until October 19, 1986, the 5.5¢ rate. That final authorization was extended to March 31, 1987, by which time stamps in the new denomination were available. The 3.4¢ School Bus stamps were withdrawn from philatelic sale on April 30, 1987.

Because these stamps were printed on the obsolete Cottrell presses, they provided a solution to a previously unsolved mystery — doubled images that had been found on two earlier Cottrell press coil stamps, the 2¢ Locomotive and 4¢ Stagecoach issues. Some philatelic publications had called these varieties "double transfers," but officials of the Bureau of Engraving and Printing had found no such marks on the proof sheets of either stamp. A committee representing the Bureau Issues Association examined the 2¢ Locomotive plates (by then the 4¢ Stagecoach plates had been destroyed), but they could find no doubled images in the engraved subjects.

I found a similar effect on a 3.4¢ School Bus coil of 500; every stamp on the roll had some doubling. With the assistance of George V.H. Godin and Belmont Faries of the Bureau Issues Association, some of my stamps were sent to the Bureau for an explanation in September 1985. The answer came in an October 3 memorandum: the effect is not a double transfer, it's set-off, sometimes called offset, but of a previously unreported origin.

Henry O. Fuchs, printing project engineer in the Bureau's Office of

A test on the Cottrell press before it was scrapped by the BEP confirmed that this image doubling was caused by set-off from the chill roller.

153

Research and Technical Services, investigated the problem and reported his findings to Edward V. Felver, chief of the Office of Engraving: "Set-off occurs on the chill rollers at the exit side of the dryer. During start up, at slow speed, when neither the drying ovens nor the chill rollers have reached equilibrium, ink is transferred to the chill rollers, and is then set-off onto the printed work.

"Normally stamps with set-off are mutilated. The samples in question, however, have such a small amount of set-off that it could easily be overlooked by the examiner."

Fuchs' report concluded with the secret of why the set-off doubling is repeated so precisely on each successive impression: "The plate cylinder and chill rollers are geared together on this press and the diameters are in a 2:1 ratio so that set-off in register could be expected." When Felver forwarded Fuchs' report to Belmont Faries, he wrote in his October 8 cover letter, "At last we have a clear, logical explanation that I hope will finally put the matter to rest."

The explanation for Cottrell-press image doubling might have remained a mystery forever had the investigation been postponed, because the last two Cottrell presses were formally taken out of service at 4 p.m. on November 20, 1985. It is no longer possible to run tests to discover and confirm the origin of varieties like this. The mystery was solved just in time.

The 11¢ Stutz Bearcat Coil Stamp

The most inexplicable coil issued in 1985 was the 11¢ Stutz Bearcat stamp, issued only in tagged form in coils of 500 and 3,000. The stamp features a 1933 Stutz Bearcat automobile printed in green ink on the Cottrell press. Four plates were used, 1 paired with 2, and 3 paired with 4. The numbers alternate at 24-stamp intervals. Numbers 5 through 8 were manufactured, but were never sent to press.

The 11¢ Stutz Bearcat coil was issued at a first-day ceremony held at the Cars of Yesteryear Museum in Baton Rouge, Louisiana. Only plates 3 and 4 are known on first-day covers.

The odd thing about this stamp is that it met no postal need, although it could have. A precancel in the 11¢ denomination could have been used for the first-class postcard rate for quantity mailings sorted to each local carrier route, in effect from November 1, 1981, through April 2, 1988. The Postal Service never did issue a stamp for that unusually long-lasting rate, although a dedicated mailer could have used the 11¢ Stutz precanceled with a mailer's permit postmark.

According to USPS, 11¢ definitive stamps had been requested by the Stamp Vendors Association as makeup postage for its stamp vending machines. These vendors sell stamps for more than face value as a convenience to people who don't want to make a trip to the post office. In 1985, many of their machines vended one 22¢ and one 11¢ stamp for 50¢, a 17¢ profit on each sale. In this way, a dollar would buy enough postage to mail three letters.

There isn't anything unusual about issuing stamps for this particular purpose, even though they meet no postal rate as such, but it does seem odd that an unnecessary stamp should have been issued during the rush of a rate-change year when other stamps were more urgently required. An 11¢ sheet stamp, the Alden Partridge stamp in the Great Americans series, had been issued earlier in 1985. A second stamp for such an offbeat purpose is excessive even by fairly liberal standards.

The stamp that never had a rate of its own is still on sale as this book is written. It is the very last Cottrell press Transportation series coil stamp still authorized to be in circulation.

The 8.3¢ Ambulance Stamps

For the second time in two months, two new coil stamps were issued at the same time and place. But unlike the 10.1¢ Oil Wagon and 12.5¢ Pushcart stamps, issued without fanfare in Oil Center, New Mexico, on April 18, the 4.9¢ Buckboard and 8.3¢ Ambulance coils got the full treatment. They were issued on June 21, 1985, at the opening ceremony of the NEVPEX-TOPEX stamp show in Reno, Nevada, sponsored by the Nevada Stamp Study Society and host of the American Topical Association's national convention that year.

The 8.3¢ Ambulance stamp, although originally intended as a B press stamp, had to be switched to the Cottrell press because the B

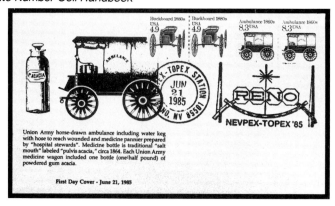

Union Army horse-drawn ambulance including water keg with hose to reach wounded and medicine pannier prepared by "hospital stewards". Medicine bottle is traditional "salt mouth" labeled "pulvis acacia," circa 1864. Each Union Army medicine wagon included one bottle (one-half pound) of powdered gum acacia.

First Day Cover - June 21, 1985

This first-day cover with a plate 3 line pair of the 4.9¢ Ambulance and a plate 1 line pair of the 8.3¢ Ambulance has the special pictorial cancel for Nevpex-Topex, the stamp show at which the two stamps were issued.

press was needed to print 22¢ Flag stamps, the only first-class letter-rate coil stamp once the D contingency stamp supply was exhausted. The design pictures a Civil War-era horse-drawn battlefield ambulance printed in green ink. Six Cottrell press plates were manufactured, but only four were actually used. Plate 1 was paired with plate 2, and 3 with 4. Lines appear where the plates adjoined on the press. Plate numbers alternate at 24-stamp intervals. Unprecanceled, tagged editions were issued for collectors in coils of 500, printed only from plates 1 and 2, the numbers found on first-day covers. Untagged versions overprinted in black ink with the service inscription "Blk. Rt. CAR-RT SORT" between parallel lines were issued in coils of 500 and 3,000. FDCs exist with precanceled plate 1 and plate 2 PNCs, but they are rare.

One of the most interesting plate varieties ever found on a Cottrell-press stamp occurred on this issue. On plate number 1, the top row's digit was engraved in the wrong place, one millimeter lower and to the right of its proper position. When the paper web is slit normally during processing, that plate number is usually cut at the edge, while the coils from the other rows have their plate numbers in the normal place clear of the edge. Naturally, when the number is cut, a piece of it appears at the top of the coil from the second row. When the web is cut a bit high, the plate 1 digit disappears completely from the top row, and a complete number appears at both the top and bottom of the second row. When the web is cut low, the low digit is whole, but in a different position from the normal coils.

The 8.3¢ Ambulance replaced the 7.4¢ Baby Buggy coil stamp. It met the minimum rate per piece for third-class bulk mail sorted to the individual carrier route that had gone into effect on February 17, 1985. That rate lasted until an increase to 10.1¢ on April 3, 1988.

Plate number 1 on the top row of stamps is misplaced one millimeter lower and to the right of its proper position. As a result, a normally slit coil will leave only part of number 1 on that row, and part will appear at the top of the second row. When the web is slit high, complete 1s will appear at the top and bottom of the second row, while the top row will have the number omitted. When the web is slit low, the 1 on the top row will be whole, but lower than on coils processed from the other rows.

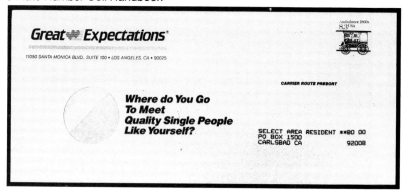

This typical cover has a plate 1 single of the 8.3¢ Ambulance Transportation coil precancel, properly used.

Even though a precanceled 10.1¢ Oil Wagon stamp existed at the time, it was not valid to cover the new rate because it had an improper overprinted service inscription. Instead the Postal Service authorized mailers to continue using the 8.3¢ Ambulance precancels as false franking for the new rate, with the balance due to be paid at the time of mailing, until October 9, 1988. By that time the 10.1¢ stamps had been reissued with a new overprint for this presort rate. The 8.3¢ Ambulance stamps were withdrawn from philatelic sale on February 28, 1989.

The 8.3¢ carrier-route presort rate outlasted the supply of stamps printed on the Cottrell press, which had been dismantled in 1985. Ironically, in order to meet the need, a new version of the stamp was printed on the intaglio B press in 1986, as had originally been intended in 1985. Sleeves for the B press were prepared from a transfer roller made from the same master die as the Cottrell-press plates, but because the recess image was not as deep, more shading detail is evident in the letters of the inscription. The B-press images are a fraction of a millimeter narrower than their Cottrell-press counterparts, and B-press coils have no joint lines adjacent to the numbered stamps as the Cottrell versions do. Single sleeve numbers repeat at 52-stamp intervals. (Discussion of the revised 8.3¢ Ambulance coil stamp begins on Page 185.)

The 4.9¢ Buckboard Stamp

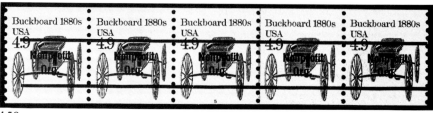

The 4.9¢ Buckboard coil stamps were issued on June 21, 1985, at the NEVPEX-TOPEX opening ceremony in Reno, Nevada, along with the 8.3¢ Ambulance. These stamps, too, had originally been scheduled to be printed on the intaglio B press, but had to be moved to the Cottrell press because the B press was overloaded with 22¢ Flag production. Unlike the 8.3¢ Ambulance, the 4.9¢ Buckboard never appeared in a B-press edition.

The stamp depicts an 1880s flat-bottom wooden wagon rendered in brown ink. Eight Cottrell-press plates were manufactured, but only six

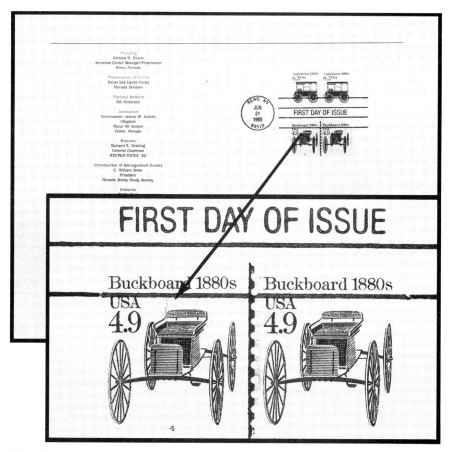

This first-day ceremony program for the 8.3¢ Ambulance and 4.9¢ Buckboard coils has a "Buggy Whip" gripper crack on the plate 4 Buckboard stamp.

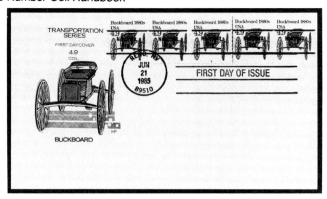

**This House of Farnam first-day cover is the only one report-
ed with plate 3 of the 4.9¢ Buckboard precancel.**

were actually used, paired consecutively. Lines appear where the
plates met on the press. Plate numbers alternate at 24-stamp intervals.
Unprecanceled tagged philatelic editions were issued in coils of 500,
printed from plates 3 and 4. These are the PNCs found on 4.9¢ Buckboard first-day covers. Untagged precancels of the 4.9¢ Buckboard
overprinted "Nonprofit Org." in black ink between parallel lines were
issued in coils of 500 and 3,000, printed from all three pairings: plate 1
with plate 2, 3 with 4, and 5 with 6. Rare FDCs of this issue exist with
precanceled number 3 and number 4 PNCs.

A type of constant plate variety called "gripper crack" is abundant
and spectacular on numbered stamps of this issue, more than on any
other Transportation coil stamp. Best known is the "Buggy Whip"
crack on plate 4 that runs upward from the rear of the wagon toward
the inscription lettering and, in some cases, between the letters. So
many cracks appeared on two adjacent rows of plate 5 that the variety
is known as the "Rain Crack," because the effect looks like a shower.
Other significant gripper cracks are found on plates 5 and 6. Besides

**Late-appearing numbers, such as this plate 6 example, often were used as
false franking after the five-digit sort nonprofit rate had risen to 6.3¢.**

these flaws that developed during press runs, the 4.9¢ Buckboard stamps include pre-printing plate varieties as well, low entries of the subject in several positions on plates 1, 3 and 4.

The 4.9¢ Buckboard stamp met the rate for bulk mail sorted to five ZIP-code digits mailed by qualified nonprofit tax-exempt and political organizations that was in effect from February 17 to December 31, 1985. It succeeded the 4¢ Stagecoach precancel. From January 1 to March 8, 1986, it was authorized as false franking for the 6.3¢ rate, and from March 9 to April 19, 1986, as false franking for the 7.2¢ rate, with the balance to be paid at the time of mailing. The rate dropped to 7.1¢ on April 20, 1986, and again false franking with the 4.9¢ Buckboard was authorized until March 31, 1987. By that time, a stamp had been issued in the proper denomination. The 4.9¢ Buckboard stamps were withdrawn from philatelic sale on October 31, 1988, long after their usefulness had passed. Even then, PNC collectors were sad to see them go. Their buggy whips, rain cracks, low entries, and literally dozens of other, subtler varieties made this stamp the specialist's delight.

The 21.1¢ Letters Stamps

The 21.1¢ Letters coil stamp was issued at a ceremony in Washington, D.C., on October 22, 1985, During a meeting of the Envelope Manufacturers Association. Postmaster General Paul N. Carlin was the featured speaker, despite the fact that this stamp exemplified the "poster art" style that Carlin had told the Citizens Stamp Advisory Committee to discontinue.

The new stamp established several precedents. It was the first multicolor coil stamp printed by the gravure process. It was the first stamp to appear with a service inscription printed as part of the design to satisfy the Postal Service's precancel requirements. It was the first stamp issued to meet an incentive discount rate based solely on the form of the address rather than on presorting.

On previous stamps printed from more than one printing base, such as precanceled stamps whose design was printed by the intaglio process but whose overprint was applied by a flexographic relief mat or plate, only one plate number appeared, that of the intaglio plate or sleeve. With the appearance of the 21.1¢ Letters stamp, one number was printed for each of the six gravure cylinders, with all six digits grouped at the bottom of a single stamp, repeating at 24-stamp intervals.

The six Andreotti press cylinders represent six different ink colors: pink, red, yellow, green, blue and black. The stamp design shows a row of five overlapped envelopes in different colors. The tagged version of the stamp has the country and denomination, "USA 21.1," in white type on a black background, a technique called reverse or drop-out printing. The service-inscribed version, which the Postal Service considers a precancel, adds "ZIP+4" in bold black figures in the foreground. The color cylinders were used interchangeably with either of the black cylinders. Both black cylinders were designated number 1. Thus the first coils of each version to appear were numbered 111111. Later a second blue cylinder was used for both versions, so both also exist numbered 111121. Only the former combination is known on first-day covers, both tagged and service-inscribed. This is the first stamp for which major cachetmakers made FDCs with both. To receive cancels, the Postal Service required that any covers submitted bearing precanceled postage had to have, in addition, full first-class postage in unprecanceled form. The September 19, 1985, *Postal Bulletin* notice confused the issue, however, when it incorrectly stated that it would affix a 1¢ Omnibus stamp "in addition to one 21.1¢ ZIP+4 coil stamp" for collectors who elected to have the Postal Service prepare FDCs on their unfranked envelopes.

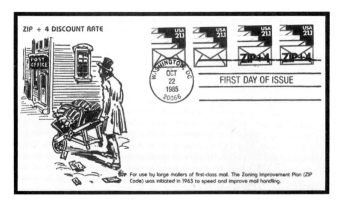

The 21.1¢ Letters coil was the first issue for which a significant number of covers bearing precanceled PNCs were prepared. This KMC Venture cover has cylinder numbers 111111 on both tagged and service-inscribed pairs.

The tagged version was issued in coils of 500 only, the untagged, service-inscribed version in coils of 500 and 3,000. Ostensibly the stamp was issued to meet the new rate that had gone into effect on February 17, 1985, and lasted until April 2, 1985, superseding the 19.1¢ rate that had been offered beginning on October 9, 1983. The rate increased to 24.1¢ on April 3, 1988, but the 21.1¢ Letters ZIP+4 stamps were authorized for use as false franking, with the balance paid at the time of mailing, until October 9, 1988. Shortly after that, a stamp of the new denomination became available.

In each rate period since the creation of this tier in 1983, mailers, were offered an incentive discount of nine-tenths of a cent per piece to use nine-digit ZIP codes in addressing mail, without any presort requirement, as long as at least 250 pieces were mailed at one time. In 1987, the Postal Service had proposed to increase the discount to 2¢, but the Postal Rate Commission denied the request after critics pointed out that this would encourage many bulk mailers to abandon presort in favor of unsorted ZIP+4 mail, adding a burden to the Postal Service that is currently handled by the mailers themselves.

Some critics have argued that the entire nine-digit ZIP code should be scrapped, that mail processing technology, including multi-line optical character readers and bar coders, have already rendered the ZIP+4 system obsolete. But the Postal Service still clings to it, despite resistance from nearly every sector of the public. The Postal Service projected only 21 million pieces of mail would have nine-digit ZIP code addresses in 1989, one-fourth of its ambitious prediction when the program was launched in 1983. In a 1988 report to Congress titled "Postal Service Operations," the U.S. General Accounting Office criticized the ZIP+4 plan, noting that mailers had received $25 million in discounts over an 18-month period on ZIP+4 mail that was not automatically sorted to carrier routes. In some instances, this was because the mail-processing centers were not automated; in others, because optical character readers rejected letters as unreadable. Even though the five-year transition from mechanization to automation has been completed, the controversy is sure to continue.

Under these conditions, the appearance of the 21.1¢ Letters stamp in gaudy poster art with its bold ZIP+4 service inscription makes a certain kind of sense, if it is regarded more as a piece of promotional advertising than as a receipt for the payment of postage. Viewed purely as postage, it's a mystery. Why would mailers avail themselves of such a small discount to begin with, then fritter it away with the added cost of affixing stamps? Meters were widely used to cover this rate, but finding a 21.1¢ ZIP+4 stamp properly used on cover during its rate period is one of the great challenges of modern postal history collecting.

On the other hand, despite its relatively low usage, the stamp was probably profitable for the Postal Service. Almost 100 million were

This properly used 21.1¢ ZIP+4-inscribed Letters stamp was probably used at its actual designated rate, judging by the dated advertising copy.

shipped during the three years they were current, of which more than 15 million were the tagged philatelic version. (Joe Brockert, a Postal Service spokesman, said these were not created solely for collectors. "We found there was a gray area in which a mailer who could meet the requirements for the ZIP+4 rate might not have a necessary permit to use precanceled stamps. Plain stamps were made for those users as well as for collectors." It would be interesting to see an example of that usage.) The stamps actually cost the Postal Service less than $300,000 to manufacture, but have a face value of more than $20.6 million. If, as I suspect, almost 30 percent of the stamps were retained in mint condition by stamp collectors, dealers and investors (approximately equal quantities of tagged and service-inscribed versions), those sales alone would have generated more than $5 million profit for the Postal Service.

The service-inscribed version of the 21.1¢ Letters stamp was the

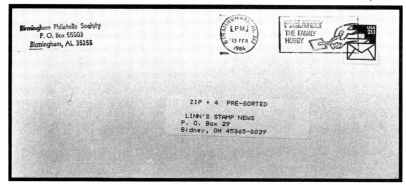

The endorsement on the label of this cover says "ZIP+4 Presort," but if it is actually from an unsorted portion of the mailing, it may be a rare, legitimate solo use of the tagged 21.1¢ Letters stamp.

first to reflect the new USPS policy on precancel format that had been announced in the September 26, 1985 *Postal Bulletin:*

"The format of precanceled stamps ordered from the Bureau of Engraving and Printing is being changed. Rather than having two highly visible lines plus type when appropriate across the face of each precanceled stamp, the cancellation will consist of either a single horizontal line or type placed across the face of each stamp. No stamp will bear both a line and type as a precancellation. The new precanceled format will first appear on the 21.1¢ Letters Coil Stamp and all subsequent stamps that require precanceling.

"At present, inventories of stamps precanceled with two lines will be used until supplies are exhausted. The existing format on current stamps and the new format on new issues will be accepted from mailers for bulk mailings. Mail bearing stamps with either precancel format is to be processed.

"Local precanceling procedures are not changed. Two parallel lines and the name and state of the post office must be imprinted on stamps precanceled at the post office. Also, the criteria for stamps overprinted by mailers are not affected."

In reality, only one of these two styles — type (a service inscription) placed across the face of each stamp — has been used to indicate that the Postal Service regards a stamp as a precancel. The single horizontal line has not been used as of this writing, but would make sense if the need arises for a precanceled version of a normal first-class-letter-rate stamp in the future.

The 21.1¢ Letters stamps were printed on coated paper thinner than those used for other gravure-printed stamps. When the first gravure coil stamp appeared, the nondenominated D coil, bulk mailers had difficulty loading coils of 3,000 into their stamp-affixing machines. The gravure process does not apply as much pressure as intaglio printing, leaving the paper thicker after passing through the press. The thinner paper solved that problem. Another innovation was the 408-subject format of the printing cylinders, 17 stamps across and 24 around.

If these stamps were intended to boost the volume of ZIP+4 mail, they must be considered a failure. It took until 1989 for the volume of mail addressed with nine-digit ZIP codes to reach the level originally projected for 1985, and by that time, even the Postal Service's own stubborn dedication to ZIP+4 seemed to be flagging. One of the services discontinued in January 1988, in response to the congressional mandate to reduce operating costs, was the "look-up service" whereby the Postal Service provided the nine-digit ZIP code when processing each change of address request. Without a system to assure that people will be familiar with their own nine-digit addresses, the end may be near.

Postal zones were pioneered in Chicago in 1895, and Boston in 1920. It has been almost a half-century since postal zones were introduced across the United States, and about a quarter-century since the Zone Improvement Plan (ZIP) began. Both were unqualified successes, despite some initial resistance from the public. Postal planners may have expected a similar experience for the nine-digit system. Perhaps in retrospect they wish they had switched to a letter-number combination, which could have encoded as much information in fewer figures, and might have met less public resistance.

If ZIP+4 does end in failure, the service-inscribed 21.1¢ Letters stamp may go down in history as a monument to the postal folly of the 1980s, an odd legacy for a stamp that brought so many postal and philatelic innovations. It was definitely a failure with collectors, beating all other contenders in the annual *Linn's* poll as the worst definitive stamp design of 1985.

The 18¢ George Washington Monument Stamps

The second multicolor gravure coil stamp printed on the Andreotti press in the new, 408-subject format appeared close on the heels of the first. The 18¢ George Washington and Washington Monument stamp was originally intended to be the first multicolor gravure coil stamp and the first to use the new precancel style incorporating the service inscription into the design without any other cancel indicator, but a series of problems delayed its appearance. Meanwhile, mailers who required stamps for first-class letters presorted to three digits of the ZIP code continued to use precanceled 17¢ Electric Auto coil stamps as false franking, with the balance paid at the time of mailing.

The June 20, 1985 *Postal Bulletin* announced that the 18¢ Washington stamp would be issued on July 23 and that its colors would be yellow, maroon, green, gray and brown, with a precancel inscription overprinted in black. All this information proved to be incorrect. The colors that were listed were intended to be "self" colors, similar to those on the 21.1¢ Letters stamp, with each doing its job independently of the others. The service inscription would not have been an overprint in any case, since it was supposed to be, and eventually was, printed from a gravure cylinder along with each of the other colors. Two sets of gravure cylinders made up for the self-colors were rejected, in all probability because the poster-art effect would have made the portrait of George Washington look like a cartoon. The third set was redone in process colors — yellow, magenta, cyan and black — screened and combined to yield full, continuous-tone color, but less sharp than self-colors at best, and visibly blurred whenever color registration is less than perfect.

These cylinders were approved, but the design was altered. The original, unveiled on February 15, 1985, at the annual meeting of the Sons of the American Revolution in Richmond, Virginia, had the letters "USA" in white, reversed, or dropped out, in the background. In the process version, "USA" became black letters, printed from the

When the design was first unveiled, the letters USA were white; as finally issued, they are black.

167

process (tone) black cylinder. On the service-inscribed edition, the words PRESORTED FIRST CLASS were printed from a separate, line black cylinder. As a result, the tagged 18¢ Washington coils have four digits on the numbered stamps, but the untagged service-inscribed stamps have five. Either way, they appear at 24-stamp intervals.

Another source of delay was financial. When Postal Service officials learned that they had to make drastic cuts in expenses to avoid a fiscal year 1985 operating deficit in excess of $500 million, they decided to postpone the issue date until after the start of the new fiscal year on September 28. The stamp was finally issued on November 6, 1985, at the first first-day ceremony ever held at the Bureau of Engraving and Printing in Washington D.C.

In issuing the 18¢ Washington Monument stamp, the Postal Service was responding to criticism that for more than a year, since the 5¢ George Washington stamps were taken off sale in April 1984, no current stamp featured the Father of this country, the only time that had been true since 1847. It was also quietly commemorating the centennial of the Washington Monument, completed on December 6, 1884, and dedicated on February 21, 1885. Whether this stamp satisfied the constituency clamoring for a George Washington stamp, or the less vocal group wishing to mark the monument's centennial, or even the mailers who had asked USPS for "colorful" stamps to spruce up their junk mail is anybody's guess. The BEP took pains to point out that the service inscription was positioned across the bottom third of the stamp so it would not obliterate Washington's face. Nevertheless, stamp collectors voted it the second worst definitive stamp design of the year in the *Linn's* poll. If you credit the third-place showing of the nondenominated D stamp to the coil version, it is clear that the three gravure-printed coil stamps struck out with collectors: 21.1¢ Letters, worst design; 18¢ Washington Monument, second worst; D stamps, third worst. The Postal Service was not to be deterred, however. The next gravure coil stamp, the nondenominated E contingency design, was already on the drawing boards.

Technically it could be argued that there was a legitimate postal use for the tagged version of the 18¢ Washington stamp, since 18¢ was the extra-ounce rate for first-class letters to Canada and Mexico, counterpart to the 17¢ domestic rate for each added ounce after the first. In reality, probably few if any of the stamps were used for that purpose. The stamp was actually issued for collectors. But demand was great for the service-inscribed version covering the basic presort first-class rate, in effect from February 17, 1985, to April 2, 1988. When the rate increased to 21¢ on April 3, 1988, the 18¢ Washington was authorized as false franking, with the balance paid at the time of mailing, until October 9, 1988. By then a stamp in the new denomination was available for use. The 18¢ Washington coils were withdrawn from philatelic sale on October 31, 1988.

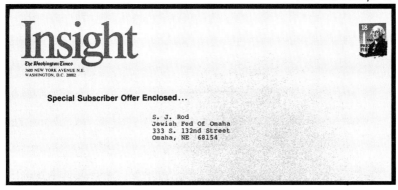

Use of the first-class presort rate has grown rapidly in the United States, rivaling third-class bulk mail. Illustrated here are typical covers franked with service-inscribed 18¢ Washington Monument stamps showing the five cylinder numbers 33333.

The unpopularity of the stamp did not detract from its collectibility. On the contrary, some of the factors that caused the stamp to be unattractive added to the collector's challenge. When the colors were not well-registered, which was most of the time, the cylinder numbers danced up and down. To find a superb example, with the image well-centered and the cylinder numbers perfectly aligned, was not easy.

The first batch of these stamps was printed from cylinders 1112 (tagged version) and 11121 (service inscribed), reading in this order: magenta, cyan, yellow, process black, line black. Perhaps the number 1 process black cylinder was defective, or maybe at that stage of development the Bureau was still attempting to print USA in dropout white instead of black ink. Later batches, and far more common with almost 10 times as many impressions printed, are numbers 3333 (tagged) and 33333 (service inscribed). Some of the service-inscribed stamps exhibit varying degrees of tagging from phosphors that unintentionally contaminated the lacquer applied over the image. Both sets of cylinders were used on paper from two different manufacturers, Henry & Leigh Slater Company of England and Rolland Company of Canada. When

169

stamps on the Rolland paper are soaked in chlorinated tap water, the printed image has a tendency to flake off. Both of these papers have shiny gum, but stamps printed from number 3 cylinders also appeared with dull gum, reported to be paper acquired for printing the nonde-nominated E stamp.

In 1988, after the 18¢ presort rate was obsolete, a different set of cylinders was sent to press, all numbered 4 except for the cyan printer, yielding the combination 43444, a service-inscribed edition only, and printed only on paper with dull gum. Any cover bearing a numbered 43444 18¢ Washington stamp mailed at the presort rate is an example of false franking.

Imperforates exist of the tagged 18¢ Washington number 1112 and the service inscribed, number 33333.

Chapter 13

A Year of Transition

Plate number coil collecting took several giant steps into the philatelic mainstream in 1985. By June, the Plate Number Coil Study Group had compiled enough information comprehensively that Stephen G. Esrati announced in round-robin number 9, "The big news is that I've assembled a catalog of the PNCs, complete with prices." Drafts were circulated, marked up, and returned. The final editing was completed in June and sent to press. Catalogs went on sale July 7. Esrati underestimated the demand, and a corrected second printing was needed in August. The first edition of the catalog priced each PNC in mint condition only, as pairs and strips of three, four and five. Precancel gap positions that appeared on these pairs and strips were also priced.

Since then, the Esrati *Catalog of Plate Number Coils,* renamed *Plate Number Coil Catalog,* has become an annual publication of the study group and an essential resource for every serious PNC collector.

Although the Scott catalogs continued to list U.S. coil stamps only as singles, pairs and line pairs, two other publishers broke rank, joining Minkus. The Brookman *Price Guide of United States Stamps,* a widely used reference in the retail stamp trade, began pricing coil plate strips of three, but without reference to specific numbers. As dealers became aware that coil collectors were not satisfied with pairs any more, Brookman provided a basis for pricing strips, especially at shows and bourses. Since the dealers didn't know scarce numbers from common ones, collectors equipped with an Esrati catalog could often find bargains.

The German *Michel USA-Spezial-Katalog 1985/86* listed the specific plate numbers known for each coil stamp (with many mistakes), so that users were more aware of what existed than collectors who used Scott, Minkus, Brookman, Harris, or the *Postal Service Guide to U.S Stamps.* But Michel did not price the plate numbers separately.

This was the year that *Linn's* inaugurated the monthly Plate Number Coils column by Stephen G. Esrati, and *Stamp Collector* began my monthly Plate Number Coils Considered column. In *Linn's*, Esrati's coverage was supplemented by Robert Rabinowitz, who frequently included PNCs in his Plate Numbers column. Tom Myers, a PNC dealer in Akron, Ohio, started a new publication called *Plate Number Coil Bulletin*, but there was little in it that could not be learned from other, more widely available, philatelic publications.

All these developments were important steps in advancing PNC collecting toward the mainstream of U.S. philately, but major obstacles still stood in the way. At the time, the biggest challenge for collectors already committed to PNCs was the problem of keeping up with new issues as all the rate-change stamps came out. For newcomers, the problem was to discover suppliers. In 1985, not one dealer could supply every PNC, so it was necessary to buy from several dealers and to find trading partners. No big dealers were yet committed to PNCs, so everyone had to follow the classified coil ads closely. Even then, some plate numbers could not be purchased from anyone.

Although used singles, mint strips of three and mint strips of five were close to achieving consensus as the preferred formats, there was still some ambiguity as several dealer price lists and the Esrati catalog continued to include strips of four as a collectible format. Fully capitalized mainstream dealerships were unlikely to make the commitment to invest in substantial PNC inventories as long as doubts lingered. And without that commitment, PNCs couldn't move up from the classifieds to the display advertising, where they would catch the attention of more casual collectors.

Finally, aside from Esrati's PNC Study Group, a closed, elite group limited to 20 working enthusiasts, there was nothing the newly converted collector could join. Even collectors who had been involved with PNCs from the beginning were only acquainted with most others my mail and phone contacts. So 1985 was a year of important advances, but the major breakthrough was yet a year away.

Chapter 14

The Coil Stamps of 1986

After a record output of new coil stamps in 1985, the year of sweeping rate changes when seven presses at the Bureau of Engraving and Printing were loaded to capacity with coil production — two Cottrells, the Andreotti gravure press, the gravure section of the A press, the intaglio B press, the intaglio C press, and the intaglio D press — 1986 was a slow year. Only eight new coil stamps were issued, counting tagged and service-inscribed editions separately, and every one was printed on the intaglio B press, with a single sleeve number appearing at 52-stamp intervals.

Of these new issues, only one really represented a new postal need, the 5.5¢ Star Route Truck stamp issued to meet the nonprofit rate presorted to the individual carrier route. All the others were new designs for denominations of stamps that had previously been printed on the Cottrell presses. The Cottrells had been taken out of production and scrapped in November 1985. Their plates could not be run on any of the other presses, so B press sleeves had to be manufactured. In some instances, a very similar stamp design was issued; in others, an entirely new one.

Actually, there would have been several more new coil stamps issued to meet the various rate tiers of nonprofit bulk mail, but those rates changed so rapidly — three times within the year — that the stamp designs were obsolete before there was time to produce them. Except for the nonprofits, rates covered by coil stamps remained stable from 1985 to 1988.

In 1986 the Postal Service announced a new design policy for the Transportation coil series that most careful observers thought had gone into effect a year earlier: henceforth the numerals of value would be at least twice as large as the size of the letters USA. But then the first new Transportation coil of the year, the re-engraved 4¢ Stagecoach stamp, failed to obey this rule. The large-numeral policy actually coincided with the disappearance of the letter c for cents from the inscription.

Although the policy on precancels announced in 1985 had proclaimed that no new precancels would include overprinted parallel lines along with service inscriptions, the revised B press version of the 8.3¢ Ambulance precancel overprint continued the old style, because the Postal Service did not consider it to be a new stamp.

The year began with no new coils at all for seven-and-a-half months. Actually more than nine months had passed since the last new coil issue in early November of 1985, the longest such drought in the history of PNCs. When the first one finally did appear, there was little advance warning.

The Re-engraved 4¢ Stagecoach Stamp

An August 19, 1986 news release from U.S. Postal Service headquarters announced:

"The four-cent Stagecoach and 8.3¢ Ambulance coil stamps, initially printed on the Cottrell presses, are now being produced on the Bureau's B Press. Additional Stagecoach stamps are needed only in coils of 3,000. Additional supplies of the Ambulance stamps are needed in precanceled form only.

"The Stagecoach stamp had reached plate number six on the Cottrell press, and the Ambulance stamp had been printed with four plate numbers. For coil stamps printed on the B Press, plate numbers appear on every 52nd stamp. Cottrell press items have plate numbers on every 24th stamp.

"Of the three stamps now being printed on new presses (third was the 50¢ Chester W. Nimitz sheet stamp in the Great Americans series), only one — the four-cent Stagecoach — was re-engraved (Kenneth Kipperman, vignette/Gary Slaght, lettering). The Postal Service explained that the image of that stamp was too large in the original Cottrell engraving for adaptation to B Press printing sleeves.

"There will be no first day of issue for the re-engraved Stagecoach stamp."

By the time the news release appeared, the re-engraved 4¢ Stagecoach coils were already in circulation. Except for the slightly smaller design and the absence of a joint line, they looked like the original 1982 Cottrell-press version described on Page 96. There are subtle differences. Because engraved lines on B press sleeves are shallower than on Cottrell plates, B press stamps do not have the depth of color that Cottrell stamps do. On the other hand, the superior wiping system on the B press leaves the unprinted portion whiter than on its Cottrell counterpart. Under shortwave ultraviolet illumination, the difference between the crisp block tagging of the B press and the much

The original 4¢ Stagecoach design, on the right, was too wide to be used on a B press sleeve, so a smaller, re-engraved version was prepared, shown on the left. Under shortwave ultraviolet illumination, the block tagging of the re-engraved stamp is easy to differentiate from the overall tagging of the Cottrell press version.

weaker, splotchy, overall tagging of the Cottrell press is striking, leaving no room for doubt about which stamp came from which press.

Like their Cottrell press predecessors, the re-engraved 4¢ Stagecoach coils were printed mainly for one large user, Disabled American Veterans. Stamps to fill the DAV order were shipped to Cincinnati on August 13, 1986. The next day, shipments were dispatched to the Philatelic Sales Division in Merrifield, Virginia, and Kansas City, Missouri. But they were not placed on sale at the L'Enfant Plaza post office philatelic counter in Washington until late in the afternoon of August 15. The only purchaser who prepared covers on that day was *Linn's* Washington correspondent, Charles Yeager.

The following month, subscribers to Artcraft first-day covers received a printed notice enclosed with their regular delivery offering "first day covers" of the re-engraved 4¢ Stagecoach stamps for three dollars each: "We were able to put through several hundred each with a strip of three of the old and a strip of three of the new so the comparison is right there." The printed notice made no mention of PNCs, but those who asked were able to purchase them for $12.50 apiece.

In the last issue of *Linn's* for 1986, dated December 29, Stephen G. Esrati reported the existence of the Artcraft covers in a front-page story. Esrati's article aroused a storm of controversy, since the Postal Service had refused to allow collectors to make their own FDCs. It seemed to many that Leo August, the owner of Washington Press, maker of Artcraft cachets, had been granted a special favor. August was unwilling to state exactly how he got the covers, but a *Linn's* investigation uncovered some facts.

"If you look carefully at the cancels on those covers, you'll see that they were made by a fixed-date device, not the changeable-date handstamp they use when I get covers canceled in Washington," said

Doug Holl, maker of Uncovers cachets, who prepares many unofficial FDCs in Washington and is very familiar with the postmarks that are available.

"That means it had to be ordered in advance. You can't just walk up to the counter the way Leo August's agent supposedly did and get a cancel like that."

John Halliday, maker of the House of Farnam cachets, made the same observation, as did *Linn's* correspondent Yeager.

So I asked Gordon Morison, assistant postmaster general for Philatelic Affairs, to explain how it happened. Morison routed my questions to Robert G. Brown, general manager of the Philatelic Sales Division. Brown's assistant Cindy Tackett supplied the pertinent document, which sheds interesting light on how the Postal Service handles large orders for special philatelic cancels.

The June 2, 1986 memorandum from Brown to the Customer Programs Division general manager says, "The Philatelic Sales Division will grant approval to The Washington Press to obtain rubber composition cancelations of stamp-affixed covers at the following post offices."

It lists nine dates in August for which Leo August would furnish from 15,000 to 30,000 covers for Washington, D.C. 20066 cancelations — including 15,000 on August 15, the date in question.

"He will have the envelopes delivered on or before the requested cancelation dates. Under no circumstances may the envelopes be backdated if received after the approval date

"A token quantity of 100 covers must be sent to each post office. In order to minimize our handling costs, the remaining quantity will be canceled at the Philatelic Sales Division.

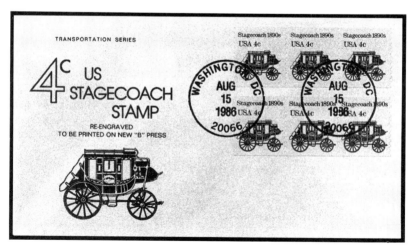

This cover has both Cottrell (bottom) and B press (top) versions of the 4¢ Stagecoach coil stamp. Although the cachet gives no indication of its origin, it came from Washington Press, maker of Artcraft cachets.

"Please have the postmasters confirm the actual number of envelopes canceled so that we may bill the customer for the five-cent per cancelation fee over the basic 50 free covers."

Brown's cover letter to me added that the August 15 handcancel "was mailed by Certified Mail No. P213860457 on July 1, 1986, to the Postmaster, Washington D.C. 20066-9998." In a later interview, Brown said that once delivered, the hand canceler would have been available that entire day to anybody who requested it.

Leo August explained that the order for 15,000 covers canceled August 15 was another product altogether — a commemorative panel observing the 72nd anniversary of the first ship passing through the Panama Canal.

The Postal Commemorative Society offered these panels and other philatelic products by subscription through direct mail promotions. The society's director, Steve Gordon, said it's covers and panels are

The August 15, 1986 datestamp on the Washington Press re-engraved 4¢ Stagecoach cover was actually created by the Postal Service for this panel prepared by the owner of Washington Press and Artcraft for the Postal Commemorative Society. The panel commemorates the 72nd anniversary of the passage of the first ship through the Panama Canal.

not available individually.

So that's the explanation for the fixed-date cancel, but what about the re-engraved 4¢ Stagecoach covers?

"I wish we had made 15,000 of those," August said. "I don't think we had more than 500, maybe fewer than that. And I sold them for just a few dollars each."

"I have an agent who checks all the time and gets covers serviced for me any time there's a new item," he said.

August refused to divulge the agent's name, or to permit an interview with the agent concerning the preparation of these covers.

"That's a trade secret," he said.

The trouble is, the regulations don't allow things to be done this way.

Section 164.21 of the *Domestic Mail Manual,* titled "Philatelic Postmarking," says: "As a free service it (handback service) is limited to transactions with fewer than 50 envelopes or other items. For 50 or more envelopes or other items, advance approval of the Stamps Division is required before service can be provided."

And rule 164.23a (3) on "Hand Back Service" repeats the structure that "there is a limit of 50 cancelations which can be provided for any single customer."

Cindy Tackett researched the records, and Robert Brown sent me the result: "Our records do not reflect any information concerning the cancelation of 400 to 500 covers with 4¢ re-engraved Stagecoach stamps affixed."

Tackett remained puzzled. "I've been handling orders from Leo August for years, and I've never seen anything like that cover. It just doesn't look like his work," she said.

This House of Farnam cover has both old (bottom) and new (top) versions of the 4¢ Stagecoach stamp. The cachet was added some time after the L'Enfant Plaza philatelic center cancel was applied.

So, even though we have learned how the cancelation device came to be, we still haven't solved the mystery of how, when and where the Artcraft FDCs of the re-engraved 4¢ Stagecoach stamps were made.

And as long as the mystery remains, critics will continue to accuse the Postal Service of giving special favors not available to all.

Early in 1987, yet another item purporting to be a "first-day cover" of the re-engraved 4¢ Stagecoach stamp appeared on the market, this one on an envelope bearing the characteristic cachet of the House of Farnam, a multicolor line engraving.

The Farnam covers differed from the Artcraft re-engraved FDCs in two significant respects. The stamps are tied to the Farnam covers with pictorial postmarks from the Washington, D.C., Philatelic Center at L'Enfant Plaza. These are changeable-date handstamps, while the Artcraft covers are canceled with plain, fixed-date large bull's-eyes.

And the Farnam covers have generic "Re-engraved Coil Series" cachets, while the Artcraft Stagecoach covers feature an illustration of the actual Stagecoach design, which Artcraft owner Leo August says was added after the covers were serviced and canceled.

From the Farnam design, which pictures an Omnibus, it is obvious that the House of Farnam cachets are add-ons also. The re-engraved 1¢ Omnibus stamps were not issued until November 26, 1986, and the original United States Postal Service announcement said that first-day cancels would not be offered for them.

That policy was subsequently changed, but not until the day the re-engraved 1¢ coils were issued. So it is likely that the Farnam cachet featuring an Omnibus was not prepared until sometime in December, or even later.

The very late arrival of these covers on the market, and the plain evidence that the cachets had been added as much as four months after the cancelation dates, caused many collectors to suspect that these covers had been backdated.

Along with the covers featuring the re-engraved 4¢ Stagecoach, the House of Farnam also issued "first day covers" of the new B press version of the 8.3¢ Ambulance precancel, postmarked August 29, 1986, the earliest known date for that stamp, discussed on Page 185.

I asked John Halliday, owner of the House of Farnam, to explain how these FDCs came into being.

"I got 200 of each cover from a contact in Washington, on the condition that I wouldn't reveal his identity," Halliday said. "About 25 of the Stagecoach covers had plate numbers, and 12 of the Ambulance.

"When I saw the *Linn's* article about the Artcraft covers, I could see that they made a special round date cancel for Leo August. This is not right.

"I could have gone to Robert Brown and complained. If he didn't agree, I could have gone to Gordon Morison. I did that once before, when Leo August got preferential treatment, and Gordon eventually let me get my covers.

"But my source must have realized the first day for each of the stamps when he read the *Linn's* stories about them. They probably were made not on the first day, but shortly after that.

"He probably knows somebody in the Postal Service who does this for him. They might have been done by somebody high up, but that's just my speculation. A lot of people in the Washington area have a good relationship with people in the Postal Service.

"When he first offered the covers to me, he wanted quite a price for them, and I wouldn't pay it. Three months later he dropped his price, and even then I paid him very well for them. I used the same cachet for all the re-engraved coils."

Halliday said his source would not agree to talk with *Linn's* about these covers, even with a pledge of anonymity.

"Why not?" I asked.

"He makes money this way. He charges an exorbitant price over the usual cost. The Postal Service doesn't like it when people can create expensive rare items that others can't get."

That's true. There's actually a rule prohibiting it, under "Philately Policy" in the *Domestic Mail Manual*. Section 161.3 states, "Uniform application of policies provides a high degree of integrity to the entire program, and all post offices, postal employees and contractors shall comply with the policies set forth in this subchapter. The Postal Service will avoid the creation of philatelic rarities."

Another rule specifically relates this to cancelations. Section 164.12 reads, "The Postal Service shall endeavor to make all unusual postmarking services widely known to collectors through advance national publicity so as to avoid such postmarks being available only to small groups of people."

Nevertheless, rarities were created somehow on these covers.

Robert Brown, general manager of the Philatelic Sales Division, and his assistant, Cindy Tackett, state emphatically that backdating of cancels is strictly prohibited, except when authorized grace periods are offered to everybody, or when damaged FDCs are being replaced.

Brown did concede that sometimes large-volume producers ask for extensions of the grace periods. They must do so in advance, and justify the request in writing, and often those requests are granted. "Sometimes I say no, if the request is unreasonable," he said.

He added that nothing like that had happened in these cases. According to Brown and Tackett, the only devices that could have canceled the House of Farnam covers are handstamps at the L'Enfant Plaza post office counter.

Mary Wood, superintendent of window services for the Philatelic Sales Division, had no specific recollection of the re-engraved 4¢ Stagecoach or the B press 8.3¢ precancel covers. She said that there have been occasions when people have brought in quantities of covers for cancelation with the pictorial handstamp.

"We won't make other customers wait while we cancel them," she said. "They leave us the covers and we'll give them a buzz when they're ready. But we don't ever cancel them with an earlier date. We never have."

Despite these assurances, John Halliday insists that special favors are done.

"Here's an example. A few years ago they let people get first-day cancels on a booklet pane. I flew to Washington to service them myself, so I could get a large number in by the 11:30 p.m. deadline.

"But when I was back in Washington on business several days later, Fleetwood and Artcraft were still bringing theirs in. That isn't fair."

Brown denies this happens.

"They're always accusing us of giving Fleetwood and Artcraft special treatment because they're the biggest, but it just isn't so. We don't show favoritism to anybody, big or small."

"Here's another example," said Halliday.

Cover maker John Halliday said the March 31, 1981 postmark on this cover was applied a year and a half or two years later, by permission of the assistant postmaster general.

"Several years ago, when they came out with the redrawn 5¢ George Washington coil stamp, Leo August got the only first-day covers.

"When I saw the preferential treatment he got, I complained. I went all the way to Assistant PMG Gordon Morison. Eventually I got the same cancel Artcraft did, a year and a half or two years later."

Asked about these covers, Gordon Morison said, "I have no recollection of it, and I can't conceive that I would have done such a thing long after the date. I certainly wouldn't do it today."

So we have charges and denials, but very little more real information about the origin of the House of Farnam first-day covers on the redesigned B press 4¢ and 8.3¢ coils than we have on the re-engraved

4¢ Artcraft FDCs. But it does seem likely that some hanky-panky was involved, somewhere along the line, despite assurances to the contrary from Postal Service officials.

But are the Artcraft and House of Farnam items really first-day covers?

Both cachets call them that, and that is how they have been collected, based on *Linn's* reports and Scott catalog listings of the earliest known use for each of the stamps.

In July 1987, John Spiehs, a writer and editor in the United States Postal Service's Philatelic Marketing Division and president of the Postal Service's Commemorative Stamp Club, sent out an album page to the club's subscribers that muddied the waters. The page featured three stamps: the B press version of the 4¢ Stagecoach, the 8.3¢ Ambulance precancel, and the 1¢ Omnibus.

The album page gives August 7, 1986, as the reissue date for the 4¢ Stagecoach, and August 15, 1986, for the B press 8.3¢ Ambulance precancel — both earlier than the dates on the first-day covers.

Spiehs told me that the album-page dates were furnished to him by the Stamps Division, "either as the dates they were printed or the dates they went into the vault, I'm not sure which. They're probably not accurate as the first day of issue, but you'll have to check with the Stamps Division on that."

Linda Foster of the Stamps Division furnished this information: The re-engraved 4¢ Stagecoach stamps went into the vault on August 11, after which they were available to fill orders. The first ones out were sent to Cincinnati, Ohio, on August 13. Supplies to fill philatelic orders were shipped to Merrifield, Virginia, and Kansas City, Missouri, on the following day.

Bureau of Engraving and Printing reports say the 4¢ coils went to press on July 31, so it's still uncertain what Spiehs' dates represent. Using Foster's dates, it appears theoretically possible, but unlikely, that some of the 4¢ Stagecoach stamps could have been sold and mailed before the August 15 date on the FDCs.

Even though doubts about the legitimacy of both the Farnam and Artcraft FDCs persist, their postmark date is clearly more believable than the ones furnished by the Postal Service on the Commemorative Stamp Club album page. I submitted examples of both FDCs to the expertizing committee of the American First Day Cover Society for an opinion. After five months of deliberation, the committee issued certificates for both.

Allison W. Cusick, the committee's chairman, explained that the covers "bear genuine USPS postmarks. However, a genuine postmark is not the sole criterion for a first-day cover."

In addition, there must be a designated official date and first-day city, the stamp must be available in the first-day city on that date, and it must be available to collectors during the grace period allowed by the USPS for covers to be submitted for servicing.

"We are issuing certificates of genuineness for the two covers bearing the re-engraved 4¢ Stagecoach coil, Scott 2228. The USPS did not designate an official first-day date for this stamp. However, we know that the stamps were sold at the Philatelic Agency on August 15, 1986," wrote Cusick.

"Yes," he continued, "the postmark might have been applied later. It probably was. But under the contemporary guidelines of the USPS, guidelines generally accepted by the philatelic community, such backdating is perfectly acceptable.

"Note that the certificate does not say that these are first-day covers. Instead, these covers have the earliest dated postmark on this issue known to the committee at the date of the certificate.

"It is conceivable that earlier dated postmarks may be found on this issue."

By the end of fiscal year 1988, more of the re-engraved 4¢ Stagecoach stamps had been shipped than of their tagged Cottrell press counterparts. (More of the Cottrell press precancels were shipped; the re-engraved version was never issued in precanceled form.) As this is being written in 1989, the re-engraved coils are still on sale. Yet six plates were required for the Cottrell press, but in all this time only sleeve 1 has ever been used to print the B press version. Cottrell press editions appeared in an array of varieties: imperforates, gripper cracks, doubled images caused by set-off. Very few comparable varieties have been found on re-engraved coils.

The greater durability of the B press sleeves, and their reduced propensity to develop flaws, reflect important improvements in intaglio printing technology. But the consequence to stamp collectors is fewer plate numbers and varieties to collect. The re-engraved 4¢ Stagecoach coil stamps brought their moments of excitement and lingering mystery, but their appearance also signified the end of the Golden Age of the Transportation series.

The 17¢ Dog Sled Stamp

The 17¢ Dog Sled stamp should go down in history as the accidental issue of the Transportation series. Had things gone according to plan, it would not exist, and in its place we would probably have a re-engraved version of the 17¢ Electric Auto stamp printed on the B press. The Dog Sled vignette would have been transitory, on a bulk-rate nonprofit decimal-denominated stamp set, including a tagged collector edition and an untagged service-inscribed version. By now it would have been obsolete and withdrawn from sale.

The problem was political, what reporters came to call Reaganomics. On December 23, 1985, the U.S. Postal Service board of governors increased rates for nonprofit and other preferred mailers substantially from 23 to 41 percent, effective January 1, 1986. But a week after the new rates had gone into effect, the board decided another increase was necessary.

The January 1 rates were set when it appeared that the Postal Service would receive a "revenue forgone" appropriation (a subsidy for nonprofit mailers) from Congress totaling $820 million for Fiscal Year 1986. But President Ronald Reagan vetoed that appropriation, and the redrafted bill included a smaller subsidy, $748 million.

The Dog Sled coil had been scheduled for release on February 21, 1986, as a 6.3¢ stamp to meet the five-digit presort nonprofit bulk-mail rate. Production ceased when the president's veto message made it clear that rates would have to be raised again. It was rescheduled as a 7.2¢ stamp, the rate that went into effect on March 9, due to be issued on June 17. But the rate dropped to 7.1¢ on April 20, so the new announcement promised a Dog Sled stamp in that denomination with an issue date of September 25. Finally, a June 4 news release said the 7.1¢ Dog Sled stamp and other previously announced nonprofit coil stamps had been "deferred indefinitely." Throughout this period of rate turbulence, the precanceled 4.9¢ Buckboard stamp remained available as false franking for nonprofit mailers using the five-digit presort discount.

On July 9, a Postal Service news release said the Dog Sled stamp would have a denomination of 17¢ and would be issued on August 20. One item had remained consistent throughout: the Dog Sled stamp would be issued at a ceremony held in the Anchorage, Alaska, Museum of History and Art, and it was. The stamp depicts a 1920s dog sled

These are some of the plans, announced and later withdrawn, for the Dog Sled coil stamp's denomination. In all, a total of six stamps — 6.3¢, 7.2¢ and 7.1¢ both tagged and service-inscribed — were scheduled for this design but never released, before the seventh actually was issued as a 17¢ stamp.

printed in blue ink on the intaglio B press, with sleeve numbers appearing at 52-stamp intervals. Only sleeve number 2 has been collected. According to USPS plate activity reports, sleeve 1 was canceled without any impressions having been printed from it.

The stamp was issued only in tagged form, not precanceled. For the first year it was sold only in coils of 100, because adequate supplies of 17¢ Electric Auto coils were still on hand in coils of 500 and 3,000. Later, the 17¢ Dog Sled was issued in the larger coils as well. Like the 17¢ Auto, the Dog Sled stamp paid the added-ounce first-class letter rate until April 2, 1988. It is still on sale as this chapter is written in 1989, although its postal purpose is obsolete. Imperforate examples of the 17¢ Dog Sled have been found.

The Revised 8.3¢ Ambulance Precanceled Stamp

The second coil stamp moved from the Cottrell press to the B press without changing its subject was the precanceled version of the 8.3¢ Ambulance stamp, overprinted "Blk. Rt. CAR-RT SORT" in black ink between parallel lines. Unlike the 4¢ Stagecoach, which had to be re-engraved for the switch because the original die was too big in its horizontal dimension, the 8.3¢ Ambulance master die was satisfactory in its original form, because it had been engraved for the B press initially. Only the press overload caused by the 1985 rate changes had forced a change of plans, so that its first year's production was printed on the Cottrells while the B press ran 22¢ Flag coils. The original 8.3¢ Ambulance coil stamps are described on Page 155.

In other respects the two B press stamps had similar histories. Both the re-engraved 4¢ Stagecoach and the revised 8.3¢ Ambulance precancel went on sale without adequate prior notice to collectors, and first-day cancels were not offered. Again, *Linn's* Washington correspondent Charles Yeager was the only one who prepared covers mailed on the date they were actually placed on sale for the first time at the L'Enfant Plaza post office philatelic center in Washington, and again, some time after that "first day covers" appeared on the market with philatelic cancels dated the same as Yeager's machine-canceled covers, August 29, 1986. As with the re-engraved 4¢ Stagecoach, the Postal Service added a layer of confusion by publishing an earlier "Re-issue date" on the album page circulated to its Commemorative Stamp Club subscribers.

Because the B press version of the 8.3¢ Ambulance was issued only in precanceled form, it is not as easy to differentiate from its Cottrell-press counterpart as other designs printed on both presses, because the tagging styles characteristic of each press are not present. On single stamps, the B press image is 1/4 millimeter narrower than the Cottrell, because the Cottrell press plates were engraved on flat pieces of steel, then curved to fit the printing plate cylinder, stretching the images. B press sleeves are cylindrical to begin with. The shallower image of the B press version leaves the shading lines in the lettering distinct; the deeper engraving on the Cottrell-press version makes the letters appear solid. The superior wiping system on the B press makes the background appear whiter and the image contrastier than on Cottrell stamps.

On plate pairs or strips, the Cottrell-press stamps have a joint line, but the B-press stamps do not. On longer strips, the two Cottrell press plate numbers alternate at 24-stamp intervals. Cottrell press precancel overprints were printed from hard vinyl or rubber composition letterpress mats nine subjects in the vertical dimension and 12 subjects in the horizontal, in sets of four. On any given roll, the precancel gap between the mats appears at 12-stamp intervals. B press precancel overprints are printed from a pair of plastic flexographic plates 18 subjects vertically by 26 horizontally, so the gap where the ends of the

Although transfer rolls made from the same master die made plates for both stamps, B press images emerged ¼ millimeter narrower than those printed on the Cottrell press.

plates meet occurs at 26-stamp intervals on each roll.

Records kept by Linda Foster at USPS headquarters show that the B press 8.3¢ precancels first reached the Bureau of Engraving and Printing vault on August 20, and the philatelic centers on September 2. Foster's shipping date is later than August 29, the date that Yeager purchased and mailed them. Evidently the explanation is that the stamps were shipped on that Friday, but the paperwork wasn't entered until the following Tuesday, after the Labor Day weekend. The earliest use date of August 29 appears unassailable.

Nevertheless the USPS Commemorative Stamp Club album page gives the "re-issue date" as August 15. That is clearly a mistake. According to BEP reports, the 8.3¢ Ambulance sleeve went to press on August 4. From then until they went into the vault on August 20, they could not have been available outside the Bureau.

The Bureau went back to number 1 on this stamp, which seems inconsistent. When Flag coil stamps are printed in sequence on different presses — the B, the C, and the D — the numbers are all in succession. No one has adequately explained why this sleeve, manufactured from the same die as the Cottrell plates, wasn't numbered sequentially. Stamps printed from sleeve 2 appeared later.

About 200 covers bearing August 29, 1986 philatelic cancels on House of Farnam cacheted envelopes appeared on the market in 1987 and were quickly snapped up. Most had a pair of the original tagged Cottrell press 8.3¢ Ambulance stamps and a pair of the new B press precancels, but about a dozen had plate number strips of both. John Halliday, owner of the House of Farnam, said he had bought them from the same source who supplied covers of the re-engraved 4¢ Stagecoach, and he added his same cachet to these as he had to the others.

The expertizing committee of the American First Day Cover Society, which had issued certificates for the re-engraved 4¢ Stagecoach covers, declined an opinion on these. The submitted House of Farnam cover bears a genuine postmark, said the committee, but it had insufficient postage — only 16.6¢ in tagged, unprecanceled stamps, when 22¢ was required. "The USPS did not designate an official first day for this [replated] stamp. However, there is ample documentation that this coil was on sale in Washington on August 29, 1986," wrote committee chairman Allison Cusick.

"Charles Yeager serviced first-day covers of No. 2231, which have Washington machine cancels and which passed through the mailstream. If these Yeager covers were submitted to the commit-

This cover mailed by Linn's *Washington correspondent Charles Yeager on August 29, 1986, has a plate 1 example of the B press precanceled 8.3¢ Ambulance stamp in the center, between a PNC of the tagged 8.3¢ Ambulance and plain 14¢ Iceboat stamp, both Cottrell press stamps.*

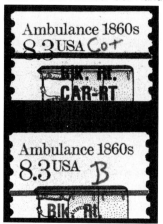

With these gauges, one can identify the press on which any 8.3¢ precanceled coil was issued.

tee, I am certain we would issue a certificate of authenticity for them.

"However, the cover which you submitted lacks proper postage and should not have been postmarked. We do not intend to encourage such illegal covers." In closing, Cusick pointed out that declining an opinion does not prejudice the covers in any way.

"It's always difficult to assess the contemporary scene. That is as true in philately as it is in public events. Time brings perspective and further knowledge. Perhaps it's too soon to evaluate these covers properly."

The easiest way to identify an unknown 8.3¢ coil stamp, on or off, cover, is to make a set of gauges.

Take a known Cottrell-press stamp and label it "Cot" near the top, then cut it in two horizontally and keep the top half. Do likewise with a B press stamp after writing "B" on it.

When faced with an unknown example, take one of the gauges and place it on top of the stamp to be measured. If the ends of the ambulance align perfectly, the two stamps are from the same press. If not, the unknown is from the other press, which can be confirmed with the second gauge.

The 8.3¢ third-class bulk rate presorted to the individual carrier route expired on April 2, 1988. The 8.3¢ Ambulance precancels were then authorized as false franking for the new 10.1¢ rate until October 9, 1988. By then, proper stamps in the new denomination were available. Both Cottrell and B press versions of the 8.3¢ Ambulance stamp were withdrawn from philatelic sale on February 28, 1989.

The Revised 14¢ Iceboat Stamp

The 14¢ Iceboat was the first of the stamps originally printed on the Cottrell press to have been assigned to the B press, but was the third to appear. Like the B press version of the 8.3¢ Ambulance precancel,

188

it was not re-engraved. The B press sleeve was manufactured from a transfer roller made from the same master die as the Cottrell-press plates, resulting in a very similar stamp, but with an image a fraction of a millimeter narrower than the original. Since the 14¢ Iceboat is a tagged stamp, its press can be conclusively determined under short-wave ultraviolet illumination. The Cottrell stamps have overall tagging; the B press stamps have block tagging. The other characteristic difference is that the paper on the B press version look whiter owing to its superior wiping system. On plate pairs or strips, the Cottrell-press stamps have a joint line, but the B-press stamps do not. On longer strips, the two Cottrell-press plate numbers alternate at 24-stamp intervals, while the single B-press sleeve number repeats at 52-stamp intervals. The original stamp is described on Page 136.

For the third time, *Linn's* correspondent Charles Yeager was the only person on hand to mail covers on the first day the revised stamps were placed on sale at the L'Enfant Plaza post office philatelic center in Washington. His September 30, 1986 covers are the only ones ever reported; no cacheted covers with philatelic cancels of that date have appeared. The first official notice of this stamp from the Postal Service came in the news release dated October 17, 1986, more than two weeks after it had been placed on sale, but *Linn's* had published a

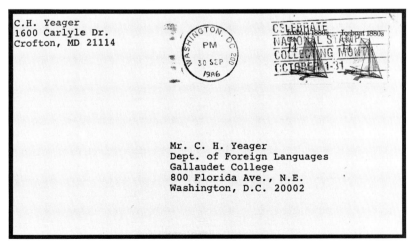

This cover showing the earliest known use of the B press 14¢ Iceboat, on the left, also has the original Cottrell press version on the right. Both are number 2 plate number coils.

front-page headline story in the July 28 issue alerting collectors that new B-press varieties of several Cottrell-press Transportation coil stamps would appear in coming months. An enlarged photograph of a 14¢ Iceboat stamp illustrated the article.

Sleeve 2 was the only one ever used to print the 14¢ Iceboat on the B press, so that is the only collectible PNC of this stamp. Sleeve 1 was defective and never used. The plate number on the B press stamp is in a different position, approximately 1/4 millimeter to the right of the Cottrell press placement, better centered to the stamp design. Both versions of the 14¢ Iceboat stamp were issued in coils of 500 and 3,000. The postcard rate increased to 15¢ on April 3, 1988. The Cottrell-press 14¢ Iceboat was withdrawn from philatelic sale on February 28, 1989, and the B-press edition four months later, on June 30.

The revised 14¢ Iceboat coil stamp was the first Transportation coil not to be listed separately in the Scott catalog, although the *Scott Specialized Catalogue of United States Stamps* does include a "no line" plate 2 strip listing.

The 5.5¢ Star Route Truck Stamps

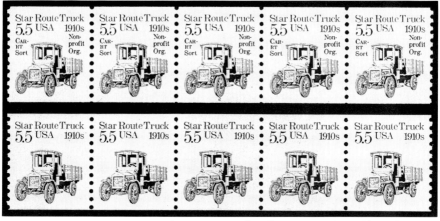

The Star Route Truck coil stamp design is yet another, like the Dog Sled, that fell victim to the tug-of-war between President Ronald Reagan and the Congress over the size of the "revenue foregone" appropriation, the subsidy to nonprofit and other favored mailers. The original March 19, 1986, announcement said that a 5.7¢ Star Route Truck coil stamp would be issued to cover the nonprofit bulk rate presorted to the individual carrier route that had gone into effect on March 9, but gave no further information. When the design was unveiled at a ceremony in Chicago on April 3, the Postal Service said the stamp would be issued on June 10 in Louisville, Kentucky.

The nonprofit carrier-route presort bulk rate fell to 5.5¢ on April 20. The following day, the Postal Service announced that the Star Route Truck coil stamp would be issued in that denomination, but that the rate change would require postponement of the issue date.

The drop in nonprofit rates resulted from the elimination of one preferred rate category, second-class out-of-county limited circulation newspapers, mostly small town weeklies, but some major metropolitan dailies, that mail fewer than 5,000 copies out of the county in which they are printed. With that subsidy eliminated, the money saved, about $20 million, was redistributed to the remaining preferred rate categories, including the nonprofits. A May 13 news release set the issue date for the 5.5¢ coil as September 12, still in Louisville, but that information was retracted in a June 4 release that said the stamp had been "deferred indefinitely."

When Fiscal Year 1986 closed at the end of September, it was clear that the rates would be stable through Fiscal Year 1987, so a new issue date and place for the 5.5¢ Star Route Truck coil stamp were announced in an October 10 news release. This time the information was accurate. The stamp, printed in maroon ink on the intaglio B press, depicts an early 20th-century truck driven by a private contract mail carrier. It was issued at a ceremony in Fort Worth, Texas, on November 1, 1986, at a joint meeting of the National Star Route Mail Contractors' Association and the Southern Region of the U.S. Postal Service.

The 5.5¢ Star Route Truck coil stamp was issued in two versions — a single-color tagged version in coils of 500, and a two-color untagged version with an engraved service inscription in black ink, "CAR-RT Sort Non-profit Org." in three lines bracketing the maroon vignette, in coils of 500 and 3,000. The latter was the first bicolor engraved stamp in the Transportation coil series. Both versions have single sleeve numbers at 52-stamp intervals. The first of each to appear has sleeve number 1, since they are rightly regarded as different issues. Eventually sleeve 2 of the service-inscribed edition also appeared.

The Postal Service regarded the engraved service inscription itself as a precancellation, so no added overprint was required. This was a

All these stamps have engraved service inscriptions, but only one, the 5.5¢ Star Route Truck, is considered a precancel by the Postal Service.

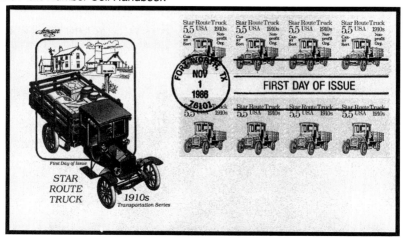

This Artmaster first-day cover has a sleeve 1 strip of the service-inscribed 5.5¢ Star Route Truck stamp. The strip of tagged stamps was required also, because the face value of the service-inscribed stamps, regarded as precancels, did not count toward the required first-class postage.

departure from past policy. From 1976 to 1984, 10 coil stamps with engraved service inscriptions were issued, but were not regarded as precanceled unless also overprinted with black lines. Two stamps issued in 1985, the 18¢ Washington Monument presort and the 21.1¢ ZIP+4, had printed service inscriptions that were considered precancels, but both of those were gravure printings, not engravings.

For the first time, the official Postal Service announcement invited collectors to prepare first-day covers using the service-inscribed precancels as well as the tagged collector editions, but with a hitch: "Precanceled Star Route Truck stamps may be affixed to covers, but at least 22¢ in mint, unprecanceled postage also must be affixed to receive first-day cancellations. At least one unprecanceled Star Route Truck stamp must be included." Some collectors attempted to get cancels on covers bearing only the service-inscribed stamps, but they were returned uncanceled, at least for the first part of the grace period, which lasted until December 1.

Philatelic Release No. 79, issued on November 20, 1986, reversed that policy before the grace period had expired.

"The Postal Service today announced that precanceled stamps and stationery items will be counted toward the total postage on covers submitted for first day or other philatelic cancellations. Formerly, these items were considered valid for postage only when used as part of a bulk mailing. For philatelic purposes, 22¢ in mint postage had to be added to any precanceled item in order to receive a first day cancellation.

"In the future, additional postage need only make up the difference between the value of the precanceled item and the 22¢ First-Class rate. . .

192

"The policy change is designed to reduce the overall cost to collectors for obtaining first day cancellations. The Postal Service noted that it also is consistent with a recent change in regulations which permits the use of precanceled stamps and stationery for non-bulk mailings."

Some FDCs franked solely with service-inscribed 5.5¢ Star Route Truck stamps received first-day cancels under the new policy, even though others submitted just days earlier had been rejected.

The long-delayed appearance of the Star Route Truck coil stamp finally allowed the Postal Service to retire the 3.4¢ School Bus coil stamp, which had actually been used for four different nonprofit carrier-route presort rates, three as false franking. On April 3, 1988, the rate was again lowered, this time to 5.3¢. Bulk mailers were authorized to continue using the service-inscribed 5.5¢ Star Route Truck stamps as false franking for the new rate, with the difference to be refunded by the Postal Service, until October 9, 1988. By then a stamp in the new denomination had been issued. The 5.5¢ Star Route Truck coil stamps were withdrawn from philatelic sale on February 28, 1989.

The 25¢ Bread Wagon Stamp

The 25¢ Bread Wagon coil stamp was issued on November 22, 1986, at a first-day ceremony at the VAPEX philatelic exhibition in Virginia Beach, Virginia. It depicts a horse-drawn 1880s bakery wagon printed in brown ink. As originally issued, it was printed on the intaglio B press with single sleeve numbers spaced at 52-stamp intervals, and processed into coils of 3,000, intended for use in post office vending machines, mainly to be purchased by after-hours patrons mailing parcels and overweight letters, in multiples or in combination with other stamps. The only single stamp franking would have been the international surface postcard rate to countries other than Canada or Mexico.

This was yet another new issue necessitated by the retirement of the Cottrell presses. The Postal Service announcement stated, "It will replace the 25¢ Paul Revere stamp issued in 1965." This wasn't quite right. It's true that the 25¢ Paul Revere coil stamp had been issued originally in 1965, companion to the sheet stamp of the same Liberty series design issued seven years earlier. It was actually the last new item in the Liberty series, which was about to be superseded by the Prominent Americans series. But the 1965 25¢ Revere coil stamp was

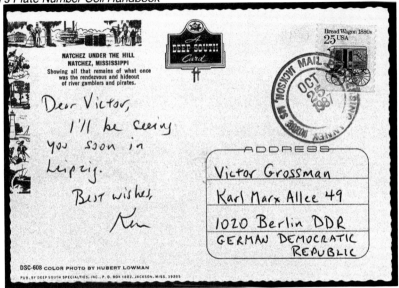

At the time it was issued, the only rate for a single 25¢ Bread Wagon stamp was the international surface postcard rate to countries other than Canada or Mexico. The plate 1 stamp carried this postcard to East Germany.

issued without phosphor tagging. The stamp that the 25¢ Bread Wagon coil replaced was the tagged 25¢ Paul Revere coil, issued on April 3, 1973, in New York City. Although the 25¢ Revere coil was withdrawn from philatelic sale on April 30, 1987, many were still in Postal Service vaults and available for use, along with the 25¢ Bread Wagon coils, when the first-class letter rate increased to 25¢ on April 3, 1988.

The rate increase dragged the 25¢ Bread Wagon from the margin to the mainstream, and transformed it in the process. The original printing sleeve, number 1 — the only plate number available on FDCs — was canceled two weeks after the rate increase. But the huge demand for 25¢ stamps meant that new printings were needed for coils of 100 and 500 as well as 3,000. Four additional sleeves were manufactured. Numbers 2, 3 and 4 have single sleeve numbers at 48-stamp intervals, for use interchangeably on the intaglio C and D presses, processed into coils of 100 stamps. Sleeve 5 was a second B press number, with the single digit spaced at 52-stamp intervals processed into rolls of 500 and 3,000. The stamps printed on the C and D presses are a different shade from those printed on the B press. Sleeve 2, 3 and 4 coils are more yellowish than those printed from sleeves 1 and 5. By the time the 25¢ Bread Wagon stamp was withdrawn from philatelic sale on April 30, 1989, six times as many C and D press stamps had been shipped as those printed on the B press, and most of the B press stamps in circulation had been printed from sleeve 1. As a result, commercial covers with number 5 PNCs are scarce.

Shortly after the rate change, imperforate rolls of the 25¢ Bread

Wagon appeared. Imperfs have been found showing sleeve numbers 2, 3, 4 and 5.

The Re-engraved 1¢ Omnibus Stamp

By the time the fourth Transportation series stamp originally printed on the Cottrell press had to be replaced by a B press version, the Postal Service had taken note that collectors had been angered by the way the previous three had been issued. Only the most alert or "connected" people in Washington had been able to obtain covers of the revised 4¢ Stagecoach, 8.3¢ Ambulance precancel, and 14¢ Iceboat stamps postmarked on their issue date. "First day covers" of those stamps that had reached the market were instant rarities, quickly soaring in value to three-figure realizations. Postal officials adamantly refused to permit a grace period for servicing covers with those stamps, but the way they handled the re-engraved 1¢ Omnibus, although confused and contradictory, was a tacit admission that they had made a mistake.

A November 6, 1986, news release announced that the new Omnibus stamps would "be available in early December," but that "no first-day cancellation will be offered."

Next, *Linn's* reported on November 17 that "the Postal Service will make every effort to have the new 1¢ Omnibus on sale November 26 at the philatelic sales counter at Postal Service headquarters."

Forewarned with that information, several Washington-area cachetmakers prepared their envelopes for the announced release date. One of them, Lorraine E. Bailey, took the Postal Service at its word and printed "NO FIRST DAY OF ISSUE CANCEL AVAILABLE" on her cachet.

Continuing to compromise its credibility in these matters, the Postal Service surprised everybody by making available a first-day-of-issue cancel on November 26 and then granting a 60-day grace period for anyone to get that cancel by mail — the very thing it had stubborn-

On the re-engraved 1¢ Omnibus coil stamp, the digit is much larger than on the original, and the "c" for cents has been deleted.

195

ly refused to do with the re-engraved 4¢ Stagecoach stamp.

At that point, only three months had elapsed since the release of the Stagecoach, so this would not have been significantly later than some of the extended grace periods that had been permitted for servicing other FDCs.

In the annual *Linn's* poll, collectors voted the re-engraved 1¢ Omnibus coil stamp the least necessary definitive stamp issued in 1986. They were wrong. Almost half a billion of these stamps were needed as vending-machine changemakers during the remainder of the 22¢ letter rate period, and as makeup postage for 25¢ letters and 15¢ postcards and postal cards in the weeks and months following the rate increase. The re-engraved 1¢ Omnibus coil stamp is still with us, and it is quite likely to see similar duty in the future.

I asked USPS to reconsider, to permit collectors to get re-engraved Stagecoach covers also. But on each step up the ladder the answer was "No" in succession: Joe Brockert, Dickey B. Rustin, Robert G. Brown, Pete Davidson and Gordon Morison.

By the time the latter three met to consider my appeal, nearly a year had passed, and they ruled that too much time had gone by to reconsider. But if they had acted when I first made the suggestion, thousands of collectors would be a lot happier today.

Unlike the re-engraved 4¢ Stagecoach, which had reproduced the original design but reduced it in size slightly, the re-engraved 1¢ Omnibus followed the new standard, with a much larger digit to denote the denomination, and dropping the c for cents, now reading "1 USA" instead of "USA 1c." It also has block tagging, in contrast to the overall tagging on the Cottrell-press version. The single sleeve numbers appear at 52-stamp intervals, without joint lines. Only number 1 exists on first-day covers, but number 2 has subsequently appeared.

Chapter 15

PNC Collecting Sweeps U.S.

If 1986 was a sleepy year for new U.S. coil stamp issues, it was the year of the decade for stamp collectors, the centerpiece being AMERI-PEX 86 in Rosemont, Illinois, from May 22 to June 1, the largest and most successful philatelic exhibition ever held in this country. It was also the year that plate number coil collecting reached maturity and entered the hobby's mainstream.

For the first time, the major obstacles to growth of the specialty had been overcome. The biggest restraint had been finding sources of supply, but by January 1986, Illinois dealer Al Haake became the first to offer his customers every reported plate number. PNCs also became auction items for the first time. Sam Houston Philatelics hammered down a complete collection in strips of three (except line pairs of 10.9¢ Hansom Cab number 3 and 4 precancels) for $1,100 on February 14, and Steve Ivy Philatelic Auctions realized $800 for a similar collection at its pre-AMERIPEX sale on May 21. A complete collection in mint strips of five, including many scarce precancel gap positions, sold at retail for $2,700 at the American Philatelic Society's STAMPSHOW in Washington, D.C., at the end of August.

The biggest marketing breakthrough came after Haake bought out the complete stock assembled by D. John Shultz of Kansas, one of the pioneer PNC collector-dealers. Shultz's was the largest accumulation of scarce earlier PNCs, and the total inventory of more than 24,000 mint strips was said to have a 1986 retail value of $280,000. The dispersal of Shultz's stock made possible the next step, when some of the best-known dealers in U.S. stamps entered the PNC market.

In the dead of summer, when the stamp business usually runs from bad to nonexistent, Dale Hendricks, proprietor of Dale Enterprises, Inc., of Emmaus, Pennsylvania, took a gamble. He took out a double-page advertisement in the July 7 issue of *Linn's* to announce his entry into the PNC trade, and the response exceeded even his optimistic expectations. Display ads from other dealers also began to appear in

By filling out Form 3620, collectors may obtain a permit to use precanceled stamps on first-class mail.

the front of *Linn's.*

The Postal Service did its part to help by easing the rules for using precanceled stamps as postage on first-class mail. Once collectors were assured that they would not be stuck with "scrap," they became eager buyers of coil precancel rolls so they could strip out the PNCs. A little-known rule had for many years allowed anyone to get a first-class precancel use permit by filling out Postal Service Form 3620 and being issued a permit number. There is no charge for a first-class permit, but those who use precancels on third-class bulk mail must pay an annual fee. The regulations for first-class precancel usage had been ambiguous, however, so the Postal Service issued a clarification in the July 10, 1986 *Postal Bulletin*:

1. Although precanceled stamps typically are used to pay postage on bulk mailings, they also may be used on single piece or limited size mailings as long as the proper amount of postage is paid. Bulk rate discounts do not apply under such usage.

2. All users of precanceled stamps must have an approved permit, Form 3620, Permit to Use Precanceled Stamps or Envelopes, on file. *

3. Those who do not have permits may purchase precanceled stamps only for philatelic purposes.

4. Mail bearing precanceled stamps may not be deposited in street collection boxes. All such mail must be presented to authorized postal employees at weigh units, window units, or detached mail units of the post office where the mailer's permit is held. When such use is not part of the qualifying bulk mailing, stamps should be canceled with a dated device by the accepting clerk.

198

5. A mailer may use precanceled stamps along with regular stamps on the same mailpiece for full payment of postage. In this event, a permit must also be on file and mail must be presented as in item 4 above.

6. Unless a bulk mailing is being made, it is not necessary to complete a Form 3602 PC, Statement of Mailing With Bulk Rate, simply because a mailer uses precanceled stamps.

7. Precanceled stamps bearing endorsements such as 'Presorted First Class' may be used in any mailing as long as the appropriate amount of total postage is reflected on each piece. **

* Possession of this permit does not require a fee. A fee must be paid only when mailing in bulk at discount rates.

** Unless an item is part of a qualified bulk mailing, the total postage must equal or exceed the First-Class rate, regardless of the type of endorsement.

(The footnotes were added by USPS in 1988.)

PNC literature achieved a new level of professionalism, and reached many thousands of collectors, during 1986. In February, Stephen G. Esrati launched his bimonthly PNC newsletter, *The Plate Number*, which has appeared at approximately two-month intervals ever since. In March, Scott announced that its *1987 Specialized Catalogue of United States Stamps* would henceforth also list and price PNCs by number in mint strips of three. The *Specialized* is issued in November of the year before its title date.

The 1986 edition of the *Catalog of Plate Number Coils* edited by Stephen G. Esrati was issued in time for distribution at AMERIPEX. It is an interesting souvenir of the year in PNCs, since the cover is illustrated with four "stamps" that turned out to be essays — the 5.7¢ Star Route Truck and 7.2¢ Dog Sled designs, both plain and service-inscribed variants, all of which fell victim to the rate roller coaster. The 1986 edition still included the anachronistic mint strip-of-four format, but it added prices for used PNC singles, broadening its usefulness significantly.

The June 1986 issue of *The American Philatelist* published my article, "Collecting U.S. Is Fun Again," about PNCs, the "newest philatelic rage." Editor Bill Welch filled the entire front cover with a full-color enlarged used single of a plate 6 18¢ Flag stamp from my collection. His teaser punned on the stamp's seashore vignette: "The Rising Tide of Plate Number Coils. See Page 540."

Also that summer, California PNC dealer Ed Denson published a 29-page booket, *An Introduction to Collecting Plate Number Coils,* an excellent comprehensive guide for beginners that covers every style of PNC collecting.

Verification of the newfound significance of PNC collecting, if any more was needed, came with the publication of the *Linn's U.S. Stamp Yearbook 1986,* which listed all the plate numbers reported for the Transportation coil series.

Besides literature, PNC collecting also made giant strides as a fellowship of collectors who shared a common interest. Before 1986, only a handful of PNC enthusiasts had met face-to-face with others who shared their passion in other parts of the country, but AMERIPEX changed all that. About 40 PNC collectors and dealers attended a meeting sponsored by the Plate Number Coil Study Group. The slide show on PNCs I had prepared for the American Philatelic Society got its premiere showing at that meeting (except for a preview a couple of weeks earlier for my local stamp club in Jackson, Mississippi, the Jackson Philatelic Society). Before AMERIPEX was over, I showed it again at the meeting of the Errors, Freaks and Oddities Collectors Club. Throughout the show, PNCs were in the air, and a lot of dealers who had paid no attention to PNCs before they arrived in Chicago knew, by the time they left, that this was a big new area of interest.

For PNC collectors and dealers, STAMPSHOW 86 in Washington was an encore performance the following August, but on a smaller scale.

Looking to the future, Scott revealed that plans were under way to publish two PNC albums, one with spaces for a plate strip of each stamp, the other with spaces for a strip of every plate number.

The year closed with a report of the first counterfeit PNCs. Tennessee collector Robert S. Rowe found several bogus plate 6 and 7 18¢ Flag coils in a large mixture, evidently rejects created by someone practicing the forger's art. Rowe was fooled until plate 8, which doesn't exist, also turned up. Under magnification he could identify the fakes. What better proof could one wish to demonstrate the importance of plate number coils?

Chapter 16

The Coil Stamps of 1987

Ten new coil stamps were issued by the Postal Service in 1987, counting tagged and service-inscribed versions separately, making it another relatively slow year. All the new coils included plate numbers. No postal rate changes that affected coil stamps occurred during 1987, but new stamps were still required from the last round of nonprofit rate adjustments of 1986.

Taken as a whole, the new coil issues covered quite a variety of innovations. One was the first postage stamp ever overprinted in red ink at the Bureau of Engraving and Printing. For the first time, pre-canceled stamps appeared on first-day-ceremony programs alongside the tagged collector editions — one overprinted and another with an engraved service inscription. Ceremonies were held for a re-engraved coil stamp and for a test coil, both firsts. One presort rate got its first stamp ever, which also turned out to be the first electronically designed coil stamp, created at the new $2.6 million Design Center at Bureau of Engraving and Printing.

The year 1987 brought some lasts as well as firsts. The last two coil stamp designs moved from the Cottrell press to the B press were issued, one re-engraved, the other using the original master die. The decision by Postal Service officials to produce new stamp designs rather than varieties of old ones meant they had to scrap their plans to issue a planned re-engraved version of the 5¢ Motorcycle stamp. It also sparked a debate in the pages of *Linn's*.

In the August 17 issue, *Linn's* editor-publisher Michael Laurence deplored the new policy, but in the September 14 issue, columnist John M. Hotchner disagreed with Laurence. But even as this discussion was unfolding, unbeknownst to all of us the Postal Service was doing the very thing it said it wouldn't: distributing a new variety of an old stamp.

The last decimal-denominated stamps issued in tagged versions without overprints or service inscriptions were issued in 1987. Those stamps had also been distributed to all Universal Postal Union member countries as samples of U.S. stamps. Henceforth, a single version would serve all the requirements of mailers, collectors and international obligations.

Beginning with the June 25, 1977 news release on the 22¢ William Faulkner commemorative stamp, the Postal Service included PMS numbers of the ink colors assigned to stamps. PMS refers to the Pantone Matching System, a standardized set of blended ink colors introduced in the graphic arts industry in 1963. For postage stamp use, the PMS system is used primarily with single-color intaglio printing and with self-colors in combination printing. Process colors do not have PMS numbers.

Half of the new coil stamps issued in 1987 had not been anticipated at the beginning of the year, and one stamp that was planned — the re-engraved 5¢ Motorcycle — didn't appear. All in all, it was an interesting year for coil collectors.

The 8.5¢ Tow Truck Stamps

The Tow Truck design had originally been announced, early in 1986, as a nonprofit third-class bulk mail coil stamp covering the basic presort rate, to be issued along with a companion embossed envelope of the same denomination picturing the Pilgrim ship *Mayflower*. These items were to replace the precanceled 6¢ Tricycle coil stamp and the 6¢ U.S. frigate *Constitution* ("Old Ironsides") embossed envelope, respectively. The 6¢ items had remained in use, as false franking, as the rate went from 6¢ to 7.4¢ on January 1, 1986, to 8.7¢ on March 9, 1986, and to 8.5¢ on April 20, 1986.

Because production on the basic Tow Truck design had begun before the change in policy declared late in 1985 — that henceforth precancel service inscriptions would be incorporated as design elements — space had not been provided for the "Nonprofit Org." letter-

Every year since 1961, the Wilkinsburg Stamp Club has issued satirical souvenir sheets that poke fun at one or more U.S. stamps issued during the previous year. Coil stamps have been frequent targets of WSC barbs since 1982. The 1987 miniature sheet lampooned the stamps and postal stationery that fell victim to the fluctuating nonprofit rates in 1986.

ing. For this issue, therefore, the Bureau of Engraving and Printing used a 468-subject flexographic plate to overprint the precancel inscription in red ink, but without the parallel lines previously used in precancel overprints. The Bureau had used red overprints in the past on revenue stamps, but this was the first time on a postage stamp.

A March 19, 1986 news release gave 8.7¢ as the denomination of the Tow Truck stamp and Mayflower envelope, but gave no issue date or city. On May 13, the denomination was changed to 8.5¢. The envelope was scheduled for release in Plymouth, Massachusetts, on July 17, and the stamp in Indianapolis, Indiana, on October 5. A June 4 news release canceled that information, saying these items had been "deferred indefinitely." The delay, as well as the change in denomination, was caused by the fluctuating "revenue foregone" appropriation, and the uncertainty about that subsidy's future. By the end of Fiscal Year 1986 (the last Friday in September), it was clear that rates would be stable through the following fiscal year, so the embossed envelope was rescheduled for release on December 4, 1986, and the 8.5¢ Tow Truck coil as the first stamp issued in the new year.

The first-day ceremony for the 8.5¢ Tow Truck stamp was held on January 24, 1987, at the ARIPEX '87 philatelic exhibition in Tucson, Arizona. For the first time, the ceremony program included both the tagged collector edition of the stamp and the precanceled edition intended for use by bulk mailers. Also for the first time, collectors were invited to frank first-day covers with precancels, on which the precancels would count as postage.

The stamps depict a 1920s tow truck with a hand-operated crane at

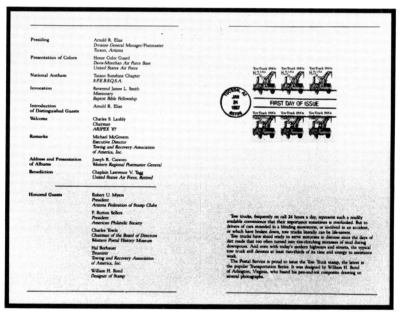

This was the first time a first-day ceremony program included both tagged and precanceled versions of a stamp.

the rear. They were printed in dark gray ink on the intaglio B press, with single plate numbers spaced at 52-stamp intervals. The tagged philatelic editions were issued in coils of 500. The untagged precancels with the overprinted red inscription were issued in coils of 500 and

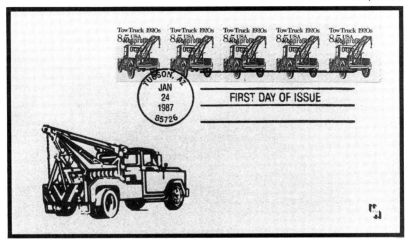

The Postal Service invited stamp collectors to submit first-day covers franked with precancels only for the first time. This plate 1 example was prepared by H & H Stamps and Coins.

3,000. Sleeve 1 was used to print both varieties. It is the only number on first-day covers. Number 2 appeared later, only on precancels.

The collector edition was more convenient to use as postage than most decimal-denominated tagged coil stamps, because a pair equaled 17¢ in face value, exactly the added-ounce first-class letter rate.

The 8.5¢ nonprofit rate continued through April 2, 1988. On April 3, the rate dropped to 8.4¢. Mailers were authorized to use the 8.5¢ Tow Truck precancels until October 9 as false franking, with the overpayment refunded by the Postal Service. By then a stamp in the new denomination was available. The precanceled 8.5¢ Tow Truck coil stamps were withdrawn from philatelic sale on October 31, 1988, and the tagged counterparts two months later, on December 31, 1988.

This plate 1 cover is a typical use of the basic nonprofit-rate 8.5¢ Tow Truck coil stamp, implicity dated by the political message as an example of true franking usage.

The 7.1¢ Tractor Stamps

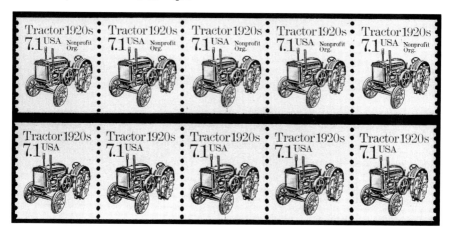

If the stamps to meet the nonprofit bulk rate presorted to five ZIP code digits had been issued on schedule, they would have had a Dog Sled design and been issued in Anchorage. Only after a series of delays was that design taken for the 17¢ first-class added-ounce rate.

The 7.2¢ Dog Sled stamp was first announced in a March 19, 1986 news release. The change to 7.1¢ was noted on April 21, and June 17 was mentioned as the possible issue date. Then a May 13, 1986 news release said the 7.1¢ Dog Sled stamp would be issued on September 25, but that announcement was nullified in a June 4 release saying it had been "deferred indefinitely." Shortly after that, the Dog Sled design was diverted to the 17¢ denomination. Meanwhile, the old 4.9¢ Buckboard precancels remained in service as false franking for the 6.3¢ rate from January 1 to March 8; for the 7.2¢ rate from March to April 19; and for the 7.1¢ rate beginning April 20, 1986.

By the close of Fiscal Year 1986, in late September, it was clear that the 7.1¢ rate would be stable through the next fiscal year, so a stamp in that denomination was rescheduled. Since the Dog Sled design had

Two different tractors were considered as subjects for Transportation coil stamp designs. This essay, showing a 1918 Waterloo Boy Model N tractor, wasn't adopted because the drawing was too detailed for a stamp.

been appropriated for a different denomination, the design showing a 1920s John Deere tractor was assigned to the nonprofit rate.

Two different B press printing sleeves, both numbered 1, were used to print the two versions of the 7.1¢ Tractor coil stamp. The plain, tagged version, printed in dark red ink only,was processed into coils of 500 for philatelic sales. The untagged, service-inscribed version was printed in two colors by the Giori system from a single intaglio printing sleeve and processed into coils of 500 and 3,000. The basic design engraved portion received dark red ink from one inking-in roller, while the service inscription "Nonprofit Org." engraved letters received black ink from a second inking-in roller.

Both sleeve 1 7.1¢ Tractor coils, tagged and service-inscribed, exist on first-day covers. Coils in both versions have single sleeve numbers spaced at 52-stamp intervals.

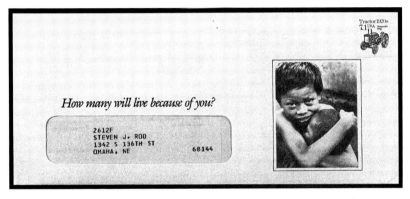

This U.N. Children's Fund mailing franked with a sleeve 1 single of the service-inscribed 7.1¢ Tractor stamp is a typical usage. It contained a UNICEF fund appeal.

Both stamps were issued in Sarasota, Florida, on February 6, 1987, at a ceremony at the SARAPEX 87 stamp show. Both versions of the stamp were included on the first-day-ceremony program, the second time a stamp considered a precancel by the Postal Service got such treatment, and the first with an engraved "precancel" inscription.

The 7.1¢ nonprofit rate for the five-digit presort lasted almost two years. On April 3, 1988, the rate rose to 7.6¢. The Postal Service authorized mailers to continue using the 7.1¢ Tractor stamps to cover the new rate as false franking, with the balance due paid at the time of mailing, until October 9, 1988. By then a 7.6¢ stamp was available.

In an interesting coincidence, a new 7.1¢ nonprofit bulk rate went into effect on the very day that the old rate rose to 7.6¢, for ZIP+4-addressed mail presorted to five digits. In 1989, a third version of the 7.1¢ Tractor coil stamp was issued, with a new service inscription, "Nonprofit 5-Digit ZIP+4." An unprecedented third sleeve numbered 1 was used for the basic design. That stamp is described on Page 264.

The first two 7.1¢ Tractor coil stamps, the plain tagged version and the "Nonprofit Org." service-inscribed version, were withdrawn from philatelic sale by the Postal Service on February 28, 1989. The third version, service-inscribed "Nonprofit 5-Digit ZIP+4," was not issued until May 26, 1989.

The Re-engraved 2¢ Locomotive Stamp

The re-engraved 2¢ Locomotive coil stamp was the first design previously printed on the Cottrell press and now, in revised form, printed on the intaglio B press, to be given a full-dress formal first-day treatment, complete with a ceremony and a program. That wasn't supposed to be, but the Postal Service had trumpeted its "commitment to the collecting community" in December by promising to hold first-day ceremonies at five stamp shows during the first half of 1987.

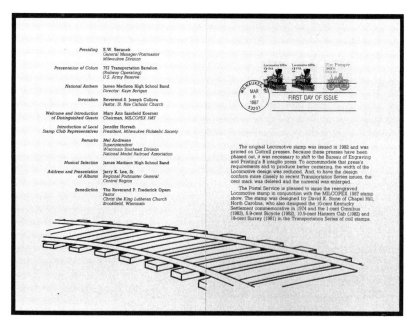

This first-day ceremony program, bearing a plate 1 pair of the re-engraved 2¢ Locomotive coil stamps, is the first such program ever created for a re-engraved stamp. According to a Postal Service spokesman, it will probably be the last.

An unintended first-day sale of the re-engraved 2¢ Locomotive coil, at the New York International Stamp Exposition, gave showgoers the opportunity to get a PNC on a cover with the show's Big Apple pictorial cancel on the very day the stamp was being issued in Milwaukee.

When the item scheduled to be released at MILCOPEX 87 in Milwaukee, the 14¢ Flag postal card, had its issue date postponed until July, a stand-in was required. The only new stamp not previously committed was the re-engraved 2¢ Locomotive coil.

So on March 6, 1987, the re-engraved 2¢ Locomotive was issued with the required fanfare in Milwaukee. However, because of the way the Postal Service routinely handles such stamps in its distribution system, it was also inadvertently placed on sale that same day in New York, at the New York International Stamp Exposition. For philatelic purposes, the Postal Service had been pressured into acknowledging that re-engraved stamps are different issues from the originals, but for inventory, accounting, filling orders and shipping, they are considered to be the same product.

The new design of the 2¢ Locomotive followed the same pattern as the re-engraved 1¢ Omnibus coil stamp issued in 1986. Both versions of the 2¢ Locomotive are printed in black ink. The re-engraved vignette is slightly smaller than the original Cottrell press stamp issued in 1982. The B press stamps, with their shallower engraving and more effective wiping, seem to have darker images and whiter paper. The inscription was changed from "USA 2¢" on the original to "2 USA"

The differences are easy to spot on these two plate number singles. The inscription on the re-engraved version, on the left, reads "2 USA." The original reads "USA 2c."

209

on the re-engraved stamp, with the 2 now doubled in size. Single sleeve numbers appear at 52-stamps intervals without joint lines. The Cottrell press 2¢ Locomotive, described on Page 92, has two alternating plate numbers, and joint lines, alternating at 24-stamp intervals. As this is written, only sleeve 1 has appeared on coils of the re-engraved stamp, and therefore that is the only PNC found on first-day covers. The re-engraved stamps have block tagging, in contrast to the overall tagging of the original.

The initial order for the re-engraved stamp was limited to coils of 3,000, but later, as the supplies of Cottrell press 2¢ Locomotives were depleted in smaller rolls as well, the re-engraved stamp was also processed into coils of 500. In 1989, the re-engraved 2¢ Locomotive stamps became the first to be processed into coils of 10,000, which were ordered by Reader's Digest Books to use in a sweepstakes promotional mailing.

Because no stamps printed from Cottrell press plate number 1 ever reached collectors, the use of sleeve 1 to print the re-engraved version on the B press did not duplicate an existing number, unlike all the other revised Transportation series issues.

The big user of 2¢ Locomotive coil stamps in both versions, as was true of tagged 4¢ Stagecoach coils, was Disabled American Veterans. During the 22¢ letter-rate era, DAV franked its return envelopes with five 4¢ Stagecoach stamps and a single 2¢ Locomotive. When the rates increased in 1988, there wasn't much call for 2¢ Locomotives, either as changemakers or makeup postage. The 1¢ and 3¢ stamps fulfilled those requirements. As I write, the re-engraved 2¢ Locomotive is still on sale, and its day may yet come.

The 10¢ Canal Boat Stamps

On April 11, 1987, a first-day ceremony was held for the 10¢ Canal Boat stamp at the ALPEX stamp show in Buffalo, New York. The show was sponsored by the Plewacki Post Stamp Society of American Legion Post Number 799. Buffalo, where the Erie Canal began, was chosen by the Postal Service for its historical tie to the stamp's subject. The first-day ceremony was held in the Marine Midland Bank auditorium.

The Erie Canal linked Albany on the Hudson River with Buffalo on Lake Erie, for more than 60 years providing efficient transportation

The only 10¢ rate covered by the 10¢ Canal Boat stamp was the surcharge for nonstandard-size first-class mail weighing one ounce or less. This cover, franked with a sleeve 1 example of the Canal Boat stamp, shows the correct usage on the first day of the 25¢ first-class letter rate.

connecting the Midwest cities on the Great Lakes to New York City at the mouth of the Hudson. The 1880s boat shown on the stamp, drawn by horses, mules or donkeys, operated during the late period of the canal's history.

The 10¢ Canal Boat stamp was printed in blue ink on the intaglio B press, with a single sleeve number spaced at 52-stamp intervals. At this writing, sleeve 1, the only number on first-day covers of this stamp, is the only PNC that has appeared. With this issue the Postal Service adopted a policy of issuing tagged collector editions in coils of 100, in addition to the coils of 3,000 for commercial users or vending machine sales (of which there were few for this issue).

The round 10¢ denomination was convenient for making up odd postage amounts, especially for parcels and mail requiring special services for which there was no single stamp. In addition, there actually was a 10¢ rate, the surcharge for nonstandard-size first-class and third-class letters and postcards weighing one ounce or less.

Nonstandard size is defined as a letter or card exceeding 11½ inches in length or 6⅛ inches in height or ¼ inch in thickness. The surcharge for such mail is not well-known, even by postal employees, so underpaid pieces franked at the regular first-class rate usually are delivered without the 10¢ postage due being assessed. It is a relatively recent innovation. As long as mail was mainly sorted by hand, the actual dimensions of a letter didn't matter much. But mechanized, and later automated, mail processing depended on near uniformity of the items being processed, so it did cost more to process an item that the machine couldn't handle.

Prior to 1981, the nonstandard surcharge was 7¢. In 1981 it rose to 9¢, and on February 17, 1985, to 10¢. It remained 10¢ after the 1988 rate changes. In the future, this may be one of the more difficult usages to collect.

The 22¢ Flag Over Capitol Test Coil Stamp

Ever since the 1960s, nearly all United States postage stamps and postal stationery, precancels excepted, have been issued with luminescent tagging applied over the printed image. It is the phosphors of the taggant, glowing brightly when illuminated under shortwave ultraviolet light, that the processing facer-canceler "sees." It then "faces" the envelope or card so that the address can be read properly, and cancels the stamp. Under ordinary light in the visible spectrum, the tagging phosphors are nearly invisible. Since the very first tagged stamps were tested in Dayton, Ohio, in 1963, the phosphors have been applied in a lacquer suspension applied on press by a roller or letterpress plate.

The lacquer-suspension method of tagging stamps has a number of problems. In printing, it tends to limit the speed of the presses, and takes space that could be used to print another ink. In processing, the abrasive qualities of the calcium silicate and zinc orthosilicate phosphors cause slitting knives and perforating pins to dull. Esthetically, the lacquer tends to dull the brightness of ink images, giving a less pleasing appearance than intended.

All those drawbacks have been regarded as tolerable by the Postal Service, but one other problem has not. Because of the lacquer, canceling inks do not penetrate as they should, making it relatively easy to remove the cancels from many used stamps. The Postal Service estimates it loses around $200 million in revenue annually from the illegal reuse of "washed" stamps.

One possible solution was to impregnate the paper itself with tagging phosphors during its manufacture. To test the feasibility of this approach, phosphor-impregnated paper was manufactured to Postal Service specifications by Harrison and Sons Ltd. of England. Twenty million 22¢ Flag Over Capitol coil stamps, the most widely used

212

prime-rate adhesives, were ordered printed on the paper, which the Postal Service calls "prephosphored." A new C press sleeve was manufactured, with the letter T in the bottom margin of each stamp, so that the test stamps could be easily distinguished from the regular ones. Since the design had been altered, number 1 was assigned to that sleeve, so the numbered stamps, which occur at 48-stamp intervals, read "T1."

Regular C press sleeves are 20 rows across, 960 subjects in all. Their products are ordinarily processed into coils of 100 only, on the Goebel coiling equipment. In this case, however, the Postal Service required coils of 3,000 for the actual test, so the sleeve was made with 18 rows across, 864 subjects total. The 18-across format allowed processing on the Huck coiling equipment into the larger rolls.

Once having decided to proceed with the experiment, the Postal Service decided to give the test coils the full philatelic treatment. The first-day ceremony was held at the NOJEX philatelic exhibition in Secaucus, New Jersey, on May 23, 1987, the first time any test stamp had been given an official first day of issue, a ceremony and a ceremony program. Coils for collectors were sold in blister-pack rolls of 100, just as the ordinary coils of 100 Flag stamps are sold. The test stamps appear whiter than the regular Flag stamps, and their colors are much brighter. The regular 22¢ Flag coil, issued in 1985, is described on Page 137.

The test stamps also used a proprietary gum called Kool Jet, previously used only on coils of 100. The Postal Service wanted to know if the Kool Jet gum would work equally well on coils of 3,000, in the high-speed stamp-affixing machines used by bulk mailers.

Of the 20 million ordered, about 100,000 were used in test mailings. Within a month after the issue date, the test had been deemed a success, and by the end of the year the Postal Service was making plans to issue other stamps on phosphored paper.

The 22¢ Flag test coils were withdrawn from philatelic sale on February 28, 1990, but the Postal Service reported in January 1989 that 204,000 are stored in its vaults for possible future reissue.

The Revised 12¢ Stanley Steamer Stamp

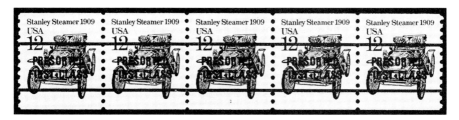

In July 1987, the Postal Service announced that no more definitive stamp varieties would be created. If new stamps were needed in a particular denomination, a new design would be issued, rather than moving the old design to a new press.

But on Saturday, August 29, I received the September-October issue of the USPS *Philatelic Catalog* in the mail. Naturally I always turn to the coil listings first, mainly to see which stamps are being withdrawn from sale.

This time there was a big surprise — a B press version of the 12¢ Stanley Steamer Steamer precancel. At first I thought this was a mistake. But when I turned to the coil listings by press at the back of the catalog, the new stamp was there too.

I called Charles Yeager at his office. The stamp was news to him, but he promised to investigate and let me know as soon as the post office opened Monday morning. I also called *Linn's* editor-publisher Michael Laurence, figuring that he might have received some advance notice. But he hadn't heard of it either.

On Monday morning I called the Stamp Information Branch in Washington, but everyone there seemed surprised to learn of the stamp's existence. Robert Brown, head of philatelic sales, hadn't known of it either.

A new stamp was coming out, and the people in charge didn't know anything about it.

Swiftly they circled the wagons. Frank Thomas at Stamp Information told me that it was policy not to discuss, in advance, when a Cottrell press stamp was being moved to the B press, unless it was being re-engraved. He remained unmoved when I pointed out that the Postal Service had forewarned the press about the 8.3¢ Ambulance, a similar stamp, in an August 19, 1986 news release.

And when I asked what had happened to the policy of not creating varieties, announced just a month earlier, Thomas said, "We don't consider them new varieties unless they're re-engraved."

Once again he was contradicting the precedent set by his philatelic marketing colleagues when they listed the B press 8.3¢ precancel as a new stamp in their Commemorative Stamp Club album.

Robert Brown said there would be no possibility of getting first-day cancellations for the revised issue, even if the issue date were known. He added, "As soon as I hang up from talking to you, I'm going to get Cindy (Tackett) on the phone and make sure there won't be any backdated cancels on these."

Wayne Anmuth of the Postal Service gave me a lecture on why I should not report news that makes the Postal Service look bad, and got angry when I mentioned the First Amendment. Assistant Postmaster General Gordon Morison wasn't taking calls that day.

When the new 12¢ precancels reached the philatelic counter at L'Enfant Plaza on September 3, Charles Yeager made up a few covers. So did Wayne Anmuth. They are so far the earliest documented usage of the stamp. Backdated covers canceled with September 3, 1987, Washington, D.C., postmarks were prepared by cachetmaker Alan

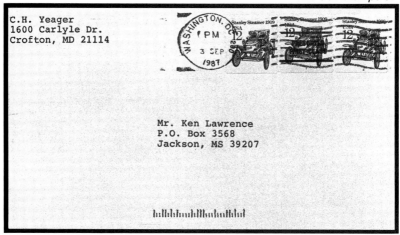

C.H. Yeager
1600 Carlyle Dr.
Crofton, MD 21114

Mr. Ken Lawrence
P.O. Box 3568
Jackson, MS 39207

Linn's *Washington correspondent Charles Yeager mailed this cover on September 3, 1987, the first day the revised 12¢ Stanley Steamer precancels were placed on philatelic sale, but more than two months after they had first been shipped to bulk mailers. The cover has a plate 1 single of the B press stamp and a plate 2 single of the tagged Cottrell version of the stamp issued in 1985.*

Tossman. Much later, House of Farnam covers appeared on the market with September 3 L'Enfant Plaza Philatelic Center cancels.

The possibility of earlier dated commercial covers exists. B press 12¢ Stanley Steamer precancels were shipped to Pennsylvania in June, and to California and Missouri in July.

Sleeve 1 of the 12¢ Stanley Steamer was assigned on April 29, 1987, and went to press on the intaglio B press on May 12. Only precancels were printed from this sleeve, with the blue ink design and the black ink PRESORTED FIRST-CLASS overprint matching the Cottrell press version described on Page 142, except for the characteristic subtle differences between similar stamps printed on those two presses.

The Cottrell press plates and the B press sleeve were all manufactured from the same master die. Its single sleeve number repeats at 52-stamp intervals without joint lines. The two Cottrell press plate numbers alternate at 24-stamp intervals, with joint lines, throughout the coil. The shallower engraving on the B press sleeve, and superior wiping on that press, give an impression of greater contrast than the Cottrell version: a darker image and whiter paper. The B press image is a fraction of a millimeter narrower than the original. The revised stamp was processed into coils of 3,000 only, the original into coils of 500 and 3,000.

This was the third time that a Cottrell press coil stamp had been moved to the intaglio B press without the necessity of re-engraving. (Only stamps that had measured more than .73 inches in their originals had to be re-engraved to meet the smaller subject-size standards.) The first, the 8.3¢ Ambulance precancel, received its own Scott catalog number different from the Cottrell press original. The revised 14¢ Iceboat did not. The B press 12¢ Stanley Steamer precancel got the same treatment as the 14¢ Iceboat. The only mention is in the *Specialized Catalogue of United States Stamps*, a line under the original listing noting the existence of a "P# strip of 3, no line, P#1."

Only sleeve 1 was needed. The 12¢ postcard first-class 5-digit presort rate, in effect since November 1, 1981, had originally been covered by two different precanceled versions of the 12¢ Torch coil stamp, described on Page 37. When supplies of these stamps were depleted in 1985, the original 12¢ Stanley Steamer printed on the Cottrell press was issued. When those ran low, the B press version was issued. The rate increased to 13¢ on April 3, 1988. The Postal Service authorized mailers to continue using the precanceled 12¢ Stanley Steamer stamps as false franking, with the balance paid at the time of mailing, until October 9. Shortly after that, a stamp to cover the 13¢ rate was issued. All the 12¢ Stanley Steamer stamps were withdrawn from philatelic sale on February 28, 1989.

The 17.5¢ Racing Car Stamps

Three new Transportation series coil stamps were issued on September 25, 1987, at a first-day ceremony at the INDYPEX stamp show in Indianapolis, Indiana: two versions of the 17.5¢ Racing Car stamp and the 5¢ Milk Wagon stamp. Only the tagged version of the 17.5¢ Racing Car appears with the 5¢ Milk Wagon stamps on the first-day ceremony program, but all three stamps were available at the show. Collectors who wished to make first-day covers using the service-inscribed 17.5¢ stamps could do so, although all coils of that stamp at the show were slit high, and all had cut sleeve numbers.

Both versions of the 17.5¢ stamp were printed from number 1

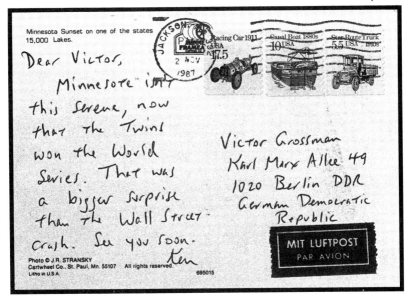

No real rates exist for tagged, decimal-denominated coil stamps. The three plate 1 single stamps used on this postcard to Germany combined to total exactly 33¢, the international airmail postcard rate in 1987.

sleeves, the only ones ever used, but they were different sleeves. The version printed for bulk mailers was service-inscribed "ZIP+4 Presort" in red ink, in addition to the vignette and main inscription, common to both stamps, printed in purple ink. The two-color untagged service-inscribed stamp was printed from a single intaglio sleeve on the B press and processed into coils of 500 and 3,000. The Postal Service regards the service inscription as a precancel.

The single-color purple tagged version without the service inscription was issued for collectors. There was no postal need for it. This was to be the last time that the Postal Service would issue a tagged, decimal-denominated collector stamp. Beginning in 1988, only un-

This essay for a 17.5¢ Transportation coil stamp showing a 1903 Winton Bullet racing car lost out to one showing the 1911 Marmon Wasp, winner of the first Indianapolis 500 auto race.

217

The photograph of the 17.5¢ Racing Car stamp released in advance to the news media made it appear that the stamp had been printed by the gravure process. It turned out that the picture had been made from artwork before the stamp's die had been engraved.

tagged service-inscribed editions intended for actual bulk-mail use were issued. This final purely philatelic stamp was sold only in coils of 100, making it the first decimal stamp processed into 100-stamp coils.

The stamp's design shows the 1911 Marmon Wasp that won the first Indianapolis 500 auto race. An earlier racing car, the 1903 Winton Bullet, was also worked into a design for a 17.5¢ stamp, but ultimately was rejected. The new stamp was the first coil to be designed at the Bureau of Engraving and Printing's new $2.6 million Design Center, which allows the artists to manipulate their artwork by computer

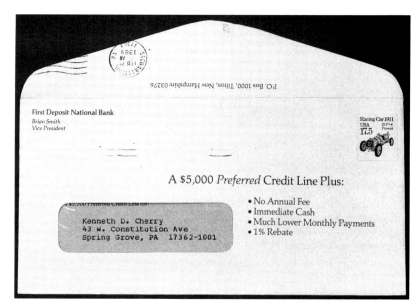

This is an exceptionally nice cover showing proper use of the service-inscribed 17.5¢ Racing Car stamp, because the dated machine cancel on the back flap, February 28, 1988, shows that it was used when 17.5¢ was the ZIP+4 presort first-class rate.

218

— changing colors, image sizes, location and shapes — using minutes to do tasks that formerly took hours, days and weeks, as well as to store design data, produce negatives for offset and gravure printing, and engrave gravure printing cylinders. That may account for the foul-up in which the design of the 17.5¢ stamp released to the press made it appear that the stamp had been printed by the gravure process instead of line-engraved intaglio. The photo had actually been made from an early stage of the design process, before the stamp's die had been engraved.

The untagged service-inscribed 17.5¢ Racing Car coil stamp prepaid quantity first-class mail addressed to nine-digit ZIP codes and presorted to five digits, a rate tier that had not previously had its own stamp. It was not as widely used as other quantity- and bulk-mail rates, so properly used examples of this stamp on cover can be difficult to collect.

The Postal Service had announced in July 1985 that it would release a 17.5¢ coil stamp in October of that year. The two-year postponement meant that when the stamp finally did appear, its rate had only another six months of use before the next round of increases and decreases. On April 3, 1988, the rate increased to 20.5¢. The Postal Service authorized use of the 17.5¢ stamps as false franking for the new rate until October 9. By then a stamp in the new denomination had been issued. At this writing in January 1990, both tagged and service-inscribed 17.5¢ Racing Car coil stamps are still on philatelic sale. The tagged version exists imperforate.

The 5¢ Milk Wagon Stamp

It is pretty obvious why the 17.5¢ Racing Car coil stamps were issued at INDYPEX in Indianapolis, but it isn't so evident why the 5¢ Milk Wagon stamp was issued at the same ceremony on September 25, 1987. The most logical answer is this: September 25 was the very last day of Fiscal Year 1987. By issuing the stamp on that date and not a day later, the cost and selling price of 23.8 million 5¢ Milk Wagon stamps was counted in the FY 1987 budget, rather than the FY 1988 budget, which everyone knew would bring a flood of rate-change stamps. Fewer than half that many were shipped in FY 1988.

The replacement for the 5¢ Motorcycle coil stamp, a Cottrell press issue, had been promised for more than a year. In the summer of 1986, the Postal Service announced that a re-engraved edition would be issued, and in the fall it said that the 5¢ Motorcycle had been re-engraved and was awaiting release. For whatever reason, it wasn't. In December, USPS reversed itself. Spokesman Joe Brockert of the Stamps Division said, "Based on our needs, we anticipate ordering the re-engraving of only the 2¢ Locomotive within the next 12 months. It may be the last of the re-engraved issues." That is exactly what happened.

But evidently some time during these 12 months, Postal Service officials decided they needed more 5¢ coil stamps after all. By the time that decision was announced in July, the policy on issuing re-engraved stamps had changed. Donald M. McDowell, general manager of the USPS Stamps Division, told *Linn's* Washington correspondent Charles Yeager, "We started off believing that, based on the initial contacts we had with collectors, they preferred a variety to a new issue. We started doing varieties, and then collectors decided they would rather have new issues, so we are now giving them new issues."

Ever since then, I have tried without success to find a single collector who was consulted by USPS, and who expressed that opinion. I haven't found one, in two years of asking. (John Hotchner published that opinion in his *Linn's* "U.S. Notes" column, but I don't think he has a lot of supporters on this issue.) My guess is that McDowell and others misinterpreted the anger collectors expressed that only certain well-connected individuals had been able to make first-day covers of the varieties, while the average collector had been denied that chance. They weren't angry that B press varieties of Cottrell press stamps were being created, but that the Postal Service method of issuing them was insensitive and inconsistent.

Whatever the validity of that analysis may be, the 5¢ stamp depicting a turn-of-the-century horse-drawn milk wagon was issued in coils of 100 and 3,000, printed in gray ink on the intaglio B press, with single sleeve numbers spaced at 52-stamp intervals without joint lines. Sleeve 1, the number found on first-day covers, is the only number used by the time of this writing in January 1990. The stamps have been used mostly as changemakers in vending machines since the 1988 rate changes, to go with 20¢ added-ounce coils for an even quarter apiece.

Chapter 17

PNCs Come of Age

In 1987, it was no longer possible for serious collectors of modern United States stamps to ignore plate number coils.

In February, Scott released its two long-awaited PNC albums. Both were designed to hold strips of three. The basic PNC pages have spaces for one plate strip of each stamp, tagged and precanceled, without reference to specific plate numbers. These were issued without a binder, but fit easily into a Scott National album. The comprehensive album includes a binder and pages with individual spaces for all reported PNCs, both tagged and precanceled.

Many collectors were unhappy that the Scott album could only accommodate strips of three. Despite that complaint, Scott quickly sold out all 3,500 albums it had printed. When a second edition was published, the pages that had shown two rows of strips side by side in the original edition had been redesigned as single-row pages. In that way, although the layout still shows strips of three, the entire album will accommodate strips of five.

At CAPEX 87, the international stamp exhibition in Toronto in June, Scott's director of marketing, Stuart Morrissey, announced that the company was also considering publishing a PNC singles album.

This was also the year that collectors began entering PNC exhibits in competition. At NAPEX, in Arlington, Virginia, at the end of May, Wayne Anmuth's exhibit, "Plate Number Coils Canceled First Day of Issue and on General Mail," was awarded a silver-bronze medal. At the Omaha Stamp Show in September, Darrell Ertzberger's entry, "Cottrell Press Issues of the Transportation Coil Series," which included PNC material, won a gold. In addition, Ertzberger's exhibit received the American Philatelic Society post-1945 award and the American Association of Philatelic Exhibitors award for presentation.

The July 13, 1987, issue of *Linn's* inaugurated in its "Trends of Stamp Values column, a new feature, which has since then appeared every six months. This feature in "Trends" gives current market prices for every plate number coil as a mint strip of five, mint strip of three and used single.

APS STAMPSHOW 87 was held in Boston at the end of August. Scott chose that opportunity to issue its pocket-size booklet, *Checklist of Plate Number Coils.* All 1,000 copies Scott brought to the show sold out there. The format is identical to Scott's U.S. checklist, with five columns of boxes after each listing, so collectors can use one row to keep track of each different collection they are assembling: mint strips of five, strips of three, used singles, PNC first-day covers, varieties and so forth.

Once again, about 40 colletors attended the PNC Study Group meeting at STAMPSHOW, with Steve Esrati presiding. We still didn't manage the chemistry to launch an open membership organization of PNC collectors (the study group is closed, limited to 20 or 21 people designated by Esrati), but a lot of interest was expressed, and Michigan collector Gene Trinks accepted responsibility for coordinating its formation.

STAMPSHOW week was the time dealer William S. Langs chose to place a full-page three-color advertisement in *Linn's* offering to pay $1,000 for a mint plate 6 strip of the 18¢ Flag coil stamp in extra-fine condition. With that backdrop, a mint strip with very-fine centering sold at the Steve Ivy STAMPSHOW auction for $1,050 plus a 10-percent buyer's premium. Even the 1987 edition of Esrati's *Catalog of Plate Number Coils,* issued just a few months earlier, had not anticipated such a leap. Esrati had priced that key strip at $650. Otherwise, though, the Esrati catalog reflected the emerging consensus, as listings for strips of four were dropped.

With the surging popularity of PNCs reaching exalted heights undreamed of just a couple of years earlier, some previous naysayers were converted to the PNC cause. In his May 11, 1987 *Linn's* "U.S. Notes" column, John M. Hotchner confessed,

"I have to tell you that I was not enthusiastic about the proposal to add plate numbers to coil stamps. I figured it would cost the collector...

"Every time I thought of this, I'd have a good laugh — until one day, not so long ago, I looked up to find that I'd joined the quest for numbers.

"I'm not sure how it happened. I was just throwing copies into a box. Then suddenly I wanted to fill in spaces.

"So three cheers for USPS! I've been converted. I'm collecting more of these items, and I like it."

The year's one sour note was struck when a post office notified a stamp dealer that if he was a holder of a permit to use precanceled stamps, he was forbidden to sell precanceled stamps. The regulation was anachronistic, dating to the era when only permit holders could purchase precancels from the post office. In effect, the Business Requirements Division of the USPS Office of Classification and Rate

Adjustment had nullified the progress that had been achieved a year earlier, when the Postal Service had eased the rules on precancel use so that collectors and dealers could use their extra precancels as postage while they built their collections and inventories. The issue festered for months before it was finally resolved, and during that time was more significant for confusing an issue that everyone thought had been settled than for any serious threats to dealers, collectors or precancel users.

The year ended with collectors well aware that 1988 would bring wholesale rate changes and the need for billions of new stamps to meet them, with the prospect for an outpouring of new coil issues comparable to the record level of 1985. The difference was that this time there were thousands more serious PNC collectors, representing a broad cross-section of mainstream U.S. philately.

Chapter 18

The Coil Stamps of 1988

Every one of the 20 new coil stamps issued in 1988 was required by the across-the-board rate increases and decreases that went into effect on April 3, with the possible exception of the 25¢ Honeybee, the most hotly collected of the entire batch. One could argue that the Honeybee stamp wasn't needed in addition to the 25¢ Flag Over Yosemite and 25¢ Bread Wagon prime rate stamps, but it would be difficult to argue that coil collectors were being gouged by the Postal Service.

The opposite was true. The reason the 20-stamp 1988 coil roster didn't exceed the 24-stamp record year for coils in 1985 was only because the Postal Service stopped issuing tagged collector editions in the same design as the untagged service-inscribed and precanceled decimal-denominated stamps issued for quantity and bulk mail. Had the old policy been followed, there would have been 29 new coil stamps issued in 1988, and a new record.

In an interview at USPS headquarters in Washington, Dickey Rustin and Frank Thomas of the Stamp Support Branch (formerly called the Stamp Information Branch) explained the change. Rustin said, "All of us involved — Gordon Morison, Don McDowell, Pete Davidson, and the rest of us — asked what was the purpose of the second version. It was limited to collector use, but it doubled the cost for collectors. It wasn't needed." Thomas added, "We changed the first-day cancel policy. Formerly we had needed tagged stamps for that."

The change did not take place soon enough to boost first-day covers to their previous level of popularity. The numbers of FDCs canceled had always fluctuated from issue to issue, but for the first year, the total for each Transportation coil issue was in the neighborhood of 200,000 or more. By mid-1982 and into 1983, significantly fewer were made, the low point being the 77,900 of the 3¢ Handcar. However, if that figure does not include the Artcraft and Fleetwood covers canceled by their manufacturers with official Postal Service encouragement, it may not be anywhere near the real quantity for that issue.

224

The high point for a Transportation coil was reached in 1985, with 327,710 FDCs of the 14¢ Iceboat. The 18¢ George Washington Monument coil, also issued in 1985, holds the record for a modern coil with 376,238 canceled. All these numbers must be regarded as approximate despite their six-figure specificity. After 1985, the FDC numbers sagged, and in 1988 they ranged from about 118,000 to 155,000, with the 3¢ Conestoga Wagon being the most popular.

Another new coil stamp policy was announced in the summer of 1988. To reduce the overall percentage of waste, the Bureau of Engraving and Printing would allow paper splices to be processed into finished coils of stamps. In the past they had been excised. Not until January 1990 did the Postal Service reveal that the policy on splices had to change in order to accommodate mailers who wished to purchase their stamps in coils of 10,000.

Some earlier coil stamps took on new duties in 1988. Most important among these was the 25¢ Bread Wagon, issued in 1986 as a utility, round denomination vending machine stamp needed only in coils of 3,000 printed on the intaglio B press. After the April 3 rate increase, it became the principal denominated prime-rate coil stamp for a period of time. This directly affected PNC collectors. For two years only one sleeve number existed, but suddenly there were four more, three of them in a new format from a different press — coils of 100 printed on the intaglio C press or the intaglio section of the D press.

Other old coils with new jobs were the 20¢ Flag Over Supreme Court, 20¢ Fire Pumper, and 20¢ Official stamps. All three had been prime-rate stamps in the 1981 to 1985 era and had been withdrawn after their day had passed. Now they were dusted off and placed back on sale, given the more modest task of meeting the added-ounce letter rate. The Postal Service counted this a huge success in its Philatelic and Retail Services annual report. "By storing 357 million 20¢ coil stamps when the prime rate became 22¢, we had them available when 20¢ became the second-ounce rate in 1988, and avoided $500,000 in new costs."

But consternation exploded among PNC collectors and dealers when previously rare plate numbers of the 20¢ Fire Pumper, numbers 12 and 14, appeared in quantity, causing prices to plummet. The 20¢ Official PNC strips also declined considerably.

This was not the first such shock to hit the PNC market, but previous jolts had come before PNCs had achieved such broad popularity and acceptance. Many collectors and accumulators suddenly grew cautious. What else might be in the Postal Service's vaults? Is there a chance that numbers now believed to be worth a thousand dollars or more are buried in a Kansas City cave, awaiting future distribution if the postcard rate becomes 18¢? These possibilities are among the hazards of collecting modern definitive stamps, but their realization caused an instant sobering in the PNC market, and prices that had been rising steadily leveled off sharply, or even declined.

In his May 16, 1988 "Editor's Choice" column, *Linn's* editor-publisher Michael Laurence pressured the Postal Service to disclose exactly which stamps were being held for future contingencies and in what quantities. Assistant Postmaster General Gordon Morison promised the report would be distributed in the fall, but at the end of the year it had not appeared. What actually happened was that the inventory revealed huge stockpiles of stamps that had taken on significant value in the philatelic aftermarket, especially among coils. Were they to be released as thoughtlessly as the 20¢ Fire Pumpers, they might deal a fatal blow to the most thriving area of U.S. stamp collecting. Postal Service officials have refused to say exactly which stamps were involved, but they immediately ordered the destruction of millions of stamps, and deferred release of their report until the purge was complete.

Four new coil stamps issued in 1988, all Officials, do not have plate numbers, following the policy adopted in 1985. First was the nonde-

These four 1988 Official coil stamps are the first modern U.S. stamps to be printed entirely by offset lithography.

nominated Domestic Mail E coil stamp, issued on March 22 along with a nondenominated E Official stamped envelope for mailing savings bonds, and the regular E Earth stamps issued in sheets, booklets and coils for the general public. The E Official stamp was issued in coils of 100 for authorized government users. It was the first modern stamp printed entirely by offset lithography. Normally lithography alone does not provide sufficient security because it is easy and cheap to counterfeit, but for stamps limited to official use, that did not seem to be a problem. The E Officials were the first Officials to be printed on phosphored paper, eliminating the need for tagging over the printed design.

Unlike the uncoated paper used to print the 22¢ Flag Over Capitol stamp, which had the tagging phosphors blended into the paper sizing, the Officials are printed on coated paper with the phosphors as part of the coating. The design was similar to that of the Official stamps issued in 1983 and 1985, except that the letters USA appeared only

Presiding — J. B. McCullough
MSC Manager / Postmaster
Corpus Christi, Texas

Presentation of Colors — U. S. Navy Color Guard
Naval Air Station
Corpus Christi, Texas

National Anthem — Veterans Band of Corpus Christi

Invocation — Monsignor Patrick Higgins
St. Patrick's Catholic Church

Welcome — Honorable Betty Turner
Mayor of Corpus Christi

Introduction of — Rex H. Stever
Distinguished Guests — Chairman
TEXPEX '88 Stamp Show

Remarks — William K. McDaniel
President
Texas Philatelic Association

Address and Presentation — William A. Campbell, Jr.
of Albums — Regional Postmaster General

Benediction — Reverend Melissa Smith-Farris
First United Methodist Church

* * * * * * *

Honored Guest — Joseph G. Schraer
Division General Manager
Postmaster
San Antonio Division

Restricted to official governmental use, Penalty Mail stamps and stationery products help the Postal Service and federal agencies keep track of postage expenses. Unauthorized use carries a fine of $300, hence the "penalty" designation.

Penalty Mail stamps were first introduced in 1873 with the withdrawal of free franking privileges for governmental agencies. Envelopes were added to the Penalty Mail line in 1879, but all such products were declared obsolete in 1884.

The present-day Penalty Mail stamps were unveiled in 1983. Since then, all such stamps are based on the original design by veteran topographer Bradbury Thompson, and feature the Great Seal of the United States.

The 15¢ and 25¢ Official stamps, postcard and letter-rate stamps, respectively, were the first Officials ever to have a first-day ceremony and a ceremony program.

once, in the top line of type. The stamps were printed in red, blue and black on a Goebel Optiforma offset press.

A 20¢ Official stamp of similar design and process was issued May 19 without a prior announcement. This stamp would have appeared later in the year, but the complaints from collectors about the reissue of the 1983 engraved 20¢ Official coils, which do have sleeve numbers, resulted in those being recalled for destruction and the earlier release of the replacement, offset-printed stamp.

In contrast to those first two 1988 Official stamps, which were rushed into circulation, the other two were the first Officials ever to be issued at a first-day ceremony complete with their own fancy ceremony program. The 15¢ and 25¢ Officials were released on June 11, 1988, at the TEXPEX exhibition sponsored by the Texas Philatelic Association. Except for the new phosphor-coated paper, offset printing, and slightly streamlined design, the 25¢ Official obeyed the tradition of the original 20¢, Domestic Letter Rate D, 22¢, and Domestic Mail E stamps, all of which were prime-rate stamps issued as coils of 100. The 15¢ Official was a departure from tradition. All the previous Officials issued in postcard denominations — 13¢, Postal Card Rate D, and 14¢ Officials — had been sheet stamps issued in panes of 100. Now the postcard Official was a coil too.

All the other new 1988 coil stamps have PNCs. Six of the new Transportation coil subjects were recommended by members of the public: Conestoga wagon, tugboat, ore (coal) car, elevator, cable car and police patrol wagon.

The 3¢ Conestoga Wagon Stamp

The first coil stamp issued in 1988, the 3¢ Conestoga Wagon, was one of the most important. It was needed as makeup postage for the 22¢ stamps that would still be in use when the first-class letter rate increased to 25¢, as everyone expected. There were still supplies of 3¢ Francis Parkman and 3¢ Handcar coil stamps in Postal Service vaults and depositories, but not enough for the anticipated rate-change requirements. Had this stamp been needed earlier, it would have been issued as a re-engraved version of the 3¢ Handcar.

The design showed an early 19th-century covered wagon used by pioneers migrating westward from Pennsylvania to the Ohio River valley, and prototype for the lighter *Prairie Schooner* that carried set-

Readers of Linn's Stamp News *suggested the covered wagon design in 1987.*

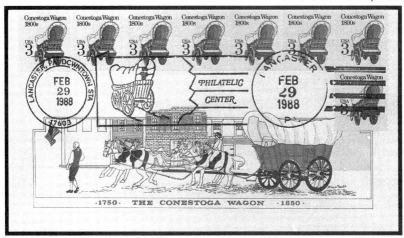

The Lancaster, Pennsylvania, pictorial cancel matches the stamp design on this unofficial first-day cover prepared by Rollin Berger on this Panda cachet. The strip of stamps includes a sleeve 1 PNC.

tlers farther west. It was the first Transportation series design that responded directly to popular demand. Commenting on an informal poll of his readers, John M. Hotchner reported in his *Linn's* "U.S. Notes" column that the Conestoga wagon, as a stamp subject, was the "people's choice."

The 3¢ Conestoga Wagon coil stamp was printed on the intaglio B press in maroon ink with block tagging. A single sleeve number appears at 52-stamp intervals. The stamps were issued in coils of 100, 500 and 3,000. The first-day ceremony was held in Conestoga, Pennsylvania, on February 29, 1988, the first time a U.S. stamp was ever issued on Leap Year Day.

Postmasters from several nearby towns took their handstamps to Conestoga for the occasion, so collectors who wanted interesting unofficial first-day covers didn't have to travel very far to get them. Present were cancels for Intercourse, Lampeter, Paradise, Mount Joy, Blue Bell and Peach Bottom, as well as a Lancaster Philatelic Center pictorial cancel showing a Conestoga wagon.

Sleeve 1 is the only PNC reported as of January 1990, and therefore the only number found on a first-day covers.

The Nondenominated E Earth Contingency Coil Stamp

The nondenominated E contingency stamps, showing the Earth as viewed from space in full color, were issued as sheet stamps in panes of 100; in booklets of 20; and in coils of 100, 500 and 3,000. They were placed on sale in Washington, D.C., on the afternoon of March 22, 1988, after the meeting of the postal board of governors earlier that day had approved the new 25¢ letter rate to begin on April 3. Because they were issued late in the day without prior notice, relatively few first-day covers were made on the actual date of issue. Unofficial FDCs of these stamps and the E contingency Official stamp and stamped envelope released along with them may be hard to find.

USPS had unveiled the E design on February 18, but it wasn't until two days after the stamps had been issued that USPS published the official announcement. Since the stamps were issued without advance notice, a 60-day grace period was given for submitting first-day covers, rather than the usual 30 days.

The previous nondenominated contingency A (15¢), B (18¢), C (20¢) and D (22¢) stamps were not popular with the public. Each had featured a single-color design with a stylized eagle and dropout white lettering. In each case, the "Letter Stamps" had been shunned by users as soon as new denominated replacements were put on sale, leaving significant waste to be destroyed. That was not the case with the E Earth stamps. The USPS Philatelic and Retail Services annual report for 1988 proudly proclaimed the E stamps a success: "The attractive, colorful design completely muted the public's vocal outcry against 'Letter Stamps,' which had been so prevalent in previous rate changes, and significantly reduced the destruction of these stamps as denominated issues became available."

One reason the E stamps were a success is because the Citizens' Stamp Advisory Committee decided to change the design, and to link the subject with the letter E. The project began a few months after the 1985 22¢ letter rate went into effect. Bradbury Thompson, a design coordinator, submitted several possible subjects, including eagle and egret as well as the one that was adopted — Earth. Pete Davidson, director of stamps and philatelic marketing at the Postal Service, was a strong advocate of Earth.

Design work under project director Jack Williams began in September 1985, and actual production took place over several months in 1986. Stamps were sent to the USPS underground storage facility near Kansas City, Missouri, in two huge shipments, one in September 1986 and the other in February and March 1987. By mistake, a coil of E stamps somehow was shipped to Hollywood, Florida, in 1986, and turned up in a routine inventory. Thus the first report on the E stamp appeared in the November 24, 1986 issue of *Linn's*, more than a year before the design was officially unveiled.

The E stamps were issued only for use as domestic postage, because Universal Postal Union regulations require denominated postage on international mail. But Canada accepted letters bearing E stamps without collecting postage due, as a courtesy, even though the new U.S. letter rate to Canada was 30¢. The E stamps were printed on the Andreotti gravure press. Each of the four colors — red, yellow, blue and black — was printed from a separate gravure cylinder, so the cylinder numbers appear in groups of four. On the coil stamps they are spaced at 24-stamp intervals. Two sets of cylinders were used to print coils, in several different press runs.

Four different cylinder number combinations exist on the E coils, reading in order red, blue, yellow, black: 1111, 1211, 1222, 2222. The 1111 and 1211 combinations are found only on coils of 100 stamps; 1222 and 2222 are both found on coils of 500; and 1222 is also found on coils of 3,000. Imperforate rolls of 1111 and 1211 have been found.

Offset plates also were prepared for the E stamps but probably never went to press, the fate of a "special blue" Andreotti press gravure cylinder.

The yellow number is sometimes difficult to read. Daylight is better than incandescent for making it out. A magnifying glass helps, as does a blue filter.

The E coil stamps must be regarded as the first successful United States coil stamps printed by the gravure process. All three previously issued gravure coil designs were issued in 1985 — the nondenominated contingency D Eagle (22¢), the 21.1¢ Letters, and the 18¢ George Washington Monument. All were unpopular with stamp collectors and the public.

The Postal Service acted quickly to place denominated 25¢ stamps and postal stationery into circulation. The E contingency items were all withdrawn from philatelic sale on June 30, 1989.

The 25¢ Flag Over Yoocmite Stamp

The 25¢ Flag Over Yosemite stamp was issued on May 20, 1988, at a ceremony at Yosemite National Park in California. Originally it had been scheduled to be released on May 13. The stamp depicts the stars and stripes over Half Dome peak, one of Yosemite's best-known natural wonders. The stamp is printed in red, blue and green ink with block tagging. The original announced intention of the Postal Service was to issue this stamp only in coils of 500 and 3,000, which meant it would have been printed only on the intaglio B press with single sleeve numbers spaced at 52-stamp intervals.

In that event, the 25¢ Flag coils would have been the prime-rate coil stamp used mainly on business mail and sold by coin vending machines in post offices, while the 25¢ Bread Wagon stamps in coils of 100 would have been more widely used by private individuals, after the supplies of nondenominated E stamps were exhausted.

The first three printing sleeves followed this plan, and the fourth — a C or D press sleeve with single plate numbers spaced at 48-stamp intervals — also had only 18 rows across, so sleeve 4 stamps, like numbers 1, 2 and 3, were suited to processing on the Huck coiling equipment into coils of 500 and 3,000. All four of those numbers are found on first-day covers, although number 3 was not even assigned until the issue date of the stamp, May 20, and number 4 was not assigned until the following August and did not go to press until September 5. These FDCs exist because some cachetmakers and servicers did not receive envelopes from their printers until very late, and were granted lengthy extensions of the 30-day grace period by the Philatelic Sales Division. Some 25¢ Flag first-day covers were being canceled more than a year after the date of issue.

As things actually worked out, despite the original announcement, 25¢ Flag stamps were issued in coils of 100. By the close of Fiscal Year 1988 in late September, almost 4.7 billion had been shipped in 100-stamp blister packs, as against 555 million in coils of 500 and 3,000. Probably three reasons contributed to the change in plans. First and most important was the popularity of the Flag Over Yosemite design. It was the first coil stamp ever chosen as the best definitive in the annual *Linn's* readership poll. Second was the unpopularity of the 25¢ Bread Wagon design, which undoubtedly contributed to the early withdrawal of that stamp. Third was the delay in issuing the 25¢ Honeybee coil stamp caused by production difficulties in combining offset and intaglio printing on a single stamp. The Honeybee was supposed to be issued on June 11, was postponed until mid- or late July, and finally actually appeared on September 2. Had the 25¢ Honeybee coils been released according to plan, the 100-stamp coils of 25¢ Flag stamps might not have been necessary. At the opposite extreme, tests were conducted in November 1988 on 10,000-stamp coils of 25¢ Flag stamps.

The 25¢ Flag Over Yosemite coil stamps were block tagged on the B, C and D presses, but later a new version was issued on phosphor-coated paper instead, described on Page 261. Sleeve numbers 1

Some 25¢ Flag Over Yosemite coil stamps have the red ink image almost completely missing.

through 9 had been used by the time the changeover was made, but at this writing no block-tagged example of a number 6 roll has ever been reported. Although numbers as low as 2 were issued on the phosphor-coated paper, higher numbers continued to appear in block-tagged form because the initial supply of phosphor-coated paper was insufficient to meet the prime-rate coil stamp requirements.

Interesting varieties have appeared on the 25¢ Flag coils. On some, the red color is almost completely omitted. Another variety, called the "Black Forest," has the trees rendered in dark brown, dark gray or black rather than green, evidently a problem of ink contamination. Imperforate strips are known of numbers 2, 3, 4, 5, 7 and 9.

The 10.1¢ Oil Wagon Stamp
Overprinted in Red

The 1985 rate for which the 10.1¢ Oil Wagon stamp had originally been issued — the third-class bulk rate presorted to five ZIP-code digits — was superseded by the 13.2¢ rate on April 3, 1988, but the stamp was acceptable to prepay that rate as false franking for six more months. Shortly after that, it was withdrawn from philatelic sale. That

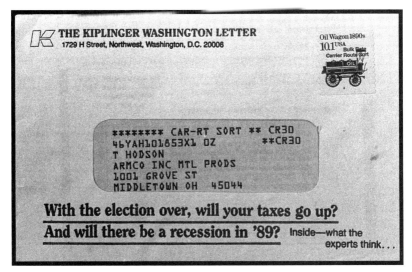

The printed advertisement on this cover indicates that it was mailed in 1988. The stamp is a number 2 plate number coil of the 10.1¢ Oil Wagon stamp with the new red overprint.

The 10.1¢ Oil Wagon coil stamp was originally issued in a tagged collector edition without a precancel overprint, and in a precanceled version with the Bulk Rate overprint in black ink between two lines to cover the 1985 third-class rate for mail presorted to five ZIP-code digits. The 1988 10.1¢ rate required a different overprint to indicate its new purpose, this time in red ink without precancel lines.

original stamp, issued in 1985, had a black precancel overprint inscription, "Bulk Rate," between lines, which was very difficult to read on top of the dark blue of the vignette. A companion tagged version was issued for collectors without the precancel overprint. Both are described beginning on Page 146.

On the same day that the old 10.1¢ rate rose to 13.2¢, the old 8.3¢ bulk rate sorted to the individual carrier route, covered by the 8.3¢ Ambulance stamp, rose to 10.1¢. To tailor a stamp to that new rate, all that the Bureau of Engraving and Printing had to do was to change the overprint. That was done, making the revised 10.1¢ Oil Wagon stamp the first issue to meet one of the new bulk rates. There wasn't enough space around the design for an engraved service inscription. This was the second time a red overprint was used on a bulk-mail stamp; the first was on the 8.5¢ Tow Truck coil issued in 1987.

The text of the overprint was changed to "Bulk Rate Carrier Route Sort," the ink color was changed to red, the precancel lines were eliminated, and the overprinted inscription was raised slightly to make it more readable.

The new stamp was issued in Washington, D.C., without a ceremony on June 27, 1988. It was announced in advance, and a first-day cancel was offered.

In fact, it was announced first in an April 11 confidential memorandum to first-day cover cachet manufacturers, 10 days before it was publicly announced.

In effect these were first-day covers of an overprint, the first time the USPS had ever promoted such a thing, but solid evidence that the officials at USPS headquarters now understood that each new variation on an old stamp was regarded as a separate issue by collectors.

The first sleeve number to appear was 2, the number that appears on first-day covers. It had been used previously with the original overprint, but was not used to print tagged stamps. In October a third

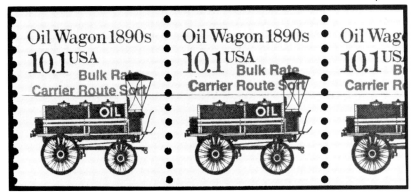

The overprints on these Oil Wagon stamps are not aligned because they are from opposite ends of the flexographic plate, which was mounted slightly askew on its form roller.

10.1¢ Oil Wagon sleeve was manufactured and was sent to press for the first time on November 18, 1988. Only red precancels appear on this number.

The red overprint, like its black predecessor, was applied by two 468-subject flexographic plates at the letterpress station of the intaglio B press. The single sleeve numbers repeat at 52-stamp intervals, on coils of 500, 3,000 and 10,000.

The 16.7¢ Popcorn Wagon Stamp

The 16.7¢ Popcorn Wagon coil stamp, issued July 7, 1988, to meet the basic third-class bulk rate presorted to three ZIP-code digits, was the first coil stamp issued according to the new policy for stamps the Postal Service considers precancels. Only an untagged service-inscribed version exists; there is no companion tagged edition for collectors without the restrictive endorsement. And the service inscription is printed in a second color from the same intaglio sleeve as the design.

The stamp depicts a turn-of-the-century Popcorn Wagon first used in Chicago. Appropriately, the stamp was issued at a first-day ceremony in the lobby of the main post office in Chicago. Only sleeve number 1 was issued, so that is the only PNC found on first-day covers. In 1990, sleeve 2 appeared on the 10,000-stamp coils.

The stamps were printed on the intaglio B press in two colors: red

235

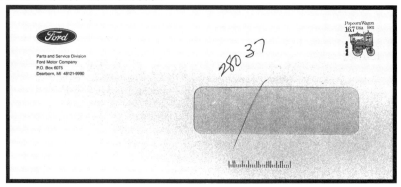

Only one commercial cover in 52 franked with a 16.7¢ Popcorn Wagon will have a PNC, as this sleeve 1 example does.

for the basic design, and black for the service inscription. Cachetmakers had been told in the April 11 memorandum to expect a single-color stamp. Earlier, they had been told the denomination would be 16.5¢, which was the amount the Postal Service had filed with the Postal Rate Commission on May 4, 1987, but which eventually was hiked an additional two-tenths of a cent. It replaced the 12.5¢ rate covered by the precanceled 12.5¢ Pushcart coil stamp. The 16.7¢ Popcorn Wagon stamps are sold in coils of 500, 3,000 and 10,000.

This imperforate miscut pair of 16.7¢ Popcorn Wagon stamps puts part of the stamp's inscription at the bottom, rather than its proper place at the top.

Imperforates exist of the 16.7¢ Popcorn Wagon coil stamps, including examples that are mis-slit also. One other "error" on this stamp occurred in the *Postal Bulletin* description, which said, "Marginal Markings: © U.S. Postal Service 1988 Use Correct ZIP Code __." Those are the marginal markings for sheet stamps. The copyright notice for coil stamps appears on the packaging label and does not include the ZIP code message.

The 15¢ Tugboat Stamp

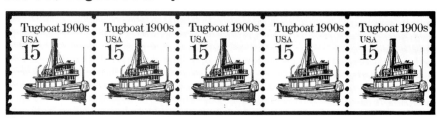

When the Postal Service board of governors applied to the Postal Rate Commission for 1988 rate increases on May 4, 1987, it requested a jump in the postcard rate from 14¢, paid by the 14¢ Iceboat coil stamp, to 16¢. New stamp designs for a 16¢ coil stamp have not been published. Had this proposed rate been adopted, we might have seen the return of the 16¢ Liberty Head coil stamp in the Americana series, a 1978 issue printed on both Cottrell and intaglio B presses. The Postal Service hasn't told us how many of those stamps were in its storage vaults in early 1988 or whether a new B press sleeve might have been prepared. A precedent of sort existed, however — the release of 12¢ Torch stamps in the Americana series, in 1981, to meet the now postcard rate.

When the 15¢ rate was adopted, supplies of two older coil stamps — the 15¢ Flag coil in the Americana series and the 15¢ Oliver Wendell Holmes coil in the Prominent Americans series — were distributed from the vaults. Those supplies must not have been sufficient, because in early April the issue date of the 15¢ Tugboat coil stamp was advanced by two months, from September 14 to July 12. The stamp was released at a first-day ceremony aboard the retired ocean liner *Queen Mary* at Long Beach, California.

The 15¢ Tugboat stamp pictures a turn-of-the-century tug in a single-color purple rendering. The stamps are printed on the intaglio B press and issued in coils of 500 and 3,000. Only sleeve number 1 was known to exist for almost a year, and that is the only PNC found on first-day covers. Number 2 appeared in the summer of 1989.

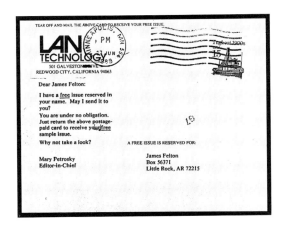

This message-and-reply postcard advertising a magazine subscription was the first reported sighting of a sleeve 2 15¢ Tugboat coil stamp.

The 13.2¢ Coal Car Stamp

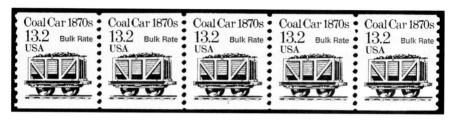

The 13.2¢ Coal Car coil stamp replaced the original 10.1¢ Oil Wagon stamp with the black precancel overprint, paying the new third-class bulk rate for mail presorted to five ZIP-code digits. It follows the 1988 policy, having been issued only in an untagged service-inscribed format, without a companion tagged collector edition. The Postal Service regards the engraved endorsement as a precancel indicator.

The design shows an 1870s coal car used by underground miners to bring coal to the surface. The vignette is printed in dark green ink and the service inscription in red, from a single seamless sleeve on the B press, with numbers repeating at 52-stamp intervals. The stamp is sold in coils of 500, 3,000 and 10,000.

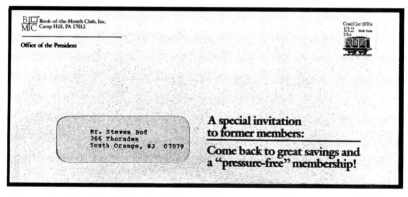

Covers bearing the 13.2¢ Coal Car coil stamp are quite common, but those with PNCs, like this number 1 example, can still be a challenge to collect.

The 13.2¢ Coal Car stamp is the first 1988 Transportation series coil to have been issued in the intended denomination on the announced date without further changes. A notice in the June 23, 1988 *Postal Bulletin* preceded the official July 5 philatelic release, reversing

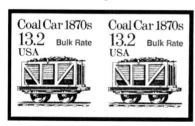

Shortly after the 13.2¢ Coal Car coil was issued, imperforate examples were found.

238

the usual protocol. It was issued at a first-day ceremony held at the Mellon Science Center of Duquesne University in Pittsburgh, Pennsylvania, on July 19.

Sleeve 2 appeared for the first time more than a year later, so only sleeve 1 is found on first-day covers. Number 1 exists imperforate also.

The 8.4¢ Wheel Chair Stamp

In the original May 4, 1987 application from the Postal Service board of governors to the Postal Rate Commission, the nonprofit rate of 8.5¢ for the basic three-digit ZIP code presort, then covered by the precanceled 8.5¢ Tow Truck coil stamp, would have risen to 8.7¢. Cachetmakers were notified that an 8.7¢ Wheel Chair stamp would appear, but were warned as always to keep the information "in strict confidence until publicly announced by the Postal Service." By the time the stamp was publicly announced, the rate had been reduced, not raised, to 8.4¢, but by holding off the public announcement, the Postal Service avoided becoming the butt of jokes about phantom stamps such as it had endured in 1985 and 1986 with the Tow Truck and other nonprofit-rate coils.

The 8.4¢ Wheel Chair stamp was issued, as its public announcement promised, on August 12, 1988, at a dedication ceremony held at the Veterans Administration Medical Center in Tucson, Arizona. Its companion 8.4¢ embossed envelope, issued April 12 in Baltimore, Maryland, depicted the historic U.S. Navy frigate *Constellation.*

The 8.4¢ Wheel Chair stamp depicted a vintage 1920s wheelchair (which most authorities regard as one word) in maroon ink, with the "Nonprofit" service inscription in red. Only one untagged version was issued; the Postal Service regards its service inscription as a precancelation. The stamps were issued in coils of 500 and 3,000.

Originally these stamps were printed on the intaglio B press from a single seamless sleeve with numbers repeating at 52-stamp intervals. The B press sleeve was number 1, and those were the only stamps available on the issue date and for the next two months. But the Bureau of Engraving and Printing was experiencing problems drying the red ink of the service inscription, which forced printers to run the press at a slow speed, greatly reducing its productivity.

For that reason, a C press sleeve was manufactured, number 2. C press numbers appear at 48-stamp intervals; otherwise the stamps are identical. C press 8.4¢ Wheel Chair stamps were not placed on sale until October 6, but a number of first-day covers showing sleeve number 2 PNCs were made on several different cachets, by cachetmakers who had been granted extensions of time to submit covers to the Philatelic Sales Division for cancelation. C press sleeves may also be used on the intaglio section of the D press. Eventually the B press drying problem was solved. In 1990, coils of 3,000 appeared printed from sleeve 3.

The 21¢ Railroad Mail Car Stamp

After the stamps for commercial users of third-class bulk mail rates, the next most widely used quantity-mail stamps are those for presorted first-class mail. When the Postal Service board of governors submitted its request for rate increases to the Postal Rate Commission on May 4, 1987, it had hoped to boost the basic three-digit presort rate from 18¢, covered by the service-inscribed 18¢ Washington Monument coil stamp, to 21.5¢. A confidential USPS memorandum circulated to cachet manufacturers advised them to expect a coil stamp in that denomination featuring a railroad mail car. But the Postal Rate Commission reduced the request by a half cent, so the first public

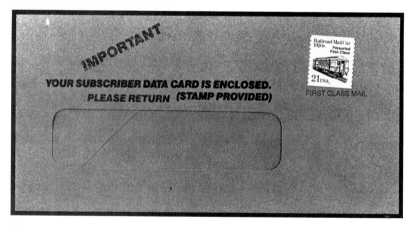

Shown is a typical use of the 21¢ Railroad Mail Car stamp on a Newsweek *subscription promotion mailing, in this case a sleeve 2 plate number coil printed on the C or D press.*

An early version of the Railroad Mail Car stamp design was prepared for a different rate that was not approved by the Postal Rate Commission.

announcement correctly stated the new stamp's 21¢ denomination.

It is interesting to speculate about whether, had the Postal Service known that the final first-class presort rate would be 21¢, they would have issued a tagged version of this stamp without a service inscription for use on postcards to Canada, instead of or in addition to the 21¢ Chester Carlton sheet stamp in the Great Americans series. As it is, the stamp would look empty and unbalanced without the "Presorted First-Class" endorsement.

An essay version of the Railroad Mail Car stamp was drawn with a 20.7¢ denomination, dropped to 20.5¢ by the Postal Rate Commission for ZIP+4 presorted first-class mail.

The 21¢ Railroad Mail Car coil stamp was issued on August 16, 1988, at a ceremony on the plaza of the Palace of the Governors in Santa Fe, New Mexico. It pictures in green ink a 1920s mail car — literally a moving post office at the time, in which mail was collected and sorted en route. The service inscription is red. The stamps were initially printed on the intaglio B press from a seamless sleeve numbered 1, with sleeve numbers spaced at 52-stamp intervals. That

Several first-day covers exist of the imperforate 21¢ Railroad Mail Car coils.

was the stamp made available on the date of issue.

But again, as happened with the 8.4¢ Wheel Chair stamp, the 21¢ Railroad Mail Car stamp production had to be moved to the C press because the red ink dried too slowly on the B press infrared drying unit. Although sleeve 2, with its 48-stamp PNC interval, did not go to press until after the date of issue, a few first-day covers of that stamp exist, submitted as replacements for faulty ones canceled during the grace period. The sleeve 2 rolls did not actually go on sale until late October.

These two strips show a series of plate gouges that match up perfectly because they were originally side by side on the same paper web before slitting, straddling both rows of stamps. The plate flaw is enlarged in the inset.

Imperforate rolls were found soon after the stamps were issued, and some were used to service first-day covers, including two with imperforate sleeve 1 PNC strips.

Another interesting variety is a series of plate gouges that straddle the edge of two rows of stamps on the paper web. PNC dealer Frank Marrelli, who discovered this flaw, calls it "railroad tracks" and "railroad tracks continued."

The 7.6¢ Carreta Stamp

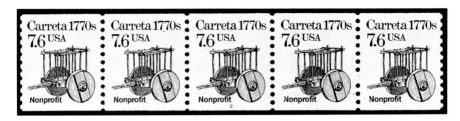

The 7.6¢ Carreta stamp replaced the original 7.1¢ Tractor stamp of 1987 to prepay the nonprofit bulk rate for mail presorted to five ZIP-code digits. The Postal Service board of governors had requested an increase to 7.8¢, but the Postal Rate Commission shaved off two-tenths of a cent from the proposed hike.

The *carreta* design — Spanish for cart — shows what may be the earliest vehicle used in North America, made entirely of wood lashed together with leather thongs, drawn by a team of oxen joined at the horns. The idea for the design originated with Theron Fox of San

Jose, California, a stamp collector and pioneer cachetmaker who had unusual access to officials of the USPS Stamps Division. As a retired newspaper reporter and former chairman of the city's Historic Landmark Commission, he was unusually knowledgeable about the history of natives and settlers of the old Southwest. His expert knowledge had saved the Postal Service embarrassment when he was able to help them correct a number of historically inaccurate design elements in the 1977 Alta California commemorative stamp. A carreta had figured in that design, and Fox believed it was certainly appropriate for the Transportation series as an authentic American original.

The stamp was issued at a ceremony held at the San Jose Historical Museum, on August 30, 1988. It was printed untagged only, in two colors on the intaglio B press — the vignette in brown ink and the service inscription in red — with single sleeve numbers spaced at 52-stamp intervals. The sleeve number digits are printed in the same red ink as the service inscription, rather than, as in the case of all the other Transportation series coil stamps, the color of the basic design elements. The Postal Service regards the service inscription as a precancelation. No tagged edition just for collectors was issued.

Three sleeve numbers have been reported at this writing. Only sleeve 1 was available on the issue date and for the next three months. But two numbers exist on first-day covers nevertheless, because a few number 2 PNCs were submitted for cancelation as replacements for spoiled covers, and were accepted by the Philatelic Sales Division despite the very late date. Sleeve 3 did not appear until late in 1989.

The 25¢ Honeybee Stamp

The 25¢ Honeybee coil stamp was issued at a first-day ceremony held at the Omaha Stamp Show on September 2, 1988. Postal Service representatives have declined to state whether they consider the 25¢ Honeybee to be one design of a set, but it appears to be the fourth in a series of definitive stamps featuring colorful fauna subjects and a common type style for the inscription elements.

The first stamp in the series, the 25¢ Pheasant horizontal-format booklet stamp, was issued in panes of 10, two panes to a $5 booklet, manufactured by American Bank Note Company in Richmond, Virginia. It was printed in four process colors on a leased J.W. Fergusson and Sons Champlain gravure press using solvent-based inks. The sec-

The 25¢ Honeybee stamp appears to be part of a set that includes three booklet stamps: the 25¢ Pheasant, and the se-tenant 25¢ Owl with 25¢ Grosbeak designs.

ond and third, the se-tenant 25¢ Owl and 25¢ Grosbeak vertical-format booklet stamps, were issued in panes of 10, two rows of five alternating stamps of each design per pane, two panes to a $5 booklet, manufactured by the Bureau of Engraving and Printing in Washington. They were printed in four process colors on the Andreotti gravure press using water-base inks. The 25¢ Honeybee horizontal-format coil stamp was printed by a combination of offset lithography and line-engraved intaglio printing on an assortment of presses at BEP. In addition to the four process colors, the Honeybee includes an additional "self" color, a shade of solid yellow chosen from the Pantone Matching System chart, and an intaglio black image. If these four stamps do constitute a deliberately created set of fauna stamps, it represents a bold departure to employ such disparate suppliers and production methods. But wildlife artist Chuck Ripper designed all four stamps, assuring stylistic continuity.

Had the 25¢ Honeybee coil stamp been issued on the originally intended date, June 11, 1988, the impression of a four-stamp set would have been much stronger. The 25¢ Pheasant booklet stamp was issued on April 29; the 25¢ Owl and 25¢ Grosbeak booklet stamps were issued on May 28. But production problems plagued the Honeybee, causing delays. The initial postponement was to mid-July, then finally to September. By then there were so many prime-rate definitives available that it was hard to keep track of them all: Bread Wagon coils; Flag Over Yosemite coils; Flag and Clouds sheet and booklet stamps; nondenominated E contingency stamps in sheets, booklets and coils; and leftovers from years past, including the Paul Revere sheet and coil stamps, and Frederick Douglass sheet stamps. With all those choices available, the design similarities of the four fauna stamps didn't stand out.

The 25¢ Honeybee was the first United States coil stamp ever to combine two different printing processes in the design itself. In the past, combination printing for coils had been limited to letterpress overprinting, usually with flexographic mats or plates, on line-engraved stamps, and tagging on both line-engraved and gravure coils. The Honeybee broke new ground by combining offset lithography with line engraving. The combination was accomplished in two different ways. For some of the Honeybee coils, the offset portion of the image — everything except the body of the bee itself, including the color foreground, the inscription, and the frame — was printed on the Goebel Optiforma press, the same press that was also being used to print the new series of four Official stamps issued in 1988. After the offset run on the Goebel press, the printed paper rolls were run again on the intaglio C press, which added the line-engraved portion — the body of the bee in black ink. Other Honeybee coils were printed on the combination offset/intaglio D press in a single run that applied the complete stamp design.

Intaglio sleeves are interchangeable on the C and D presses, a convenient feature for coil production. In the past, for intaglio-only Transportation and Flag series coil production, sleeves could be moved easily from one to the other as needed, but infrequently were. Only the D press has the capability to combine offset lithography with line-engraved intaglio, a combination first used on the 20¢ Smokey the Bear commemorative sheet stamp in 1984. For standard definitive-size coil stamps, the intaglio sleeves are 48 subjects in circumference, with a single sleeve number that appears at 48-stamp intervals on the finished stamps. Two different sleeves were prepared for the Honeybee stamps. Sleeve 1, 18 rows across, yields 864 subjects per impression. Sleeve 2, 20 rows across, yields 960 subjects per revolution. A third 960-subject intaglio sleeve was manufactured but had a low spot and could not be used.

Offset plates are not interchangeable between the Goebel Optiforma press and the D press. Plates for the Optiforma press are 25 subjects in the rotary (horizontal) dimension, while those for the D press are 24 subjects. Both can be either 18 or 20 subjects across, yielding 450- and 500-subject offset plates for the Goebel, 432- and 480-subject offset plates for the D. Since the Goebel's 25-subject on-press circumference does not divide evenly into the 48-stamp circumference of the intaglio sleeve, its images "float" in relation to the intaglio images. But the D press offset plate's 24-stamp circumference is exactly half the 48-stamp intaglio sleeve circumference, so the relative positions repeat throughout a D press run.

Offset plates are prepared in sets of five, but because they wear out much more quickly than intaglio sleeves and therefore must be replaced frequently, their plate numbers are not printed on the stamps. The five plates represent each of the process colors whose halftone dot patterns combine to reproduce "full" color — yellow, magenta, cyan and black — plus an additional deep solid yellow for the background chosen from the Pantone Matching System color scheme. In an early

Loss of register caused the bee to wander in and out of the stamp, as well as up and down within the frame. The misregistered stamps on the left and right here, with a normal example in the middle, make the bee appear to fly toward the flower, land, and take off.

test on the Optiforma press, its sixth offset station was used to apply tagging, but that proved to be unsatisfactory and the printed impressions were destroyed. The tagging was then switched to the letterpress station of the C press and printed in blocks over both ink impressions. This meant that all three basic printing methods were being used in combination: planographic (flat-image lithography), recess (line-engraved intaglio), and relief (raised-image letterpress).

Registering the Optiforma offset impressions with the C press intaglio design was a production nightmare for BEP printers, and the way they solved the problems affected the final product. Originally, the plate numbers engraved on sleeve 1 looked like all the others we've seen on the other stamps. But during test runs of the Honeybee, the number was so tall that it poked into the bottom of the frame as registration varied. The sleeve was dechromed and sent back to siderographers in the design and engraving division of the BEP to shorten the plate numbers at each of the 18 positions, but a master die with a smaller number wasn't available. So, using a flat engraving tool, the siderographer went into the metal below the engraved image and threw up a mound of steel. He "stabbed it up, tiled it and trimmed it," filling in the top portion of the existing digit.

The printing sleeve was then rechromed and returned to production. In that way the plate numbers were all shortened, so that on

On this sleeve 2 strip, the misregistration is in the vertical dimension. With the bee printing high in relation to the background, the sleeve number is entirely inside the frame of the stamp design, as shown in the inset, rather than properly positioned below it.

The top serif of the sleeve 1 digit of the Honeybee coil appears on only one coil out of every 15 to 20, indicating that it is probably present on just one of the 18 positions on the sleeve.

loosely registered stamps they would still be clear of the bottom of the frameline most of the time. But because the repair was done by hand, there is some variation from one row to the next. One or more positions has a top serif. Another has a rounded swelling at the top, while most seem to be cleanly chopped. Stamps from the initial press runs with the taller uncut number are much scarcer than those with truncated digits.

By the time sleeves 2 and 3 were prepared, the BEP had acquired smaller dies for the digits. The number 2 Honeybee digit is only one-half millimeter tall, compared with three-fourths of a millimeter on other PNCs.

To improve horizontal registration of the stamp design, the BEP added a servo mechanism to the intaglio C press, to compensate for the mechanical differences between the Optiforma and C presses that tended to preclude precise registration.

This device regulates the speed of a chill roller, and the resulting speed of the paper web, stretching or shrinking the paper to keep the images in register by keeping the repeat length "twenty-one seven fifty" (21-¾ inches) every 25 stamps.

One source of the registration difficulty is that the space between two stamp images straddling the seam where the two ends of each offset plate meet on the Goebel press is not identical to the spaces between the other stamps.

Sometimes the edge of the plate is marked by a seam line, or pair of seam lines, similar in appearance to Cottrell press joint lines. Sometimes only a speck or two of ink appears there. When those lines or markings appear at 25-stamp intervals, the stamps were printed on the Goebel Optiforma press. On those stamps, the gutter between the adjacent stamp images at the offset plate seam is two-tenths of a millimeter wider than the 4mm spacing between the rest of the

This photographically cropped 25¢ Honeybee stamp on cover shows the offset black ink image shifted to the left. The intaglio black and the other four offset colors are properly registered.

stamps, measuring frame to frame.

Seam lines are more commonly found on D press rolls. The lines are caused by wear at the edge of the plate, which picks up ink. That ink transfers to the blanket and then prints along with the offset image. When the lines are spaced at 24-stamps intervals, they are D press lines. In that event, they repeat throughout a roll in exactly the same positions relative to the sleeve number position. In fact, collectors have identified many constant D press seam line positions, and some find them as interesting to collect by position as precancel gaps. Although the seam lines are unintended freaks, unlike Cottrell press joint lines, the overall effect of moving production to the D press was

Sometimes the seam, where the two ends of an offset plate adjoin, prints a line, or a pair of lines as shown here. In this example, the D press offset plate ends were not perfectly aligned, so the stamp image on the right is lower than that on the left. Photo credit: Peter P. Chiesa.

The gutter between the two stamps at the edge of the Goebel offset plates is two-tenths of a millimeter wider than the spacings between the rest of the stamps. Photo credit: Peter P. Chiesa.

to solve many of the registration problems and to reduce spoilage significantly.

Besides problems registering the offset impressions to the intaglio, some stamps show registration problems just among the five offset images. Dirty offset blankets transfer ink in blotches to areas that are not supposed to be printed. Normally Bureau examiners notice such defects and remove them for destruction. But the effect isn't always so easy to detect when it happens with yellow ink, so some examples have been collected. In philately, production varieties like these are considered freaks.

In addition to such freaks, some interesting major errors have been found. Imperforate coils printed from both sleeves have been found.

The blotches of yellow color in the margins of this pair of 25¢ Honeybee stamps were caused by a dirty offset rubber blanket. The blanket transfers the printed image from the metal plate to the paper.

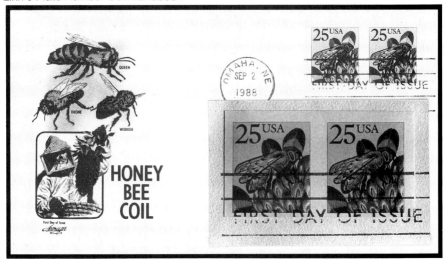

Imperforate rolls of the 25¢ Honeybee coil appeared so soon after the date of issue that several first-day covers were serviced with imperforate pairs.

Finds of sleeve 1 imperforate rolls occurred soon enough after the issue date that a number of first-day covers were serviced with imperforate pairs, and at least one with an imperforate plate number strip. Another interesting variety has the complete offset image in five colors, but the intaglio black is omitted, making it appear that the bee has vanished.

One variety that has not made its way to collectors as I write is a production run of 25¢ Honeybee coils on phosphor-coated paper. Be-

This error stamp has the complete five-color offset printing but is missing the black intaglio image showing the details of the bee.

Chuck Ripper's original sketch for the 25¢ Honeybee stamp included a lot of white space. Had it been adopted, the stamp could have been printed on phosphor-coated paper.

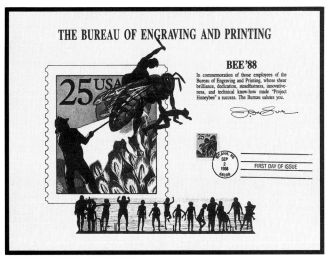

This souvenir card was a reward to Bureau of Engraving and Printing employees for seeing the Honeybee stamp through the success despite all the difficulties.

cause the design covers almost the entire stamp with ink, the border area alone does not include enough luminescence to meet the USPS minimum tolerance to assure that the phosphor glow will activate mail-processing facer-canceler machines. An entire production run was scrapped, and only block-tagged Honeybee stamps have been shipped.

For their successful efforts to produce this difficult, innovative stamp, BEP employees were rewarded with a limited-edition souvenir card, "produced largely at personal expense" on the Bureau's six-color Miller offset press. The text of the card, titled "BEE '88," reads: "In commemoration of those employees of the Bureau of Engraving and Printing, whose shear (sic) brilliance, dedication, steadfastness, innovativeness, and technical know-how made 'Project Honeybee' a success. The Bureau salutes you." The illustration on the card showed three BEP employees struggling to keep the bee in register on the stamp, with a group of people cheering below.

About 80 of the cards were printed. A Bureau employee traveled with the cards at his own expense to the Omaha Stamp Show, affixed a stamp to each card, and canceled them "First Day of Issue." When word of these cards' existence spread, some collectors offered as much as $100 for one, but at this writing it has been impossible to find evidence that any of them have actually been sold. *Linn's* published an editorial criticizing the Bureau for issuing the souvenir cards and a reply I wrote defending the Bureau.

The *Postal Bulletin* announcement of the 25¢ Honeybee stamp, and the notices sent to the philatelic press, said the stamp would be issued only in coils of 100. Actually it has been available since the very first day in coils of 100 and 3,000.

The saga of the 25¢ Honeybee coil stamp isn't over, but it has already, in its first year, proven itself to be one of the most interesting modern United States stamps, and one of the most challenging to collect in all its facets.

The 5.3¢ Elevator Stamp

The 5.3¢ Elevator coil stamp was issued at a ceremony held in the lobby of the Waldorf-Astoria Hotel in New York, on September 16, 1988. It depicts a turn-of-the-century Otis elevator in black ink with a red service inscription, "Nonprofit Carrier Route Sort," which the Postal Service considers a precancel. The B press stamps are untagged and sold in coils of 500 and 3,000. Single sleeve numbers repeat at 52-stamp intervals.

The 5.3¢ rate for nonprofit third-class bulk mail presorted to the individual carrier route is the lowest per-piece U.S. rate, except for mail that is delivered free. The rate declined from 5.5¢, prepaid by the service-inscribed 5.5¢ Star Route Truck coil stamp, on April 3, 1988, but that is one-tenth of a cent higher than the rate originally proposed by the USPS board of governors to the Postal Rate Commission on

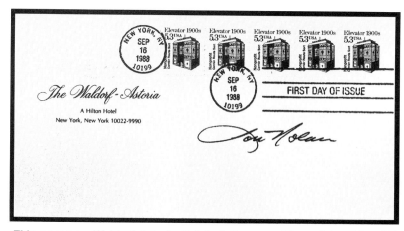

This cover on Waldorf-Astoria Hotel stationery, with a plate strip of the stamp issued in the hotel's lobby, was canceled at the first-day ceremony and autographed by Lou Nolan, the 5.3¢ Elevator stamp's designer.

May 4, 1987. The Postal Service had told cachetmakers to expect a 5.2¢ Elevator stamp, but only in a confidential memorandum that was not distributed to the press.

At this writing, only sleeve 1 has been reported, so that is the only number collectible on first-day covers.

The 20.5¢ Fire Engine Stamp

The 20.5¢ Fire Engine coil stamp was issued at a ceremony in San Angelo, Texas, on the grounds of the Fort Concho National Historic Landmark, on September 28, 1988. It depicts a turn-of-the-century fire engine in red ink with a black service inscription, "ZIP+4 Presort," which the Postal Service considers a precancel. The B press stamps are untagged and sold in coils of 500 and 3,000. Single sleeve numbers repeat at 52-stamp intervals.

The 20.5¢ rate, for first-class mail addressed to nine-digit ZIP codes and presorted, replaced the short-lived 17.5¢ rate prepaid by the service-inscribed 17.5¢ Racing Car coil stamp. The rate is two-tenths of a cent lower than the amount proposed by the USPS board of governors to the Postal Rate Commission on May 4, 1987 (almost five months before even the 17.5¢ stamp had been issued!). Cachetmakers had been told to expect a 20.7¢ Fire Engine stamp, but only in a confidential memorandum that was not distributed to the press.

At this writing, only sleeve 1 has been reported, and that is the only number collectible on first-day covers. The 20.5¢ Fire Engine stamp was issued five days after the close of Fiscal Year 1988, yet the fiscal year report includes 18,875,000 of these stamps shipped. That is the amount shipped for philatelic sales, all in coils of 500. No coils of 3,000 were shipped in Fiscal Year 1988.

The 24.1¢ Tandem Bicycle Stamp

The 24.1¢ Tandem Bicycle coil stamp was issued at a ceremony held at the Sahalee Country Club in Redmond, Washington, which

bills itself "The Bicycle Capital of the Northwest." It depicts a fin-de-siecle "bicycle built for two" immortalized in Harry Dacre's 1892 song *Daisy Bell*, in blue ink with a red service inscription, "ZIP+4," which the Postal Service considers a precancel. The B press stamps are untagged and sold in coils of 500 and 3,000. Single sleeve numbers repeat at 52-stamp intervals.

The 24.1¢ rate for unsorted mail with nine-digit ZIP-code addresses preserves the same nine-tenths of a cent discount per piece off the prime rate that the previous 21.1¢ rate, prepaid by the 21.1¢ ZIP+4 Letters coil stamp during the 22¢ letter-rate era, saved mailers then.

The Postal Service board of governors had sought to increase the discount when the proposal for a 23¢ rate was submitted to the Postal Rate Commission on May 4, 1987. A debate ensued, and those who opposed enhancing the incentive argued that with a larger discount, many mailers might opt to pay the one-time cost of computerizing nine-digit ZIP-code addresses, but leave all the sorting to the Postal Service. To avoid the possibility that mailers would take this as an invitation not to presort their bulk mailings, the Postal Rate Commission raised the rate to 24.1¢. Meanwhile the Postal Service had told cachetmakers to expect a 23¢ Tandem Bicycle coil stamp, but only in a confidential memorandum that was not distributed to the press.

At this writing, only sleeve 1 has been reported, so that is the only number collectible on first-day covers.

The 20¢ Cable Car Stamp

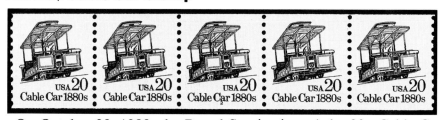

On October 28, 1988, the Postal Service issued the 20¢ Cable Car coil stamp in San Francisco's Union Square. It depicts an 1880s cable car riding over the crest of a hill. The one illustrated is a composite incorporating elements of several cable cars, but mainly the "dummy"

The original designer envisioned the Cable Car stamp as a service-inscribed bulk mail issue.

or "grip" car that carried just a few riders and pulled other passengers cars. Although the original design included a service inscription, the stamp as issued appeared only in tagged form, to cover the added-ounce first-class letter rate.

The design had originally been proposed by the Citizens' Stamp Advisory Committee as a service-inscribed stamp, but stamp specialists at the BEP pointed out that when images in two colors are too close to each other on a Giori-type inking-in system, the risk of ink contamination can lead to excessive spoilage.

In a confidential memorandum not issued to the press, cachetmakers were told that a 26¢ Cable Car coil stamp would be issued, and a 20¢ Circus Wagon coil stamp. But the Circus Wagon design was deferred, and the 20¢ denomination went to the Cable Car.

Although the 20¢ Cable Car stamps were printed on the intaglio C press, they were printed from 864-subject sleeves, 18 rows across, because the initial order was only for coils of 500 and 3,000, which are processed on the 18-row Huck coiling equipment. At that time, USPS vaults had sufficient supplies of 20¢ Flag and 20¢ Fire Pumper stamps in coils of 100 to meet the demand. But when those supplies ran low, 20¢ Cable Car stamps were ordered in coils of 100, which are processed on the 20-row Goebel coiling equipment. Future C press sleeves may make use of the full 20-row, 960-subject capacity, if USPS continues to require large quantities of 100-stamp coils.

Single sleeve numbers repeat at 48-stamp intervals. At this writing, numbers 1 and 2 exist, and both are found on first-day covers, even though sleeve 2 did not go to press until after the issue date.

In the original announcement for the stamp, the color was described as purple (PMS 276). But after the stamp was issued, the Postal Service reported that difficulties in production had required a change to dark blue (PMS 532). According to a Bureau official quoted in the *Linn's 1988 U.S. Stamp Yearbook*, the purple ink "didn't behave," failed to meet the proper density standard, and "came up much too pale." Had the Postal Service not announced the change, no one would have known the difference. PMS 276 and PMS 532 are both so dark as to be almost indistinguishable even when they are held side by side on a Pantone color products selector fan.

The 13¢ Patrol Wagon Stamp

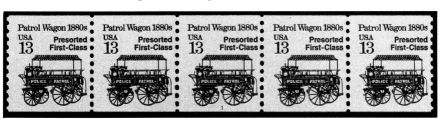

The 13¢ Patrol Wagon coil stamp was issued on October 29, 1988, in Anaheim, California, at a ceremony opening the second day of the American First Day Cover Society's annual convention. It depicts an 1880s horse-drawn police wagon in black ink with a red service inscription, "Presorted First-Class," which the Postal Service considers a precancel. The B press stamps are untagged and sold in coils of 500 and 3,000. Single sleeve numbers repeat at 52-stamp intervals.

The 13¢ basic presort rate for first-class postcards mailed in quanti-

If the 10.1¢ Oil Wagon stamp had not conveniently ended up meeting the new third-class bulk-mail rate presorted to the carrier route, the Patrol Wagon design would have been used for that rate.

ty replaced the 12¢ rate, covered by the precanceled 12¢ Stanley Steamer coil stamp, on April 3, 1988. The Postal Service board of governors had asked the Postal Rate Commission to approve a 14¢ postcard presort rate, on May 4, 1987. Had that rate been approved, we might have seen an untagged service-inscribed version of the 14¢ Iceboat coil stamp. When the Postal Rate Commission approved a 13¢ rate instead, USPS was able to use the Patrol Wagon design for that purpose because it wasn't needed for the third-class carrier route presort rate, conveniently met by a new overprint on the old 10.1¢ Oil Wagon coil stamp.

At this writing, only sleeve 1 has been reported for the 13¢ Patrol Wagon stamp, the last coil issue of 1988, so it is the only number collectible on first-day covers.

Chapter 19

Over the Top with PNCs

The year 1988 saw plate number coil collecting outstrip all other specialized areas of United States stamp collecting. A scientific poll of *Linn's* readers showed that 32.6 percent collect PNCs, that 30.9 percent had purchased PNCs within the previous 12 months, and that 34.9 percent are regular readers of *Linn's* monthly PNC column. To place these results in context, the comparable figures for one of the most popular established areas of collecting, U.S. first-day covers, are 26.8, 24.6, and 24.6 percent, respectively. In round numbers, about 25,000 *Linn's* readers collect PNCs.

It was also the year when PNC collectors finally got organized. The new Plate Number Coil Collectors Club, called "PNC3" by its members, grew so quickly that the American Philatelic Society waived its usual rule requiring an organization to exist for two years before granting it affiliate status. By the end of the year, PNC3 membership exceeded 300; the organization became APS Affiliate Number 185 on March 11, 1989. The first issue of PNC3's popular monthly newsletter *Coil Line*, edited by Tom Maeder, appeared in May. Gene C. Trinks, who as the voluntary acting president oversaw the birth and initial growth of the group, handed it over to the first elected president, Don Eastman, at a meeting in Detroit at APS STAMPSHOW in August.

In the fourth edition of the *Plate Number Coil Catalog* edited by Stephen G. Esrati, the editor included a new system of catalog numbers based on the denomination of each coil stamp and its series. Although other catalogs don't assign a separate number to each PNC, and Esrati's system does, it has not caught on among collectors and dealers. Other PNC literature published in 1988 included *The Transportation Coils and Other Plate Number Coil Issues* by Joseph Agris, a coffee-table book with eight pages of color plates whose text is marred by an unacceptable number of factual mistakes, and *Denson's Specialized Catalog of Plate Number Coils on First Day Covers, Souvenir Pages and Ceremony Programs* by Ed Denson. PNC dealer Robert

Rabinowitz, began contributing a column to the controversial paper *The Stamper Monthly* (which appeared only every several months) and launched his own gossipy and polemical newsletter called *Coil Number Expose.*

The *Scott 1989 U.S. First Day Cover Catalogue and checklist* edited by Michael A. Mellone was published in the summer of 1988. It included a new section I compiled, "Plate Number Coil FDCs," that gave an introductory overview of PNC FDCs and priced every known PNC FDC individually. In the most extreme difference between a scarce plate number and a relatively common one of the same stamp, FDCs of the 9.3¢ Mail Wagon were valued at $30 with numbers 1 or 2, as against $2,000 with numbers 3 or 4. Of course the latter two are believed to be among the rarest PNCs on first-day covers, but a surprising number of PNCs are sufficiently scarce to be priced in the hundreds or thousands of dollars.

Scott also issued its comprehensive plate number singles album pages in 1988, stiff 8½-by-11-inch loose-leaf illustrated pages that fit a standard three-ring binder, with spaces for each different plate number. This album was an instant hit with collectors of used PNC singles. At the opposite pole, Lighthouse published the Mercedes Benz of PNC albums in 1988 — expensive luxury albums with illustrated hingeless pages showing spaces for mint strips of five, and sometimes longer, including most precancel gap positions, as well as a hingeless PNC singles album. Lighthouse offers padded binders and slipcases for their top-of-the-line PNC albums.

The grandest proof that PNCs had "arrived" came when dangerous counterfeits of the most expensive plate numbers appeared on the PNC market, manufactured by a skilled Canadian forger. Fortunately he was discovered quickly by a *Linn's* investigation, and the Canadian authorities shut down his operation. The complete story is told beginning on Page 76. *Linn's* editor-publisher Michael Laurence cited that as one of the top stamp news stories of 1988.

Chapter 20

The Coil Stamps of 1989

The year 1989 began with no new coil stamps on the roster of forthcoming issues, the first time that was true since PNC collecting began. A USPS confidential memorandum to cachetmakers had told them to expect a 20¢ Circus Wagon coil stamp in the Transportation series, deferred from a previously scheduled September 26, 1988 issue date. But as I write, that stamp has been announced to the philatelic press and the public as a new 5¢ coil stamp to be issued in the spring of 1990.

The two new coil stamps that were issued during the first half of 1989 were modifications of previously issued designs, not new designs. But nobody was complaining; after the rate-change outpouring of 1988, most PNC collectors were ready for a breather.

The final "coil" stamp of 1989 was the most unusual ever — an experimental pressure-sensitive self-adhesive 25¢ Eagle and Shield stamp issued on November 10 at the Vapex stamp exhibition in Virginia Beach, Virginia. For the next 30 days it was test-marketed in 15 cities. Plate numbers were printed on the 18-stamp rectangular panes of these stamps, called "booklets," but not on the 5,004-stamp coils printed from the same gravure cylinders. In both versions, these EX-TRAordinary stamps, as the Postal Service called them, sold for more than face value — $5 for 18 stamps. They were manufactured by American Bank Note Company. The pressure-sensitive stamps were printed for ABNC on a leased Champlain gravure press at J.W. Fergusson & Sons, of Richmond, Virginia. The single printed row of coil stamps was slit from the web, die cut, and stripped by Fergusson. The rest of the web, 228-subject sheets, were die cut by Label Systems, Inc., of Bridgeport, Connecticut, and then processed into 18-subject unfolded panes and shipped by ABNC of Chicago, Illinois.

There were important developments on the coil front besides new stamp issues, however. The January 5, 1989 *Postal Bulletin* carried notice of the new policy on precanceled stamps that finally laid to rest the anachronistic rule barring precancel-use permit holders from selling precanceled stamps to collectors: "Text has been added in DMM 143.31 Nonpermit Holders, specifying (for clarity) that precanceled postage bought for philatelic purposes includes collecting and exchange of collection items. Since stamp collectors may also be permit holders, the prohibition in former DMM 143.22, constraining permit holders from selling unprecanceled stamps obtained under their permit, is unnecessary and impossible to administer. It has been deleted."

The problem had first been reported in the November 1987 issue of *The Plate Number*, Stephen G. Esrati's bimonthly PNC magazine. Throughout 1988, *Linn's* had called for the Postal Service to change the policy. Having finally prevailed, *Linn's* hailed the announcement in a January 23 editorial.

Also in January, the Postal Service issued its long-awaited inventory of stamps stored in USPS vaults for future contingencies. This included every kind of stamp, but the demand for it arose from plate number coil collectors who had been stunned by the reissue in early 1988 of 20¢ Fire Pumper plate numbers previously considered rare. *Linn's* editor-publisher Michael Laurence had called upon the Postal Service to provide the inventory list in a May 16, 1988 column, and in a June 13 letter, Assistant Postmaster General Gordon C. Morison had promised he would provide it. At the end of August Morison said it would be mailed "in about two more weeks," but we all were still waiting as the year ended.

What really happened was that Postal Service officials were surprised by much of what had been stored and forgotten, so they ordered the destruction of huge quantities of stamps that would not be required in the future. Only after the purge had been completed, which took much longer than anticipated, did Morison supply the inventory of what remained. Among the shredded stock were millions of Transportation coil stamps, an average of 700,000 of each issue, that had been held in reserve by the Philatelic Sales Division for possible future release as a mint set. The volatile aftermarket that had developed for these stamps in the years since 1981 made such a project unwise, and the idea was scrapped.

The Postal Service had come through the 1988 rate-change rush smoothly, but some adjustments were made at the beginning of 1989. First, a decision was made to phase out the 25¢ Bread Wagon stamp in coils of 100. The 25¢ Flag Over Yosemite was its replacement, although it had originally been intended only for coils of 500 and 3,000. Because of scheduling conflicts, supplies of 25¢ Honeybee stamps could not be shipped during the first five months of 1989, but as soon as supplies were replenished, they were again made available. New 1989 supplies were printed only on the offset/intaglio D press, not the combined Goebel Optiforma offset and intaglio C press method originally used. And at the end of April, collectors learned that

Reader's Digest had become the first mass mailer to devise a use for a tagged decimal-denominated coil stamp, the 12.5¢ Pushcart stamp originally issued for collectors in 1985. That story is told beginning on Page 144.

The 25¢ Flag Over Yosemite Stamp on Phosphor-Coated Paper

Ever since the successful experiment with the 22¢ Flag test coil stamp on phosphored paper, Postal Service planners had wanted to switch to that system of tagging for prime-rate stamps, and perhaps eventually for all stamps. The main purpose is to thwart those who re-use postage by making it more difficult for them to remove cancelation ink. But the paper used for the "T" coils manufactured by Harrison and Son Ltd. of England, with the taggant applied in the sizing bath during paper manufacture, was expensive.

To bring down the cost of phosphored paper, the Bureau of Engraving and Printing, at the end of 1988, began to experiment with phosphor-coated paper, that is, paper on which the phosphor is added after it is manufactured. In the initial tests, the coating was too heavy. Part of the phosphor particles flaked off during press runs. According to Charles Yeager in the April 1989 issue of *The United States Specialist*.

"There was some concern among printers whether the 'flying phosphor' was toxic and thus a health hazard. The phosphor was tested and found to be non-toxic.

"The BEP also tried another approach. Regular Flag stamp paper was run through the Andreotti gravure press. The 25¢ Flag design was printed over the gravure phosphor coating. After printing, the intaglio Flag inks began to flake off and that ended the experiment.

"According to a BEP spokesman, the problem of excessive phosphor was finally solved by returning all rolls of the phosphor-coated paper to the paper supplier. The supplier reduced the heavy coating of phosphor by 'shaving off' the top of the phosphor particles that were 'standing up.' I interpret this to mean that the BEP returned some of the phosphor-coated paper rolls to the paper finisher where the rolls were scuffed or brushed to remove loose phosphor particles. The rolls were then probably calendered and shipped back to the BEP. Subsequent test printings using the 'shaved' paper produced stamps acceptable to the USPS and regular production runs began.

"The BEP used rolls of phosphor-coated paper that were 18½-inches wide during the test period. Rolls of paper 18½-inches wide are regularly used with 864-subject (18 x 48) C press printing sleeves or 936-subject (18 x 52) B press sleeves. Rolls of paper 20½-inches wide are regularly used with 960-subject (20 x 48) printing sleeves to print stamps on the C press for processing into coils of 100.

"Flag Over Yosemite test press runs were conducted using a 960-subject printing sleeve and 18½-inch wide rolls of paper. This combination produced printed rolls of Flag stamps 19 rows across the roll and left one row of stamp subjects on the printing sleeve unused. Complicated? Yes, but rolls of paper 18½-inches wide cost less than the wider 20½-inch rolls."

And the rolls of phosphor-coated paper cost only half as much as the Harrison and Sons phosphor-impregnated paper. Although the Postal Service announcements and news releases call both papers "pre-phosphored," the differences are easy to see under shortwave ultraviolet illumination. The original phosphored test paper appears smooth, brilliant and uniform. The phosphor-coated paper appears uneven and splotchy, a good match for the overall tagging applied by the old Cottrell presses.

By January 1989, the experiment was deemed a success. The January 26 *Postal Bulletin* carried this notice:

"A prephosphored 25-cent Flag Over Yosemite coil stamp goes on sale February 14 in Yosemite, California. The prephosphored stamp can be distinguished from the regular 25-cent Flag Over Yosemite coil stamp by the whiter paper and colors that appear appreciably brighter . . .

"This coil issue is assigned Item 7737, the same number as the current conventionally tagged 25-cent Flag Over Yosemite coil of 100. To distinguish the prephosphored 25-cent Flag coil issue from the current one, the shipping cartons will be marked Item 7737P. If personnel remove those coils for philatelic centers from the carton, they should identify it in some manner as prephosphored stock.

"Because of the commingling in its inventory of the conventionally tagged stamps and those printed on prephosphored paper, the Bureau of Engraving and Printing will not fill requisitions specifically for one or the other type of coil. The prephosphored coils will gradually replace the conventionally tagged 25-cent Flag Over Yosemite coils."

The philatelic news release appeared on February 10, just four days before the issue date, stating that there would be no dedication ceremony but that a first-day-of-issue cancellation would be offered, with a grace period of 60 days for submitting covers. Because of the long grace period, and even longer extensions granted to some cachetmakers and FDC servicers, first-day covers exist of numbers 5, 6, 7, 8, 9 and 10, although only number 8 was available on the issue date. The original block-tagged version of the stamp issued in 1988 is described on Page 231.

A lot of people were on hand for the dedication ceremony at Yosemite National Park when the original 25¢ Flag stamp was issued on May 20, 1988, but only a few braved the weather to be present on February 14, 1989, when the stamp was reissued on phosphor-coated paper. Ed Denson was present on both occasions, to make these FDCs. Both have unofficial cancels on PNC strips, as well as first-day-of-issue cancels on singles.

The phosphor-coated variety of the 25¢ Flag Over Yosemite coil stamps went on sale in many post offices before the February 14 official first day, probably because postal clerks who had not read the *Postal Bulletin* announcement failed to notice a difference between the new and old versions of the stamp. As a result, there are probably a lot of predated covers to be found for this issue, covers bearing the phosphor-coated version canceled before February 14.

There was no first-day ceremony at Yosemite National Park this time. In fact, as PNC first-day cover specialist Ed Denson wrote, "The week prior to the release was the coldest on record here since the winter of '36." Denson was one of only five collectors who actually went to the Yosemite post office on February 14 to prepare FDCs.

Although the aim of the Postal Service had been to replace the block-tagged version of the stamp with the new version printed on phosphor-coated paper, the Bureau did not have a sufficient supply of the new paper to make the switch immediately. Several of the later sleeve numbers re-appeared on the older paper with block tagging, although at this writing sleeve 6 is known only on phosphor-coated paper. The scorecard for the first year's production of 25¢ Flag Over Yosemite coil stamps looks like this:

Sleeve Number	Press	Subjects per Sleeve	Block Tagged	Phosphor-Coated
1	B	936 (18X52)	X	
2	B	936 (18X52)	X	X
3	B	936 (18X52)	X	X
4	C/D	864 (18X48)	X	
5	C/D	960 (20X48)	X	X
6	C/D	864 (18X48)		X
7	C/D	960 (20X48)	X	X
8	C/D	864 (18X48)	X	X
9	C/D	960 (20X48)	X	X
10	C/D	960 (20X48)		X
11	C/D	960 (20X48)		X
13	C/D	960 (20X48)		X
14	C/D	960 (20X48)		X

Although the 864-subject sleeves do not use the full production capacity of the C and D presses, their 18-across format conveniently fits the Huck coiling equipment when orders call for processing into coils of 500 and 3,000 stamps.

Experiments with 10,000-stamp coils, begun with the block-tagged 25¢ Flag stamps in 1988, continued using phosphor-coated rolls in 1989. These were deemed successful, and the 10,000-stamp coils went into general distribution in 1990.

This is the history of a stamp in mid-passage, certain to be enriched further before its reign ends with the next rate increase. Already numbers 5 through 11 exist imperforate.

The 7.1¢ Tractor Stamp (5-Digit ZIP+4)

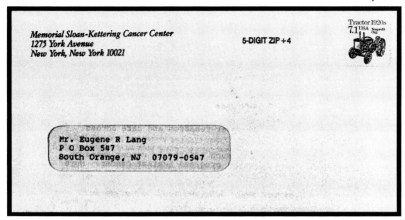

In some instances the 7.1¢ Tractor stamp with the original inscription was used to prepay the new 7.1¢ rate, as indicated by the added endorsement on this cover. The contents are dated September 19, 1988.

The original 7.1¢ Tractor coil stamps were issued in Sarasota, Florida, on February 6, 1987. The tagged version was a relic of a policy on its way out, to issue a collector version of each bulk-mail stamp. (Until November 20, 1986, such stamps had been required to service first-day covers.) The untagged version bore the service inscription "Nonprofit Org." to cover the third-class bulk rate for mail presorted to five ZIP-code digits by nonprofit mailers that was in effect from April 20, 1986, to April 2, 1988. Both of those stamps are described beginning on Page 206.

The original service-inscribed stamp had a brief reprieve for false franking at the 7.6¢ rate that went into effect on April 3, 1988, but eventually it was superseded by the 7.6¢ Carreta stamp. Both original versions were withdrawn from philatelic sale on February 28, 1989.

Ironically, however, a new 7.1¢ nonprofit rate began at the very moment the old one ended, for a rate tier that had not previously existed: third-class mail addressed with 9-digit ZIP codes and presorted to five digits. Some nonprofit mailers used the stamps with the original service inscription to cover the new 7.1¢ rate, although this usage was not specifically authorized.

Just two weeks before the stamp's issue date, the Postal Service announced that the 7.1¢ Tractor stamp would be reissued on May 26, 1989, with a new, more restrictive service inscription, "Nonprofit 5-Digit ZIP+4."

The dedication ceremony was held at COMPEX in Rosemont, Illinois, near Chicago. The stamp's basic design and color scheme were identical to the original. The typeface of the service inscription was changed from a serif font on the original to sans-serif on the reissue. The new stamp was issued only in untagged form, in coils of 500 and

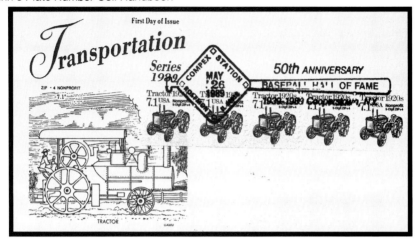

This Gamm first-day cover is canceled with the special commemorative postmark used at Compex, the stamp show at which the new version of the 7.1¢ Tractor coil stamp was issued.

3,000, printed on the intaglio B press, with single sleeve numbers spaced at 52-stamp intervals. Because the inking-in Giori press system prints both colors — dark red of the vignette and the black service inscription — from the same sleeve, a new sleeve was required, numbered 1, just as the previous ones had been. That is the number that appears on first-day covers.

Chapter 21

PNCs Today and Tomorrow

There are always risks attached to writing history as it happens. Unexpected developments can render a writer's work foolish or obsolete. The perspective of time can add insights and alter interpretations of the most ordinary observations, the most confident conclusions. Nevertheless, the close of 1989 and the start of a new decade seems a good time to pause, to look back on the first nine years of plate number coil collecting, take stock of where we are, and try to imagine our future direction.

Although in relative terms 1989 was relaxed year for coil collecting, we have continued to advance. One of the most marvelous pieces of PNC literature is Ed Denson's March 15, 1989, illustrated newsletter, *The Point*, describing his adventure in pursuit of unofficial first-day covers of the reissued 25¢ Flag Over Yosemite coil stamps during a near-record cold spell in the California mountains. Robert M. Washburn published two booklets *PNC Varieties* and *PNCs on Cover* that bring PNC reference material closer to classic standards. The former includes every plate or production variation from major errors to flyspecks that occur on PNC coil rolls. The latter is a compendium of earliest reported usages for each PNC on a cover that actually passed through the mails, as well as a scale of relative scarcity of each PNC on commercially used cover. Both will be updated in future editions.

The fifth edition of the *Catalog of Plate Number Coils* edited by Stephen G. Esrati continued to set the standard as the serious PNC collector's required reference. The Postal Service streamlined its bimonthly *Philatelic Catalog*, re-arranging coil stamps to include denominations consecutively, rather than by year of issue. This should speed the handling of over-the-counter philatelic sales. (Other definitive stamps are similarly re-arranged, but the effect will be most profound with coils, since coil stamps are the runaway best-sellers at philatelic counters.) The 1989 edition of the H.E. Harris and Company, Inc. *Postage Stamp Catalog* of United States and British North

America for the first time listed precanceled and service-inscribed coil stamps as unnumbered mint singles and as plate strips of three, but still without regard for specific plate numbers.

Cumulatively, these small incremental developments indicate that we have come a long way since the first plate number coils appeared in April 1981, the initial wave of enthusiasm for PNC collecting in 1983, the start of specialized PNC publications in 1985, the meeting at AMERIPEX in 1986, the market surge in 1987, and the founding of the Plate Number Coil Collectors Club in 1988. We began at the fringes of United States stamp collecting, and we now have full catalog recognition, albums with annual supplements, and popular columns in the philatelic press.

Our future depends largely on what the Postal Service decides to do and how we respond. Although a rumor has circulated for some time that the Transportation coil series is nearing its end, USPS officials deny that. The series began with a decision to unite two concerns — the desire of mailers for attractive coil stamps whose subjects have broad appeal and do not generate controversy, and the desire of stamp collectors for line-engraved stamps. The series has been so successful in both respects that it has survived several significant postal policy changes: switching from plain line precancel overprints to putting restrictive endorsements into the overprints, to eliminating overprints and returning service inscriptions to the basic engraved design; from issuing tagged versions of every new design to abolishing them for decimal values; from small digits to large for a stamp's denomination; from deep engraving to shallow; and so on. Postal Service officials insist that no decision has been made, or even discussed to end the Transportation coil series any time soon, and they still have several designs awaiting future issue. One of them, the circus wagon, was planned for 1988 but never materialized.

On the other hand, discussions have taken place and are continuing about what kind of new series should replace the Transportation coils when the time comes. Designs do exist for one or more new series, but USPS spokesmen refuse to give any details about them. They decline to state whether the 25¢ Honeybee coil stamp was issued as a pilot for a possible future series.

The biggest factors affecting future coil stamp production will be pressures from the marketplace. In seeking bids for production of the nondenominated F contingency stamp, the U.S. Postal Service advertisement offered a variety of production options: gravure, or combinations of offset and intaglio, flexography and gravure, flexography and intaglio, or gravure and intaglio. The aim is security against counterfeiting at the lowest possible cost, while yielding an attractive, colorful stamp. Besides a low bidder from the private sector, who will print the sheet stamp version, the Bureau of Engraving and Printing is also doing the booklet and coil F stamps. F stamp coil production began at BEP in October 1988 and continued into 1989, using the gravure process. The design of the F stamp is a flower, referred to in internal BEP documents as an orchid.

The USPS Philatelic and Retail Services annual report for 1988 made this prediction: "As rates become more complex (more rate tiers), more denominations of coil stamps may be required . . . Commemoratives in booklets, and perhaps eventually in coils, may require additional quantities of stamps in both formats." But commemorative-size coils may have to wait a bit. In a 1988 interview, Dickey B. Rustin, then manager of the USPS Stamp Information Branch, said, "Doubling the size of coils would drive costs up. We're not interested in that at the moment."

Other changes are likely to come first. Current research aims at improving the adhesive used on stamps, the quality of stamp paper and the effectiveness of phosphor taggants. Battelle Memorial Institute has a $700,000 research contract with the Postal Service to identify a better stamp adhesive. American Bank Note Company has a research contract to develop specifications for a superior gravure stamp paper. Experiments with phosphored and phosphor-coated papers have been conducted at the Bureau of Engraving and Printing since 1987. As solutions are found in each of these areas, they will have an effect on the stamps we collect. Today the plurality of all United States postage stamps is coils — 46 percent — significantly ahead of sheet and booklet stamps, at 27 percent each, but booklet stamps are inching up while coil stamps are beginning to decline.

If fiscal concerns continue to dominate future stamp-issuing policies, we are likely to see more and more multicolor gravure and offset coil stamps, less and less line engraving. To date, plate number coil collecting has adjusted to every unforeseen change that has come, and has grown stronger from every challenge. Many changes are in store for the stamps we love to collect. We can expect a lively, fascinating adventure ahead.

Bibliography

Official Publications of the United States Postal Service

Accountable Paper Items Shipped During Fiscal Year 1987.
Accountable Paper Items Shipped During Fiscal Year 1988.
Accountable Paper Items Shipped During Fiscal Year 1989.
Accountable Paper Items Shipped During Fiscal Year 1989, revised January 9, 1990.
Actual Shipments of Accountable Paper Items During Fiscal Year 1980.
Actual Shipments of Accountable Paper Items During Fiscal Year 1981.
Actual Shipments of Accountable Paper Items During Postal Fiscal Year 1982.
Actual Shipments of Accountable Paper Items During Postal Fiscal Year 1983.
Actual Shipments of Accountable Paper Items During Postal Fiscal Year 1984.
Actual Shipments of Accountable Paper Items During Postal Fiscal Year 1985.
Actual Shipments of Accountable Paper Items During Postal Fiscal Year 1986.
The Americana Series Issues of 1975-1981. 1981.
Domestic Mail Manual.
Monthly Postage Stamp Plate Activity Report.
Philatelic and Retail Services Annual Report, FY 1988.
Philatelic Catalog.
Postal Bulletin.
The Postal Service Guide to U.S. Stamps. 9th edition. 1982.
The Postal Service Guide to U.S. Stamps. 10th edition. 1983.
The Postal Service Guide to U.S. Stamps. 11th edition. 1984.
The Postal Service Guide to U.S. Stamps. 12th edition. 1985.
The Postal Service Guide to U.S. Stamps. 13th edition. 1986.
The Postal Service Guide to U.S. Stamps. 14th edition. 1987.
The Postal Service Guide to U.S. Stamps. 15th edition. 1988.
The Postal Service Guide to U.S. Stamps. 16th edition. 1989.
Stamp News USA.
Stamps and Stories. 8th edition. 1981.
United States Postage Stamps. Transmittal Letter 8. Publication 9. 1984.
The United States Postal Service Mint Set of 1981 Definitive Stamps and Postal Stationery.
The United States Postal Service Mint Set of 1982 Definitive Stamps and Postal Stationery.

United States Postal Service Mint Set of Definitive Stamps and Postal Stationery 1983.

United States Postal Service Mint Set of Definitive Stamps and Postal Stationery 1984.

Books and Monographs

Joseph Agris. *The Transportation Coils and other Plate Number Coil Issues.* Eclectic Publishing. 1988.

George Amick. *Linn's U.S. Stamp Yearbook 1988.* Linn's Stamp News. 1989.

Fred Boughner. *Linn's U.S. Stamp Yearbook 1983.* Linn's Stamp News. 1984.

Fred Boughner. *Linn's U.S. Stamp Yearbook 1984.* Linn's Stamp News. 1985.

Fred Boughner. *Linn's U.S. Stamp Yearbook 1985.* Linn's Stamp News. 1986.

Fred Boughner. *Linn's U.S. Stamp Yearbook 1986.* Linn's Stamp News. 1987.

Fred Boughner. *Linn's U.S. Stamp Yearbook 1987.* Linn's Stamp News. 1988.

Dennis D. Chamberlain. *The Great Philatelic Treasure Hunt.* Dennis D. Chamberlain. 1983.

Dennis D. Chamberlain. *The Great Philatelic Treasure Hunt 1986 Update.* Dennis D. Chamberlain. 1986.

Ed Denson. *An Introduction to Collecting Plate Number Coils.* Second revised edition. Ed Denson. 1986.

Herman Herst Jr. *Nassau Street.* Seventh edition. First revised edition. Linn's Stamp News. 1988.

Linn's World Stamp Almanac. Fourth edition. Linn's Stamp News. 1982.

Linn's World Stamp Almanac. Fifth edition. Linn's Stamp News. 1989.

Stanley B. Segal. *Errors, Freaks and Oddities on U.S. Stamps — Question Marks in Philately.* Bureau Issues Association. 1979.

Robert M. Washburn. *PNC Varieties.* Robert M. Washburn. 1988 and 1990.

Robert M. Washburn. *PNCs on Cover.* Robert M. Washburn. 1988 and 1990.

Les Winick. *The Transportation Series of Coil Stamps.* The Washington Press. 1989.

Catalogs

Stephen R. Datz. *U.S. Errors 1986.* General Philatelic Corporation. 1986.

Stephen R. Datz. *U.S. Errors 1988.* General Philatelic Corporation. 1987.

Stephen R. Datz. *U.S. Errors 1990.* General Philatelic Corporation. 1989.

Denson's Specialized Catalog of Plate Number Coils on First Day Covers, Souvenir Pages and Ceremony Programs. First edition. Ed Denson. 1988.

George V.H. Godin, Vahe Nazar, and G. William Patten, eds. *Durland Standard Plate Number Catalog 1984.* Bureau Issues Association Inc. 1984.

George V.H. Godin, Vahe Nazar, and G. William Patten, eds. *Durland Standard Plate Number Catalog 1986.* Bureau Issues Association Inc. 1986.

Harris Illustrated Postage Stamp Catalog for United States, Canada & United Nations. Winter-spring 1982 edition. H.E. Harris & Co. Inc. 1981.

Hebert's Standard Plate Number Single Catalogue 1988. 12th edition. Trans Pacific Stamp Company 1988.

Michael A. Mellone. *Scott 1989 U.S. First Day Cover Catalogue & Checklist.* Scott Publishing Company 1988.

Michael A. Mellone. *Scott 1990 U.S. First Day Cover Catalogue & Checklist.* Scott Publishing Company 1989.

Michel USA-Spezial-Katalog 1985/86. Schwaneberger Verlag GMBH. 1985.

Michel USA-Spezial-Katalog 1989. Schwaneberger Verlag GMBH. 1989.

Minkus New 1982 American Stamp Catalog. Minkus Publications Inc. 1981.

Minkus 1988 Specialized American Stamp Catalog. Minkus Publications Inc. 1987.

The Noble Official Catalog of United States Bureau Precancels. 63rd edition. Gilbert W. Noble. 1981.

Scott Pelcyger. *Mellone's Specialized Catalogue of First Day Ceremony Programs & Events.* FDC Publishing Company 1989.

Plate Number Coil Study Group. *Catalog of Plate Number Coils.* Stephen G. Esrati. 1985.

Plate Number Coil Study Group. *Catalog of Plate Number Coils.* Corrected first printing. Stephen G. Esrati. 1985.

Plate Number Coil Study Group. *Catalog of Plate Number Coils.* Stephen G. Esrati. 1986.

Plate Number Coil Study Group. *Catalog of Plate Number Coils.* Third edition. Stephen G. Esrati. 1987.

Plate Number Coil Study Group. *Plate Number Coil Catalog 1988.* Fourth edition. Stephen G. Esrati. 1988.

Plate Number Coil Study Group. *Plate Number Coil Catalog 1989.* Fifth edition. Stephen G. Esrati. 1989.

Precancel Stamp Society Bureau Precancel Catalog. Second edition. Precancel Stamp Society Inc. 1982.

Price Guide of United States, Canada & United Nations Stamps. 1987 Revised edition. Brookman Stamp Company 1987.

Scott 1982 Specialized Catalogue of United States Stamps. Scott Publishing Company 1981.

Scott 1987 Specialized Catalogue of United States Stamps. Scott Publishing Company 1986.

Scott 1988 Specialized Catalogue of United States Stamps. Scott Publishing Company 1987.

Scott 1989 Specialized Catalogue of United States Stamps. Scott Publishing Company 1988.

Scott 1990 Specialized Catalogue of United States Stamps. Scott Publishing Company 1989.

1982-83 Stamp News. Marshall Field's. 1982.

Periodicals

The American Philatelist. Published monthly by the American Philatelic Society. Bill Welch, ed.

Coil Collector. Published monthly by United States Coil Collectors Society. Ron Bowman, ed. January 1984 - September 1985.

Coil Line. Published monthly by the Plate Number Coil Collectors Club. Tom Maeder, ed. May 1988-.

Coil Number Expose. Published irregularly by Robert Rabinowitz. May 1988-.

EFO Collector. Published bimonthly by the Errors, Freaks and Oddities Collectors Club. Howard Gates, ed.

First Days. Published 8 times a year by the American First Day Cover Society. Sol Koved, ed.

Label Mania. Published infrequently by the Coil Label Study Group. David E. Barrie LaVergne, ed. January 1989-.

Linn's Stamp News. Published weekly by Amos Press Inc. Michael Laurence, ed.

Mekeel's Weekly Stamp News. Published weekly by Philatelic Communications Corporation. John F. Dunn, ed.

Modern Postal History Journal. Published quarterly by the Modern Postal History Society. Terence Hines, ed.

Plate Block and U.S. Single Newsletter. Published monthly by Robert Rabinowitz.

The Plate Number. Published six times per year by Stephen G. Esrati. February 1986-.

Plate Number Coil Bulletin. Published monthly by Tom Myers. February 1985-?

The Point. Published occasionally by Ed Denson. May 1988-.

Scott Stamp Monthly. Published monthly by Scott Publishing Company Richard L. Sine, ed.

S.P.A. Journal. Monthly publication of the Society of Philatelic Americans. Belmont Faries, ed. Ceased publication with the December 1983 issue.

Stamp Collector. Published weekly by Van Dahl Publications. Dane Claussen, ed.

Stamp Wholesaler. Published 28 times a year by Van Dahl Publications. James A. Magruder II, ed.

Stamps. Published weekly by H.L. Lindquist Publications. Al Starkweather, ed.

Topical Time. Published bimonthly by the American Topical Association. Glen Crago, ed.

The United States Specialist. Published monthly by the Bureau Issues Association. Charles Yeager, ed.

Appendix

Modern Coil Stamp Production

Postage stamps are a 19th-century invention, but coil stamps are a 20-century invention (although classic coil expert Joseph Agris says the first patent for coil stamps was issued in 1889). Truly efficient coil stamp production is a development of recent years. Advances have continued throughout the period since plate number coils were introduced in 1981.

The first United States coil stamps were privately perforated by vending machine operators from imperforate 400-subject sheets. The Post Office Department sold the sheets in the fall of 1906, and the first private coils appeared in 1907. The following year saw the first coil stamps manufactured by the Bureau of Engraving and Printing, also prepared from sheets printed on flatbed presses. Neither the private nor the Bureau coils were economical to produce, since both required paste-up splices every 20th stamp.

To overcome this problem, Stickney rotary presses were developed. The first rotary-press coil stamps were issued in 1914, and from that time until 1956, all United States coil stamps were printed on the Stickney presses. As we have seen in Chapter 2, the production bottleneck in those years was not in the printing, but in the coil processing, essentially a labor-intensive manual system. The introduction of the Cottrell presses in 1956, capable of high-speed printing, using pre-gummed paper since 1972, and the mechanized Huck coiling equipment in 1959, introduced the modern age of coil stamp produc-

The first coil stamps were privately perforated from imperforate sheets sold by the U.S. Post Office Department. The example shown here was manufactured in 1907.

275

The first coil stamps manufactured by the Bureau of Engraving and Printing were issued in 1908.

tion. This was the basic method being used when PNCs were introduced in 1981.

The Stickney and Cottrell machines were single-color intaglio printing presses. In addition to developing more efficient production of single-color stamps, especially coils, the Bureau of Engraving and Printing and the Postal Service were also developing multicolor presses, which were especially in demand for printing Flag stamps. The 6¢ and 8¢ Flag Over White House coil stamps of 1969 and 1971, the 10¢ Crossed Flags coil stamp of 1973, and the 13¢ Flag Over Independence Hall coil stamp of 1975 were printed on the short-lived nine-color Huck press. The Huck press had been touted as the most advanced stamp printing press in the world when it made its appearance in 1968. It used a complicated system of 90 40-subject (2 x 20) small plates attached to three separate printing cylinders. Each print-

Coil stamp production became practical with the introduction of the Stickney rotary presses. The first rotary press coil stamps, shown here, were issued in 1914.

ing unit could print up to three colors. The Huck press proved to be a monumental failure in practice, with an unacceptable rate of spoilage and plate usage. It was scrapped in 1978.

Meanwhile, the Giori three-color intaglio B press had been obtained in 1973 to print booklet and coil stamps. The first coil stamps printed on the B press were the three-color 13¢ Flag Over Independence Hall design of 1976 (previously printed on the Huck press) and two 1978 Americana coils; the three-color 15¢ Fort McHenry Flag and the blue 16¢ Statue of Liberty Head, which originally had been printed as a Cottrell press product.

That was the situation as the new plate number coil system went into effect in 1981: The Bureau of Engraving and Printing had two proven ways of printing coil stamps, on the single-color Cottrell intaglio presses or on the three-color intaglio B press. Webs printed on either of those presses had 18 subjects across, the format accepted by the Huck coil-processing equipment that had been installed in 1959. BEP also possessed two presses that had never before been used to print coil stamps, the Andreotti gravure press acquired in 1969 and the Giori combination gravure/intaglio A press obtained in 1973, both of which would eventually be used to print coils. Over the next several years, additional coil production equipment would go on line.

The Intaglio B Press

The paper web is shown here on the Bureau of Engraving and Printing's B press as it approaches the intaglio sleeve to be printed.

The first coil stamps with the new plate numbers printed on them were the 18¢ Flags printed on the Giori intaglio B press. Officially called Press 701 at the Bureau of Engraving and Printing, the B press was built by Koenig and Bauer of Wurzburg, West Germany. It was acquired in 1973, but its first stamp production, the 13¢ Flag Over Independence Hall coil previously printed on the Huck press, did not appear until the early part of 1976.

The B press prints up to three colors from a single line-engraved sleeve, using the Giori system, which applies each color selectively from separate inking-in rollers. In the beginning a solvent wipe was used to remove excess ink before the sleeve printed the paper web. Now a water wipe is used. Only coil and booklet stamps are printed on the B press, so it prints only roll-to-roll without an on-press capability for sheeting or perforating. The B press prints on rolls of uncoat-

In the Giori system, up to three different ink colors can be deposited on the B press sleeve at one time by separate inking-in rollers. Here the cutaway design of the inking-in rollers can be seen.

ed, pregummed paper. Flag coil stamps have been printed on paper backed with glossy resin dextrin "wet" or "shiny" gum, or a synthetic "shiny-gum" equivalent made from polyvinyl acetate.

Transportation coils have been printed on paper backed with "dry" or "dull" matte-textured Davac gum, also incorporating polyvinyl acetate. Official stamps have been printed on both. From its first use, the B press has been able to apply tagging phosphor blocks in a lacquer suspension. In 1984 the B press gained the capability to apply relief-printed (letterpress) precancel overprints.

The B press employs a two-roll "flying paster" feed system, now common to all BEP rotary presses. This system automatically fastens a new roll of paper to the end of the previous roll as it runs out, without the necessity of stopping the press.

Coil stamps are printed from seamless 936-subject intaglio sleeves, 18 subjects across by 52 in circumference, at a rate of about 5,000 impressions (4,500,000 stamps) per hour. The 18-across format was dictated by the Huck coil-processing equipment, purchased many years earlier for use with the Cottrell presses. The first plate used to apply precancel overprints was simply a seamless routed-out tagging roller that applied two plain lines to each of the 18 rows across the web. This was used to print 11¢ Caboose and 20¢ Flag Over Supreme Court precancels.

Later B press precancels were printed from rubber paired composition 468-subject flexographic plates, 18 subjects across by 26 in the

This B press flexographic plate was used to apply Bulk Rate precancel overprints to 12.5¢ Pushcart and 10.1¢ Oil Wagon coil stamps.

rotary dimension. The seam where the two flexographic plates meet shows as a gap in the overprinted lines that occurs at 26-stamp intervals throughout each coil.

Flag series coil stamps of each design issued since 1975 have been printed on the B press. Since 1984, many single-color Transportation series coil stamps have been printed on the B press, and most of the two-color intaglio Transportation coils beginning in 1987. After the intaglio C press went on line in 1984, most production of 100-stamp intaglio coils was shifted to that press or, more recently, to the intaglio section of the D press, leaving the B press to print coils processed into rolls of 500, 3,000 and 10,000.

The Cottrell Intaglio Presses

The Cottrell single-color intaglio presses were the second to print PNCs, beginning with the 18¢ Surrey coil stamps of 1981 that launched the popular Transportation series. These were the oldest rotary printing presses still in use at the Bureau of Engraving and Printing. Transportation series stamps were the last coils printed on them before their retirement. The prototype for these presses was built to Bureau specifications by the Huck company of New York City and delivered in 1950. Further development refined the design, and in 1955 BEP ordered five of the new presses from the Cottrell Company of Westerly, Rhode Island, the first of which was delivered in late 1955 and the rest in 1956. By 1981, these five presses accounted for 60 percent of all BEP stamp production.

The webfed single-color Cottrell intaglio presses — designated Presses 801, 802, 803, 804, and 805 — printed line-engraved commemorative and regular stamps at a rate of 5,400 impressions (2,160,000 to 4,665,600 stsamps, depending on format) per hour. The commemoratives were normally processed into 50-stamp panes, and the regular stamps into 100-stamp panes or various sizes of booklets and coils.

The Cottrell presses printed roll-to-roll from two curved plates mounted together around the cylinder, thus printing joint lines on coil stamps at the seam between two plates. Cottrell press coil plates were laid out in a 432-subject format, 18 subjects across by 24 in the rotary direction, so the joint lines (and on most coils printed since 1981, plate numbers) appear at 24-stamp intervals on each roll. Phosphor tagging ink was applied continuously by a roller, resulting in somewhat uneven overall tagging quite different in appearance from the block tagging applied by the other presses.

When the Cottrell presses were first acquired, two of the 29 old Stickney rotary presses were kept to print precancels, but in 1959 a letterpress overprinting station was added to one of the Cottrells. Thus, precanceled coil stamps manufactured before 1959 were printed by the Stickneys' "wet" process, while those manufactured from 1959 and after were "dry" printed on the Cottrells. Several denominations in the Liberty series were printed by both methods.

The relief image hard vinyl or rubber composition letterpress plates used on the Cottrell press to apply precancel overprints to coil stamps were laid out as 108-subject "mats," nine subjects across and 12 subjects in the rotary dimension, used in sets of four so that two mats yielded 18 subjects across the web, and the two mats (24 subjects) around the cylinder yielded gaps in the precancel lines at 12-stamp intervals. On occasions when mats manufactured at different times with different overprint type styles were used together in the four-mat set, se-tenant overprints resulted, with different type styles at the right and the left of the gap.

Until the late 1970s, the Cottrell presses applied adhesive to the paper web during printing. After that, Cottrell press stamps were printed on uncoated paper pregummed with Davac, a matte-textured resin-dextrin adhesive in a solvent emulsion containing a small amount of polyvinyl acetate.

Early on the morning of March 5, 1982, a fire at BEP's annex building damaged the four remaining Cottrell presses. Press 802, which had been printing 20¢ Fire Pumper coil stamps, and Press 804 had to be scrapped. The other two presses were lightly damaged. Both were returned to production within 72 hours, Press 801 for tagged stamps and Press 803 for precancels.

Although Cottrell press printing has been called "dry," in contrast to the "wet" printing of the old Stickney presses, the terms are relative. As the web entered the press, it passed first through a water fountain that applied moisture to the side of the paper that next came into contact with the plate. But the old Stickney system had required 15 to 30 percent moisture by weight, whereas the Cottrell required dampening of only 5 to 10 percent. True dry printing came only with the introduction of pregummed paper.

The first stamp printed on the prototype Huck press was the 3¢ International Red Cross commemorative of 1952. It was a two-color stamp, with the blue design printed from the intaglio plates, and the red cross printed on a letterpress attachment later used for precanceling. The first Cottrell press stamp was the 3¢ Statue of Liberty definitive of 1954; the first Cottrell commemorative was the 3¢ Wheatland stamp of 1956.

For the first three years of plate number coils, the largest number were printed on the Cottrell presses: prime rate 18¢ Surrey and 20¢ Fire Pumper stamps, second-ounce 17¢ Electric Auto stamps, all tagged issues; bulk mail issues including 9.3¢ Mail Wagon, 5.9¢ Bicycle, 10.9¢ Hansom Cab, 4¢ Stagecoach, 5.2¢ Sleigh precancels and their tagged counterparts for collectors; tagged 2¢ Locomotive, 4¢ Stagecoach, 3¢ Handcar, 1¢ Omnibus, and 5¢ Motorcycle changemakers and makeup postage stamps. Another Cottrell PNC stamp was the prime-rate 20¢ Consumer Education coil.

As newer, more modern presses were ordered, delivered, and placed into production, the Bureau planned to phase out the Cottrell presses. Two were scheduled to be taken out of service in May 1982, and the others by the end of the year. The fire on March 5 moved up the retirement of the first two by two months, but the target date for the retirement of the other two was not met. Lack of press capacity meant the two were needed to reprint older single-color definitive stamps, and occasional new issues. But after the 5¢ Motorcycle stamp was printed (it was issued on October 10, 1983) the Cottrells got no new assignments for over a year.

New 1984 Transportation series coils, the 11¢ Caboose and 7.4¢ Baby Buggy designs, were assigned to the B press. But before the Cottrells could be shut down for good, the 1985 rate increases revived them. Six new coil stamps were assigned to the two remaining 29-year-old machines: the 14¢ Iceboat, 8.3¢ Ambulance, and 4.9¢ Buckboard coils, all in tagged editions, and all but the 14¢ Iceboat and 11¢ Stutz Bearcat in precanceled form. This time, though, the end really was in sight. The last stamps printed on Press 803 in November 1985 were dummy coil testing stamps. On November 17, Press 801, the only operating Cottrell press after Press 803 had been used for the final time, printed an order of $5 postage due stamps. At 4 p.m. on Wednesday, November 20, 1985, those two Cottrell presses were permanently removed from service, ending an era.

No longer would collectors see new stamps with the characteristic Cottrell features: high relief prints from the deep recessed images of line-engraved plates, on paper tinted in the ink's shade because of the presses' less-than-perfect paper wiping system, and frequent printed gripper cracks caused by the stress of the plate fasteners on the fatigued metal of the curved steel plates. These presses were not only the workhorses of BEP's stamp printing operation for three decades, they must also be credited with playing the key role in ushering in modern stamp production methods: from "wet" to "dry" intaglio printing, using fast-drying inks; from on-press gumming to the use of pre-gummed paper; the birth of phosphorescent tagging on U.S. stamps; and as a necessary adjunct to their high productivity, from manual to mechanized coil processing.

The products of the Cottrell presses represent the Golden Age of modern postage stamps. It is certain that future generations of stamp collectors will study them and admire them with the same passion that classics lovers apply to flat-plate line-engraved 19th-century United States stamps.

The Andreotti Gravure Press

After the Cottrells, the next presses to print plate number coils were the two that employ the gravure process: the Andreotti and the combination A press. Both were used to print the nondenominated D contingency coil stamps in 1982, stamps that were not placed on sale until just before the 1985 rate changes. Their face value was established as 22¢.

Originally the D coil stamps were supposed to be printed on the Cottrell presses. Six Cottrell plates had been manufactured for that purpose, between July 1981 and February 1982, but no stamps were printed from them, despite the fact that the Cottrells' ability to print stamps of the same general design had been proven with the A, B and C contingency stamps. Undoubtedly the decision to switch to the gravure process with the D stamps was essentially a decision to experiment with the gravure presses for coil stamp production, using a stamp that would not be needed immediately.

Gravure printing, also called rotogravure or photogravure, is an intaglio method using printing cylinders with shallower recesses than those of line-engraved intaglio plates. The resulting printed image is smooth to the touch, not raised in relief as is true of line-engraved prints. Cylinders are chemically etched using a sophisticated technical process that prepares a fine-grained image consisting of screened dots to produce tones or shades of color, with a separate cylinder for each color of ink. In printing, the cylinders are inked and then wiped by a doctor blade. Ink remaining in the recesses prints on the paper web.

Two methods of multicolor printing are possible with the gravure system: process printing or self-color printing. The two can also be used in combination. In process printing, the original colors are separated into their primary color components either through color separation photography (hence the term photogravure) or a simulated computerized equivalent. The separations are screened into halftone dot patterns with the diameters of the dots proportional to the intensity of the printed image. When the four halftone dot separations are printed in register in their respective process colors — yellow, magenta, cyan,* and black — they combine visually to yield the illusion of full color in continuous tonal gradations.

In order to avoid optical moire patterns, which appear as smears or shimmering images, the screen for each color's dot pattern image must be rotated at a precise predetermined angle from the other colors' screens. Under high magnification, process color dots of ink will appear to be in rows at odd angles to one another, a feature that can assist experts in determining whether a particular stamp is really a missing-color error.

Self colors are used when each color stands alone, without needing to be blended with others to achieve the illusion of other intermediate colors. Self colors may be any shade of ink; they are not restricted to the primary colors used in process printing. Of the coil stamps printed

*Earlier generations of printers referred to the process colors as yellow, red, blue, and black. Except for the fact that the chemistry of modern inks is more advanced, the terms process magenta and process red are equivalent, as are process cyan and process blue, although descriptively magenta and cyan are more accurate. Even today, printers often call a magenta printing cylinder "the red printer," and the cyan, "the blue printer."

to date on the Andreotti gravure press, only the 18¢ George Washington Monument stamp was printed using process colors. The single-color nondenominated D contingency coil, the multicolor 21.1¢ Letters and nondenominated E Earth contingency stamps were all printed in self colors.

Most gravure stamps are printed on coated paper that facilitates color registration and drying at high printing speeds. Fine dot patterns can yield exceptionally clear and sharp images, but these require expensive paper of the sort used to print the 1982 20¢ State Birds and Flowers commemorative stamps.

Nearly all BEP gravure printed stamps, including the coil issues, have employed coarser dot patterns printed on cheaper paper that have an appearance of being slightly hazy or out of focus. The paper used to print the non-denominated D contingency stamps was thick, yielding 3,000-stamp coils too large in diameter to fit some bulk mailers' stamp-affixing machines. Later gravure coils were printed on thinner paper. Both dextrin and Davac PVA gum have been used on gravure coil issues.

In 1969, in response to a request from the Post Office Department that BEP take over the printing of aerograms, previously supplied by the Government Printing Office, the Bureau solicited bids for a rotogravure press. The contract was awarded to Miehle Company of Chicago, and the press was built by Andreotti S.P.A. of Ceprano, Italy. As delivered in 1970, it had seven printing units with provision for an eighth to be added later. The Andreotti press also has the capability to print on the front and back of the paper web simultaneously, using letterpress plates on the back, a feature used in printing the 1973 8¢ Postal People commemoratives and the 1975 Contributors to the Cause set. It is ironic that a press purchased to print aerograms became the one that solved the Bureau's problem of producing multicolor stamps. The first stamp printed on the Andreotti was the 1971 8¢ Missouri Statehood commemorative. Since that time it has accounted for the majority of U.S. commemorative stamps.

Press 601, as the Andreotti is officially called, is webfed, capable of operating roll-to-roll (with later sheeting and perforating or coil precessing), roll-to-sheet, and roll-to-sheet with in-line perforating, although the cylindrical in-line "bull's-eye" perforator is no longer used because it slows the speed of production. Some of the commemorative stamps printed on the Andreotti are among the most attractive and popular U.S. issues, including the previously mentioned 20¢ State Birds and Flowers, the 1981 15¢ Coral Reefs and 18¢ Space Achievements, and the 1983 20¢ Balloons issues. But the first three gravure coil stamp designs, all issued in 1985 — the non-denominated D contingency stamp, the 18¢ Washington Monument, and the 21.1¢ Letters stamps — were duds, poorly printed and unpopular with users and collectors alike.

The nondenominated E Earth contingency stamp, issued in 1988, was the first Andreotti coil issue to achieve popular acceptance. Evidently spurred by this success, BEP has assigned production of the nondenominated F contingency stamp booklets and coils, whose design is said to be a flower, an orchid, to Press 601.

The Combination Intaglio/Gravure A Press

The non-denominated D contingency coil stamps, printed on the Andreotti gravure press in 1982, were also printed from the same two gravure cylinders on Press 702, the Giori combination intaglio/gravure A press, but using only its gravure printing capability. As with the Andreotti press run, this was probably an experiment, exhibiting the same problems as the Andreotti product, ugly and unpopular stamps on paper too thick to accommodate bulk mailer stamp-affixing machines. The D stamps from the two presses appear to be identical, except they are wound in opposite directions on finished coils.

A BEP publication prepared for the Citizens' Stamp Advisory Committee calls the A press "the most versatile press in the Bureau." It can print roll-to-roll or roll-to-sheet, either perforated or imperforate, but the on-press perforator is no longer used because it slows the operating speed too much, and the sheeter has been removed from the press. Although the versatility of the A press is undeniable, it took a long time — more than a decade — to overcome its problems and use it for its intended purpose. When bids were solicited in 1971, BEP had not contemplated using the new press to print coil stamps. "This press had to be capable of producing high quality, close register, process gravure printings in combination with line-intaglio printings and be specifically suitable and equipped for four primary printing formats: 400-subject ordinary size sheet postage stamps, 200-subject commemorative size sheet postage stamps, and 400-subject and 360-subject book postage stamps.

"The press had to be able to process print with five gravure colors in combination with up to three line-intaglio colors, overprint with phosphorescent ink by a dry offset unit having the capability of perfecting,** imprint (precancel) by a letterpress unit, accurately perforate, cut to sheets, and deliver the finished sheets into units of exactly 100 sheets per unit."*

In its initial form, the press delivered only sheets, not rewound rolls, but it was later modified for roll-to-roll printing, and thus could be used to print coil stamps.

The A press was built by Koenig and Bauer of Wurzburg, Germany. The intaglio portion of the press is similar to the B press, using the Giori inking-in system capable of printing up to three colors using a single sleeve. The five gravure units were supplied by Andreotti of Italy. The A press was installed in 1973.

*Russell E. Tudor, "Web 8-Color Gravure/Intaglio Press," *The United States Specialist*, April 1982, page 150.
**"Perfecting" means printing on the back.

The first stamp issued from the A press was the 13¢ Currier and Ives "Winter Pastime" Christmas stamp of 1976, printed from the gravure section only. An Andreotti press version of the stamp was also issued at the same time. Several other commemoratives were printed on the A press gravure section between 1976 and 1981. The first stamp printed on the intaglio section of the A press was the 13¢ Flag Over Independence Hall sheet stamp of 1975, originally printed on the nine-color Huck press. The A press version appeared in 1981.

The original version of the 39¢ Grenville Clark stamp has "floating" plate numbers because it was printed from a 920-subject A press intaglio sleeve. The later edition, printed from an 800-subject sleeve, has its plate numbers in the corner selvage only.

Other intaglio-only A press definitives and commemoratives followed. The first stamp to combine both the intaglio and gravure capabilities of the A press successfully was the 1982 20¢ Touro Synagogue commemorative. But even it did not fulfill the promise of the designers, because the two types of printing were on separate portions of the stamp. Not until the 1984 20¢ Douglas Fairbanks commemorative were the two printing methods fully integrated in a single registered multicolor image.

By 1981, all presses except the A had restored the traditional corner plate number block-of-four format for sheet stamps, conforming with the policy announced by the Postal Service in December 1980. But the A press sleeve and cylinder formats were not easily adapted to stamp collectors' desires for corner plate blocks, because the 460-subject commemorative and 920-subject definitive layout on the printing sleeve did not divide equally into 400- or 800-stamp sheets. The same ratio existed for the gravure cylinders, with exactly half the intaglio sleeve circumference. As a result, plate numbers "floated" from position to position along the selvage when the printed web was cut into 50- or 100-stamp panes.

As long as perforating had to be done on press, or using the old sheetfed L perforators, there was no practical answer to the problem. But after new high-speed off-press Eureka perforators were acquired in 1985, the A press sleeve and cylinder layouts were reformatted to 800 subjects for definitives and 400 for commemoratives, with wide gutters between panes. The slight waste of paper was more than compensated by the faster cheaper processing on the Eurekas. The 1985 22¢ Madonna and Child Christmas stamp was the first A press gravure printing without the "floaters," and the 1986 25¢ Jack London stamp was the first line-engraved definitive without them. After 1985, all sheet stamps once again had corner plate number blocks.

The gravure section uses the same doctor-blade wiping system that the Andreotti uses, and the intaglio section uses the same water wip-

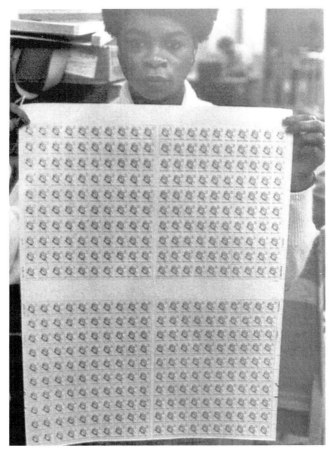

The 25¢ Jack London stamp was the first line-engraved definitive stamp printed on the A press from an 800-subject sleeve.

ing system that the intaglio B press uses. The single-color letterpress unit, originally intended for precanceling, is actually used for tagging with phosphorescent ink. The perfecting unit uses dry offset, an indirect relief printing system also known as letterset. Both the letterpress and dry offset stations print from magnetic plates. The normal operating speed of the A press is 300 feet per minute, which equals 2 to 2.5 million stamps per hour.

By 1982, Bureau planners had ordered a rewind rollstand to make coil stamp printing possible, but to date a portion of the non-denominated D contingency coil stamp production is the only existing A press coil. The Postal Service has promised more gravure coils in the future, so PNC collectors probably haven't seen the last of the A press.

The Intaglio C Press

In its 1984 report to the Citizens' Stamp Advisory Committee, the Bureau of Engraving and Printing hailed the Goebel three-color intaglio C press as "the most productive intaglio press in the world." Press 901, as it is officially known, operates only in a roll-to-roll mode. It has no in-line perforating or sheeting capability.

The press was acquired from Goebel of West Germany in 1982, built to design specifications developed in 1978. Its principal purpose is to print Flag stamps, booklets and coils, from single seamless 960-subject sleeves, suitable to be processed on companion equipment also supplied by Goebel. It can also print sheet stamps from 800-subject sleeves.

The maximum running speed of the C press is 500 feet per minute, which works out to more than 7 million stamps per hour. It uses the Giori-type inking-in system to print up to three colors from the intaglio sleeve, followed by a water wipe. When the product is to be processed on different equipment, sleeve formats with fewer subjects are used. Tagging is applied at a letterpress station. The C press accommodates paper webs ranging in width from 14½ to 22½ inches, with a print width one-half inch narrower than the web.

The first stamp printed on the C press was the 20¢ Flag Over Supreme Court stamp from sleeve number 4. The product was acceptable, and was placed on sale without prior notice, circulating with the rolls printed on the B press issued in 1981. Although there was no first day of issue, covers are known with sleeve 4 stamps used in the summer of 1982; the earliest reported use at this writing is July 29, 1982.

The first C press booklet stamps, also 20¢ Flag Over Supreme Court stamps, were printed the following year. Unlike the coils, these did get a proper first-day sendoff, at the National Postage Stamp Show in New York City on November 17, 1983. The C press 20¢ Flag booklet panes were processed into 20-stamp two-pane $4 counter booklets, whereas the earlier B press counterparts had been processed into six-stamp and 10-stamp single-pane booklets to be sold in vending machines for $1.20 and $2, respectively.

The typical coil stamp 960-subject sleeve format is 20 subjects across, too wide to fit the old 18-across Huck coil-processing equipment, and 48 subjects in circumference. Thus the distinguishing feature of C press coils is the 48-stamp interval from one plate number to the next. After C press production reached capacity, the strategy for Flag coil production changed. The C press product was processed into 100-stamp coils on the new equipment, while B press stamps were processed into larger 500-stamp and 3,000-stamp coils on the old equipment.

The first Transportation series coil stamps printed on the C press were 25¢ Bread Wagon coils assigned in 1988, when 25¢ became the prime rate. In 1986 and 1987, the large B press rolls had been adequate to supply the requirements for the stamp. The need for 100-stamp counter coils after the rate increase made the switch logical. Other Transportation coils moved from the B press to the C press in 1988 were the 7.6¢ Carreta, 8.4¢ Wheel Chair, and 21¢ Railroad Mail Car stamps, not to supply them in small rolls, but because the B press was exhibiting problems drying the red ink of the service inscriptions on those stamps. The first Transportation coil printed originally on the C press was the 20¢ Cable Car stamp of 1988, issued in 100-stamp rolls to cover the new added-ounce rate.

Another 1988 challenge for the C press arose from the demands of the 25¢ Honeybee coil stamp, which combined an offset-printed background applied by a Goebel Optiforma offset press with an intaglio foreground image and tagging block printed on the C press. Registering the images printed on two separate presses was an unprecedented problem for the production of U.S. coil stamps. The C press was fitted with an electric-eye feedback servo mechanism, causing a chill roller to shrink the paper when the intaglio print began drifting out of register. The makeshift two-press system worked, but with an unacceptably large amount of spoilage, and causing two postponements in the issue dates announced for the Honeybee stamp. Later, production of the 25¢ Honeybee was moved to the combination intaglio/offset D press, where the spoilage rate fell to normal levels.

The C press will probably be the Bureau's flagship press for prime-rate definitive stamp production over the next several decades.

The Combination Intaglio/Offset D Press

The Goebel combination six-color offset and three-color intaglio D press, officially designated Press 902 at the Bureau of Engraving and Printing, was acquired in 1984. It prints only roll-to-roll, with no in-line perforating or sheeting capability. Unlike the combination intaglio/gravure A press, which waited more than a decade before proving its capability to integrate the two printing methods, the D press printed a difficult stamp integrating both systems as its acceptance trial: the 20¢ Smokey Bear commemorative issued August 13, 1984. Spoilage was high on that stamp, but printers mastered the press, which went on to become one of BEP's most reliable machines.

In offset printing, ink impressions are transferred from the plate to the paper web by a rubber blanket rather than printed directly.

In effect, the D press is a C press plus a six-color offset press combined. C and D press intaglio sleeves and tagging plates are interchangeable.

The first coil stamps printed on the D press were 22¢ Flag Over Capitol stamps, using sleeves previously employed on the C press.

A view of the Bureau of Engraving and Printing's D press.

The products are indistinguishable, so they cannot be collected as separate items. The 960-subject C/D seamless intaglio sleeves are 20 subjects across and 48 in circumference, with plate numbers spaced at 48-stamp intervals. Transportation series coil stamps printed on both the C and D press are also indistinguishable.

The first coil stamp printed on both presses in collectible varieties was the 25¢ Honeybee. This was the first U.S. coil stamp to combine offset and intaglio printing on the same stamp. Both presses used the same intaglio sleeves and tagging plates, but because the D press has an offset unit and the C doesn't, the background color images are different. On the D press, the offset stations use magnetic plates exactly half the dimension of the intaglio sleeves in the rotary direction — 24 subjects in this case — so the two are perfectly synchronized with two offset repeat lengths for one intaglio on the printed roll.

The Goebel Optiforma offset press used in combination with the C press to print 25¢ Honeybee coils also used magnetic plates, but they are 25 subjects in the rotary direction, so their repeat lengths "float" in relation to the intaglio prints. Both systems print evidence of the offset plate edge, as well as occasional other offset plate varieties, so the intervals between them can be counted and the press determined from that evidence.

The main purpose of the D press is to print colorful commemorative stamps. But it will continue to be used for intaglio coil stamp production on a space-available basis, and may come into its own if future coil stamps use the combination intaglio/offset method pioneered by the Honeybee stamps.

The Goebel Optiforma Offset Presses

The two webfed six-color Goebel Optiforma presses at the Bureau of Engraving and Printing were not designed as stamp printing presses and were not acquired for the purpose of printing postage. They are called the "Jimmy Carter presses," because they were purchased in the late 1970s when President Carter thought it might be necessary to issue gasoline rationing coupons in the event of a petroleum shortage. The two presses are built to their West German manufacturer's standards specifications for high-quality multicolor webfed offset presses. They use one magnetic plate for each color of ink, and to apply phosphor tagging. Ink is transferred from the plate to the paper web by a rubber blanket.

Officially at BEP the Optiforma presses are designated Press 42 and Press 43. They were used in 1985 to print the colorful multicolor covers for the 22¢ Seashells stamp booklets of the original design, in which a floating pattern of 25 different seashells was cut into individual booklet covers, requiring a set of seven consecutive covers to show the complete design.

In 1987 and 1988, the Optiforma presses were used to print postage. Press 43 was used in December 1987 to print non-denominated E Official coil stamps on phosphor-coated paper from 450-subject plates, 18 subjects across and 25 subjects in the rotary direction. The 39¢ Graphic Design aerogram went to press in April 1988 on Press 42, the first aerogram to be printed on a press other than the Andreotti gravure press since BEP had taken over aerogram production from outside suppliers and the Government Printing Office in 1971.

Usually offset printing alone is not regarded as sufficiently secure for stamp printing, because it is easy to counterfeit. But the tagging block on the 39¢ Graphic Design aerogram and the phosphor-coated paper on the Official stamps provided sufficient additional security, in the opinion of senior Postal Service officials. Also, since only government agencies can use Official stamps as postage, the likelihood of someone creating postal forgeries for this use is remote. Subsequent

Official stamp issues have all been printed on the same Optiforma press.

The Optiforma press came to the attention of plate number coil collectors with the appearance of the 25¢ Honeybee coil stamp in 1988. The first printings began on Press 43, printed from five 450-subject plates, one for each process color — yellow, magenta, cyan and black — plus a background self color, a PMS (Pantone Matching System) blended yellow ink. Tests using the sixth plate to apply phosphor tagging were unacceptable. The rolls were then run on the intaglio C press, which applied a black intaglio image from an 864-subject sleeve, and block tagging. Later, Press 43 printed five colors from 500-subject Honeybee plates, with the C press image added by a 960-subject sleeve.

Printers had a difficult time registering the images printed under tension by two different presses under different humidity and ink-drying conditions. When the combination D press was no longer needed to print commemoratives, 25¢ Honeybee production was moved there, where offset and intaglio printing were combined in a single operation, bringing the spoilage rate way down. Since then, all Honeybee stamps have been printed on the D press, using the same sleeves previously employed on the C press, but new 432- and 480-subject offset plates.

Despite all the difficulties experienced in combining Optiforma

The Huck coiling equipment processes stamps from a web with 18 subjects across. The dashes at the right edge, perpendicular to the web, are used by an electric eye to place the perforations properly. The parallel dashes at the right align the web for proper slitting. The crow's foot marginal marking at the top left appears only once on the sleeve, to allow "sheet" counting of B press stamps.

offset and C press intaglio printing, there will probably be more stamps printed by the two-press method in the future to satisfy the public's desire for colorful stamps, most easily met by offset printing, and the security needs of the Postal Service, best assured by intaglio printing. So we'll most likely be seeing more products from "the Jimmy Carter presses."

The Huck and Goebel Coiling Equipment

The coil-processing equipment at the Bureau of Engraving and Printing consists of machines manufactured by the Huck Company of New York, first installed in 1958 and 1960, and machines built by Goebel of West Germany, in use since 1982.

The printed web of paper, as it emerges from the press, is rewound, and visually examined as the rewinding occurs. The rewound rolls are then fed into the processing equipment that perforates, slits and winds the stamps into coils of the desired length. The Huck equipment employs a rotary perforator. After coiling, the rolls are automatically packaged and labeled. Because examining is done before processing, errors and freaks that occur during processing, such as imperforates, shifted perforations, and mis-slit rolls, regularly escape detection and are sold over post office counters. The Huck equipment is designed to accommodate rolls printed with 18 subjects across the web — the format of the now-defunct Cottrell presses designed by Huck originally, and of the intaglio B press. Today nearly all coils processed on the Huck equipment are made into rolls of 500 and 3,000. The machines were built to be modified easily to manufacture 10,000-stamp coils

The Huck coiling equipment includes a rotary perforator.

After perforating, the 18 rows across the web are slit into single strips, as shown on the 25¢ Flag Over Yosemite stamps being processed in this photograph.

The labeling machine cuts a paper disc from a continuous tape, prints it, and affixes it to coil wrappers after they are processed on the Huck equipment.

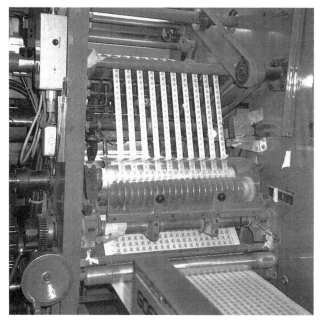

The Goebel coiling equipment uses a stroke perforator ahead of its slitting station.

also. That capability was tried experimentally in late 1988 and throughout 1989. Normal production of 10,000-stamp coils began in early 1990.

Stamps are visually examined during rewinding before they are loaded onto the Goebel equipment also. The Goebel machines accept coils up to 20 subjects across the printed web. Perforating is by a stroke perforator; the rows are slit and rolled into the proper length. On the Goebel equipment, the proper length is always coils of 100. These are packaged into 50-roll transparent plastic trays. The trays are sealed with thin plastic covers, die cut and rouletted, so that each roll is in its individual blister package, easily separated from the other rolls in the same tray. The trays are packed 800 to a case, and stored in the Bureau vault to await shipping.

GLOSSARY

A Press — Five-color gravure and three-color intaglio Giori webfed combination stamp printing press acquired by the Bureau of Engraving and Printing in 1973. Officially called Press 702.

Accountable Paper Depository — A regional **Stamp Distribution Office** designated as the source of supply for limited-use postal items and emergency supplies for other Stamp Distribution Offices in the region.

Aerogram or Aerogramme — An officially issued lettersheet bearing an imprinted stamp indicium for international airmail used to send written messages without enclosures.

AFDCS — See **American First Day Cover Society**.

American First Day Cover Society — The principal organization of first-day cover collectors in the United States; an affiliate of the **American Philatelic Society**. Publisher of the journal *First Days*, which appears eight times annually. Every serious collector of first-day covers should be a member of AFDCS. For information, write to William Simpson, Executive Director, American First Day Cover Society, 1611 Corral Drive, Houston, Texas 77090.

American Philatelic Society — The principal organization of stamp collectors in the United States and publisher of the monthly journal *The American Philatelist*. Every serious stamp collector in this country should be a member of APS. For information, write to American Philatelic Society, P.O. Box 8000, State College, Pennsylvania 16803.

American Philatelist — Monthly journal of the **American Philatelic Society**.

American Topical Association — The principal organization of topical or thematic collectors; an affiliate of the **American Philatelic Society**. Publisher of bimonthly journal *Topical Time*. Everyone who collects philatelic material by topic or theme should be a member of ATA. For information,

write to Donald W. Smith, Executive Director, American Topical Association, P.O. Box 630, Johnstown, Pennsylvania 15907.

Andreotti Gravure Press — Seven-color webfed gravure printing press acquired by the Bureau of Engraving and Printing in 1970 to print aerograms. This has been the main press for printing multicolor commemorative stamps since 1973. Not used to print coil stamps until the 1980s. Officially called Press 601.

APS — See **American Philatelic Society**.

ATA — See **American Topical Association**.

B Press — Three-color webfed Giori intaglio stamp printing press acquired by the Bureau of Engraving and Printing in 1973, in production since 1976. Officially called Press 701.

Bar Code — A machine-readable row of short and tall ink bars on a piece of mail, coding the addressee's five-digit or nine-digit ZIP code, permitting automated high-speed sorting on modern Postal Service equipment. Bar codes can be sprayed on by the Postal Service's optical character readers, which translate the written or typed address into the digital bar codes, or they can be printed on envelopes in advance of mailing.

Basic Presort — Bulk or quantity mail presorted to the first three ZIP-code digits and bundled by the mailer before posting.

BEP — See **Bureau of Engraving and Printing**.

BIA. See **Bureau Issues Association**.

Blanket — The rubber surface on the transfer cylinder of an offset press that takes the ink from the plate and prints it on the paper.

Block Tagged — Stamps with phosphor tagging applied over the printed subject in a rectangle that does not touch or straddle the perforations when properly registered.

Brookman Catalog — A retail price guide for United States, Canadian and

United Nations stamps. The guide is issued once or twice a year by the Brookman Stamp Company and is organized according to the Scott numbering system.

Bulk Mail — Third-class commercial and nonprofit mail, presorted and bundled, mailed in bulk at reduced rates by authorized permit holders.

Bureau Issues Association — The principal organization of collectors of United States stamps, also called the **United States Stamp Society**; an affiliate of the **American Philatelic Society**. Publisher of the monthly journal, *The United States Specialist*. Every serious collector of U.S. stamps should belong to the BIA. For information, write to Executive Secretary, Bureau Issues Association, Inc., P.O. Box 1047, Belleville, Illinois 62223.

Bureau of Engraving and Printing — The branch of the United States Treasury Department responsible for printing United States currency and securities. Nearly all U.S. postage stamps have been printed at the Bureau since 1894, although the Postal Service has increased the use of private stamp printing contractors in recent years. To date, all U.S. coil stamps have been printed at BEP, except the pressure-sensitive issue of 1989.

Bureau Precancel — A stamp issue precanceled at the Bureau of Engraving and Printing, differentiated from **local precancel**.

C Press — Three-color webfed Goebel intaglio stamp printing press acquired by the Bureau of Engraving and Printing in 1982. Officially called Press 901.

Cachet — An inscription or pictorial design, or both, printed, stamped or hand-drawn on a **cover**.

Carrier-Route Presort — Bulk mail presorted by the mailer and bundled for the delivery route of each postal carrier before posting.

Ceremony Program — An officially or privately issued card or folder listing participants and features of a stamp dedication ceremony, handed out to those in attendance. In recent years, ceremony programs include examples of the new stamp or other postal item canceled with the official first-day-of-issue postmark. Beginning in 1989, officially issued ceremony programs have been available from the U.S. Postal Service by subscription.

Chill Roller — Press rollers that rapidly reduce the temperature of the paper web either before or after printing, sometimes to facilitate tagging or drying, and sometimes to regulate color registration.

Chromed — The hardened state of a printing plate, sleeve or cylinder after the steel has been plated with chrome to prolong its productivity.

Coated Paper — Paper with a slick, glossy surface.

Coil — A full roll of stamps as issued by the Postal Service. Also, an individual coil stamp.

Coil Collector — Newsletter of the United States Coil Collectors Society edited by Ron Bowman, published monthly from January 1984 until September 1985.

Coil Line — Newsletter of the **Plate Number Coil Collectors Club (PNC3)** edited by Tom Maeder, published monthly since May 1988.

Coil Stamp — A stamp issued in a roll, rather than in a pane, booklet or souvenir sheet. In the United States, coil stamps typically have parallel straight edges at the top and bottom or the left and right, with perforations only between stamps on the roll.

Collector Edition — See **Philatelic Edition**.

Color Omitted — A major error, in which one or more colors of ink is completely missing from a stamp. If even a faint tiny trace of the color is present, the stamp is considered a freak, not a major error.

Color Shift — A freak misregistration of one or more ink colors in relation to the other elements of the stamp design and perforations.

Combination Intaglio/Gravure A Press — See **A Press**.

Combination Intaglio/Offset D Press — See **D Press**.

Commercial Cover — A cover used as business mail. The term is often used to mean any **nonphilatelic cover**.

Constant Mat Variety — Any variation from the basic overprinted design caused by an irregular feature present in the relief image area of the letterpress precancel mat.

Constant Plate Variety — Any printed variation from the basic stamp design caused by an irregular feature in the printing base image area. Constant plate varieties can be located exactly by subject position.

Contingency Stamp — A postage stamp printed for use at a time when previously circulating stamps may not be adequate for postal needs, usually at the time of a rate change.

Cottrell Presses — Single-color webfed intaglio stamp printing presses in use at the Bureau of Engraving and Printing from 1956 to 1985, designed by the Huck Company, Inc., of New York, and built by the Cottrell Company of Westerly, Rhode Island. Officially called Presses 801, 802, 803, 804 and 805.

Cover — An entire envelope, wrapper, lettersheet, postcard, postal card or aerogram that has passed through the mails or been canceled as a souvenir.

Cylinder — See **Gravure Cylinder**.

Cylinder Number — The plate number of a gravure printing cylinder used on the Andreotti or A Press.

D Press — Six-color offset and three-color intaglio Goebel webfed combination stamp printing press acquired by the Bureau of Engraving and Printing in 1984. Officially called Press 902.

Dampener Fountain — On a lithographic press, the reservoir that holds the aqueous solution applied to the portion of the plate that does not contain an etched image, to repel oily ink so that only the etched area receives ink.

Davac Gum — See **Dull Gum**.

Dechromed — The softened state of a printing plate, sleeve or cylinder after the chrome plating has been removed so that its surface can be repaired and restored.

Decimal Denomination — A stamp whose denomination includes a decimal fraction of a cent.

Denson Catalog — *Denson's Specialized Catalog of Plate Number Coils on First Day Covers, Souvenir Pages and Ceremony Programs*, edited by Ed Denson, published loose-leaf in the fall of 1988 and subsequently updated with supplement pages.

Dextrin Gum — See **Shiny Gum**.

Die — In intaglio stamp printing, a die is a piece of steel bearing an original line-engraved design, later multiplied on a printing plate by the hardened relief image of a **transfer roller**.

Dig — A minor flaw in a printing plate, sleeve or cylinder. Also, the printed image of such a flaw.

Doctor Blade — The device to wipe excess ink from a gravure cylinder before it is pressed against the paper web to print the image.

Double Transfer — Partial or complete duplication of an engraved image caused by shifting the transfer roller slightly as the intaglio image is being entered into the printing plate. The term also refers to the appearance of the printed image of a double transfer. Reports of double transfers on modern coil stamps are erroneous, mimicked by set-off from unintentionally inked printing press rollers.

Dropped Transfer — See **Low Transfer**.

Dry Gum — See **Dull Gum**.

Dry Offset — Indirect printing from an inked image on a relief plate to a transfer cylinder or blanket, and from there to paper. Because the plate image is raised, water dampening of the plate required for **lithography** is not needed to keep ink away from the nonprinting areas. Also called letterset.

Dry Printing — Intaglio printing on paper first dampened to a relatively low moisture content, 5 to 10 percent by weight, a term often applied to U.S. stamps printed on Cottrell presses, to differentiate them from similar stamps printed on Stickney rotary presses. Oddly, the term is rarely applied to truly dry-printed stamps, on paper that is not premoistened.

Dull Gum — Water-activated stamp adhesive with a dry matte finish, usually a proprietary product called Davac, consisting mainly of a synthetic, usually polyvinyl acetate, or occasionally polyvinyl alcohol, blended with some corn dextrin.

Durland Catalog — The *Durland Standard Plate Number Catalog*, in recent years edited by George V.H. Godin and published every several years by the **Bureau Issues Association**. Between editions, new plate number reports are published monthly in *The United States Specialist*, the BIA's journal.

Earliest Known Use — The earliest date on which a particular stamp or postal item is proven to have been used. The term is applied especially to stamps that had no official issue date and, among plate number coils, to PNCs that are not known on first-day covers.

EFO — Errors, Freaks and Oddities.

EFO Collector — Newsletter of the **Errors, Freaks and Oddities Collectors Club**, published six times annually.

EFOCC — See **Errors, Freaks and Oddities Collectors Club**.

EKU — Earliest known use.

Embossed Envelope — An item of postal stationery on which the stamp imprint is embossed as a security measure.

Endorsement — On a piece of mail, the written, printed, stenciled or handstamped class or service designation is an endorsement. The endorsement may be supplied as a **service inscription** on a stamp.

Engraving — See **Line Engraving**.

Error — A stamp or postal stationery item exhibiting a mistake in production sufficiently serious that an essential element is completely omitted, duplicated or reversed. Examples would be imperforates, omitted colors, double prints or inverts.

Errors, Freaks and Oddities Collectors Club — The principal U.S. organization for collectors of stamp errors, freaks, oddities and all types of varieties in stamp and postal stationery production; an affiliate of the **American Philatelic Society**. Publishes *The EFO Collector* six times annually. For information, write to CWO James E. McDevitt, USCG Ret., Secretary, EFO Collectors Club, 1903 Village Road West, Norwood, Massachusetts 02062-

2524.

Esrati Catalog — The *Plate Number Coil Catalog* edited by Stephen G. Esrati, published annually since 1985 (originally called *Catalog of Plate Number Coils)* organized according to a numbering system devised by the editor.

Facer Canceler — A piece of mail-processing equipment that orients ("faces") an envelope to be read easily, and cancels its stamp.

False Franking — Postage on a piece of mail whose denomination does not equal the actual prepaid per-piece rate, with the balance due in addition paid at the time of mailing or the overpayment refunded. False franking of bulk and quantity mail is authorized at the time of rate changes, pending the issuance of new stamps in the proper denomination.

FDC — See **First-day cover**.

First-Class Mail — Ordinary mail with the highest processing priority.

First-Day Cover — A cover bearing a cancel dated with the official issue date. First-day covers are typically canceled earlier or later than the date of the postmark.

First Day of Issue — The official date on which a stamp or postal stationery item is placed on sale. Also applies to the cancelation denoting the official issue date.

First Days — Journal of the **American First Day Cover Society**.

Five-Digit Presort — Bulk or quantity mail presorted to five ZIP-code digits and bundled by the mailer before posting.

Flexographic Plate — A flexible rubber composition or plastic letterpress (relief) plate used in many stamp and postal stationery printing operations, including B press precancel overprints.

Flexography — A type of **letterpress** (relief) printing using a flexible rubber composition or plastic plate instead of a metal plate to apply the ink image to paper.

Flyspeck — A minute stamp printing variety, often requiring magnification to be appreciated.

Font — Typeface; type style.

Frank — Literally, a postal marking that allows a piece of mail to be carried free. For lack of an adequate alternative, philately has appropriated this verb to mean any marking, including a postage stamp, imprint or meter, required to authorize the carriage of mail, whether fee-paid or free.

Freak — A stamp or postal stationery item exhibiting a mistake in production of a partial or ephemeral nature. Freaks include shifted perforations, miscuts, preprint paper folds, crazy perfs and misregistered colors. In countries other than the U.S., stamp freaks are often called errors.

Gap — The unprinted space between the ends of two printed precancel overprints, indicating the seam between adjacent mats or flexographic plates on the press. When the gap straddles the **joint line**, it is called a **line gap**. When it appears at any other position, it is labeled by its relation to the joint line. Thus a gap two perforation rows to the left of the line is called Gap two left, abbreviated GAP 2L.

Giori Combination Intaglio/Gravure A Press — See **A Press**.

Giori Intaglio B Press — See **B Press**.

Giori System — A system of delivering ink to intaglio plates or sleeves using cutaway inking-in rollers, allowing a single plate or sleeve to print up to three colors with a minimum of bleeding one color into another.

Glossy Gum — See **Shiny Gum**.

Goebel Coiling Equipment — Machines installed at the Bureau of Engraving and Printing in 1982 that process printed rolls of paper up to 20 rows across by slitting into individual rows, stroke perforating, rolling and packaging coils of 100 stamps in 50-coil transparent plastic trays, each one separately detachable in its own sealed blister pack.

Goebel Combination Intaglio/Offset D Press — See **D Press**.

Goebel Intaglio C Press — See **C Press**.

Goebel Optiforma Presses — See **Optiforma Presses**.

Gouge — A flaw in a printing plate, sleeve or cylinder. Also, the printed image of such a flaw.

Gravure Cylinder — The printing base of a gravure press, bearing a shallow recessed image area consisting of screened dots. A separate cylinder is required for each color of ink.

Gravure Printing — A method of intaglio printing in which a shallow recessed cylinder is required to print each color of ink. Each cylinder is chemically etched, yielding a fine-grained image of screened dots. These may be combined in register to simulate full, continuous-tone color, or printed separately to yield a poster-like effect. Bec use gravure cylinders are usually manufactured photographically, the process is often called **photogravure**. Nearly all gravure work is done on rotary presses, so the old term **rotogravure** tends to be redundant.

Gripper Crack — A plate crack that occurs along the last row of subjects at either end of a plate, caused by stress of the grippers that fasten it to the press cylinder. Gripper cracks print as jagged lines.

Halftone — A simulation of continuous tonal gradations between black and white achieved by a pattern of printed dots varying in diameter, below the resolution limit of ordinary vision.

Harris Catalog — A retail price guide for United States, Canadian and United Nations stamps issued once or twice a year by the H.E. Harris Company, organized according to the Scott numbering system.

Hi-Brite Paper — Paper impregnated with brighteners that glow under longwave ultraviolet illumination.

Huck Coiling Equipment — Machines installed at the Bureau of Engraving and Printing in 1958 and 1960 that process printed rolls of paper 18 rows across by slitting into individual rows, rotary perforating, rolling and wrapping, into coils of 100, 500, 3,000 or 10,000 stamps. In recent years, the Huck equipment has been used almost exclusively for coils of 500 and 3,000. The 10,000-stamp coil capacity is a recent modification.

Huck-Cottrell Press — A single-color or webfed intaglio stamp printing press, prototype for the **Cottrell presses**, designed and built by the Huck Company, Inc., of New York between 1948 and 1952, first used in stamp production in 1952.

Imperforate — Coil stamps with perforations entirely omitted are major errors, but on some stamps such errors are widely available and inexpensive. However, not every stamp that appears to be imperforate actually is. If the slightest trace of a perforation dent can be detected, it is a "blind perforation" freak, not an imperforate error. Imperforates are collected in pairs or larger multiples.

Imperforate Between — A pair of stamps perforated normally on the outside, but completely missing the row of perforations between the two. A major error.

Ink Fountain — The trough from which a press is supplied with ink. Usually ink travels on oscillators and rollers that spread it consistently and uniformly before depositing it on the printing plate.

Inscription — The portion of a stamp design comprising letters and numbers, including such things as the name of the stamp-issuing entity, the denomination, the service designation, and the title of the vignette.

Intaglio B Press — See **B Press**.

Intaglio C Press — See **C Press**.

Intaglio Cottrell Presses — See **Cottrell Presses**.

Intaglio Plate — In stamp printing, a flat or curved line-engraved piece of steel that delivers the inked image to the paper. A plate, which may be curved to fit a rotary press printing cylinder (paired with a similarly manufactured mate), first has its image subjects entered on the flat piece of steel, which differentiates it from an **intaglio sleeve**.

Intaglio Printing — Another term for **recess printing**.

Intaglio Sleeve — A cylindrical seamless **printing base** tapered internally to fit the press **mandrel**, used to print stamps on the intaglio **B** or **C** presses, or the intaglio section of the **D press**. Using the **Giori System**, a sleeve can print up to three colors of ink.

Joint Line — Printed line of ink marking the place where the edges of two curved plates adjoin on Cottrell or Stickney press. See **Line Pair**.

Lacquer — The transparent base for printing tagging phosphors on stamps.

Letter Rate — See **Prime Rate**.

Letterpress — The generic term for all forms of **relief printing**, from medieval block printing and modern handstamps to moveable type and **flexography**.

Letterset — See **Dry Offset**.

LG — See **Line Gap**.

Line Engraving — A method of intaglio or recess printing in which the image to be printed is cut (recessed) into the printing base. Printed line engravings yield a characteristic raised relief ink image. See **Recess Printings**.

Line Gap — A precancel **gap** straddling the coil **joint line**.

Line Pair — Pair of Cottrell or Stickney press coil stamps with the printed **joint line** on or adjacent to the row of perforations between them.

Linn's Stamp News — The world's largest weekly stamp newspaper; carries a monthly column on Plate Number Coils by this book's author. For information, write to Linn's Stamp News, P.O. Box 29, Sidney, Ohio 45365.

Lithography — A planographic printing process operating on the principle that oil and water do not mix. The portion of the printing surface dampened with an aqueous solution repels oily ink, while the etched or greasy surface accepts ink. In commercial printing, the lithographic image is printed indirectly by an **offset** process, so that a minimum amount of dampening solution reaches the paper along with the desired amount of ink.

Local Precancel — A stamp issue overprinted locally with the city and state names or abbreviations, overprinted on a press or by a handstamp device. Differentiated from **Bureau precancel**.

Low Transfer — A stamp subject entered below its normal position on a plate or sleeve because of an improperly positioned **transfer roller**, yielding a low print in relation to other stamps on the same roll or pane. Also called dropped transfer.

Mailer's Postmark — A postal cancelation applied to mail by an authorized mailer before posting. A type of precancelation.

Mailer's Postmark Permit — Authorization to use a **mailer's postmark**.

Mandrel — A shaft on which a cylinder turns. On most rotary presses, plates are mounted on cylinders that are mounted on mandrels, but on the B, C and D presses at the BEP, intaglio sleeves are mounted directly on tapered mandrels.

Master Die — See **Die**.

Mat — A hard rubber letterpress (relief) plate used to apply overprints on Stickney and Cottrell presses.

Mat Variety — Any variation in the basic overprinted design resulting in an irregular precancel image. Some mat varieties are ephemeral, owing mainly to the flexible and relatively fragile rubber medium; others are constant. See **Constant Mat Variety**.

Matte Gum — See **Dull Gum**.

Mekeel's Weekly Stamp News — The oldest weekly stamp collector newspaper in the United States which carries occasional coverage of plate number coils. For information, write to Mekeel's, P.O. Box 5050, White Plains, New York 10602.

Mellone Catalog — The *Scott U.S. First Day Cover Catalogue and Checklist*, edited by Michael A. Mellone, published annually, using the Scott numbering system.

Meter Stamp — A franking label or imprint stating the postage amount and the location (and, for first-class mail, the date) of mailing. Modern U.S. meter stamps must be printed with ultraviolet-luminescent ink.

Michel Catalog — The German-language *Michel USA-Spezial-Katalog* published every few years by Schwaneberger Verlag GMBH in Munich, West Germany, using the Michel numbering system.

Minkus Catalog — The *Minkus New 1982 American Stamp Catalog* and the *Minkus 1988 Specialized American Stamp Catalog*, the two most recent editions published by Minkus Publica-

tions, Inc., using the Minkus numbering system.

Mint — (1) Unused, post-office fresh condition, describing stamps and postal stationery. (2) Flavoring in dextrin gum applied to some Flag coil stamps.

Miscut — See **Mis-slit**.

Misperforated — Stamps showing freak perforations shifted strongly from their proper position, so that they cut into the stamps' design, are the most common type of misperfs on coils. Double or triple perforation errors are rare.

Misregistration — The misalignment of a printed or embossed image in relation to others on the same printed product. Also applies to tagging blocks, perforations and roulettes.

Missing Color — See **Color Omitted**.

Mis-slit — A freak coil stamp occurrence when the paper web is misaligned in the coiling equipment so that the rows of stamps are separated too high or too low. Mis-slit coil stamps will sometimes show subjects from two adjacent rows of stamps, or marginal markings. Coils mis-slit so that the plate numbers appear at the top instead of the bottom are avidly sought by many collectors.

Modeler — The person responsible for working an approved stamp design into the form required by an engraver, so that it can be successfully translated into a line-engraved image in a piece of steel.

Modern Postal History Journal — Quarterly newsletter of the **Modern Postal History Society**.

Modern Postal History Society — Organization of collectors of modern **nonphilatelic covers** and 20th-century rates, routes and postal markings; an affiliate of the **American Philatelic Society**. Publishes the quarterly *Modern Postal History Journal*. For information, write to Terence Hines, P.O. Box 629, Chappaqua, New York 10514-0629.

MPHS — See **Modern Postal History Society**.

Nine-Digit ZIP Code — Postal code permitting sorting to the individual address or carrier route.

Nondenominated Stamp — A **contingency stamp** printed and stored in advance of need, then released to fulfill a specific designated postal rate need, usually a prime-rate increase, when the circulating stamps are inadequate to cover the new rate.

Nonphilatelic Cover — A cover used as ordinary mail without any intent to create a collectible item.

Nonprofit Mail — A category of reduced-rate third-class bulk permit mail for specially qualified organizations, typically churches, charities, tax-exempt educational institutions and, in recent years, political campaign organizations.

Official Mail Stamp — A stamp for use only by authorized agencies of government.

Offset — (1) An indirect printing process in which the inked image is printed first on a transfer cylinder, usually covered with rubber called a **blanket**, and from there to the paper. Offset printing is either a planographic process called **lithography**, or a **letterpress** process called letterset. Offset plates are right-reading, rather than mirror-image. (2) An inadvertently transferred ink image, also called **set-off**.

Offset Blanket — See **blanket**.

Optical Character Reader — A piece of mail-processing equipment capable of reading a written or typed address, translating it into a system of short and tall bars, and spraying the **bar code** on the envelope to facilitate automated high-speed sorting.

Optiforma presses — Six-color webfed Goebel offset presses acquired by the Bureau of Engraving and Printing in the late 1970s, but not used in stamp production until 1985. Officially called Presses 42 and 43.

Overall Tagged — Stamps with phosphor tagging applied in a lacquer suspension or ink over the entire usable surface of the paper web, not divided into individual blocks to cover each stamp subject.

Overprint — A printed image applied over the basic stamp design. Overprinted U.S. coil stamps are precancels. Before 1978, precancel overprints consisted of city and state names or abbreviations between parallel horizontal lines, printed in black ink. Between 1978 and 1985, precancel overprints consisted of plain parallel horizontal lines, or lines plus a restrictive service inscription, in black ink. Beginning in late 1985, precancel inscriptions have been printed by gravure cylinders or intaglio sleeves as part of the stamp designs, except for reissued versions of earlier precancels employing flexographic overprints in black ink, and two stamps issued in 1987 and 1988 with red precancel overprints. The red overprints are service inscriptions only, without lines.

Pairings — See **Plate Pairings**.

Pane — The booklet- or retail-size portion cut down from an original printed **sheet** of stamps. U.S. definitive sheet stamps are normally issued in 100-stamp panes, and commemoratives in 50-stamp panes, but other formats also exist.

Pantone Matching System — A standardized system of blended colors, each with a PMS number, used throughout the graphic arts industry since the 1960s, but officially used by the Bureau of Engraving and Printing and the Postal Service to designate postage stamp colors only since 1987.

Paper Wipe — The system of removing excess ink from Cottrell press plates before they are pressed against the paper web to print the image.

Penalty Mail — Official U.S. mail bearing the printed warning, "Penalty for private use to avoid the payment of postage $300." On Official stamps, called Penalty stamps by the Postal Service, this has been shortened to read, "Penalty for private use $300."

Penalty Stamp — The Postal Service designation for **Official Mail stamp** since Fiscal Year 1985.

Perfecting — Printing on the back side of a web of paper simultaneously with printing on the front.

Perforating — Punching rows of small holes between printed stamp subjects to facilitate separation. Modern U.S. coil stamps are rotary perforated on **Huck coiling equipment** or stroke perforated on **Goebel coiling**

equipment, 9.8 perforations per two centimeters.

Philatelic Cover — A cover manufactured to be a collectible item. Philatelic covers include such things as canceled cacheted souvenir covers that never entered the mailstream, covers commemorating particular events, and covers mailed to document specific postal rates, routes and usages.

Philatelic Edition — A stamp printed for stamp collectors, without a real postal need.

Philatelic Sale — Sale at a post office philatelic counter or by the Philatelic Sales Division of USPS.

Phosphor-Coated Paper — Paper that has tagging phosphors coated onto its surface during manufacture.

Phosphor Tagged — See **Tagged**.

Phosphored Paper — Paper that has tagging phosphors incorporated into the sizing at the time of manufacture.

Photogravure — A system of shallow **recess printing** in which the image to be printed is transferred to the printing cylinder by a photographic negative and etched into the surface.

Photo-Offset — A system of indirect printing in which the image on a plate, produced from a photographic negative and etched in, is transferred first to a rubber **blanket**, then printed onto paper from the blanket.

Piece — A portion of a cover bearing a canceled stamp or stamp imprint.

Planographic Printing — Printing from a **plate** in which the surface to be printed is in the same plane as the unprinted area rather than recessed or raised in relief; also called **lithography**.

Plate — In its generic meaning, any **printing base**. In its specific meaning, a printing base that begins as a flat rectangular surface, though it may later be curved to fit a printing cylinder. Stamp printing plates are made of steel for **intaglio** printing, aluminum for **lithography**, and rubber or plastic for **flexography**.

Plate Crack — A flaw in the surface of a steel printing plate that accepts ink and prints onto the paper along with the desired image.

Plate Number — The serial number assigned to a printing plate, sleeve or cylinder at the Bureau of Engraving and Printing. The numbers began with 1 in the 1890s and reached five digits in recent years. For internal accounting reasons, the BEP began using six-digit numbers instead in the 1980s. Beginning in 1981, single-digit suffixes, beginning with 1 for each new stamp design, were added to the five- and six-digit serial numbers, and since then only the suffix digits have been printed on the coil stamps, pane selvage and booklet binding stubs.

Plate Number Coil — Since 1981, a U.S. coil stamp showing a small plate number below the design in the stamp's bottom margin. Before 1981, a mis-slit coil stamp from the edge of the printing web showing part or all of the plate number printed outside the stamp's intended image area.

Plate Number Coil Collectors Club — The principal open membership organization of U.S. plate number coil collectors; an affiliate of the **American Philatelic Society**. Publisher of the monthly newsletter *Coil Line*. Every PNC enthusiast should be a member of PNC3. For information, write to Eric Russow, Secretary, Plate Number Coil Collectors Club, P.O. Box 7386, Des Moines, Iowa 50309.

Plate Number Coil Study Group — A closed working group of approximately 20 members appointed by Stephen G. Esrati to research all aspects of plate number coils and to assist in preparing each year's *Plate Number Coil Catalog* edited by Esrati.

Plate Pairings — Both the Stickney rotary presses, in use from 1914 to 1962, and the Cottrell presses, from 1956 to 1985, required two curved plates in tandem, together forming a complete cylindrical surface, to print stamps. Each printed roll of paper would contain the numbers of both plates, and on Cottrell press coil stamps printed from 1981 to 1985, the numbers of both paired plates would appear on a single coil of stamps. Over the life of a stamp, a single plate was often paired with more than one other plate.

Plate Strip — In modern coil collecting, a strip of stamps, one of which includes the plate number. Coil collectors usually prefer the numbered stamp to be at the center of a mint strip of three or five. The term also applies to the plate number/imprint strips of three sheet stamps collected by early plate number specialists, later superseded by plate number blocks.

Plate Variety — See **Constant Plate Variety**.

PMS — See **Pantone Matching System**.

PNC — Plate number coil.

PNC3 — See **Plate Number Coil Collectors Club**.

PNCSG — See **Plate Number Coil Study Group**.

PNS — Plate number strip.

Polyvinyl Acetate — See **Dull Gum** and **Shiny Gum**.

Postcard — Privately printed mailing cards requiring postage in the form of an adhesive stamp, meter or permit imprint. Not to be confused with a **postal card**, an item of postal stationery that includes an imprinted stamp indicium.

Postcard Presort Rate — The perpiece discounted cost of mailing postcards in quantity, presorted and bundled by mailers before posting.

Postcard Rate — The cost of mailing a single postcard, or the per-piece cost of postcards mailed in quantity.

Postal Card — An officially issued card bearing an imprinted postage stamp indicium. A similar privately issued card requiring the addition of postage is a **postcard**.

Postal Rate — The amount of money required to prepay postage for an individual piece or specific weight of mail, at a specified class of service to a given location, zone, country or geographic area.

Postal Rate Commission — An independent federal regulatory agency established by Congress in the Postal Reorganization Act of 1970. It serves as a legal forum for proposed changes in postal rates, fees, mail classifications and postal service, and investigates complaints in these areas.

Postal Stationery — An officially issued postal card, envelope, wrapper, letter card or aerogram bearing an imprinted postage stamp indicium.

Pre-Bar-Coded — Mailing bearing a machine-readable **bar code** of the addressee's nine-digit ZIP code printed on the items to be mailed by the mailer prior to posting.

Precancel — A stamp, stamped envelope or postal card that is considered by the Postal Service to have been canceled before mailing, either during its production at the Bureau of Engraving and Printing, or applied locally by a printing plate, handstamp device or a mailer's permit postmark. Precanceled postage properly used on third-class bulk mail, first-class quantity mail and certain special first-class mail categories do not require additional postal cancelations. Precancels used on ordinary first-class mail by permit holders must receive dated cancels at the time of mailing.

Precancel User's Permit — A permit authorizing a mailer to buy and to use precanceled stamps and postal stationery. A first-class precancel user's permit is issued free, but fees in addition to postage must be paid by holders of bulk-mail precancel permits.

Prephosphored Paper — Paper that has been impregnated with tagging phosphors (**phosphored paper**) or coated with tagging phosphors (**phosphor-coated paper**) during manufacture.

Presort — Bulk or quantity mail presorted and bundled by the mailer before posting.

Press 42 — See **Optiforma Presses**.

Press 43 — See **Optiforma Presses**.

Press 601 — See **Andreotti Press**.

Press 701 — See **B Press**.

Press 702 — See **A Press**.

Press 801 — See **Cottrell Presses**.

Press 802 — See **Cottrell Presses**.

Press 803 — See **Cottrell Presses**.

Press 804 — See **Cottrell Presses**.

Press 805 — See **Cottrell Presses**.

Press 901 — See **C Press**.

Press 902 — See **D Press**.

Primary Colors — See **Process Colors**.

Prime Rate — The cost of postage to mail a domestic letter weighing one ounce or less.

Printing Base — The generic term for a plate, sleeve, cylinder, stencil or other medium used to deliver repeatable inked images to paper.

Process Colors — Four primary ink colors — yellow, magenta, cyan and black — which can be combined as screened halftones printed in combination to achieve a simulation of full, continuous-tone color.

Process printing — Printing four **process colors** in combination from individual **halftone** separations that, when combined, simulate full, continuous-tone color.

PS — **Plate Strip**. Usually followed by the number of stamps in the strip. Thus "PS5" means a strip of five stamps with a plate number on the center stamp.

PVA — Polyvinyl acetate. see **Dull Gum** and **Shiny Gum**.

Quantity Mail — First-class and postcard mail, presorted and bundled, mailed in bulk at reduced rates by authorized permit holders.

Rate — See **Postal Rate**.

Rate Tier — Within a class of mail, a specific level of surcharge or discount.

Recess Printing — Printing from a plate, sleeve or cylinder in which the image to be printed is engraved or etched into the printing base. Ink is forced into the recesses of the plate, the excess is wiped from the surface, and the print is pulled by putting paper (often premoistened) under pressure against the inked plate. Etching, line engraving and gravure are all recess printing techniques.

Rechromed — The hardened state of a printing plate, sleeve or cylinder after it has been repaired or restored, and then replated with chrome to prolong its productivity.

Redesigned Stamp — A stamp design differing from one issued previously by altering subtle details only.

Re-Engraved Stamp Design — A stamp virtually identical to an earlier one, but from a newly engraved master **die**.

Registration — In printing generally, the proper placement of each separately printed ink or embossed image in relation to others. In stamp production, registration also applies to tagging

blocks, perforations and roulettes.

Reissued Stamp — Either a new release of a stamp previously withdrawn from sale, or an altered version of an existing stamp.

Relief Printing — Any printing process in which the area not to be printed is cut away, leaving the printing plate image raised in relief. The world's oldest printing process, wood block printing, and some of the most common, such as rubber handstamps, are examples of relief printing, as is the earliest example of printing from moveable type, the Gutenberg Bible.

Revised Stamp Design — A stamp design differing from one issued previously in subtle details only, either deliberately or inadvertently (for example, changed solely by switching production from one press to another).

Rotary Presses — Presses that print from curved plates, sleeves or cylinders, as opposed to flat plates or other flat printing bases. All presses used to print U.S. coil stamps since 1914 are rotary presses, but the term is often used to mean the **Stickney rotary presses**.

Rotogravure — **Gravure Printing** on a rotary press; as a practical matter, nearly all gravure printing is rotogravure.

Rouletting — A form of stamp separation achieved by slitting or scoring, similar to **perforating**, but without any paper being removed.

Scott Catalog — The *Scott Standard Postage Stamp Catalogue* and the *Scott Specialized Catalogue of United States Stamps*, both issued annually, using the Scott numbering system. The stamp reference books most widely used by collectors in the United States.

Seam — The edge of a printing plate where it is fastened to the printing cylinder, usually applied to **offset** plates.

Seam Line — A printed line marking the edge of a plate, applied especially to **offset** plates.

Self Color — A single color of ink printed on a separate area, yielding its hue directly. Differentiated from **process colors,** which yield a full range of hues by combining overlapping **halftone** images of four primary colors. For example, green can be printed either as green ink separately, a self color, or by combining halftone printings of two process colors, cyan and yellow, in the same space.

Service Inscribed — A stamp with a printed **service inscription** in its design or overprint.

Service Inscription — The restrictive wording printed as part of a stamp design or overprint designating the service for which the stamp is intended to be used, and serving as an **endorsement** when affixed to a piece of mail. Service inscriptions include "Airmail," "Bulk Rate," "Presorted First-Class," "Nonprofit CAR-RT Sort," "Special Delivery," "Postage Due" and many others. In most cases, stamps bearing restrictive service inscriptions can also be used by permit holders on regular first-class mail bearing an endorsement to that effect.

Se-tenant Overprint — The 17¢ Electric Auto stamps exist with three different precancel overprints, differing in their fonts (type styles). Two of the three fonts, called Type A and Type B, are sometimes found on the same rolls of stamps, alternating in 12-stamp strips. The stamps straddling the gap between the two overprint styles are a Type AB or BA se-tenant pair.

Set-off — The inadvertent transfer of printed ink onto paper where it doesn't belong. Sometimes wet or tacky ink on one printed sheet or web will transfer onto the back of the adjacent sheet or turn of the web. Sometimes **chill rollers**, tagging rollers or other parts of a printing press will pick up wet ink and transfer it back to another part of the paper web, yielding a ghost or shadow image that appears to be doubled. Also called offset.

Shade — A discernible difference in the color of ink used to print a stamp.

Sheet — The piece of paper containing the entire original printed layout of stamps, which is normally cut into smaller units called **panes** before being distributed. In less precise usage, the term sheet is often used to mean a pane of stamps, and the individual stamps issued in panes are called sheet stamps.

Shiny Gum — Water-activated stamp adhesive with a glossy or "wet" physical appearance, made of corn dextrin or a combination of dextrin and synthetics, such as polyvinyl acetate.

Siderography — The craft of making printing plates by transferring repeating multiple engraved subjects to flat or cylindrical steel printing bases.

Sizing — Glue or similar substance incorporated into paper during manufacture, essential to the integrity of ink images, written or printed. On unsized paper, such as a blotter or paper towel, ink runs rather than staying in place.

Sleeve — See **Intaglio Sleeve**.

Sleeve Number — The plate number of an intaglio printing sleeve used on the B, C or D press.

Slitting — Separating printed rolls of coil stamps into individual rows one stamp deep, with straight edges top and bottom of horizontal-format stamps, or left and right of vertical-format stamps.

Solvent Wipe — The system originally used to remove excess ink from intaglio printing sleeves on the B press before they were pressed against the paper web to print the image; later replaced by a water wipe.

Souvenir Cover — A cover deliberately created as a collectible item, featuring the stamp(s), cancelation(s) or other postal markings(s), or commemorating an event or anniversary. Most souvenir covers are decorated with cachets.

Souvenir Page — An officially issued letter-size stamp data sheet bearing one or more of the stamp or stamps described and pictured, canceled with the official first-day-of-issue postmark.

Splice — The taped joint or seam connecting two rolls of printed stamp paper, or repairing a break in a single roll. Except on coils of 10,000 stamps, splices are supposed to be removed and destroyed, but when they escape detection and reach the stamp market, they are eagerly sought by EFO collectors.

Stamp Collector — A weekly stamp

newspaper that carries occasional articles related to plate number coils, but has some very useful technical articles on developments in stamp production technology. For information, write to Stamp Collector, P.O. Box 10, Albany, Oregon 97321.

Stamp Distribution Office — The supplier of retail quantities of stamps, postal stationery, and other postal, fiscal, and philatelic products to the post offices within a Management Sectional Center, the local administrative unit of the Postal Service.

Stamp Imprint — See **Stamp Indicium**.

Stamp Indicium. The franking imprint on an item of **postal stationery**.

Stamps — A weekly stamp newspaper that carries sparse coverage of plate number coils and related news. For information, write to Stamps, 85 Canisteo Street, Hornell, New York 14843.

Stickney Rotary Presses — Intaglio webfed stamp printing presses designed by Benjamin F. Stickney, in use at the Bureau of Engraving and Printing from 1914 until 1962.

Subject — The individual design for a single stamp as it appears on a printing plate, sleeve, mat or cylinder; or as printed on a sheet or web of paper.

Tagged — Stamps bearing luminescent phosphors that glow under ultraviolet illumination, used to activate post office facer-canceler machines. Phosphor tagging may be applied by any of several different methods: prior to printing, impregnated into paper sizing or coated onto the paper surface; at the time of printing, blended into ink or in a separate lacquer suspension; or after stamp printing, in a separate pass through a printing press.

Tagging Shift — Displacement of a printed block of tagging phosphor out of register with the printed image.

The Plate Number — A commercial bimonthly newsletter on U.S. plate number coil stamps edited by Stephen G. Esrati, published since February 1986, abbreviated *TPN*.

Thematic Collecting — The common international term for **topical collecting**.

Third-class Mail — Low-priority reduced-rate mail, including printed matter and merchandise, but excluding individualized text letters. Third-class matter may be mailed as individual pieces or, by permit holders, in presorted bundled bulk quantities at reduced rates.

Topical Collecting — A system of collecting in which the organizing principle is the common subject matter of stamps, postal stationery, meters and postal markings, rather than their country of origin, period of use, rate study or other traditional method of classification.

Topical Time — Journal of the **American Topical Association,** published every two months.

TPN — See *The Plate Number.*

Transfer Roller — A steel cylinder bearing a raised image taken from an engraved master **die,** used to transfer a single original intaglio design to the multiple-subject positions of a printing **plate** by a rocking motion under pressure. Each stage — die, transfer roller, plate — begins with a soft piece of steel, later hardened after its image is complete.

True Franking — Postage on a piece of mail whose denomination exactly equals the actual prepaid per-piece rate.

Typography — (1) The design and layout of printing subjects. (2) Anachronistically, in philatelic texts this term is used in its archaic meaning of **letterpress** printing.

Uncoated Paper — Matte-finish paper without an added surface treatment.

United States Coil Collectors Society — Publisher of *Coil Collector* from January 1984 to September 1985; no longer exists.

United States Specialist — The monthly journal published by the **Bureau Issues Association**.

United States Stamp Society — See **Bureau Issues Association**.

Unsorted — Quantity mail delivered to the post office without presorting by the mailer.

Untagged — A stamp printed without phosphor tagging, either deliberately, because the stamp does not need to be canceled, or in error.

USPS — United States Postal Service.

Variety — Any stamp that differs in some respect from a normal stamp of its type.

Vignette — The pictorial portion of a stamp design.

Water Wipe — The system of removing excess ink from intaglio printing sleeves on the B, C and D presses before one is pressed against the paper web to print the image.

Web — A continuous roll of paper. Presses are typically either sheetfed (printing onto a succession of stacked individual sheets of paper) or webfed (printing onto a continuous roll of paper). All U.S. coil stamps since 1914 have been printed on webfed presses.

Wet Gum — See **Shiny Gum**.

Wet Printing — Intaglio printing on paper first dampened to a high moisture content, 15 to 30 percent by weight; a term often applied to U.S. stamps printed on Stickney rotary presses, to differentiate them from similar stamps printed on Cottrell presses.

Wiping System — The device that removes excess ink from an intaglio plate, printing sleeve or gravure cylinder before it is pressed against a sheet or web of paper to print an image.

Withdrawal Date — In the United States, the date a stamp or other postal item is removed from sale at philatelic counters and at the Philatelic Sales Division of the Postal Service.

Withdrawn From Philatelic Sale — Removed from sale by philatelic counters and the Philatelic Sales Division, but kept on sale at ordinary post office counters until supplies are exhausted.

ZIP Code — ZIP is the acronym for Zone Improvement Plan, the system of five-digit postal codes introduced in the 1960s to speed the processing of mail, and to render mail processing susceptible to mechanization.

ZIP+4 — The augmented system of nine-digit postal codes, adding four to the basic **ZIP code**, introduced in the 1980s to render mail processing susceptible to automation.

ZIP+4 Presort — Bulk or quantity mail presorted to nine ZIP-code digits and bundled by the mailer before posting.

ZIP+4 Unsorted — Bulk or quantity mail bearing the full nine-digit **ZIP code** for each addressee, but delivered to the post office without presorting by the mailer.

Checklist of Imperforate Plate Number Coils

Stamp	1	2	3	4	5	6	7	8	9	10	11	12	13	14	15	16	17	18	19	20	21	22
Transportation Series																						
1¢ Omnibus					X	X																
2¢ Locomotive			X	X			X		X													
4¢ Stagecoach, precanceled					X	X																
5¢ Motorcycle	X	X																				
5.9¢ Bicycle, precanceled			X	X																		
6¢ Tricycle, precanceled		X																				
9.3¢ Mail Wagon, precanceled	X	X	X	X																		
10.1¢ Oil Wagon, precanceled (black)	X																					
10.9¢ Hansom Cab, precanceled	X	X																				
12.5¢ Pushcart, precanceled	X																					
13.2¢ Coal Car	X																					
14¢ Iceboat	X	X																				
16.7¢ Popcorn Wagon	X																					
17¢ Electric Auto	X	X	X	X																		
17¢ Electric Auto, precanceled Type A		X	X																			
17¢ Dog Sled		X																				
17.5¢ Racing Car	X																					
18¢ Surrey		X					X	X	X													
20¢ Fire Pumper	X	X	X	X	X			X	X					X	X							
20¢ Cable Car		X																				
21¢ Railroad Mail Car	X																					
25¢ Bread Wagon		X	X	X	X																	
Flag Series																						
18¢ Flag		X	X	X	X																	
20¢ Flag Over Supreme Court	X	X	X	X	X	X		X	X	X	X	X	X	X								
22¢ Flag Over Capitol	X	X	X	X	X	X	X	X		X	X	X			X		X	X	X	X		X
25¢ Flag Over Yosemite		X	X	X	X		X		X													
25¢ Flag, phosphored paper						X	X	X	X	X	X	X										
Other Coil Issues																						
20¢ Consumer Education	X	X	X	X																		
25¢ Honeybee	X	X																				
(22¢) Green D Eagle	X	X																				
(25¢) E Earth	1111, 1211																					
18¢ Washington Monument	1112																					
18¢ Washington Monument, service inscribed	33333																					
Officials																						
20¢ Official	X																					

Official Data on Coil Stamps

Stamp	Issue Date	City	Designer	Modeler	Vignette Engraver	Lettering Engraver	Press
1981							
18¢ Flag	4/24/81	Portland, Maine	P. Cocci	P. Cocci	T.R. Hipschen	K.C. Wiram & R.G. Culin, Sr.	Intaglio B
18¢ Surrey	5/18/81	Notch, Mo.	D. Stone	C. Holbert	E.P. Archer	T.J. Bakos	Cottrell
17¢ Electric Auto	6/25/81	Greenfield Village, Mich.	C. Jaquays	C. Holbert	E.P. Archer	T.J. Bakos	Cottrell
17¢ Electric Auto, precanceled	11/81	nationwide	C. Jaquays	C. Holbert	E.P. Archer	T.J. Bakos	Cottrell
20¢ Fire Pumper	12/10/81	Alexandria, Va.	J. Schleyer	C. Holbert	K. Kipperman	R.G. Culin Sr.	Cottrell
9.3¢ Mail Wagon	12/15/81	Shreveport, La.	J. Schleyer	C. Holbert	G.M. Chaconas	G.J. Slaght	Cottrell
9.3¢ Mail Wagon, precanceled	12/81	nationwide	J. Schleyer	C. Holbert	G.M. Chaconas	G.J. Slaght	Cottrell
20¢ Flag Over Supreme Court	12/17/81	Washington, D.C.	D. Ellis	F.J. Waslick	E.P. Archer	R.G. Culin Sr.	Intaglio B or Intaglio C
1982							
5.9¢ Bicycle	2/17/82	Wheeling, W.Va.	D. Stone	C. Holbert	G.M. Chaconas	T.J. Bakos	Cottrell
5.9¢ Bicycle, precanceled	2/82	nationwide	D. Stone	C. Holbert	G.M. Chaconas	T.J. Bakos	Cottrell
10.9¢ Hansom Cab	3/26/82	Chattanooga, Tenn.	D. Stone	C. Holbert	E.P. Archer	T.J. Bakos	Cottrell
10.9¢ Hansom Cab, precanceled	3/82	nationwide	D. Stone	C. Holbert	E.P. Archer	T.J. Bakos	Cottrell
20¢ Consumer Education	4/27/82	Washington, D.C.	J. Boyd	none	J.S. Creamer Jr.	A. Saavedra	Cottrell
2¢ Locomotive	5/20/82	Chicago, Ill.	D. Stone	C. Holbert	J.S. Wallace	R.G. Culin Sr.	Cottrell
4¢ Stagecoach	8/19/82	Milwaukee, Wis.	J. Schleyer	C. Holbert	T.R. Hipschen	G.J. Slaght	Cottrell
4¢ Stagecoach, precanceled	11/82	nationwide	J. Schleyer	C. Holbert	T.R. Hipschen	G.J. Slaght	Cottrell
1983							
20¢ Official	1/12/83	Washington, D.C.	B. Thompson	P. Cocci	E.P. Archer	G.J. Slaght	Intaglio B
5.2¢ Sleigh	3/21/83	Memphis, Tenn.	W. Brooks	R.C. Sharpe	E.P. Archer	R.G. Culin Sr.	Cottrell
5.2¢ Sleigh, precanceled	3/83	nationwide	W. Brooks	R.C. Sharpe	E.P. Archer	R.G. Culin Sr.	Cottrell
3¢ Handcar	3/25/83	Rochester, N.Y.	W. Brooks	C. Holbert	E.P. Archer	T.J. Bakos	Cottrell
1¢ Omnibus	8/19/83	Arlington, Va.	D. Stone	C. Holbert	G.M. Chaconas	R.G. Culin Sr.	Cottrell
5¢ Motorcycle	10/10/83	San Francisco, Calif.	W. Brooks	R.C. Sharpe	K. Kipperman	D. Brown	Cottrell

312

Colors	Tagging	Precancel Overprint or Inscription	FDCs Canceled[12]	Image Area (Inches)	Plate No. Interval	Pl. Nos. per Coil	Stamps per Coil	Quantities Shipped through Fiscal Year 1989	Withdrawal Date
Red, Blue, Purple	Block	none	691,526[1]	.71x.82	52	1	100, 500, 3000	3,683,325,000	7/31/82
Brown	Overall	none	207,801	.75x.82	24	2	100, 500, 3000	2,230,675,000	2/28/86
Blue	Overall	none	239,458	.75x.82	24	2	100, 500, 3000	904,587,000	4/30/87 (100s) 10/31/87 (500s)
Blue	none	PRESORTED FIRST-CLASS, lines	— —	.75x.82	24	2	500, 3000	363,035,000	6/30/87
Red	Overall	none	304,668	.75x.82	24	2	100, 500, 3000	2,392,106,000	10/31/87 (reissued April 1988)
Red	Overall	none	199,645	.75x.82	24	2	500	23,300,000	6/30/85
Red	none	lines	— —	.75x.82	24	2	500, 3000	864,976,000	6/30/85
Black, Blue, Red	Block	none	598,169[1]	.71x.82	52 or 48	1	100, 500, 3000	33,665,035,000	10/31/85 (reissued April 1988)
Blue	Overall	none	814,419[3]	.75x.82	24	2	500	18,925,000	1/31/84
Blue	none	lines	— —	.75x.82	24	2	500, 3000	352,674,000	1/31/84
Purple	Overall	none	— —	.75x.82	24	2	500	18,750,000	3/31/84
Purple	none	lines	— —	.75x.82	24	2	500, 3000	611,147,000	3/31/84
Blue	Overall	none	— —	.74x.87	24	2	100, 500, 3000	545,654,000	11/30/83
Black	Overall	none	290,020	.75x.82	24	2	500, 3000	321,683,000[2]	8/31/88
Brown	Overall	none	152,940	.75x.82	24	2	500, 3000	112,951,000[2]	2/28/89
Brown	none	Nonprofit Org., lines	— —	.75x.82	24	2	500, 3000	237,995,000	8/31/85
Red, Blue, Black	Block	none	840,841[4]	.71x.82	52	1	100	60,440,000	8/31/85
Red	Overall	none	141,979	.75x.82	24	2	500	19,050,000	6/30/85
Red	none	lines	— —	.75x.82	24	2	500, 3000	928,939,000	6/30/85
Green	Overall	none	77,900	.75x.82	24	2	500, 3000	118,055,000	8/31/88
Purple	Overall	none	109,463	.75x.82	24	2	500, 3000	543,858,000[2]	6/30/88
Greenish Gray	Overall	none	188,240	.75x.82	24	2	500, 3000	357,125,000	2/28/89

313

Stamp	Issue Date	City	Designer	Modeler	Vignette Engraver	Lettering Engraver	Press
1984							
11¢ Caboose	2/3/84	Rosemont, Ill.	J. Schleyer	C. Holbert	J.S. Creamer Jr.	G.J. Slaght	Intaglio B
11¢ Caboose, precanceled	2/84	nationwide	J. Schleyer	C. Holbert	J.S. Creamer Jr.	G.J. Slaght	Intaglio B
7.4¢ Baby Buggy	4/7/84	San Diego, Calif.	J. Schleyer	F.J. Waslick	K. Kipperman	D. Brown	Intaglio B
7.4¢ Baby Buggy, precanceled	4/84	nationwide	J. Schleyer	F.J. Waslick	K. Kipperman	D. Brown	Intaglio B
20¢ Flag, precanceled	7/9/84	nationwide	D. Ellis	F.J. Waslick	E.P. Archer	R.G. Culin Sr.	Intaglio B
1985							
(22¢) nondenominated D	2/1/85	Los Angeles, Calif.	B. Thompson	F.J. Waslick	T.R. Hipschen	R.G. Culin Sr.	Andreotti or A, Gravure section
(22¢) nondenominated D Official	2/4/85	Washington, D.C.	B. Thompson	P. Cocci	E.P. Archer	G.J. Slaght	Intaglio B
14¢ Iceboat	3/23/85	Rochester, N.Y.	W.H. Bond	E.F. Porter	G.M. Chaconas	G.J. Slaght	Cottrell
22¢ Flag Over Capitol	3/29/85	Washington, D.C.	F.J. Waslick	F.J. Waslick	T.R. Hipschen	R.G. Culin Sr.	Intaglio B, Intaglio C or Intaglio D
12¢ Stanley Steamer	4/2/85	Kingfield, Maine	K. Dallison	E.F. Porter	G.M. Chaconas	G.J. Slaght	Cottrell
12¢ Stanley Steamer, precanceled	4/85	nationwide	K. Dallison	E.F. Porter	G.M. Chaconas	G.J. Slaght	Cottrell
10.1¢ Oil Wagon	4/18/85	Oil Center, N.M.	J. Schleyer	— —	E.P. Archer	R.G. Culin Sr.	Intaglio B
10.1¢ Oil Wagon, precanceled (black)	4/85	nationwide	J. Schleyer	— —	E.P. Archer	R.G. Culin Sr.	Intaglio B
12.5¢ Pushcart	4/18/85	Oil Center, N.M.	J. Schleyer	— —	G.M. Chaconas	R.G. Culin Sr.	Intaglio B
12.5¢ Pushcart, precanceled	4/85	nationwide	J. Schleyer	— —	G.M. Chaconas	R.G. Culin Sr.	Intaglio B
6¢ Tricycle	5/6/85	Childs, Md.	J. Schleyer	— —	K. Kipperman	T.J. Bakos	Intaglio B
6¢ Tricycle, precanceled	5/85	nationwide	J. Schleyer	— —	K. Kipperman	T.J. Bakos	Intaglio B
3.4¢ School Bus	6/8/85	Arlington, Va.	L. Nolan	R.C. Sharpe	K. Kipperman	G.J. Slaght	Cottrell
3.4¢ School Bus, precanceled	6/85	nationwide	L. Nolan	R.C. Sharpe	K. Kipperman	G.J. Slaght	Cottrell
11¢ Stutz Bearcat	6/11/85	Baton Rouge, La.	K. Dallison	R.C. Sharpe	T.R. Hipschen	R.G. Culin Sr.	Cottrell
4.9¢ Buckboard	6/21/85	Reno, Nev.	W.H. Bond	E. Porter	G.M. Chaconas	R.G. Culin Sr.	Cottrell
4.9¢ Buckboard, precanceled	6/85	nationwide	W.H. Bond	E. Porter	G.M. Chaconas	R.G. Culin Sr.	Cottrell
8.3¢ Ambulance	6/21/85	Reno, Nev.	J. Schleyer	R.C. Sharpe	G.M. Chaconas	J.S. Creamer Jr.	Cottrell

Colors	Tagging	Precancel Overprint or Inscription	FDCs Canceled[12]	Image Area (Inches)	Plate No. Interval	Pl. Nos. per Coil	Stamps per Coil	Quantities Shipped through Fiscal Year 1989	Withdrawal Date
Red	Block	none	1	.75x.82	52	1	500	24,350,000	8/31/85
Red	none	lines	— —	.75x.82	52	1	500, 3000	512,680,000	8/31/85
Brown	Block	none	187,797	.75x.82	52	1	500	20,550,000	8/31/85
Brown	none	Blk. Rt. CAR-RT SORT, lines	— —	.75x.82	52	1	500, 3000	241,824,000	8/31/85
Black, Blue, Red	none	lines	— —	.71x.82	52	1	500, 3000	43,760,000	10/31/85
Green	Block	none	513,027[1]	.75x.82	38	1	100, 500, 3000	3,029,956,000	12/31/85
Red, Black, Blue	Block	none	— —	?	52	1	100	27,160,000	12/31/85
Blue	Overall	none	324,710	?	24	2	500, 3000	306,033,000[2]	2/28/89
Red, Blue, Black	Block	none	268,161[1]	.71x.82	52 or 48	1	100, 500, 3000	39,437,838,000[5]	2/28/89
Blue	Overall	none	173,998	.71x.82	24	2	500	32,325,000	2/28/89
Blue	none	PRESORTED FIRST-CLASS, lines	— —	.71x.82	24	2	500, 3000	106,792,000[2]	2/28/89
Blue	Block	none	[7]	?	52	1	500	28,800,000	12/31/88
Blue	none	Bulk Rate, lines	— —	?	52	1	500, 3000	1,455,840,500[6]	10/31/88
Olive	Block	none	[7]	?	52	1	500, 3000	28,270,000	— —
Olive	none	Bulk Rate, lines	— —	?	52	1	500, 3000	1,666,316,000	4/30/89
Brown	Block	none	151,494	.71x.82	52	1	500	23,925,000	2/28/89
Brown	none	Nonprofit Org., lines	— —	.71x.82	52	1	500, 3000	706,352,000	12/31/88
Green	Overall	none	131,480	.71x.82	24	2	500	15,700,000	4/30/87
Green	none	Nonprofit Org. CAR-RT SORT, lines	— —	.71x.82	24	2	500, 3000	122,144,000	4/30/87
Green	Overall	none	135,037	.71x.82	24	2	500, 3000	79,120,000	— —
Brown	Overall	none	[8]	.71x.82	24	2	500	19,400,000	10/31/88
Brown	none	Nonprofit Org., lines	— —	.71x.82	24	2	500, 3000	204,388,000	10/31/88
Green	Overall	none	[8]	.71x.82	24	2	500	18,975,000	2/28/89

315

Stamp	Issue Date	City	Designer	Modeler	Vignette Engraver	Lettering Engraver	Press
8.3¢ Ambulance, precanceled	6/85	nationwide	J. Schleyer	R.C. Sharpe	G.M. Chaconas	J.S. Creamer Jr.	Cottrell
21.1¢ Letters	10/22/85	Washington, D.C.	R. Sheaff	C. Holbert	— —	— —	Andreotti
21.1¢ Letters, service inscribed	10/85	nationwide	R. Sheaff	C. Holbert	— —	— —	Andreotti
18¢ Washington Monument	11/6/85	Washington, D.C.	T. Szumowski	C. Holbert	— —	— —	Andreotti
18¢ Washington Monument, service inscribed	11/85	nationwide	T. Szumowski	C. Holbert	— —	— —	Andreotti
1986							
4¢ Stagecoach, re-engraved	8/15/86 ⁹	Washington, D.C.	J. Schleyer	C. Holbert	K. Kipperman	G.J. Slaght	Intaglio B
17¢ Dog Sled	8/20/86	Anchorage, Alaska	L. Nolan	C. Holbert	E.P. Archer	G.J. Slaght and M. Ryan (numerals)	Intaglio B
8.3¢ Ambulance, redesigned, precanceled	8/29/86 ⁹	Washington, D.C.	J. Schleyer	R.C. Sharpe	G.M. Chaconas	J.S. Creamer Jr.	Intaglio B
14¢ Iceboat, redesigned	9/30/86 ⁹	Washington, D.C.	W.H. Bond	E.F. Porter	G.M. Chaconas	G.J. Slaght	Intaglio B
5.5¢ Star Route Truck	11/1/86	Fort Worth, Texas	D.K. Stone	— —	J.S. Creamer Jr.	D. Brown	Intaglio B
5.5¢ Star Route Truck, service inscribed	11/1/86	Fort Worth, Texas	D.K. Stone	— —	J.S. Creamer Jr.	D. Brown	Intaglio B
25¢ Bread Wagon	11/22/86	Virginia Beach Va.	W.H. Bond	— —	E.P. Archer	M.J. Ryan	Intaglio B or Intaglio C
1¢ Omnibus, re-engraved	11/26/86	Washington, D.C.	D.K. Stone	C. Holbert	G.M. Chaconas	R.G. Culin Sr.	Intaglio B
1987							
8.5¢ Tow Truck	1/24/87	Tucson, Ariz.	W.H. Bond	— —	E.P. Archer	M.J. Ryan	Intaglio B
8.5¢ Tow Truck, service inscribed	1/24/87	Tucson, Ariz.	W.H. Bond	— —	E.P. Archer	M.J. Ryan	Intaglio B
7.1¢ Tractor	2/6/87	Sarasota, Fla.	K. Dallison	— —	G.M. Chaconas	R.G. Culin Sr.	Intaglio B
7.1¢ Tractor, service inscribed	2/6/87	Sarasota, Fla.	K. Dallison	— —	G.M. Chaconas	R.G. Culin Sr.	Intaglio B
2¢ Locomotive, re-engraved	3/6/87	Milwaukee, Wis.	D.K. Stone	— —	G.M. Chaconas	M.J. Ryan	Intaglio B
10¢ Canal Boat	4/11/87	Buffalo, N.Y.	W.H. Bond	— —	E.P. Archer	R.G. Culin Sr.	Intaglio B

Colors	Tagging	Precancel Overprint or Inscription	FDCs Canceled[12]	Image Area (Inches)	Plate No. Interval	Pl. Nos. per Coil	Stamps per Coil	Quantities Shipped through Fiscal Year 1989	Withdrawal Date
Green	none	Blk. Rt. CAR-RT SORT, lines	– –	.71x.82	24	2	500, 3000	394,830,000[1]	2/28/89
Pink, Red, Yellow, Green, Blue, Black	Block	none	119,941	.71x.82	24	1	500	14,775,000	6/30/89
Pink, Red, Yellow, Green, Blue, Black	none	ZIP+4	– –	.71x.82	24	1	500, 3000	83,084,000	6/30/89
Yellow, Magenta, Cyan, Black	Block	none	376,238	.71x.82	24	1	500	23,850,000	10/31/88
Yellow, Magenta, Cyan, Black, Line Black	none	PRESORTED FIRST-CLASS	– –	.71x.82	24	1	500, 3000	801,708,000	10/31/88
Red, Brown	Block	none	– –	?	52	1	3000	283,948,000[1]	– –
Blue	Block	none	112,009	.71x.82	52	1	100, 500, 3000	438,257,000	– –
Green	none	Blk. Rt. CAR-RT SORT, lines	– –	?	52	1	500, 3000	435,936,000[1]	2/28/89
Blue	Block	none	– –	?	52	1	500, 3000	195,788,000[1]	6/30/89
Maroon	Block	none	136,021	.71x.82	52	1	500	16,900,000	2/28/89
Maroon	none	CAR-RT Sort Non-profit Org. (black)	– –	.71x.82	52	1	500, 3000	189,252,000	2/28/89
Brown	Block	none	151,950	.71x.82	52 or 48	1	100, 500, 3000	8,402,956,000	4/30/89
Purple	Block	none	57,845	?	52	1	3000	472,084,000	– –
Dark Gray	Block	none	224,285	.71x.82	52	1	500	17,600,000	12/31/88
Dark Gray	none	Nonprofit Org.	– –	.71x.82	52	1	500, 3000	593,252,000	10/31/88
Dark Red	Block	none	167,555	.71x.82	52	1	500	18,700,000[1]	2/28/89
Dark Red and Black	none	Nonprofit Org.	– –	.71x.82	52	1	500, 3000	344,948,000	2/28/89
Black	Block	none	169,484	.71x.82	52	1	500, 3000, 10000	85,528,000[1]	– –
Blue	Block	none	171,952	.71x.82	52	1	100, 3000	49,608,000	– –

Stamp	Issue Date	City	Designer	Modeler	Vignette Engraver	Lettering Engraver	Press
22¢ Flag, phosphored paper	5/23/87	Seacaucus, N.J.	F.J. Waslick	F.J. Waslick	T.R. Hipschen	R.G. Culin Sr.	Intaglio C
12¢ Stanley Steamer, redesigned, precanceled	6/87	nationwide	K. Dallison	E.F. Porter	G.M. Chaconas	G.J. Slaght	Intaglio B
5¢ Milk Wagon	9/25/87	Indianapolis, Ind.	L. Nolan	C. Holbert	G.M. Chaconas	D. Brown	Intaglio B
17.5¢ Racing Car	9/25/87	Indianapolis, Ind.	T. Broad	P. Cocci	G.M. Chaconas	G.J. Slaght	Intaglio B
17.5¢ Racing Car, service inscribed	9/25/87	Indianapolis, Ind.	T. Broad	P. Cocci	G.M. Chaconas	G.J. Slaght	Intaglio B
1988							
3¢ Conestoga Wagon	2/29/88	Conestoga, Pa.	R. Schlecht	— —	T.R. Hipschen	D. Brown	Intaglio B
(25¢) Nondenominated E Earth	3/22/88	Washington, D.C.	R.T. McCall	E.F. Porter	— —	— —	Andreotti
25¢ Flag Over Yosemite	5/20/88	Yosemite, Calif.	P. Cocci	P. Cocci	T.R. Hipschen	D. Brown	Intaglio B, Intaglio C or Intaglio D
10.1¢ Oil Wagon, service inscribed (red)	6/27/88	Washington, D.C.	J. Schleyer	— —	E.P. Archer	R.G. Culin Sr.	Intaglio B
16.7¢ Popcorn Wagon	7/7/88	Chicago, Ill.	L. Nolan	R.C. Sharpe	G.M. Chaconas	D. Brown	Intaglio B
15¢ Tugboat	7/12/88	Long Beach, Calif.	R. Schlecht	C. Holbert	G.M. Chaconas	D. Brown	Intaglio B
13.2¢ Coal Car	7/19/88	Pittsburgh, Pa.	R. Schlecht	— —	T.R. Hipschen	M.J. Ryan	Intaglio B
8.4¢ Wheel Chair	8/12/88	Tucson, Ariz.	C. Calle	— —	G.M. Chaconas	G.J. Slaght	Intaglio B or Intaglio C
21¢ Railroad Mail Car	8/16/88	Santa Fe, N.M.	D. Stone	C. Holbert	G.M. Chaconas	D. Brown	Intaglio B or Intaglio C
7.6¢ Carreta	8/30/88	San Jose, Calif.	R. Schlecht	— —	E.P. Archer	G.J. Slaght	Intaglio B

Colors	Tagging	Precancel Overprint or Inscription	FDCs Canceled[12]	Image Area (Inches)	Plate No. Interval	Pl. Nos. per Coil	Stamps per Coil	Quantities Shipped through Fiscal Year 1989	Withdrawal Date
Red, Blue, Black	Phosph. paper	none	151,686	.71x.82	48	1	100	20,000,000	2/28/90
Blue	none	PRESORTED FIRST-CLASS, lines	--	?	52	1	3000	91,968,000[1]	2/28/89
Gray (PMS 425U)	Block	none	10	.71x.82	52	1	100, 3000	55,152,000	--
Purple (PMS 268U)	Block	none	10	.71x.82	52	1	100	17,300,000	--
Purple (PMS 268U) and Red (PMS 186U)	none	ZIP+4 Presort	--	.71x.82	52	1	500, 3000	101,572,000	--
Maroon (PMS 209)	Block	none	155,203	.71x.82	52	1	100, 500, 3000	132,324,000	--
Red, Blue, Yellow and Black	Block	none	363,639[1]	.71x.82	24	1	100, 500, 3000	1,613,984,000	6/30/89
Red, (PMS 185U) Blue (PMS 295U) and Green (PMS 562U)	Block	none	144,339	.71x.82	52 or 48	1	100, 500, 3000	995,473,000[11]	--
Blue	none	Bulk Rate Carrier Route Sort	136,428	?	52	1	500, 3000, 10000	82,962,500[2]	--
Red (PMS 186U) and Black (PMS 701B)	none	Bulk Rate	117,908	.71x.82	52	1	500, 3000, 10000	782,387,000	--
Purple	Block	none	134,926	.71x.82	52	1	500, 3000	452,807,000	--
Dark Green (PMS 330) and Red (PMS 185)	none	Bulk Rate	123,965	.71x.82	52	1	500, 3000, 10000	1,028,783,000	--
Maroon (PMS 209) and Red (PMS 186)	none	Nonprofit	136,337	.71x.82	52 or 48	1	500, 3000	556,084,000	--
Green (PMS 455) and Red (PMS 186)	none	Presorted First-Class	124,430	.71x.82	52 or 48	1	500, 3000	586,352,000	--
Brown (PMS 168) and Red (PMS 186)	none	Nonprofit	140,024	.71x.82	52	1	500, 3000	418,332,000	--

319

Stamp	Issue Date	City	Designer	Modeler	Vignette Engraver	Lettering Engraver	Press
25¢ Honeybee	9/2/88	Omaha, Neb.	C. Ripper	P. Cocci	E.P. Archer	— —	Goebel Optiforma & Intaglio C or Offset/ Intaglio D
5.3¢ Elevator	9/16/88	New York, N.Y.	L. Nolan	— —	G.M. Chaconas	D. Brown	Intaglio B
20.5¢ Fire Engine	9/28/88	San Angelo, Tex.	C. Calle	C. Holbert	T.R. Hipschen	G.J. Slaght	Intaglio B
24.1¢ Tandem Bicycle	10/26/88	Redmond, Wash.	C. Calle	— —	G.M. Chaconas	M.J. Ryan	Intaglio B
20¢ Cable Car	10/28/88	San Francisco, Calif.	D. Romano	F.J. Waslick	E.P. Archer	M.J. Ryan	Intaglio C
13¢ Patrol Wagon	10/29/88	Anaheim, Calif.	J. Brockert	C. Holbert	E.P. Archer	D. Brown	Intaglio B
1989							
25¢ Flag, phosphor-coated paper	2/14/89	Yosemite, Calif.	P. Cocci	P. Cocci	T.R. Hipschen	D. Brown	Intaglio C or Intaglio D
7.1¢ Tractor, service-inscribed, ZIP+4	5/26/89	Rosemont, Ill.	K. Dallison	— —	G.M. Chaconas	R.G. Culin Sr. (lettering & numerals) G.J. Slaght ("Nonprofit 5-digit ZIP+4")	Intaglio B

[1] Total includes FDCs of companion sheet and booklet stamps
[2] Approximate total. Fiscal year reports do not differentiate between original and re-engraved/redesigned stamps.
[3] Probably erroneous; may include FDCs of 5.9¢ embossed envelopes released simultaneously.
[4] Total includes sheet stamps of other denominations
[5] 953,924,000 in storage as of January 1989
[6] Approximate total. Fiscal year reports do not differentiate precancel overprints.
[7] 319,953 FDCs of 10.1¢ Oil Wagon and 12.5¢ Pushcart canceled.
[8] 338,765 FDCs of 4.9¢ Buckboard and 8.3¢ Ambulance canceled.
[9] Earliest known use.
[10] 162,571 FDCs of 5¢ Milk Wagon and 17.5¢ Racing Car canceled.
[11] Approximate total. Fiscal year reports do not differentiate between block-tagged and phosphor-coated 25¢ flag stamps.
[12] Totals include 40,000 to 50,000 Souvenir Pages each issue.

Colors	Tagging	Precancel Overprint or Inscription	FDCs Canceled[12]	Image Area (Inches)	Plate No. Interval	Pl. Nos. per Coil	Stamps per Coil	Quantities Shipped through Fiscal Year 1989	Withdrawal Date
PMS Yellow, Process Yellow, Magenta, Cyan, Process Black and Intaglio Black	Block	none	122,853	.71x.82	48		100, 3000	3,310,948,000	– –
Black and Red (PMS 185)	none	Nonprofit Carrier Route Sort	142,705	.71x.82	52	1	500, 3000	213,088,000	– –
Red (PMS 185U) and Black	none	ZIP+4 Presort	123,043	.71x.82	52	1	500, 3000	240,956,000	– –
Blue (PMS 295) and Red (PMS 186)	none	ZIP+4	138,593	.71x.82	52	1	500, 3000	99,653,000	– –
Dark Blue (PMS 532)	Block	none	150,068	.71x.82	48	1	100, 500, 3000	310,729,000	– –
Black and Red (PMS 185)	none	Presorted First-Class	132,928	.71x.82	52	1	500, 3000	137,349,000	– –
Red (PMS 185U) Blue (PMS 295U) and Green (PMS 562U)	Phos.- coated paper	none	118,874	.71x.82	48	1	100, 500, 3000, 10000	8,651,556,000[11]	– –
Dark Red (Picture and Type) Black (Service Inscription)	none	Nonprofit 5-Digit ZIP+4	202,804	.71x.82	52	1	500, 3000	75,421,000	– –

321

Plate Number Coil First Day Data

Stamp	Issue Date	City	Plate Numbers on First Day Covers	Plate Numbers on Souvenir Pages	Plate Numbers on Ceremony Programs
1¢ Omnibus	8/19/83	Arlington, VA	1, 2	1, 2	1, 2
1¢ Omnibus, re-engraved	11/26/86	Washington, DC	1	no SP	no ceremony
2¢ Locomotive	5/20/82	Chicago, IL	3, 4	3, 4	NR
2¢ Locomotive, re-engraved	3/6/87	Milwaukee, WI	1	1	1
3¢ Handcar	3/25/83	Rochester, NY	1, 2, 3, 4	1, 2, 3, 4	1, 2
3¢ Conestoga Wagon	2/29/88	Conestoga, PA	1	1	1
3.4¢ School Bus	6/8/85	Arlington, VA	1, 2	1, 2	1, 2
3.4¢ School Bus, precanceled				no SP	no ceremony
4¢ Stagecoach	8/19/82	Milwaukee, WI	1, 2, 3, 4	1, 2, 3	2
4¢ Stagecoach, precanceled	11/82		none	no SP	no ceremony
4¢ Stagecoach, re-engraved	8/15/86[1]	Washington, DC	1	no SP	no ceremony
4.9¢ Buckboard	6/21/85	Reno, NV	3, 4	3, 4	3, 4[2]
4.9¢ Buckboard, precanceled			3, 4	no SP	no ceremony
5¢ Motorcycle	10/10/83	San Francisco, CA	1, 2, 3, 4	1, 2, 3, 4	1, 2
5¢ Milk Wagon	9/25/87	Indianapolis, IN	1	1	1[3]
5.2¢ Sleigh	3/21/83	Memphis, TN	1, 2	1, 2	no ceremony
5.2¢ Sleigh, precanceled			1, 2	no SP	no ceremony
5.3¢ Elevator	9/16/88	New York, NY	1	1	1
5.5¢ Star Route Truck	11/1/86	Fort Worth, TX	1	1	1
5.5¢ Star Route Truck, precanceled	11/1/86	Fort Worth, TX	1	no SP	
5.9¢ Bicycle	2/17/82	Wheeling, WV	3, 4	3, 4	no ceremony
5.9¢ Bicycle, precanceled			3, 4	no SP	no ceremony
6¢ Tricycle	5/6/85	Childs, MD	1	1	no ceremony
6¢ Tricycle, precanceled			1	no SP	no ceremony
7.1¢ Tractor	2/6/87	Sarasota, FL	1	1	1
7.1¢ Tractor, precanceled	2/6/87	Sarasota, FL	1	no SP	1
7.1¢ Tractor, Zip+4	5/26/89	Rosemont, IL	1	NR	1
7.4¢ Baby Buggy	4/7/84	San Diego, CA	2	2	2[4]
7.4¢ Baby Buggy, precanceled			2	no SP	no ceremony
7.6¢ Carreta	8/30/88	San Jose, CA	1, 2	1	1
8.3¢ Ambulance	6/21/85	Reno, NV	1, 2	1, 2	1, 2[2]
8.3¢ Ambulance, precanceled			1, 2	no SP	no ceremony
8.3¢ Ambulance, precanceled, B press version	8/29/86[1]	Washington, DC	1	no SP	no ceremony
8.4¢ Wheel Chair	8/12/88	Tucson, AZ	1, 2	1	1
8.5¢ Tow Truck	1/24/87	Tucson, AZ	1	1	1
8.5¢ Tow Truck, precanceled	1/24/87	Tucson, AZ	1	no SP	1
9.3¢ Mail Wagon	12/15/81	Shreveport, LA	1, 2, 3, 4	3, 4	no ceremony
9.3¢ Mail Wagon, precanceled				no SP	no ceremony
10¢ Canal Boat	4/11/87	Buffalo, NY	1	1	1
10.1¢ Oil Wagon	4/18/85	Oil Center, NM	1	1	no ceremony
10.1¢ Oil Wagon, precanceled, black overprint				no SP	no ceremony
10.1¢ Oil Wagon, precanceled, red overprint	6/27/88	Washington, DC	2	2	no ceremony
10.9¢ Hansom Cab	3/26/82	Chattanooga, TN	1, 2	1, 2	1, 2
10.9¢ Hansom Cab, precanceled			1, 2	no SP	no ceremony
11¢ Caboose	2/3/84	Rosemont, IL	1	1	no ceremony
11¢ Caboose, precanceled				no SP	no ceremony
11¢ Stutz Bearcat	6/11/85	Baton Rouge, LA	3, 4	3, 4	4
12¢ Stanley Steamer	4/2/85	Kingfield, ME	1, 2	1, 2	1, 2
12¢ Stanley Steamer, precanceled			1	no SP	no ceremony
12¢ Stanley Steamer, precanceled, B press version	9/3/87[1]	Washington, DC	1	no SP	no ceremony
12.5¢ Pushcart	4/18/85	Oil Center, NM	1	1	no ceremony
12.5¢ Pushcart, precanceled				no SP	no ceremony
13¢ Patrol Wagon	10/29/88	Anaheim, CA	1	1	1
13.2¢ Coal Car	7/19/88	Pittsburgh, PA	1	1	1
14¢ Iceboat	3/23/85	Rochester, NY	1, 2, 3, 4	1, 2	1, 2
14¢ Iceboat, B press version	9/30/86[1]	Washington, DC	2	no SP	no ceremony
15¢ Tugboat	7/12/88	Long Beach, CA	1	1	1
16.7¢ Popcorn Wagon	7/7/88	Chicago, IL	1	1	1
17¢ Electric Auto	6/25/81	Greenfield Village, MI	1, 2	1, 2	no ceremony
17¢ Electric Auto, precanceled	11/81			no SP	no ceremony

322

Stamp	Issue Date	City	Plate Numbers on First Day Covers	Plate Numbers on Souvenir Pages	Plate Numbers on Ceremony Programs
17¢ Dog Sled	8/20/86	Anchorage, AK	2	2	2
17.5¢ Racing Car	9/25/87	Indianapolis, IN	1	1	1[3]
17.5¢ Racing Car, precanceled	9/25/87	Indianapolis, IN	1	no SP	
18¢ Surrey	5/18/81	Notch, MO	1, 2, 3, 4, 5, 6, 7, 8, 9, 10	1, 2	2
20¢ Fire Pumper	12/10/81	Alexandria, VA	1, 2, 3, 4, 5, 6, 7, 8, 10	5, 6	no ceremony
20¢ Cable Car	10/28/88	San Francisco, CA	1, 2	1	1
20.5¢ Fire Engine	9/28/88	San Angelo, TX	1	1	NR
21¢ Railroad Mail Car	8/16/88	Santa Fe, NM	1, 2	1	1
24.1¢ Tandem Bicycle	10/26/88	Redmond, WA	1	1	1
25¢ Bread Wagon	11/22/86	Virginia Beach, VA	1	1	1
18¢ Flag	4/24/81	Portland, ME	1, 2, 3, 4, 5	1	NR
20¢ Flag Over Supreme Court	12/17/81	Washington, DC	1, 2, 3	1	no ceremony
20¢ Flag, precanceled	7/9/84	Washington, DC		no SP	no ceremony
22¢ Flag Over Capitol	3/29/85	Washington, DC	1, 2	2	2
22¢ Flag Over Capitol test	5/23/87	Secaucus, NJ	T1	T1	T1
25¢ Flag Over Yosemite	5/20/88	Yosemite, CA	1, 2, 3, 4	1	1
25¢ Flag Over Yosemite, phosphored paper	2/14/89	Yosemite, CA	5, 6, 7, 8, 9, 10	8	no ceremony
(22¢) D Eagle	2/1/85	Los Angeles, CA	1, 2	2	no ceremony
20¢ Consumer Education	4/27/82	Washington, DC	1, 2, 3, 4	3, 4	1
21.1¢ Letters	10/22/85	Washington, DC	111111	111111	111111
21.1¢ Letters, precanceled			111111	no SP	
18¢ Washington Monument	11/6/85	Washington, DC	1112, 3333	3333	3333
18¢ Washington Monument precanceled			11121, 33333	no SP	
(25¢) E Earth	3/22/88	Washington, DC	1111, 1211, 1222, 2222	1211, 1222	no ceremony
25¢ Honeybee	9/2/88	Omaha, NE	1, 2	1	1
20¢ Official	1/12/83	Washington, DC	1	1	no ceremony
(22¢) D Official	2/4/85	Washington, DC	1	1	no ceremony

[1] Earliest known use

[2] The 4.9¢ Buckboard and 8.3¢ Ambulance coil stamps were issued at the same ceremony, and are both included in one ceremony program.

[3] The 5¢ Milk Wagon and 17.5¢ Racing Car coil stamps were issued at the same ceremony, and are both included in one ceremony program.

[4] The souvenir folder for the 7.4¢ Baby Buggy coil stamp was produced locally by the San Diego postmaster.

NR No report.

323

Selected Domestic U.S. Postal Rates, 1981-1990

Minimum per piece, with typical coil stamp usages, including authorized false frankings

First-class letter, first ounce

Dates	Rate	Authorized Stamps
5/29/78 to 3/21/81	15¢	Nondenominated A
		15¢ Flag
		15¢ Oliver Wendell Holmes
3/22/81 to 10/31/81	18¢	Nondenominated B
		18¢ Flag
		18¢ Surrey
11/1/81 to 2/16/85	20¢	Nondenominated C
		20¢ Flag
		20¢ Fire Pumper
		20¢ Consumer Education
		20¢ Official (government mail only)
		20¢ Flag, plain lines overprint
2/17/85 to 4/2/88	22¢	Nondenominated D
		22¢ Flag
		Nondenominated D Official (government mail only)
		22¢ Official (government mail only)
		22¢ Flag, phosphored paper
4/3/88 continuing	25¢	25¢ Paul Revere
		25¢ Bread Wagon
		Nondenominated E
		25¢ Flag
		Nondenominated E Official (government mail only)
		25¢ Official
		25¢ Flag, phosphor-coated paper
		25¢ Eagle and Shield

First-class letter, first ounce, nonstandard size surcharge

Dates	Rate	Authorized Stamps
7/15/79 to 3/21/81	7¢	none
3/22/81 to 2/16/85	9¢	9¢ Capitol Dome
		9¢ Capitol Dome, plain lines overprint
		9¢ Capitol Dome, overprinted PRESORTED FIRST-CLASS
		9¢ Capitol Dome, overprinted PRESORTED FIRST-CLASS, narrow spaced
2/17/85 continuing	10¢	10¢ Crossed Flags
		10¢ Jefferson Memorial
		10¢ Justice
		10¢ Justice, plain lines overprint
		10¢ Canal Boat

First-class letter, added ounce

Dates	Rate	Authorized Stamps
5/29/78 to 3/21/81	13¢	13¢ Flag
		13¢ Liberty Bell
		13¢ Liberty Bell, city/state overprint
		13¢ Liberty Bell, plain lines overprint
		13¢ Liberty Bell, overprinted PRESORTED FIRST-CLASS
		13¢ Liberty Bell, overprinted PRESORTED FIRST-CLASS, narrow spaced
3/22/81 to 4/2/88	17¢	17¢ Electric Auto
		17¢ Electric Auto, overprinted PRESORTED FIRST-CLASS, Type A
		17¢ Electric Auto, overprinted PRESORTED FIRST-CLASS, Type B
		17¢ Electric Auto, overprinted PRESORTED FIRST-CLASS, Type C
		17¢ Dog Sled
4/3/88 continuing	20¢	20¢ Flag
		20¢ Fire Pumper
		20¢ Consumer Education
		20¢ Official (government mail only)
		20¢ Official, phosphor-coated paper (government mail only)
		20¢ Flag, plain lines overprint
		20¢ Cable Car

First-class letter, quantity mailing, ZIP+4 addressed, unsorted, first ounce

Dates	Rate	Authorized Stamps
Before 10/9/83	none	none
10/9/83 to 2/16/85	19.1¢	none
2/17/85 to 4/2/88	21.1¢	21.1¢ Letters, inscribed ZIP+4
		21.1¢ Letters
4/3/88 continuing	24.1¢	21.1¢ Letters, inscribed ZIP+4, until 10/9/88[1]
		24.1¢ Tandem Bicycle

First-class letter, quantity mailing, sorted to 3 or 5 ZIP code digits, first ounce

Dates	Rate	Authorized Stamps
5/29/78[4] to 3/21/81	13¢	13¢ Liberty Bell, city/state overprint
		13¢ Liberty Bell, plain lines overprint
		13¢ Liberty Bell, overprinted PRESORTED FIRST-CLASS
		13¢ Liberty Bell, overprinted PRESORTED FIRST-CLASS, narrow spaced
3/22/81 to 10/31/81	15¢	13¢ Liberty Bell, plain lines overprint, 3/22/81 to 7/1/81, 7/16/81 to 10/1/81, 10/6/81 to 10/31/81[1]
		13¢ Liberty Bell, overprinted PRESORTED FIRST-CLASS, 3/22/81 to 7/1/81, 7/16/81 to 10/1/81, 10/6/81 to 10/31/81[1]
		13¢ Liberty Bell, overprinted PRESORTED FIRST-CLASS, narrow spaced, 3/22/81 to 7/1/81, 7/16/81 to 10/1/81, 10/6/81 to 10/31/81[1]
11/1/81 to 2/16/85	17¢	13¢ Liberty Bell, plain lines overprint, until 12/1/81[1]
		13¢ Liberty Bell, overprinted PRESORTED FIRST-CLASS, until 12/1/81[1]
		13¢ Liberty Bell, overprinted PRESORTED FIRST-CLASS, narrow spaced, until 12/1/81[1]
		17¢ Electric Auto, overprinted PRESORTED FIRST-CLASS, Type A
		17¢ Electric Auto, overprinted PRESORTED FIRST-CLASS, Type B
		17¢ Electric Auto, overprinted PRESORTED FIRST-CLASS, Type C
2/17/85 to 4/2/88	18¢	17¢ Electric Auto, overprinted PRESORTED FIRST-CLASS, Type A, until 1/1/86[1]
		17¢ Electric Auto, overprinted PRESORTED FIRST-CLASS, Type B, until 1/1/86[1]
		17¢ Electric Auto, overprinted PRESORTED FIRST-CLASS, Type C, until 1/1/86[1]
		18¢ George Washington Monument, inscribed PRESORTED FIRST-CLASS
4/3/88 continuing	21¢	18¢ George Washington Monument, inscribed PRESORTED FIRST-CLASS, until 10/9/88[1]
		21¢ Railroad Mail Car

First-class letter, quantity mailing, presorted, first ounce, nonstandard surcharge

Dates	Rate	Authorized Stamps
Before 4/3/88	Same as regular first-class, first ounce, nonstandard surcharge	
4/3/88 continuing	5¢	none[5]

First-class letter, quantity mailing, sorted to carrier route

Dates	Rate	Authorized Stamps
Before 3/22/81	none	none
3/22/81 to 10/30/81	14¢	none
11/1/81 to 2/16/85	16¢	none
2/17/85 to 4/2/88	17¢	none[6]
4/3/85 continuing	19.5¢	none

First-class letter, quantity mailing, ZIP+4 addressed, sorted to 3 or 5 ZIP code digits, first ounce

Dates	Rate	Authorized Stamps
Before 10/9/83	none	none
10/9/83 to 2/16/85	16.5¢	none
2/17/85 to 4/2/88	17.5¢	17.5¢ Racing Car, inscribed ZIP+4 Presort
4/3/88 continuing	20.5¢	17.5¢ Racing Car, inscribed ZIP+4 Presort, until 10/9/88[1]
		20.5¢ Fire Engine, inscribed ZIP+4 Presort

325

First-class letter, quantity mailing, ZIP+4 addressed, barcoded, sorted to 3 or 5 ZIP code digits, first ounce

Dates	Rate	Authorized Stamps
Before 4/3/88	none	none
4/3/88 continuing	20¢	none[7]

Postcard, single

Dates	Rate	Authorized Stamps
5/29/78 to 3/21/81	10¢	10¢ Crossed Flags
		10¢ Jefferson Memorial
		10¢ Justice
3/22/81 to 10/31/81	12¢	12¢ Torch
11/1/81 to 2/16/85	13¢	13¢ Flag
		13¢ Liberty Bell
2/17/85 to 4/2/88	14¢	14¢ Iceboat
		14¢ Iceboat, redesigned
4/3/88 continuing	15¢	15¢ Flag
		15¢ Oliver Wendell Holmes
		15¢ Tugboat

Postcard, quantity mailing, ZIP+4 addressed, unsorted

Dates	Rate	Authorized Stamps
Before 10/9/83	none	none
10/9/83 to 2/16/85	12.1¢	none
2/17/85 to 4/2/88	13.1¢	none
4/3/88 continuing	14.1¢	none

Postcard, quantity mailing, sorted to 3 or 5 ZIP code digits

Dates	Rate	Authorized Stamps
5/29/78[4] to 3/21/81	9¢	9¢ Capitol Dome, plain lines overprint
		9¢ Capitol Dome, overprinted PRESORTED FIRST-CLASS
		9¢ Capitol Dome, overprinted PRESORTED FIRST-CLASS, narrow spaced
3/22/81 to 10/31/81	11¢	9¢ Capitol Dome, plain lines overprint, 7/16/81 to 10/1/81, 10/6/81 to 10/31/81[1]
		9¢ Capitol Dome, overprinted PRESORTED FIRST-CLASS, 7/16/81 to 10/1/81, 10/6/81 to 10/31/81[1]
		9¢ Capitol Dome, overprinted PRESORTED FIRST-CLASS, narrow spaced, 7/16/81 to 10/1/81, 10/6/81 to 10/31/81[1]
11/1/81 to 4/2/88	12¢	9¢ Capitol Dome, plain lines overprint, until 12/1/81[1]
		9¢ Capitol Dome, overprinted PRESORTED FIRST-CLASS, until 12/1/81[1]
		9¢ Capitol Dome, overprinted PRESORTED FIRST-CLASS, narrow spaced, until 12/1/81[1]
		12¢ Torch, plain lines overprint
		12¢ Torch, overprinted PRESORTED FIRST-CLASS
		12¢ Stanley Steamer, overprinted PRESORTED FIRST-CLASS
		12¢ Stanley Steamer, overprinted PRESORTED FIRST-CLASS, redesigned
4/3/88 continuing	13¢	13¢ Patrol Wagon[8]

Postcard, quantity mailing, sorted to carrier route

Dates	Rate	Authorized Stamps
Before 3/22/81	none	none
3/22/81 to 10/31/81	10¢	10¢ Justice, plain lines overprint
11/1/81 to 4/2/88	11¢	none
4/3/88 continuing	11.5¢	none

Postcard, quantity mailing, ZIP+4 addressed, sorted to 3 or 5 ZIP code digits

Dates	Rate	Authorized Stamps
Before 10/9/83	none	none
10/9/83 to 4/2/88	11.5¢	none
4/3/88 continuing	12.5¢	none

Postcard, quantity mailing, ZIP+4 addressed, barcoded, sorted to 3 or 5 ZIP code digits

Dates	Rate	Authorized Stamps
Before 4/3/88	none	none
4/3/88 continuing	12¢	none

Third-class, bulk mailing, sorted to 3 or 5 ZIP code digits

Dates	Rate	Authorized Stamps
5/29/78 to 3/21/81	8.4¢	8.4¢ Piano, city/state overprint
		8.4¢ Piano, plain lines overprint

3/22/81 to 10/31/81	10.4¢	8.4¢ Piano, city/state overprint, 3/22/81 to 7/1/81, 7/16/81 to 10/1/81, 10/6/81 to 10/31/81[1]
		8.4¢ Piano, plain lines overprint, 3/22/81 to 7/1/81, 7/16/81 to 10/1/81, 10/6/81 to 10/31/81[1]
11/1/81 to 5/21/83	10.9¢	8.4¢ Piano, city/state overprint, 11/1/81 to 12/1/81, 12/31/81 until further notice[1]
		8.4¢ Piano, plain lines overprint, 11/1/81 to 12/1/81, 12/31/81 until further notice[1]
		10.9¢ Hansom Cab, plain lines overprint
5/22/83 to 2/16/85	11¢	10.9¢ Hansom Cab, plain lines overprint, 5/22/83 to 10/1/83, 10/27/83 until further notice[1]
		11¢ Caboose, plain lines overprint
2/17/85 to 4/2/88	12.5¢	11¢ Caboose, plain lines overprint, until 6/16/85[1]
		12.5¢ Pushcart, overprinted Bulk Rate
4/3/88 continuing	16.7¢	12.5¢ Pushcart, overprinted Bulk Rate, until 10/9/88[1]
		16.7¢ Popcorn Wagon

Third-class, bulk mailing, sorted to 5 ZIP code digits

Dates	Rate	Authorized Stamps
Before 3/22/81	none	none
3/22/81 to 10/31/81	8.8¢	8.4¢ Piano, city/state overprint, 3/22/81 to 7/1/81, 7/16/81 to 10/1/81, 10/6/81 to 10/31/81[1]
		8.4¢ Piano, plain lines overprint, 3/22/81 to 7/1/81, 7/16/81 to 10/1/81, 10/6/81 to 10/31/81[1]
11/1/81 to 2/16/83	9.3¢	8.4¢ Piano, city/state overprint, 11/1/81 to 12/1/81, 12/31/81 until further notice[1]
		8.4¢ Piano, plain lines overprint, 11/1/81 to 12/1/81, 12/31/81 until further notice[1]
		9.3¢ Mail Wagon, plain lines overprint
2/17/83 to 4/2/88	10.1¢	9.3¢ Mail Wagon, plain lines overprint, until 6/16/85[1]
		10.1¢ Oil Wagon, overprinted Bulk Rate (black)
4/3/88 continuing	13.2¢	10.1¢ Oil Wagon, overprinted Bulk Rate (black), until 10/9/88[1]
		13.2¢ Coal Car

Third-class, bulk mailing, sorted to carrier route

Dates	Rate	Authorized Stamps
4/23/80 to 3/21/81	6.7¢	none
3/22/81 to 10/31/81	6.4¢	none
11/1/81 to 5/21/83	7.9¢	7.9¢ Drum, overprinted CAR-RT SORT
5/22/83 to 2/16/85	7.4¢	7.9¢ Drum, overprinted CAR-RT SORT, 5/22/83 to 10/1/83, 10/27/83 until further notice[2]
		7.4¢ Baby Buggy, overprinted Blk. Rt. CAR-RT SORT
2/17/85 to 4/2/88	8.3¢	7.4¢ Baby Buggy, overprinted Blk. Rt. CAR-RT SORT until 8/18/85[1]
		8.3¢ Ambulance, overprinted Blk. Rt. CAR-RT SORT
		8.3¢ Ambulance, overprinted Blk. Rt. CAR-RT SORT, redesigned
4/3/88 continuing	10.1¢	8.3¢ Ambulance, overprinted Blk. Rt. CAR-RT SORT, until 10/9/88[1]
		8.3¢ Ambulance, overprinted Blk. Rt. CAR-RT SORT, redesigned, until 10/9/88[1]
		10.1¢ Oil Wagon, overprinted Bulk Rate Carrier Route Sort (red)

Third-class, bulk mailing, ZIP+4 addressed, sorted to 3 to 5 ZIP code digits

Dates	Rate	Authorized Stamps
Before 4/3/88	none	none
4/3/88 continuing	16.2¢	none

Third-class, bulk mailing, ZIP+4 addressed, sorted to 5 ZIP code digits

Dates	Rate	Authorized Stamps
Before 4/3/88	none	none
4/3/88 continuing	12.7¢	none

Third-class, bulk mailing, ZIP+4 addressed, barcoded, sorted to 5 ZIP code digits

Dates	Rate	Authorized Stamps
Before 4/3/88	none	none
4/3/88 continuing	12.2¢	none

Third-class, nonprofit bulk mailing, sorted to 3 or 5 ZIP code digits

Dates	Rate	Authorized Stamps
7/6/80 to 7/5/81	3.5¢	3.1¢ Guitar, plain lines overprint, until 9/1/80[1]

327

		3.5¢ Violins, plain lines overprint
7/6/81 to 1/9/82	3.8¢	3.5¢ Violins, plain lines overprint, 7/6/81 to 12/1/81, 12/31/81 until further notice[1]
1/10/82 to 7/27/82	5.9¢	3.5¢ Violins, plain lines overprint, until further notice[1]
		5.9¢ Bicycle, plain lines overprint
7/28/82 to 1/8/83	4.9¢	5.9¢ Bicycle, plain lines overprint, until 12/31/82[2]
1/9/83 to 2/16/85	5.2¢	5.9¢ Bicycle, plain lines overprint, 1/9/83 to 7/6/83, 8/4/83 until further notice[2]
		5.2¢ Sleigh, plain lines overprint
2/17/85 to 12/31/85	6¢	5.2¢ Sleigh, plain lines overprint, until 6/16/85[1]
		6¢ Tricycle, Nonprofit Org. overprint
1/1/86 to 3/8/86	7.4¢	6¢ Tricycle, Nonprofit Org. overprint[1]
3/9/86 to 4/19/86	8.7¢	6¢ Tricycle, Nonprofit Org. overprint[1]
4/20/86 to 4/2/88	8.5¢	6¢ Tricycle, Nonprofit Org. overprint, 4/20/86 to 10/19/86, 10/23/86 to 3/31/87[1]
		8.5¢ Tow Truck, overprinted Nonprofit Org.
4/3/88 continuing	8.4¢	8.5¢ Tow Truck, overprinted Nonprofit Org., until 10/9/88[1]
		8.4¢ Wheel Chair

Third-class, nonprofit bulk mailing, sorted to 5 ZIP code digits

Dates	Rate	Authorized Stamps
Before 3/22/81	none	none
3/22/81 to 7/5/81	3.3¢	none
7/6/81 to 1/9/82	2.9¢	none
1/10/82 to 7/27/82	5¢	none
7/28/82 to 1/8/83	4¢	4¢ Stagecoach, overprinted Nonprofit Org.
1/9/83 to 2/16/85	4.3¢	4¢ Stagecoach, overprinted Nonprofit Org., 1/9/83 to 7/6/83, 8/4/83 until further notice[1]
2/17/85 to 12/31/85	4.9¢	4¢ Stagecoach, overprinted Nonprofit Org., until 8/18/85[1]
		4.9¢ Buckboard, overprinted Nonprofit Org.
1/1/86 to 3/8/86	6.3¢	4.9¢ Buckboard, overprinted Nonprofit Org.[1]
3/9/86 to 4/19/86	7.2¢	4.9¢ Buckboard, overprinted Nonprofit Org.[1]
4/20/86 to 4/2/88	7.1¢	4.9¢ Buckboard, overprinted Nonprofit Org., 4/20/86 to 10/19/86, 10/23/86 to 3/31/87[1]
		7.1¢ Tractor, inscribed Nonprofit Org.
4/3/88 continuing	7.6¢	7.1¢ Tractor, inscribed Nonprofit Org., until 10/9/88[1]
		7.6¢ Carreta

Third-class, nonprofit bulk mailing, sorted to carrier route

Dates	Rate	Authorized Stamps
7/6/80 to 3/21/81	3.2¢	none
3/22/81 to 7/5/81	3.1¢	none[9]
7/6/81 to 1/9/82	1.9¢	none
1/10/82 to 7/27/82	4¢	none
7/28/82 to 1/8/83	3¢	3¢ Francis Parkman, overprinted Nonprofit Org. CAR-RT SORT
1/9/83 to 2/16/85	3.3¢	3¢ Francis Parkman, overprinted Nonprofit Org. CAR-RT SORT, 1/9/83 to 7/6/83, 8/4/83 until further notice[1]
2/17/85 to 12/31/85	3.4¢	3¢ Francis Parkman, overprinted Nonprofit Org. CAR-RT SORT, until 6/16/85[1]
		3.4¢ School Bus, overprinted Nonprofit Org. CAR-RT SORT
1/1/86 to 3/8/86	4.8¢	3.4¢ School Bus, overprinted Nonprofit Org. CAR-RT SORT[1]
3/9/86 to 4/19/86	5.7¢	3.4¢ School Bus, overprinted Nonprofit Org. CAR-RT SORT[1]
4/20/86 to 4/2/88	5.5¢	3.4¢ School Bus, overprinted Nonprofit Org. CAR-RT SORT, 4/20/86 to 10/19/86, 10/23/86 to 3/31/87[1]
		5.5¢ Star Route Truck, inscribed CAR-RT SORT Non-profit Org.
4/3/88 continuing	5.3¢	5.5¢ Star Route Truck, inscribed CAR-RT SORT Non-profit Org., until 10/9/88[1]
		5.3¢ Elevator

Third-class, nonprofit bulk mailing, ZIP+4 addressed, sorted to 3 or 5 ZIP code digits

Dates	Rate	Authorized Stamps
Before 4/3/88	none	none
4/3/88 continuing	7.9¢	none

Third-class, nonprofit bulk mailing, ZIP+4 addressed, sorted to 5 ZIP code digits

Dates	Rate	Authorized Stamps
Before 4/3/88	none	none
4/3/88 continuing	7.1¢	7.1¢ Tractor, inscribed Nonprofit 5-Digit ZIP[1][4]

Third-class nonprofit bulk mailing, ZIP+4 addressed, bar coded, sorted to 3 or 5 ZIP code digits

Dates	Rate	Authorized Stamps
Before 4/3/88	none	none
4/3/88 continuing	6.6¢	none

Footnotes

[1] Authorized false franking, with the difference between the amount of postage required and the face value of the stamps paid at the time of mailing.

[2] Authorized false franking, with the difference between the face value of the stamps and the amount of required postage refunded.

[3] Presorted first-class mailings with nonstandard pieces did not require surcharge postage on each piece until September 1, 1979. Until then, surcharge postage could be paid as a lump sum at the time of mailing.

[4] Precanceled stamps were first allowed on presorted first-class mail September 7, 1978.

[5] In 1987 the Postal Service advised cachetmakers that a 26¢ Cable Car stamp would be issued in 1988. That did not happen, but the intention may have been to issue a stamp to prepay this rate (21¢ presort + 5¢ surcharge = 26¢). If so, it would have been inscribed Presorted First-Class at least, possibly adding words calling attention to the newly reduced nonstandard surcharge.

[6] This rate could legitimately have been franked with any of the 17¢ Electric Auto stamps overprinted PRESORTED FIRST-CLASS, with a CAR-RT SORT endorsement added to each piece.

[7] This rate could legitimately be franked with precanceled 20¢ Flag stamps, if any are still in circulation.

[8] The March 25, 1988, *Postal Bulletin* failed to authorize false franking with 12¢ precancels, but this was probably an oversight. It is likely that all overprinted 12¢ Torch and 12¢ Stanley Steamer coils could have paid the 13¢ rate until October 9, 1988, with the difference due paid at the time of mailing.

[9] This rate could legitimately have been franked with the 3.1¢ Guitar stamp overprinted with plain lines, with a CAR-RT SORT endorsement added to each piece.

329

Plate Number Coil Checklist

Transportation Series	1	2	3	4	5	6	7	8	9	10	11	12	13	14	15	16	17	18	19	20	21	22
1¢ Omnibus	X	X	X	X	X	X																
1¢ Omnibus, re-engraved B Press	X	X																				
2¢ Locomotive		X	X	X		X		X		X												
2¢ Locomotive, re-engraved B Press	X																					
3¢ Handcar	X	X	X	X																		
3¢ Conestoga Wagon	X																					
3.4¢ School Bus	X	X																				
3.4¢ School Bus, precanceled	X	X																				
4¢ Stagecoach	X	X	X	X	X	X																
4¢ Stagecoach, precanceled			X	X	X	X																
4¢ Stagecoach, re-engraved B Press	X																					
4.9¢ Buckboard					X	X																
4.9¢ Buckboard, precanceled	X	X	X	X	X	X																
5¢ Motorcycle	X	X	X	X																		
5¢ Milk Wagon	X																					
5.2¢ Sleigh	X	X	X		X																	
5.2¢ Sleigh, precanceled	X	X	X	X	X	X																
5.3¢ Elevator	X																					
5.5¢ Star Route Truck	X																					
5.5¢ Star Route Truck, service inscribed	X	X																				
5.9¢ Bicycle					X	X																
5.9¢ Bicycle, precanceled					X	X	X	X														
6¢ Tricycle	X																					
6¢ Tricycle, precanceled	X	X																				
7.1¢ Tractor	X																					
7.1¢ Tractor, service inscribed Nonprofit Org.	X																					
7.1¢ Tractor, service inscribed 5-Digit Zip+4	X																					
7.4¢ Baby Buggy		X																				
7.4¢ Baby Buggy, precanceled		X																				
7.6¢ Carreta	X	X	X																			
8.3¢ Ambulance	X	X																				
8.3¢ Ambulance, precanceled	X	X	X	X																		
8.3¢ Ambulance, B Press precanceled	X	X																				
8.4¢ Wheel Chair	X	X	X																			
8.5¢ Tow Truck	X																					
8.5¢ Tow Truck, precanceled	X	X																				
9.3¢ Mail Wagon	X	X	X	X	X	X																
9.3¢ Mail Wagon, precanceled	X	X	X	X	X	X		X														
10¢ Canal Boat	X																					
10.1¢ Oil Wagon	X																					
10.1¢ Oil Wagon, precanceled black	X	X																				
10.1¢ Oil Wagon, precanceled red		X	X																			
10.9¢ Hansom Cab	X	X																				
10.9¢ Hansom Cab, precanceled	X	X	X	X																		
11¢ Caboose	X																					
11¢ Caboose, precanceled	X																					
11¢ Stutz Bearcat	X	X	X	X																		
12¢ Stanley Steamer	X	X																				
12¢ Stanley Steamer, precanceled	X	X																				
12¢ Stanley Steamer, B press precanceled	X																					
12.5¢ Pushcart	X	X																				
12.5¢ Pushcart, precanceled	X	X																				
13¢ Patrol Wagon	X																					
13.2¢ Coal Car	X	X																				
14¢ Iceboat	X	X	X	X																		
14¢ Iceboat, B Press		X																				
15¢ Tugboat	X	X																				

	1	2	3	4	5	6	7	8	9	10	11	12	13	14	15	16	17	18	19	20	21	22
16.7¢ Popcorn Wagon	X	X																				
17¢ Electric Auto	X	X	X	X	X	X	X															
17¢ Electric Auto, precanceled, Type A		X	X	X	X	X																
17¢ Electric Auto, precanceled, Type B		X	X	X	X																	
17¢ Electric Auto, precanceled, Type C	X	X	X	X	X		X															
17¢ Electric Auto, precanceled, Type BA					X	X																
17¢ Dog Sled		X																				
17.5¢ Racing Car	X																					
17.5¢ Racing Car, service inscribed	X																					
18¢ Surrey	X	X	X	X	X	X	X	X	X	X	X	X	X	X	X	X	X	X				
20¢ Fire Pumper	X	X	X	X	X	X	X	X	X	X	X	X	X	X	X	X						
20¢ Cable Car	X	X																				
20.5¢ Fire Engine	X																					
21¢ Railroad Mail Car	X	X																				
24.1¢ Tandem Bicycle	X																					
25¢ Bread Wagon	X	X	X	X	X																	

Flag Series

	1	2	3	4	5	6	7	8	9	10	11	12	13	14	15	16	17	18	19	20	21	22
18¢ Flag	X	X	X	X	X	X	X															
20¢ Flag Over Supreme Court	X	X	X	X	X	X			X	X	X	X	X	X								
20¢ Flag, precanceled															X							
22¢ Flag Over Capitol	X	X	X	X	X	X	X	X			X	X	X	X	X	X	X	X	X	X	X	X
22¢ Flag phosphored paper test	X																					
25¢ Flag Over Yosemite	X	X	X	X	X			X	X	X												
25¢ Flag, phosphored paper		X	X			X	X	X	X	X	X	X			X	X						

Other Coil Issues

	1	2	3	4
(22¢) Green D Eagle	X	X		
20¢ Consumer Education	X	X	X	X
18¢ Washington Monument	1112, 3333			
18¢ Washington, service inscribed	11121, 33333, 43444			
21.1¢ Letters	111111, 111121			
21.1¢ Letters, service inscribed	111111, 111121			
(25¢) E Earth	1111, 1211, 1222, 2222			
25¢ Honeybee	X	X		

Officials

	1
20¢ Official	X
(22¢) D Official	X

331

Precancel Gap Position Checklist - Cottrell Press Issues

Stamp	Plate #	On strips of five			"No Gap" on strips of five[3]								
		2L	1L	Line	1R	2R	3R	4R	5R	6R/L	5L	4L	3L
3.4¢ School Bus	1			X	X	X	X						
	2			X	X	X	X						
4¢ Stagecoach	3	X	X	X									
	4	X	X	X									
	5	X	X	X									
	6	X	X	X									
4.9¢ Buckboard	1				X	X	X						
	2				X	X	X						
	3	X	X	X									X
	4	X	X	X									X
	5	X		X	X	X	X					X	X
	6	X		X	X	X	X					X	X
5.2¢ Sleigh	1						X		X	X	X		X
	2						X		X	X	X		X
	3	X	X	X			X			X	X	X	X
	4	X										X	X
	5	X	X	X			X			X	X	X	X
	6	X										X	X
5.9¢ Bicycle	3			X					X	X	X	X	
	4			X					X	X	X	X	
	5			X									
	6			X									
8.3¢ Ambulance	1	X	X	X	X	X							
	2	X	X	X	X	X							
	3				X	X							
	4				X	X							
9.3¢ Mail Wagon	1	X						X	X			X	X
	2	X						X	X			X	X
	3			X	X	X	X			X	X	X	
	4	X	X		X	X	X	X		X	X	X	X
	5	X			X	X	X		X	X	X	X	X
	6	X			X	X	X		X	X	X	X	X
	8	X											
10.9¢ Hansom Cab	1			X	X	X	X	X					
	2			X	X	X	X	X					
	3			X	X			X				X	X
	4			X	X			X				X	X
12¢ Stanley Steamer	1		X	X							X	X	X
	2		X	X							X	X	X
17¢ Electric Auto Type A	3	X	X	X				X	X	X	X	X	
	4	X	X	X				X	X	X	X	X	
	5	X	X					X	X				
	6	X	X					X					
	7							X	X				
Type B	5		X	X				X					
	6		X	X				X					
Type AB[1] Se-Tenant	3								X				
	4								X				
	5							X	X				
	6							X					
	7							X	X				
Type BA[2] Se-Tenant	3							X					
	4							X					
	5		X	X					X				
	6		X	X					X				

Stamp	Plate #	On strips of five				"No Gap" on strips of five[3]							
		2L	1L	Line	1R	2R	3R	4R	5R	6R/L	5L	4L	3L
Type C	1			X									
	2			X									
	3			X	X							X	X
	4			X	X							X	X
	5									X	X	X	X
	7									X	X	X	X

[1] On 17¢ Electric Auto strips with se-tenant Type AB precancel overprints, only the Type A overprint appears on a plate strip of five or fewer stamps.

[2] On 17¢ Electric Auto strips with se-tenant Type BA precancel overprints, only the Type B overprint appears on a plate strip of five or fewer stamps for those strips where the gap appears at positions 4R and 5R.

[3] Strips up to 10 stamps in length may be required to show these gap positions in the usual way, keeping two stamps past the numbered stamp at one end and two past the gap at the other.

NOTE ON B PRESS PRECANCEL GAP POSITIONS: B press precancel gaps occur at 26-stamp intervals or not at all. Only two reported positions are collectible on strips of five or fewer stamps: Line Gap and Gap 1R on sleeve 2 strips of the 10.1¢ Oil Wagon. All others require longer strips. For listings of all reported B press gap positions, consult the latest edition of the *Plate Number Coil Catalog* edited by Stephen G. Esrati. Strips up to 18 stamps in length may be required to show certain gap positions.

Topical Checklist of Coil Stamps Issued Since 1981

The list is intended to be illustrative, not comprehensive, in showing how the stamps that are the subject of this book can be collected and organized by topic. Since nearly all these coil stamps pertain to transportation, commerce, and history, those subjects are not included in the itemized list.

Advertising	1¢ Omnibus (Madison Ave.)
Architecture	5.3¢ Elevator, 18¢ Flag (lighthouse), 20¢ Flag Over Supreme Court, 22¢ Flag Over Capitol
Agriculture	4.9¢ Buckboard, 5¢ Milk Wagon, 7.1¢ Tractor, 25¢ Honeybee
Arctic	17¢ Dog Sled, (25¢) E Earth
Automotive	3.4¢ School Bus, 5¢ Motorcycle, 5.5¢ Star Route Truck, 7.1¢ Tractor, 8.5¢ Tow Truck, 11¢ Stutz Bearcat, 12¢ Stanley Steamer, 17¢ Electric Auto, 17.5¢ Racing Car, 20.5¢ Fire Engine
Aviation	5.9¢ Bicycle (Wright brothers)
Bees	25¢ Honeybee
Bicycles	5.9¢ Bicycle, 6¢ Tricycle, 24.1¢ Tandem Bicycle
Big Apple	1¢ Omnibus, 5.3¢ Elevator, 12¢ Liberty Torch, 12.5¢ Pushcart
Birds	B, C and D nondenominated stamps, all Officials
Black Heritage	3.4¢ School Bus, 20¢ Flag Over Supreme Court
Botany	12.5¢ Pushcart (vegetables), 25¢ Flag Over Yosemite (forest), 18¢ Washington Monument (boughs), 25¢ Honeybee (flower)
Cattle	7.6¢ Carreta (oxcart)
Children	6¢ Tricycle, 7.4¢ Baby Buggy
Christmas	5.2¢ Sleigh
Civil War	8.3¢ Ambulance
Dairy	5¢ Milk Wagon
Dogs	17¢ Dog Sled
Eagles	B, C and D nondenominated stamps, all Officials
Earth's Physical Features	25¢ Flag Over Yosemite, (25¢) E Earth
Education	3.4¢ School Bus, 20¢ Consumer Education
Electricity	17¢ Electric Auto
Fire Fighting	20¢ Fire Pumper, 20.5¢ Fire Engine
Fish/Fishing	14¢ Iceboat, 18¢ Flag
Flags	18¢ Flag, 20¢ Flag Over Supreme Court, 22¢ Flag Over Capitol, 25¢ Flag Over Yosemite
Flowers	25¢ Honeybee
Food	5¢ Milk Wagon, 7.1¢ Tractor, 12.5¢ Pushcart, 16.7¢ Popcorn Wagon, 25¢ Bread Wagon, 25¢ Honeybee
Forestry	2¢ Locomotive and 11¢ Caboose (lumber trains), 25¢ Flag Over Yosemite
Geology/Fossils/Minerals	2¢ Locomotive and 13.2¢ Coal Car (coal), 10.1¢ Oil Wagon, 25¢ Flag Over Yosemite, (25¢) E Earth
Globes	(25¢) E Earth
Handicapped	8.3¢ Ambulance, 8.4¢ Wheel Chair
Harbors/Rivers/Lakes/Oceans	10¢ Canal Boat, 14¢ Iceboat, 15¢ Tugboat, 18¢ Flag, 25¢ Flag Over Yosemite, (25¢) E Earth
Health	8.3¢ Ambulance, 8.4¢ Wheel Chair
Horses	1¢ Omnibus, 3¢ Conestoga Wagon, 4¢ Stagecoach, 4.9¢ Buckboard, 5¢ Milk Wagon, 5.2¢ Sleigh, 8.3¢ Ambulance, 9.3¢ Mail Wagon, 10¢ Canal Boat, 10.1¢ Oil Wagon, 10.9¢ Hansom Cab, 13¢ Patrol Wagon, 18¢ Surrey, 20¢ Fire Pumper, 25¢ Bread Wagon
Law	13¢ Patrol Wagon, 20¢ Flag Over Supreme Court, 22¢ Flag Over Capitol
Lighthouses	18¢ Flag
Medical Subjects	8.3¢ Ambulance, 8.4¢ Wheel Chair
Military	8.3¢ Ambulance, all Officials, 5¢ George Washington and 18¢ Washington Monument
Mining	13.2¢ Coal Car
Monuments/Statues	20¢ Flag Over Supreme Court, 22¢ Flag Over Capitol, 18¢ Washington Monument
Motorcycles	5¢ Motorcycle
Mountains	25¢ Flag Over Yosemite

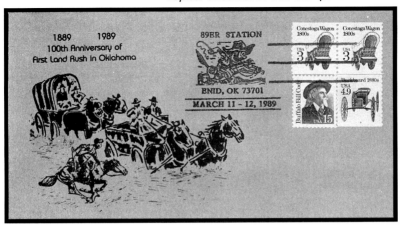

The 3¢ Conestoga Wagon coil ties in with several topicals, including Western Americana and horses.

Murder	10.9¢ Hansom Cab (scene of a celebrated murder)
Music	1¢ Omnibus and 12.5¢ Pushcart ("East Side, West Side"), 5.2¢ Sleigh ("Jingle Bells"), 7.9¢ Drum, 10¢ Canal Boat ("Erie Canal"), 18¢ Surrey ("Surrey with the Fringe on Top"), 24.1¢ Tandem Bicycle ("Daisy Bell"), 18¢ Flag ("America the Beautiful")
National Parks	25¢ Flag Over Yosemite
Navigation	10¢ Canal Boat, 14¢ Iceboat, 18¢ Flag
Petroleum	10.1¢ Oil Wagon
Pharmacy/Drugs	8.3¢ Ambulance
Police/Law Enforcement	13¢ Patrol Wagon, 20¢ Flag Over Supreme Court
Politics	22¢ Flag Over Capitol
Postal History	4¢ Stagecoach, 5.5¢ Star Route Truck, 9.3¢ Mail Wagon, 21¢ Railroad Mail Car, 21.1¢ Letters
Presidents	1¢ Omnibus (Madison Avenue), 5¢ George Washington and 18¢ Washington Monument
Railroads/Trains	2¢ Locomotive, 3¢ Handcar, 11¢ Caboose, 13.2¢ Coal Car, 21¢ Railroad Mail Car
Religion	20¢ Flag Over Supreme Court (Church and State)
Sailing Vessels	14¢ Iceboat
Ships/Watercraft	10¢ Canal Boat, 15¢ Tugboat
Space	(25¢) E Earth
Sports	17¢ Dog Sled, 17.5¢ Racing Car
Statue of Liberty	12¢ Liberty Torch
Streetcars	20¢ Cable Car
Theater	1¢ Omnibus (Broadway), 18¢ Surrey ("Oklahoma")
Tourism	25¢ Flag Over Yosemite
Trees	25¢ Flag Over Yosemite
Trucks	5.5¢ Star Route Truck, 8.5¢ Tow Truck, 20.5¢ Fire Engine
Umbrellas	12.5¢ Pushcart
War	8.3¢ Ambulance
Waterfalls	25¢ Flag Over Yosemite
Western Americana	2¢ Locomotive, 3¢ Conestoga Wagon, 4¢ Stagecoach, 4.9¢ Buckboard, 7.6¢ Carreta, 18¢ Surrey, 25¢ Flag Over Yosemite

Stamp Index

In this index, "essay" means a stamp design that was not adopted; "not issued" refers to a stamp design that was approved, but then changed before being issued.

Name Index

341

General Index

344

About the Author

Ken Lawrence, 47 years old, has collected stamps since he was 11. A native of Chicago, he has lived in Mississippi for almost 20 years. He has worked as a writer, editor, researcher and lecturer on culture, politics and history.

He has been active in the civil rights movement since his teens. His articles have appeared in more than 100 periodicals worldwide. His largest project in writing and editing, five volumes on slavery in Mississippi, received an Award of Merit from the Mississippi Historical Society.

During the past eight years, he has become active in more than a score of philatelic societies. Currently, he is editor of *The Philatelic Communicator*, the quarterly publication of the American Philatelic Society Writers Unit.

He is a governor of the Bureau Issues Association and vice president of the Jackson Philatelic Society. He writes a monthly column in *Linn's Stamp News* on plate number coils and frequent articles on his many other philatelic passions, ranging from modern postal history to Walt Disney topicals, from Germany to Cuba.